DATE DUE FOR RETURN

Collected Essays on Economic Theory
Volume III

CLASSICS AND MODERNS

Collected Essays on Economic Theory

I   WEALTH AND WELFARE
II   MONEY, INTEREST AND WAGES
III   CLASSICS AND MODERNS

John Hicks

Classics and Moderns

Collected Essays on Economic Theory
Volume III

Basil Blackwell

© in this collection Sir John Hicks 1983

First published 1983
Basil Blackwell Publisher Limited
108 Cowley Road
Oxford OX4 1JF
England

British Library Cataloguing in Publication Data

Hicks, John, 1904–
    Classics and moderns. – (Collected essays on
    economic theory; v. 3)
    1. Economics
    I. Title   II. Series
    330.1   HB171

    ISBN 0-631-12538-8

Typesetting by Unicus Graphics Ltd, Horsham.
Printed in Great Britain by TJ Press Ltd, Padstow

Contents

Contents   ix

x   *Contents*

Acknowledgements

I again have to thank Dieter Helm, of New College, Oxford, for his important assistance in the preparation of this further volume. This one owes more to him than did its predecessors.

The following have kindly given permission to reprint the more recently published papers: Croom Helm Ltd Publishers (essay 13); Lexington Books (essay 9); Oxford University Press and Springer-Verlag (essay 8); Weidenfeld (Publishers) Limited (essay 3); John Wiley & Sons, Inc. (essay 4).

Abbreviations

For an explanation of the abbreviations used for books by the author and for journals, see pp. 376ff. below.

Other books

J. S. Mill, *Essays on Unsettled Questions* (1844)   *EUQ*

J. Robinson, *Economics of Imperfect Competition* (1932)   *EIC*

R. Dorfman, P. A. Samuelson and R. Solow, *Linear Programming and Economic Analysis* (1958)   DOSSO

Preface

It was possible, when making selections for the preceding volumes of this collection, to take them in such a way that each volume had a more or less connected theme. By arranging the papers in the order in which they were originally written, the theme could be shown to be unfolding. But when the *Wealth and Welfare* papers had been taken out, and the (broadly) monetary papers had been taken out, though enough were left to fill a third volume, they would not fit together, even to the extent that the others had done. There was not one theme; there were several. So the most orderly thing I have been able to do has been to group the papers into separate parts: I. History of theory, II. Monopoly and competition, III. International trade; the papers within the parts having some relation to one another, but between the parts there being little connection. There still remained a miscellaneous part IV, consisting of papers that had little more in common than their concern with the development of some mathematical, or quasi-mathematical, technique. A number of reviews make up part V.

I began by thinking that the papers on history of theory, which here form part I, would be extensive enough to form a centre of the book. That was why I announced its title as *Classics and Neo-classics*, the title I have since withdrawn. It became clear, as the volume began to take shape, that the title was not suitable. The history of theory papers form less than half of it, and the rest have nothing particular to do with 'neo-classics'. However, a more substantial reason for the change was my increasing dislike for that expression itself. It is such a favourite of modern controversialists, but it has been so over-used that its meaning has become blurred. How often would the clarity of an article (or of a book) have been improved if the author had denied himself the use of it! I do think it has become muddling and I do not want to encourage its use.

The meaning which I had in mind, when I was proposing to use it, was the simple historical meaning. I was just thinking of those economists who flourished between the two 'revolutions' — that which we associate with Jevons and his contemporaries and that which we associate with Keynes. I shall still want a word to express that meaning; it had better be a new word, which can be given that meaning, and will suggest no other. I think I have found it in the title I have given to part I — Classics and Post-classics.

There is a good reason for thinking that, for this particular meaning, *post-classic* is better. What we usually denote by the prefix 'neo' is a revival, the re-introduction of some message from the past which (it is held) had come to be overlooked. Thus we speak of neo-Platonist and neo-Kantian, and in economics (quite properly) of neo-Mercantilist. (I would not claim that usage, in other fields, is in this respect consistent; but that, to my ear, is what 'neo' most naturally suggests.) The economists of the middle period were not in that sense 'neo-classical'. Some of them, most notably Jevons, were attacking what they understood to be classical doctrine; others, perhaps Marshall, thought of themselves as continuing a classical tradition, which they did not recognise as having been broken. In neither case was there a revival of classicism, as there should have been if the prefix 'neo' had been right.

As time has gone on, this has become increasingly awkward. For we are now confronted with genuine revivals of classical economics, so that to them the term neo-classical would be quite properly applied if it were not already occupied. We try to escape by labelling them 'neo-Ricardian'; but Ricardo was a classic, was he not? And it is not only in the Ricardian movement, that descends from Sraffa, that one sees signs of a revival of classicism. Indeed, if the term neo-classic were available, to be properly used, it would be quite fair to apply it to some of the work which has come down from that of Keynes himself.

So it is not at all surprising that 'neo-classic' has become so muddling. Post-classic has associations which are much less confusing. The post-impressionists, in painting, carried on from the impressionists, but with a difference. We have those among us who call themselves post-Keynesians. I think that what they mean by that is that they are taking what they have learned from Keynes and seeing what they themselves can make of it. If that is so, I am very much with them. But is not this just what Jevons and the others did with the classical economists — standing back from them but still learning from them?

I am not at all denying that 1870 is a divide. Jevons was quite right about that. As I shall be showing in the 'Revolutions' paper, which I have put first in part I (for it will serve as a general introduction to part I) the chief thing which then happened was the rise of micro-economics. The use of mathematical methods, marginalism and the rest, was subsidiary to that. Classical economics, in the pre-1870 sense, was essentially *macro*; in my terminology, its subject was 'plutology'. Or, as those economists themselves would have said, it was political economy, the production and distribution of the wealth of *nations*. (*Nationalökonomie*, as the Germans put it, a shade more frankly.) The new generation shifted attention in a *micro* direction, towards the economics of the individual, consumer or worker, and of the firm, and to the theory of exchange (catallactics) which tied them together.

It is true that there is another aspect of their work, or of most of their work, which strikes a modern reader. This is its predominantly static character. This was partly a consequence of the first; 'catallactics' has a natural tendency to be static. But historically it was also due to a fading of interest in the things which had impelled the classics proper towards growth theory – as I shall be explaining in my essay on Mill (one of the new papers which I have added).

What will be found in part I is by no means the whole of my writings on history of theory. A full list would include several things which are not in this volume, or in any of these volumes. They are bits of other books, which are still available, and from which they could not readily be detached. The chapters on Smith and Ricardo, and on Marshall (4 and 5 of *Capital and Growth*) are parts of the general discussion of static–dynamic methodology, the first part of that book; the same holds for what is said on Smith and Ricardo in chapter 4 of *Causality*. The historical essays (8, 9 and 10) in *Critical Essays in Monetary Theory* are also best left in their own context.

When all these had been set aside, what was left looked rather a rump. Two papers on Ricardo, but nothing particular on Smith or Mill. To make Ricardo the sole representative of classical economics, though it is the modern fashion, is not a fashion I care for. Something was clearly needed to restore the balance.

I have therefore turned to some notes for lectures, which I had given in Oxford, for some years before my retirement. From these I have constructed two papers, one on Smith and his *theoretical* background, the other on Mill and the transition to the post-classics. Accordingly, after the 'Revolutions' survey, there are four on classics, and four on post-classics (including two, which are associated with my *Capital and Time*) on the 'Austrians'. I hope that I may offer this as a fairly balanced menu.

Most of the reviews, which appear as part V, are of editions or translations of post-classical writings, thus they need to be read with part I.

I do not find anything about the papers included in parts II, III and IV which needs to be said in this general introduction. But there remains part VI.

I became very conscious, as this collection drew near to completion – when I thought of this volume together with what had gone in to the other volumes – that something was needed to pull it together. I do have a view about the nature of economic theory, which finds indirect expression in many of these essays; but it is so indirect that it can hardly make the impression I desire, if these scattered passages alone represent it. Something more was needed in the way of summing up.

A part of the answer could be found by using a sketch of an intellectual autobiography, which I wrote, on request, for my friends in Italy. That should help, but even that would not be enough. For when I wrote it, I had not yet completed my *Causality in Economics* (*CE*, 1979). Some of the ideas which appear in that book were not yet clear to me; I had not appreciated how important it was to stress them, in order to tie the rest of my work together. There are indeed, among the more recent papers included in this collection, some in which these ideas are beginning to come out.[1] But they appear in very different contexts; it is not shown how they belong together, and what is the methodological standpoint – what many will regard as the rather peculiar methodological standpoint – which they imply. Thus there were threads which still needed to be tied together; I hope that in what is here the concluding paper I have done something to tie them.

---

[1] See the introductory section of the second 'Austrian' paper (9 below) and the concluding part of the *IS–LM* 'Explanation' (volume II, essay 23).

Part I
Classics and Post-classics

1

'Revolutions' in Economics

This paper arose out of a conference on methodology, in memory of Imre Lakatos, that was held at Nafplion, Greece, in September 1974. It was not itself given at that conference, but was written after it, as my personal reaction to the papers which I had heard at it. It was nevertheless published in the second volume of its proceedings: *Method and Appraisal in Economics* (ed. Spiro Latsis, Cambridge University Press, 1976).

As will be seen, I was unconvinced by the Lakatos approach, in its application to economics. I do not here discuss the other application, to the physical sciences, to which some of the best papers that had been given at Nafplion were devoted. Although I learned much from those papers, they also left me unconvinced. But they greatly helped me to form my own views on these matters, which are set out in chapter III of *CE* (1979).

It should also be said that this paper was written at about the same time as 'The Scope and Status of Welfare Economics' which has already appeared as essay 10 in volume I of this collection. Some of the things I wanted to say had to be said in both places, so there are passages which appear in both. But they are not so extensive as to make the one paper supersede the other. There are things of importance which come up here but could not come up there.

The study of scientific 'revolutions', in which one system of thought (or 'research programme') has given place to another, has been shown, by Lakatos and his followers, to be a powerful tool in the methodology of natural science. Economics also has had its 'revolutions'; it is fruitful to study them in much the same manner. I think, however, that when one looks at them comparatively, one finds that their significance is very largely different.

This is a matter of importance, for economics itself. Economics is more like art or philosophy than science, in the use that it can make of its own history. The history of science is a fascinating subject; it is important (as has been shown) for the philosophy of science; but it is not important to the working scientist in the way that the history of economics is important to the working economist. When the natural scientist has come to the frontier of knowledge, and is ready for new exploration, he is unlikely to have much to gain from a contemplation of the path by which his predecessors have come to the place where he now stands. Old ideas are worked out; old controversies are dead and buried. The Ptolemaic system may live on in literature, or it may form the framework of a mathematical exercise; it has no direct interest to the modern astronomer.

Our position in economics is different; we cannot escape in the same way from our own past. We may pretend to escape; but the past crowds in on us all the same. Keynes and his contemporaries echo Ricardo and Malthus; Marx and Marshall are still alive. Some of us are inclined to be ashamed of this traditionalism, but when it is properly understood it is no cause for embarrassment; it is a consequence of what we are doing, or trying to do.

The facts which we study are not permanent, or repeatable, like the facts of the natural sciences; they change incessantly, and change without repetition. Considered as individual events, they are often events of great interest. Every business has a history of its own, every consumer a history of his own; any of these histories may have its own drama when we come close to it. But, as a general rule, it is not our business as economists to come close. We are trying to detect general patterns amid the mass of absorbing detail; shapes that repeat among the details that do not repeat. We can only do this if we select something less than the detail which is presented to us. In order to analyse, we must simplify and cut down.

Further, in practice, we must simplify quickly. Our special concern is with the facts of the present world; but before we can study the present, it is already past. In order that we should be able to say useful things about what is happening, before it is too late, we must select, even select quite violently. We must concentrate our attention, and hope that we have concentrated it in the right place. We must work, if we are to work effectively, in some sort of blinkers.

Our theories, regarded as tools of analysis, are blinkers in this sense. Or it may be politer to say that they are rays of light, which illuminate a part of the target, leaving the rest in the dark. As we use them, we avert our eyes from things that may be relevant, in order that we should see more clearly what we do see. It is entirely proper that we should do this, since otherwise we should see very little. But it is obvious that a theory which is to perform this function satisfactorily must be well chosen; otherwise it will illumine the wrong things. Further, since it is a changing world that we are studying, a theory which illumines the right things now may illumine the wrong things another time.[1] This may happen because of changes in the world (the things neglected may have grown relatively to the things considered) or because of changes in our sources of information (the sorts of facts that are readily accessible to us may have changed) or because of changes in ourselves (the things in which we are interested may have changed). There is, there can be, no economic theory which will do for us everything we want all the time.

Accordingly, while we are right to allow ourselves to become wrapped up in those theories which are useful now, we are unwise if we allow ourselves to forget that the time may come when we shall need something different. We may then be right to reject our present theories, not because they are wrong, but because they have become inappropriate. Things which we formerly left unnoticed (more or less deliberately unnoticed) may rise up and become essential; we shall have to bring them in, even if that means averting our attention from things we thought important before. That is the *special* reason why economics is prone to revolutions – revolutions which appear, while they are occurring, to be steps in advance, though from a different point of view they may take on quite another character.

The revolutions may be large or small. Big revolutions are (fortunately) rare. The Keynesian revolution is the obvious example of a big revolution; there are not more than two or three others which might conceivably be compared to it. It is possible that big revolutions are more likely to take their origins outside the ranks of academic economists in the narrow sense (Keynes was only a part-time academic economist). For big revolutions can only occur when something rather far away from the previous concentration of attention comes to the forefront, so that its recognition compels a major readjustment. Small revolutions, that are revolutions in my sense nonetheless, can more easily be made by academics. Working in 'blinkers' is uncongenial to the academic mind; it is difficult to teach the concentration without keeping an eye on what is around it. So it comes naturally to us to be on the watch for ways of bringing into attention things

---

[1] As an example of this, see the discussion of the evolution of market theory in ch. 5, of my *CG* (1965).

which have been only just left out; we have a bias in favour of inclusiveness and generality, even at the cost of ineffectiveness. We do keep that sort of watch fairly well.

There are, however, two ways in which we may keep our watch. One is by generalisation, by constructing 'more general' theories, theories which put more things into their places, even if we can do less with them when we have put them there.[2] This is a perfectly respectable activity; but what I am here concerned to point out is that it is not the only way in which we can do that particular business. The same function can be performed by the history of economics in another way. If we seek to discover how it was, and why it was, that concentrations of attention have changed, and theories (effective theories) have changed with them, we find ourselves 'standing back' just as we do when we pursue the generalisation method; we get something of the same gain, and it may be that we run less risk of losing our appreciation of 'effectiveness' as we get it. But I have no need to champion one of these ways of broadening our minds against the other. There is plenty of room for both.[3]

The first of the 'revolutions' which I shall be considering is that which led to the establishment of 'classical' economics — the system of thought which was taken over by Adam Smith from the Physiocrats in France. If one asks what it is that distinguishes those great (and highly 'effective') economists from their relatively ineffective pre-decessors, the answer is surely to be found in the vision of the economic process which they possessed, a vision which made it possible for them to think economic problems through, not in separate bits, but together. This vision was not a vague sense of everything being inter-related; it had content that is capable of being identified and described.

There is an exact indication of that content in the full title of Adam Smith's book — *An Inquiry into the Nature and Causes of the Wealth of Nations.* If we take that title, not as a mere label in the modern manner, but as a description which means what it says, its meaning is apparent: wealth is production; the wealth of a nation is

---

[2] Keynes's theory is of course not a general theory in this sense; it is a superbly effective theory, which gains power by what it leaves out.

[3] I have emphasised another set of reasons why we should study the history of economics — its function as a means of communication — in my paper on 'Capital Controversies' (*EP*, 1977). See also volume II of this collection, p. 238, and pp. 372-3 below.

what we now call the national product.[4] Adam Smith is to tell us what the social product of a nation is, what is meant by its being large or small; what is meant by its growing. That is 'nature'. Then he is to tell us why the social product is large or small, and why it grows. That is 'causes'.

Much of what we say, and much of what Smith said, on these matters seems uncontroversial. The social product is large when the quantities of the factors of production that are used to make it are large, and when those large quantities are used with high efficiency. The social product grows by growth in the factors of production, by increase in the numbers and in the efficiency of labour, and by the accumulation of capital. And it grows by improvements in the efficiency with which capital is applied to labour; that is, by improvements in the efficiency with which the factors of production are combined. These statements sound obvious but when we take them to be obvious, we are not taking them literally, as (I believe) Smith did, or was at the least beginning to do.

There is, of course, no question that the flow of wealth is production; things are produced, and it is in these products that the flow of wealth consists. But the things that are produced are heterogeneous; it is not obvious that we can take them together and reduce them to a common 'stuff'. What is implied in the classical approach is that for essential purposes we can take them together. We can represent them by a flow of wealth, which is so far homogeneous that it can be greater or less. It was the study of this flow of wealth which the classics called *political economy*.[5]

How did Smith and his successors come to think in this way? By analogy, surely, with the experience of business. The products of a business may be heterogeneous, but they are reduced to a common measure by being valued in terms of money. It is in money terms that we can tell whether the turnover of one business is greater than

[4] We are nowadays so accustomed to thinking of wealth as capital wealth that it may not be easy to realise that in Smith wealth is normally taken in a 'flow' sense. Even in the first sentence of his book there is a snag which worries the modern reader. 'The annual labour of every nation is the fund which originally supplies it with all the necessities and conveniences of life which it annually consumes.' The repeated *annual* emphasises *flow*; but what about *fund*? I suggest that we get nearest to Smith's meaning if we interpret *fund* to mean *revolving fund*. This would square with what he says later (in book 2) about capital. The *flow* interpretation of the sentence, which is meant to set course for the whole work, and must therefore be coherent with the title, would then become clear.

[5] *Political economy* is identified by Smith with 'the nature and causes of the wealth of nations' (Smith, 1976, vol. 2, pp. 678–9). For the subject as defined by Smith's title, it was, I would maintain, a most appropriate name. It is not appropriate for a great part of what we now call economics, so one can understand why it was abandoned.

that of another; cannot we do the same for nations? Adam Smith always found it easy, indeed too easy, to jump from the firm to the whole economy; it is not surprising that he found the analogy compelling. That, at the least, is the way he must have begun.

He soon found, however, that the money measure could not be used without precaution. It was necessary to distinguish between market values (which might not be significant as a means of valuation) and 'natural' or normal values which should be; and it was necessary to find a 'standard of value' so as to be able to correct for changes in the value of money. Thus, already in Smith, *political economy* is based upon a theory of value. It is of the first importance to emphasise that the primary purpose of that theory of value is not to explain prices, that is to say, to explain the working of markets; its primary purpose is to identify the values which are needed for the *weighting* of the social product, the reduction of the heterogeneous commodities which compose it to a common measure.

This, admittedly, is not very clear in Smith; it is much clearer in Ricardo. It was as a means of reducing heterogeneous commodities to a common measure that Ricardo used his labour theory of value. But it is not simply that device which marks the originality of Ricardo. The transition from Smith to Ricardo was itself a minor 'revolution'; but it did not come about, in the scientific manner, because of the need to take account of new facts, revealed by experiment or observation, facts which, however, had been *there* all the time. It did come about as a result of the need to accommodate new facts, but they were genuinely new facts, facts which had come into existence in the course of history – new *events*. Ricardo's rent theory, and the growth theory which followed from it, were reactions to the problems of his own time – the problems of feeding a growing population, forced upon attention, first by the Napoleonic blockade, and then in terms of reconstruction after the War. Ricardian economics is a remarkable intellectual achievement; but it could not have taken the form it did, except under the pressure of particular events.

As time went on, the land problem became less acute; thus though Ricardo's theory remained, for it had no intellectual rival, it became less and less *relevant*. So the time came when economics was ready for another 'revolution'. In fact there were two revolutions, at about the same time; one made by Marx, the other by Jevons, Walras and Menger. As a result of these two revolutions, economics was divided; economists proceeded, for many years, on quite separate tracks. How do we describe these revolutions, and how do we explain them?

In relation to the classical political economy, the distinguishing feature of the work of Marx is its distributism. Classical economics had been a theory of production and distribution, but production came first. *The Wealth of Nations*, as indicated, is a book about production ('nature' and 'causes'); though Adam Smith says much, incidentally, about distribution, what he says is unsystematic. It is true that if one judges Ricardo by that famous passage in the preface to his *Principles*, he is stressing distribution, against what he held to be its neglect by Adam Smith. 'To determine the laws which regulate this distribution is the principal problem of Political Economy.' (That, of course, is the way Marx took Ricardo; it explains why Marx, and Marxists, have always had some affection for Ricardo.) Nevertheless, in spite of this passage, the general tendency of Ricardo's work is to treat distribution as secondary. He was interested in distribution because of the importance which he attached to the effects of distribution on production, not because he had much interest in distribution *per se*. It is only in the third of the major classics, in John Stuart Mill's *Principles*, that there is much attention to distribution for its own sake. By that change of emphasis Mill opened the way to Marx.

The half-way house which we find in Mill explains a good deal. At the date when Mill was writing, the fact of the Industrial Revolution was unmistakable; a great increase in productive power had already occurred. But it had not brought with it the social gains which 'friends of humanity' (Ricardo's phrase) had expected from it. Thus already, to Mill, increase in production had come to seem to be of less importance than improvement in distribution. Further increase in production did not much matter; so the achievement of a distributive or 'socialist' society seemed near at hand. That was where the classical vision, in Mill, appeared to have led; and from that point Marx could fairly easily take over.

The other revolution is not so easy to describe, or to explain. The economists who led it are commonly called 'marginalists'; but that is a bad term, for it misses the essence of what was involved. The 'margin' is no more than an expression of the mathematical rule for a maximum (or minimum); any sort of economics is marginalist when it is concerned with maximising.[6] (Ricardo himself could be quite marginalist at times.) The essential novelty in the work of these economists was that instead of basing their economics on production and distribution, they based it on exchange. I therefore propose to make use of a term which was sometimes used, at the time in question, to mean the

---

[6] I am, of course, aware that there are problems of maximising which cannot be developed in terms of marginal *equations*.

theory of exchange; it was called catallactics.[7] So I shall re-name the so-called marginalists as catallactists.

There is, of course, no doubt that exchange is a basic feature of economic life, at least in a 'free', or what Marx would have called a 'capitalist' economy. By none of the classical economists would that have been denied. But while the classics looked at the economic system primarily from the production angle, the catallactists looked at it primarily from the side of exchange. It was possible, they found, to construct a 'vision' of economic life out of the theory of exchange, as the classics had done out of the social product. It was quite a different vision.

How do we explain the rise of catallactics? It can, I think, be explained in more than one way. Some will want to explain it as a reaction against socialism – hardly, at first, against Marx who must have been practically unknown to the first catallactists, but against the more general socialist tendencies which were already 'in the air'. One can make a case for that. It can be claimed that political economy is always in some sense socialist, catallactics individualist; though one cannot make that fit the history unless one distinguishes between means and ends. The Old Political Economists were socialists (or at least 'social') in the ends they set up; but they were individualist in practice, because they held that individualism was the way to the achievement of their social ends. As long as that was tenable, the conflict between ends was not acute. Whether one's objective was the 'welfare' of society or the freedom of the individual, the path to be followed was the same. Those to whom the one mattered more and those to whom the other mattered more could march under the same banner; they did not need to emphasise their differences. But as faith in the 'hidden-hand' declined, as the 'socialists' became socialist, the die-hard individualist was bound to cut adrift. He perceived, as he had not had to perceive before, that his objectives differed from those of his former allies. He was bound to insist upon his rejection of purely social ends, and to make a fuss about his rejection of them.

I admit that this is one strand which can be recognised in the work of the more politically minded catallactists. It appears in Pareto, at some stages of his work, and in an extreme form in some members of the Austrian school, especially Ludwig von Mises.[8] It is certainly one

[7] See for instance Edgeworth, *Mathematical Psychics* (1881), p. 30. The term has been used more recently by von Mises in *Human Action* (1949).

[8] See in particular von Mises's book *Die Gemeinwirtschaft* (1922) which was translated into English under the title *Socialism* (1959).

way in which the catallactic approach can be used; there are living writers, in America and elsewhere, who continue to use it in this manner. The exchange economy is a free economy; so to those who put freedom at the head of their values, it is bound to have a particular attraction. For it seems to show that a world is workable in which we are all allowed to go our own ways, our different ways, with a minimum of interference from other people.[9]

There is this individualist strand, especially in later work, but it will hardly do as an explanation of the 'revolution'. One can find it in Pareto, and perhaps even in Wicksell,[10] but in the work of the first generation (Jevons, say, or Menger) where is it? The most that could be argued in their case is that they were responding to a challenge. The socialists had made it impossible for the exchange economy to be taken for granted; whether one was for it, or against it, the time had come when it needed to be better understood. There may be something in that; but even that does not have to be the main answer.

I have insisted that the Old Political Economy, like other 'powerful' economic theories, was a concentration of attention. It gained strength by its omissions, by the things it put on one side. Some of the things it put on one side were rather obvious. Thus throughout the century in which it was dominant, there had been numerous writers who had refused to put on the Smithian 'blinkers'; they had been unwilling to think in the way in which that system of thought required them to think. But they had been unable to develop any system of thought with comparable potency. That is just what it was that Walras and Menger did.[11]

I would therefore maintain that the principal reason for the triumph of catallactics – in its day it was quite a triumph – was nothing to do with socialism or individualism; nor did it even have much to do with the changes that were then occurring in the 'real world'. The construction of a powerful economic theory, based on exchange, instead of production and distribution, had always been a

---

[9] *'Ce n'est pas qu'elle gouverne bien, mais elle gouverne peu'* as someone in Anatole France says of the Third Republic. The British classical economists would never have said that of *their* state.

[10] It is in his book on public finance (*Finanztheoretische Untersuchungen*, 1896) that Wicksell carries his individualism to the most extreme lengths.

[11] The Lausanne and the Austrian versions of catallactics are by no means identical, and it is possible that Jevons's version, if he had completed it, would have constituted a third variety. But it is noticeable that as time has gone on, these versions, at first distinct, have grown together. Later catallactists, such as Wicksell and Schumpeter and many more modern writers, have drawn upon Menger and upon Walras in equal measure. So the distinction between them is not one which we shall need to emphasise for our present purpose.

possibility. The novelty in the work of the great catallactists is just that they achieved it.

The appeal of catallactics lay in its intellectual quality, much more than in its individualism. The first catallactists were poor mathematicians, but they were thinking mathematically; and the mathematics that is implied in their theories has proved to be capable of enormous development. Already, before that happened, there was enough of intellectual interest to set its mark on the minds of many economists (who were now, it should be noticed, to a large extent academic economists). Though 'marginal utility' had its difficulties (difficulties of which we in our time have become increasingly aware) it was becoming easier to think of 'individuals' having given wants, or given utility functions, than to swallow the homogeneous 'wealth' of the Old Political Economy. It was easier to think of the economic system as a system of inter-related markets (Walras) or as an adjustment of means to ends (Menger) than to keep up the fiction of the social product any longer.

I have devoted this much space to the 'marginal revolution' (or 'catallactist revolution') because it seems to me to be the best example in economics of something which fits the Lakatos scheme. It provided a new way of taking up the economic problem; not just a new theory, but a new approach which was capable of much development. It was not (I have tried to show) in the main a reaction to contemporary events. The possibility of a utility theory had been there all the time; what the catallactists showed was that something could be done with it.

I pass on to what happened afterwards, in this century. That, from the point of view I am here adopting, was not just the Keynesian revolution; there was another thing too. You may be thinking that what I have called catallactics should be given a more familiar name – micro-economics; it is true that what I have called the catallactist revolution can be regarded as the rise of micro-economics. But if I used that term I might find myself saying that Keynesianism was macro-economics; and that is not right. There are two kinds of modern macro-economics. One is Keynesian; the other is quite different.

If we must have a founder for this other kind of macro-economics, it must be Pigou. Pigou of the *Economics of Welfare*,[12] or perhaps of *Wealth and Welfare*.[13] Long before the (relevant) work of Keynes! But what I mean by the other kind of macro-economics is not welfare

[12] First edition 1920.
[13] (1912).

economics in the modern sense; for what happened in the new welfare economics (in which I myself played my part) was that welfare economics was captured by the catallactists and it has never got quite free. If one looks at the whole of Pigou's book, not just at its (now) misleading title, one sees that it is a revival of the classical political economy. It is a book on production and distribution, in the classical manner. The definition of the real social product; how it can be increased; and how it is divided up. There is a line of descent, from Pigou, through my own *Theory of Wages*[14] to a great deal of modern growth theory (which, if one looks at it critically, is quite un-Keynesian). I think, for instance, of much of the work of Professor Solow. It is surely in Lakatos's sense a 'research programme'; it has been capable of much development, and it is by no means extinct.

If we are to think clearly about it, we must give it a name. I tried, at one time, to keep the classical name, and to call it political economy. But that does not do. I am now inclined to match catallactics, and to call what I am now talking about as plutology. (I know that the only writer who has previously used that term was a catallactist! But he was not of great importance; his ghost will doubtless forgive us.) Plutology is good Greek for theory of wealth.

Classical political economy, then, is the old plutology; that which descends from Pigou is the new. Why has it come up, and why has it flourished? Surely the reason for its success is the availability of the statistical material on which it can feed. We now have vast quantities of statistical material, on the macro-level; much more abundant (at least apparently) than the empirical material for micro-economics. The old plutologists did not have this material; that is why their work appears so abstract. They did not have the statistics to give it flesh and blood.

Why do we have these statistics, which they did not? It is not the case, as might be supposed from natural science analogies, that the lack of statistics, of this kind, was shown up by the classical theories; and that gave an incentive to collect them. There was something of this, but it was not the main thing. The statistics are a by-product of a great historical change, the great extension of the powers of the State which has occurred in this century. That, in its turn, is partly to be ascribed to political changes; but it is also, very importantly, a consequence of the cheapening of the costs of administration, which has made it possible for modern governments to collect information on a vastly greater scale than was previously practicable. One must always remember, when reading the older economists, that they were

14 *TW* (1932).

desperately short of facts. Nowadays we are swamped by floods of facts, or what appear to be facts, welling, all the time, out of the machines.[15]

I turn, finally, to Keynes. Keynesianism also, as it has developed, has had to accommodate the flood of facts; but it is clear that it did not start in that way. The 'social accounting Keynesianism' which is now in all the textbooks (and in the articles of journalists) was quite a late development; it is not really present even in the *General Theory*. If one looks at that book in terms of what led up to it (not in terms of what happened afterwards), one sees where it comes out. Where it belongs, when it is so considered, is not in the field of general (or 'real') economics – to which nearly all I have hitherto been saying refers. Where it belongs is in monetary economics; and since monetary statistics have long been abundant (much more abundant than most other statistics until the present century) monetary economics has always been topical; it has always had a close relation to the circumstances of the time in which it has been written; it has had to change as they have changed.

As I have stated elsewhere (at more length)[16] it is my own view that if the Keynes story is to be told properly (in its historical context) it should begin before Keynes. It begins with Hawtrey: *Currency and Credit* (1919). It must begin there, for there is a large part of Keynes's *Treatise* (1930) which is a reply to Hawtrey. A reply, on the matters where Keynes and Hawtrey differed; these are important, but they can only be seen in proper proportion once we have realised that on the most basic matter they were on the same side. Neither of them held that the economic system is automatically self-righting. The 'instability of capitalism' is nowadays commonly held to be a characteristically Keynesian doctrine; but it is already there – in Hawtrey. It has never been better stated than in the first chapter of Hawtrey's book, the chapter that is called 'Credit without Money'. In Hawtrey as in Keynes, the system has to be stabilised, by policy and by some instrument of policy. It was over the instrument of policy that they differed.

As the difference began, it looked rather small. Both agreed that the instrument was a rate of interest; but Hawtrey looked to the short rate, Keynes to the long. At this point I would accept that Keynes was more up to date. It was a change in the structure of the industrial system which Keynes perceived, and one on which Hawtrey

---

[15] Cf. what I say on the 'Administration Revolution' in *TEH* (1969), pp. 99, 162–6.
[16] In my paper on Hawtrey (*EP*, 1977).

was much less clear, making fixed capital investment of greater importance than it had been in the past, which impelled Keynes to make his first departure from the Hawtrey system. Another example, you will notice, of a theoretical development echoing a historical process.

But then Keynes discovered that his long rate was not only less directly susceptible to banking control than Hawtrey's short, but that it was very likely to be found that just when it was wanted it could not move enough. So he moved away from monetary methods to the 'fiscal' methods which have later been so largely associated with his name. That is a process that is taking place *inside* the *General Theory*. The structure of the book dates from the time when the long rate was pre-eminent; but as the work develops he cuts the ground under his own feet. Thus it was, that what began as monetary theory became 'fiscalism'.

It was nevertheless the particular circumstances of the 1930s which had this effect; it was because of his desire (his very proper desire) to apply his theory to the particular conditions of the time in which he was living that he moved in this way. At other times he might have reacted differently; one can even be fairly sure, from a general knowledge of his work, that he would have reacted differently. So it does no honour to Keynes to go on applying his theory, without drastic amendment, to the very different circumstances of the time in which we are now living. The Keynes theory has 'dated', just as the Hawtrey theory 'dated'. That does not mean that we must go back to the Hawtrey theory, or to still older theories, as many contemporaries would like to do. We must still push on. One can yet recognise that there may be something dramatically appropriate – nice for the historian, though not for those who have to live through it – if it should turn up, as now seems to be likely, that it is on the field of primary commodities (which Hawtrey emphasised, but Keynes, at least in the *General Theory*, so much under-emphasised) that the Age of Keynes will have met its nemesis.

I have covered a wide field – I had to! Let me sum up by returning to what I said at the beginning. What we want, in economics, are theories which will be useful, practically useful. That means that they must be selective. But all selection is dangerous. So there is plenty of room for criticism, and for the filling in of gaps, building some sort of bridge between one selective theory and another. There is plenty of room for academic work, doing that sort of a job. Much of it, I am well aware, works in its own 'blinkers', seeing the mote that is in one's brother's eye but not the beam that is in one's own. That,

I am afraid, is the nature of the case. Still, one could learn a little humility.

There is also, one must not forget, the application to history – not to the history of thought, with which I have here been concerned, but to economic history in the other sense. It is not only for application to the present that we need economics; we need it also for the interpretation of the past. If what I have said is true, this is a most delicate matter. We should not analyse (say) nineteenth-century history in terms of nineteenth-century theories; for our knowledge of the facts of that time is different from that of contemporaries, and the questions we ask are different from those that contemporaries asked. Yet we have to be careful in the application of modern theories, which arise out of modern experience. Neither is necessarily right.

2

The Social Accounting of Classical Models

I

The line of descent which I shall here be attempting to follow through begins before Adam Smith; it is necessary, for the understanding of Smith, to see him in relation to his predecessors. Where should one start? Not with Aristotle or Aquinas, who did not have models. The first trace of a model I can find is in Petty.[1]

Petty is so much at the beginning of economics that he is hardly an economist. If one demands (as Letwin[2] does) that a statistician should make some use of probability theory then he could not be a statistician; to call him an econometrist (as Schumpeter[3] so curiously does) is absurd. His true place is as the Father of Social Accounting. That was what he meant by his *Political Arithmetic*, of which he was so proud.

His first economic job was to make a survey of the land of Ireland, for the division of that land among Cromwellian settlers; it was the job of a surveyor or valuer. One can see how he would have looked up from that to consider the valuation of the whole wealth of a country, its labour wealth as well as its land wealth.[4] He had no income tax data at his disposal, and very little in the way of wage statistics; but even if he had had them, it is doubtful that he would

[1] Sir William Petty (1625–87) had a romantic career. The son of a tradesmen at Portsmouth, he ran away to sea, broke his leg, and was set ashore, by cruel sailors, on the coast of France. He was picked up and educated by the Jesuits; but he next emerges in the company of English exiles in Paris, one of his patrons being Thomas Hobbes. He then went to study in Holland, where he learned such secrets that we next find him teaching anatomy in the University of Oxford (1651). A better job was to be medical officer to Cromwell's army in Ireland; but a still better job was to do this survey, the 'Down Survey' as it was called. In spite of these Cromwellian associations, he made his peace with Charles II, was knighted in 1663 and became a leading member of the Royal Society, then forming. His reward for his Irish survey was a substantial piece of the county of Kerry, which he bequeathed to his distinguished descendants, Earls of Shelburne and Marquesses of Lansdowne.

[2] W. Letwin, *Origins of Scientific Economics* (1963), p. 114.

[3] J. Schumpeter, *History of Economic Analysis*, p. 209.

[4] All this is most clearly set out in his *Political Anatomy of Ireland* (1672), see esp. pp. 63–7.

have wanted to use them. For it was the normal value (rental value) of the land which, like any valuer nowadays, he would have been assessing; so it would have been the normal value of the labour which he would have wanted to set against it. How could one establish a relation between these normal values? How, as he put it, could one establish a Par between land and labour?

That, in Petty, was little more than a question; the first attempt to answer it was made, more than a half a century later, by Cantillon.[5] He also, in the first part of his book, the only part that here concerns us, was proceeding as a social accountant. He appears to have collected a mass of figures, now lost, which would surely, if they had survived, have made this more evident. He clearly knew that in a closed economy (that qualification is quite explicit) the social product is equal to the sum of incomes; and that the equality is maintained by valuing each individual product at its inclusive cost in terms of productive factors. (The other equality, between income and expenditure, is less explicit; but in the course of his work it seems to be implied.) It is, however, already apparent, from the first equality, that the significance of the aggregate (income or product) depends on Petty's Par, as Cantillon shows, much more clearly than Petty had done.

Cantillon's explanation is best expressed algebraically. He has two sectors in his model, agricultural and non-agricultural, and it is evidently in the agricultural sector that rent is to be determined. If the production of a unit of corn (taken to represent the agricultural product) requires a units of labour and b units of land, if w is the wage of labour, in terms of corn, and r is rent, per unit of land, also in terms of corn, the equation of value and cost can be written

$$aw + br = 1 \qquad (1)$$

for the value of corn in terms of itself is unity. So if a and b are given, and w is given, r is determined, and the ratio r/w is determined. But what determines w?

[5] Richard Cantillon (1685–1734) is the most distinguished economist who is known to have been murdered. He remained for long a mystery man, but research has shown that he was in fact of Irish origin, the son of a Jacobite exile, who settled in Paris. He was thus brought up in Paris, where he became a financier. He made a fortune as a bear of Law's Mississippi stock. (Thus a share of what was lost by the unsuccessful speculators went into his pockets.) Like Ricardo, having made his money he turned to economics; but unlike Ricardo he spent freely on factual research. He met his end in London, where he was murdered by a servant with whom he had quarrelled, and who then burned down the house (thus destroying his master's papers) to conceal his misdeed. All that survived was the little book we have, published in French (but it may have been originally written in English) twenty years after his death. (*Essai sur la nature de Commerce en general*, ed. Henry Higgs, Royal Economic Society, 1931)

There are, says Cantillon, two sorts of labour in agriculture: (1) common labour and (2) the labour of the farmer, which he calls 'entrepreneurial' labour. w_1, the wage of common labour, is determined, in *normal* conditions, by what is needed by the labourer to maintain his efficiency and to bring up a family; it is thus a 'subsistence' wage. The reason why w_1 must be at that level in normal conditions (or, as we might say, in equilibrium conditions) is that the supply of common labour is perfectly elastic at that wage. 'Men multiply like mice in a barn if they have unlimited means of subsistence' as he puts it himself.[6] As for his 'entrepreneurial labour' its normal wage w_2 must include a premium over w_1, to cover costs of acquiring skills, and also a risk element (since this labour is not employed contractually, but gets a residue which may vary from year to year). Nevertheless, again in normal conditions, w_2 will exceed w_1 by a constant proportion (again, it appears, because of perfect elasticity of supply). So, since the two sorts of labour are used in fixed proportions and their wages are in a constant proportion, the wage that appeared in equation (1) above is in fact determined. For if L_1 and L_2 are the amounts employed of the two sorts of labour, and L_1/L_2 is given,

$$wL = w(L_1 + L_2) = w_1 L_1 + w_2 L_2$$

Thus from w_1 and w_2, w is determined.

Now if we write $(1/a) = p$, as will henceforward be more convenient, multiplication of equation (1) by pL gives

$$wL + R = pL \qquad (2)$$

where R is the total of rents, also in terms of corn.

Now consider the non-agricultural sector, which Cantillon calls the 'handicraft' sector. Rent here is negligible, but the wage is normally higher than the wage of common labour in agriculture (for there are similar extra costs in acquiring particular skills). So if L^* is the labour employed in this sector, and w^* its wage per unit, the value of its output is w^*L^*, with $w^* > w_1$ (and probably also $> w$).

The social accounting table that is implied in Cantillon's work can then be set out as follows. There are three classes of income receivers:

A   workers in agriculture (including entrepreneurial workers);
B   landed proprietors;
C   workers in non-agriculture.

[6] Cantillon, *Essai*, p. 83.

The number in A is L, the number in C is L^*. All we require, to complete the table, are parameters α, β, γ, indicating the fractions of the incomes of the three classes that are spent on corn. So we have the situation in table 2.1:

Table 2.1

	A	B	C
Income	wL	$(p-w)L$	w^*L^*
Spent on corn	αwL	$\beta(p-w)L$	γw^*L^*
Spent on 'non-corn'	$(1-\alpha)wL$	$(1-\beta)(p-w)L$	$(1-\gamma)w^*L^*$

If the value of corn output is to equal what is spent on it, the sum of the items in the second row must equal pL. It will then follow that the sum of the items in the third row will equal w^*L^*; for the sum of these sums must equal $pL + w^*L^*$, which is the sum of the income items in row 1. There is thus just this one equation of consistency

$$pL = \alpha wL + \beta(p-w)L + \gamma w^*L^* \qquad (3)$$

an equation which can be shown to have a clear economic meaning.

This comes out more neatly if the equation is re-arranged. Write it as

$$(1-\alpha)wL + (1-\beta)(p-w)L = \gamma w^*L^* \qquad (4)$$

The two terms on the left-hand side of (4) show what is spent by the agricultural classes, A and B, on the product of C, while the right-hand side is the corn (or the value of the corn) which C gets in exchange. Thus the consistency equation is a balance-of-payments equation between the two sectors, agricultural and non-agricultural. It is the balancing of this balance of payments which ensures the consistency of the model.

I do not pretend that this balance-of-payments equation is explicit in Cantillon, but something of that sort does seem to be implied. The consequences he draws are those he would draw if he were working with such an equation.

Since the equation relates to normal conditions, it can be regarded as an equilibrium equation; and one cannot, of course, from an equilibrium equation, infer anything about causality. But the workers in C must have food, while to those in A (if not to those in B) the products of C must be less essential; so it is plausible to think of the left-hand side of (4) being given exogenously, while the right-hand side adjusts to it. If it is then granted that β is probably small, while α is large (approaching unity) the total of rents, $(p-w)L$, becomes a fair approximation to the left-hand side of the equation. So it is the spending of those rents, largely upon the products of C, which provide the exports from C, by which it pays for its imports (food). One can certainly recognise that much in Cantillon.

Later economists (including Adam Smith) have thought this an odd doctrine, but there are conditions, which may well have been those of Cantillon's own environment, which it fits. It is still true, in some 'less developed countries' that government is supported out of an agricultural surplus. Part of this is devoted to feeding (and clothing) the government's own servants, while part, in the modern case, is sold abroad. These exports pay for imports; so the goods required by the government (and indeed by other people in the C sector) which cannot be produced at home are acquired by way of exchange. It is still true, in such countries, that the population $(L+L^*)$ which can be supported at reasonable wages (w and w^*) will be larger the larger is the agricultural surplus. That is what Cantillon says.

II

It may have seemed surprising that I should have associated Cantillon with the beginning of social accounting (Petty had shown no more than that there was a need for it). I have not claimed that in Cantillon it is more than implicit; should I not have ascribed the true beginning to Quesnay[7] and the Physiocrats, who carried on from Cantillon[8] and in whose work something that looks like a social accounting table does without doubt explicitly appear? I have not done that, because I think that what is implied in Cantillon is a consistent model, so far as it goes, while the famous *Tableau Economique* of Quesnay, though it is more ambitious, has less consistency. It has in consequence set the most tantalising problems to later

---

[7] François Quesnay (1697–1774) had a distinguished career in medicine, and did not turn to economics until he was sixty years of age. He was chief physician to Madame de Pompadour, the most celebrated and the most influential of the mistresses of Louis XV. So, in spite of his association with dangerous thinkers, who were later accused of having prepared the way for Revolution, his *Tableau* was printed on the private press of the Palace of Versailles.

[8] R. L. Meek, *Economics of Physiocracy* (1961), p. 267.

commentators,[9] but to get involved in those mazes would be a distraction from my purpose.

There is nevertheless one thing emerging in Quesnay which is important. It can be explained, without reference to Quesnay's awkward examples, in terms of what has here been set out in the Cantillon table. Once one accepts that the consistency of Cantillon's table depends on a balance-of-payments equation, it is tempting to use it, as such equations have often been used by present-day economists. Suppose that the demand from A and B (the agricultural classes) for the products of C increases. That is to say, there is an increase in the total of the items on the left-hand side of equation (4) above; the right-hand side must then also be increased, to restore equilibrium. If w^* is unchanged, and γ is unchanged, L^* must increase.

That there should be an increase in employment as a result of an increase in exports was not surprising; but the balance-of-payments equation said more than that. If $\gamma < 1$ (it was natural to take it that it would be less than 1) the increase in employment in C would be greater than that directly caused by the increase in exports; $(1/\gamma)$ is a multiplier. There is a secondary increase in employment in C, due to the fact that the C people, whose incomes are increased by the initial expansion, spend part of their increased incomes on C products. Just the same story as with the Keynes multiplier! There is what mathematicians would call an *isomorphism* between them.

So, much the same problem came up with the Quesnay Multiplier as was to do, so many years later, with that of Keynes. It was impossible to believe that the secondary increase in L^*, which was to follow from the increase in 'exports', could appear all at once; it was a consequence of the primary rise, so that would surely have to happen *first*. So to make the model 'work' one had to introduce lags. The Kahn multiplier this time! That did happen with Quesnay too. There is no question that in some of his versions he does introduce lags.

Why did this not happen with Adam Smith? We shall see.[10]

[9] *ibid.*, pp. 364ff.
[10] It is tempting, at this point, to insert a passage about Turgot's *Reflections* (published, in parts, between 1769 and 1773). It is a great work, and much more readable than those of the Physiocrats. But I don't think it quite belongs in this story. Whether Smith was influenced by Turgot has been much disputed (see J. Viner, *Guide to the Rae Life of Smith*, 1954, pp. 128ff.). It is safer to assume that he was not influenced.

III

The obvious way in which Smith's model differs from those of his predecessors (the Physiocrats and also Cantillon) is that he divides into sectors differently. He also has one sector that produces a surplus and one that does not, but his 'productive' sector is not confined to agriculture. This is surely a reflection of the environment in which he was living, the kind of economy he therefore had in mind.

It is true that modern historians find their most significant date for the beginning of the Industrial Revolution in Britain at about 1780 – just *after* the publication of the *Wealth of Nations* (1776). But they have also shown that there was plenty of industrial activity, in a wider sense, much before that. What marks the difference between this proto-industrialism and what began just after Adam Smith, is that in the latter the leading form of capital came to be fixed capital (plant and machinery) while in the former it was working capital (goods in process). It has been suggested that a major reason for the importance of working capital at the proto-industrial stage was slowness of transport.[11] When goods could only be transported over land by pack-animals or carts, the production period, which was associated with many sorts of production processes, was inevitably quite long.

So Adam Smith's model is characteristically a working capital model. (Not that he entirely neglects fixed capital, but he does not give it the central place that he might have given it if he had been writing later.) His 'productive' sector comprises those activities which have a significant production period; so that, at any particular date, they have capital that is embodied in goods in process. His 'unproductive' sector comprises those which have no such production period, and hence no capital embodied. Their labour 'perishes in the very instant of its performance' as he says.[12]

Now it is important to notice that Smith's distinction (between activities which require working capital and those that do not) and that which was made by his predecessors (between agricultural and non-agricultural) are not incompatible. There could exist (and must surely have existed) economies in which agriculture was the main form of *productive* activity, in Smith's sense. It is indeed convenient, and proves to be illuminating, to begin the discussion of Smithian

---

[11] T. S. Ashton, *Economic History of England; the eighteenth century* (1955), pp. 100–2.
[12] Smith, *Wealth of Nations* (Oxford edition, 1976), p. 330.

models by considering that of such an economy. I shall even venture to call it the First Smithian model. For I find it hard to believe that Smith himself did not often work with such a model in mind. (And the same would be true of many of his successors.)

What is characteristic of this First Model is that it has an accounting period which dictates itself. It is just the agricultural year, from harvest to harvest. A capital is carried over to that period, in the form of last year's harvest; out of that stock all the labour that is employed during the year will have to be fed. All of the labour, 'unproductive' as well as 'productive'. It must be fed out of that carry-over, since the product (harvest) of the current year has not yet been produced. So what Smith would say had gone wrong with the Cantillon 'consistency equation' was that it had got its timing wrong. (That would not have mattered if it were applied to static conditions, as Cantillon would surely have applied it; but Smith was looking for something more general.) It was wrong to write equation (3) above, as we wrote it, without temporal suffixes; for the items on the right-hand side refer to the current period, and what should stand on the left is $p_{t-1}L_{t-1}$, the production of the period before.

Take the simplest case, in which $\alpha = 1$ and $\beta = 0$. The Cantillon equation then reduces to

$$pL = wL + \gamma w^*L^*$$

but what Smith would have to write in replacement of it is

$$p_{t-1}L_{t-1} = w_t L_t + \gamma w_t^* L_t^* \qquad (5)$$

This cannot be used for a balance-of-payments exercise, as appeared to be possible with the Cantillon form. It is not a static equilibrium equation; it is a difference equation. But it is not even a difference equation in L_t unless L_t^* is given.

I think it is clear that this is the way Smith would have wanted to use it. If L_t^* were zero, so that there was no 'leak' into 'unproductive' labour, (5) would reduce to

$$p_{t-1}L_{t-1} = w_t L_t$$

whence

$$p_t L_t = (p_t/w_t)\, p_{t-1}L_{t-1} \qquad (6)$$

Write $(p_t/w_t) = 1 + G_t$. Then G_t is the growth rate of the economy (as measured by the growth in its capital stock) as it would be if there were no leak into unproductive labour. If there is a leak, it is obvious that the growth rate will be lower.

That is indeed the main point which Smith wanted to have emerging. It already appears in what I have called the First Smithian model. But the assumptions of that model are not Smith's assumptions. We have to see what happens if we follow him more closely.

His productive sector was to extend far outside agriculture. That made it impossible for him to make the basic simplification of the First Model – the identification of the accounting period with the agricultural year.

The stock that is carried over at the beginning of the accounting period can then no longer be reckoned to consist entirely of finished goods. It must mainly consist of goods in process – goods which will have to have further work done on them before they can pass into consumption. If they are finished during the period, they will be available to satisfy consumption demands during the period; but they may not be finished until after the end of the period, so that they will still be goods in process at the end. And of the productive labour (L_t) that is engaged during the period, some will be finishing the consumption goods of the period, but some will be making things which will go into the final capital stock. What (keeping as close to Smith as possible) would be the accounting table that would fit this situation?

All of the items in an accounting table are in value terms. The inputs (of the period) now consist of: (1) the initial stock; (2) the flow of labour. There is a problem (the old problem of Petty's Par) of how to make them comparable. Smith is valuing at cost, so the value of the initial stock, K_t, should be the value of the labour that has gone to produce it. But that is not labour *of the period*; it is past labour. It is not obvious how to reduce it into terms of current labour. But that does not matter so much as might perhaps be expected, for the purpose of the accounting table. (Of course it does matter for other purposes.) For the difference between the value of the final stock and the value of the initial stock, $K_{t+1} - K_t$, is a matter of things that are done during the period. These should be capable of being valued in terms of current labour.

Consider first the 'productive' labour that is engaged during the period (L_t). If the whole of that labour were devoted to increasing the final stock, without any flow of consumption goods being taken out, we should have

$$K_{t+1} = K_t + p_t L_t$$

where p_t (as before) is labour productivity. But in fact consumption goods are taken out, which are acquired by members of the three classes: (A) productive labourers; (B) owners of capital, and (C) unproductive labourers. It will be noticed that it is the whole capitalist class, including landowners, who here take the place of the landowners in the Cantillon model. The values of these consumptions must be deducted from the (gross) product $p_t L_t$. So if α, β, γ, now denote the fractions of their incomes which the three classes spend on consumption *goods* (the finished products of the productive sector) while α', β', γ' denote the fractions spent on services (the products of the unproductive sector), we get table 2.2, which is comparable with that which was written out for Cantillon. (All items in this table relate to period t, so I suppress the suffixes.)

Table 2.2

	A	B	C
Income	wL	$(p-w)L$	w^*L^*
Spent on consumption goods	αwL	$\beta(p-w)L$	γw^*L^*
Spent on services	$\alpha'wL$	$\beta'(p-w)L$	$\gamma'w^*L^*$
Residues	$(1-\alpha-\alpha')wL$	$(1-\beta-\beta')(p-w)L$	$(1-\gamma-\gamma')w^*L^*$

Smith would clearly reckon these residues to be saved; so the sum of the items in the last row is S, the sum of saving.

Now w^*L^*, the income derived from services, is clearly equal to the amount spent on them; so

$$[\alpha'wL + \beta'(p-w)L + \gamma'w^*L^*] - w^*L^* = 0$$

So we may add this last expression to S, leaving it unaffected. Thus

$$S = (1-\alpha)wL + (1-\beta)(p-w)L - \gamma w^*L^*$$
$$= pL - \alpha wL - \beta(p-w)L - \gamma w^*L^* \qquad (7)$$

The deductions here shown from pL are the values of what has been taken out of it for consumption; so what remains is the increase in the capital stock. Saving = (net) investment, as would be said nowadays. The consumption corresponds to the 'leak', which was identified in the First Smithian model.

There is nevertheless one important difference between the two models, to which, one would think, Smith did not give enough attention. In the First Model, the harvest comes into the hands of farmers, who themselves make the decisions of how it is to be used.

The 'investors' and the 'savers' are effectively the same people. But in the Second Model that is not at all necessarily the case. The people who make the decisions to start the new processes are those who here are reckoned into class (B), the capitalists; but though their savings $(1-\beta-\beta')pL$ are a part, and may be a large part, of total savings, they are clearly revealed as not necessarily the whole. There is then a problem of transmission: how the savings that are made elsewhere are to be transmuted into the investment that is made in the productive sector. Adam Smith did not attend to that problem — presumably because he thought that in the conditions of his day it was not of 'normal' importance. On that he may well have been right; it is in more sophisticated economies that it has been revealed to be of such importance. But even in his day there were problems of money and banking; and this is where they ought to have been fitted in.

It is also remarkable that with equation (7) before him — and he must have had something like that equation before him — he paid so much attention to the deductions, and so little to the positive element (pL). 'Parsimony, and not industry, is the immediate cause of the increase of capital'.[13] Should he not, on his own principles, have said 'both parsimony and industry'? Again, one supposes, it was because of the environment in which he was living that he thought he could take the positive element for granted.

It should finally be emphasised that table 2.2, which is a perfectly good table for a 'working capital economy', such as (I have shown) Smith must have had mainly in mind, itself makes no assumption about 'normality', as Cantillon did for his corresponding table. The accounting relations hold, whether the economy is in a 'normal', or equilibrium, state or not. They would of course hold if the economy were in a *steady state* of regular progress; but it is impossible that Smith can have been thinking in terms of steady states. He could nevertheless say that if there were an accumulation of capital during the period, so that the end-stock was greater than the beginning stock, when suitably valued, this would mean that more processes were under way at the end of the period than at the beginning; so that, when comparing this period with its successor, it would be likely that there would be more input of labour (L) in the second period than in the first. And because of his reliance on economies of scale (the division of labour, so crucial an element in Smith's thinking — not so far mentioned, because there was not so far any need to mention it) he could be confident that from the increase

---

[13] *ibid*., p. 337.

in labour input a more than proportional increase in output would follow. Not much like the modern constant returns to scale 'steady state'!

This is also consistent with what he says about wages. He will not follow Cantillon (to whom he expressly refers[14]) in supposing the supply of labour to be perfectly elastic, so that the real wage is kept constant. Though he admits some element of 'cost of living' in wage determination, he is clear that an increase in demand will raise wages. It follows that in his progressive economy, with positive accumulation, the wage will rise, in successive period (and that, of course, is in itself to be welcomed); but since the bulk of savings comes out of profits, the rise in wages, by itself, will be tending to slow up the rate of growth. However, he does not lay much stress upon this, for he believes that scale economies will offset it. He thinks of p_t rising over time, and offsetting the effect of w_t on profits. So the growth can go on, as far ahead as one needs to look.

IV

After all this on Smith, it is unnecessary, here, to say much on Ricardo.[15] What has caused so much trouble in the interpretation of Ricardo is that he has several models, and moves from one to another without much warning. All of them are present in the famous first chapter 'On Value' of the *Principles* but not all are present in the rest of his work.

The First Model, clearly that from which he began, is easily distinguishable, for it is presented, by itself, in another work, the *Essay on Profits*[16] which he published in 1815, two years before the *Principles*. It is impossible not to recognise that this was the first stage, from which the work that was later presented in the *Principles* took its origin. This First Model is evidently an adaptation of what has here been called the First Smithian model.

The Second Ricardian, which is that which is used, fairly consistently, in the central chapters of the *Principles* (II–VIII) has a similar relation to the Second Smithian model. It is a working capital model, like the Second Smithian. It is a similar adaptation of the Second Smithian.

---

[14] *ibid.*, p. 85.
[15] For further discussion of Ricardo, see essays 3 and 4.
[16] *Essay on the Influence of a Low Price of Corn on the Profits of Stock* (1815).

That such a model should have been used by Ricardo, as extensively as it was, shows how directly he was carrying on from Smith. Yet in his time England had become industrialised, in a different sense from Smith's; so he came to realise (though I think he was a bit slow in realising) that this was inadequate. He needed a model which should pay more attention to fixed capital – to machinery. So there is also a Third Model, never worked out fully, which is represented in the last section of the *Value* chapter and of course in the chapter on machinery, which was not in the first edition of the *Principles*, but was added later.

To return to the First Model, that of the *Essay on Profits*. Even this cannot have been the beginning; there were steps, on the road from Smith to Ricardo, which must have preceded it.

The first was the recognition that Smith, in playing down the distinction between agriculture and non-agriculture, of which his predecessors had made so much, had gone too far. The scale economies (increasing returns) on which he had based his comfortable doctrine were most obviously a characteristic of the non-agricultural part of his 'productive' sector. The production of food, as Malthus was already emphasising at the turn of the century,[17] was subject to diminishing returns – in the first place in the simple sense that product would usually increase less fast than labour applied. But all that followed from that, if no more than that had been seen, was that there was another possible check to Smith's growth process, not noticed by Smith. There was not only a possible check from rising wages (w_t); even if there was no rise in wages, there would be this Malthusian effect on p_t, as labour (L_t) increased. It might, or might not, be offset by Smith's scale economies.

And there was then a more subtle point which could come into sight. If it so happened that the accumulation process led to no great expansion in employment, its main effect being a rise in the real wage (w_t), the proportion of the wage that was spent on food would be likely to diminish, while the proportion spent on those things where increasing returns were important would be likely to increase. There would thus be a good hope that in this case, the Smithian increasing returns would be dominant. In that case, it would be the rise in wages itself which would be the main impediment to growth. But if, on the other hand, the increase in the labour supply was such as to prevent the real wage rising, the Malthusian check would take its place. It was easiest to exhibit this by taking

[17] *Essay on Population* (1798 and 1802).

the real wage to be constant – as Ricardo did in his First Model, the first sketch of his theory.

The next step, which led directly to that First Model, was the observation that a general tendency to diminishing average returns (as in Malthus) implied diminishing *marginal* returns. This was no doubt first seen in terms of an *extensive* margin: land of various qualities, the land just taken into cultivation being the worst land. The cultivation of that land involved the investment of capital for the regular agricultural period; on that capital a normal rate of profit must be earned. On the marginal land there need be no further surplus; but on better land, even when the normal profit had been deducted, there would be a surplus. With a landlord–tenant system, such as was usual in England in Ricardo's time, this would be collected as rent.

The model which emerged when these considerations were taken together (that of the *Essay on Profits*) is discussed in the paper which follows (essay 3). A formal discussion of the Second Ricardian model, that which is implied in the central chapters of the *Principles* and which has a similar relation, as has been explained, to the Second Smithian, will be found in essay 4. The issues which arise in these places are special to Ricardo. On the main issue which has come up in this paper, where Smith and Ricardo are on one side, while Cantillon and the Physiocrats – and Keynes – are on the other, there is a little more to be said.

V

When the game was re-played in the 1930s, with Keynes taking the parts of Cantillon and Quesnay, who was taking the part of Smith? Obviously it was Hayek.[18] When Hayek attacked Keynes for leaving out the 'structure of production', he was making the same point as had been made by Smith. His 'Austrian' structure of production was a time-structure, like Smith's. Inputs come before outputs. An increase in employment, at unchanged real wages, involves an increase in the *wage-fund* – the total of the real goods on which wages are spent. (There is no wage-fund mysticism about that; it is just a matter of arithmetic.) This total cannot be increased out of the produce of the labour that is newly employed, for that is not yet ready. It must therefore come from some other source.

[18] Articles in *Economica*, 1931 onwards.

Smith took it that it must come from additional saving; voluntary saving, he clearly supposed. (But he could, quite logically, have admitted that it could come from increased taxation, the proceeds of which were saved.) Hayek took the same line. That would not do for Keynes. He had another way out, though he did not emphasise it, I suppose because he thought it obvious. The extra goods needed, now, could come from reserves: surplus stocks of goods, at all stages, and (in the case of a single country, in an international system) reserves of foreign exchange. Especially at the time when he, and Hayek, were writing, it was most important that that should have been allowed for.

It is rather easy, when it is allowed for, to give a re-statement of Multiplier theory, which gives due, but not undue, weight to the Smith–Hayek objection. I have done it myself, in the chapter on the Multiplier in my *Crisis in Keynesian Economics*.[19] That chapter, it would seem, has been fairly non-controversial. So the old dispute – I have shown in this essay what an old dispute it is – may now, perhaps at last be concluded.

As will be shown in a later essay (5 below) there was one Classical Economist who could see both sides.[20] There are excellent statements of both sides of the argument to be found in his works. But there were so many other things on which he wanted to preach, that he never found occasion to bring the two sides together. He left it to my generation, after much toil and many squabbles, to arrive at the point he had already reached, more than a century ago.

[19] *CKE* (1973), ch. 1.
[20] pp. 62–4.

3

Ricardo's Theory of Distribution

Reprinted from *Essays in Honour of Lord Robbins*, edited by Maurice Peston and Bernard Corry (Weidenfeld and Nicolson, 1972). It is chiefly concerned with the amendments required to Ricardo's theory, here taken essentially in its *Essay on Profits* form, when the linearity assumption, that was surreptitiously made in that *Essay* is dropped. I think I have shown that the abandonment of linearity makes less difference than has often been supposed.

I see no inconsistency between this paper and the Hicks–Hollander paper which follows, though that, of course, was written several years later.

It has been the general impression, ever since Cannan (*Theories of Production and Distribution*, pp. 339ff.), that there is something wrong with Ricardo's theory of distribution, even on his own assumptions. His arithmetical examples are not sufficient to support his conclusions; they do not show them to be necessary. The matter has been further explored by H. Barkai (*Economica*, 1959), whose more sophisticated technique seems to support the Cannan criticism. I accepted it myself, until impelled by some correspondence with Dr K. V. S. Sastri, of Andhra University (Guntur) India, to look at the matter again. He convinced me that there is more to be said for Ricardo than is allowed by these critics, even when the question at issue is taken as they take it. But I have also been convinced – and I am now inclined to think that this is a more important matter – that the distribution question on which the critics have fastened is only one of the questions which was in Ricardo's mind. There is another, on which Ricardo's position is stronger; and for his central thesis (his theory of Growth, or Retardation of Growth) it is a more important question. Even for us in our day, when we are interested in that aspect, it is a more important question.

I begin, nevertheless, with the 'conventional' problem, which I do not dispute was one of Ricardo's problems. He says, in his *Introduc-*

tion, that he is going to study the ways in which 'the whole produce of the earth...will be allotted...to rent, profits, and wages'. It is there in black and white.

The central model, on which the answer that he gives is based, requires neither arithmetical examples nor algebra for its exposition. If we make two *simplifications* (which Ricardo very frequently, but not invariably, allows himself) it can easily be represented on a diagram. I shall begin with this simplified version, but shall not omit before I have done, to consider the adjustments which are needed when the simplifications are removed.

Production, in the Ricardo model, is of two 'goods' – 'food', produced under diminishing returns, and 'manufactures', produced under constant returns. The first of the simplifications is to suppose that the two goods are demanded, throughout, in fixed proportions. Analytically, therefore, they can be reduced to a single good, a 'bundle', which I shall call Output. Output, it will be observed, is produced, by these assumptions, under *diminishing* returns.

The second simplification is to neglect fixed capital, and to make all capital circulate with a uniform fixed period. Input, therefore, is solely input of labour. Wages, however, are advanced to labourers, so that the wage of the labourer is his discounted marginal product. But since the supply of labour is taken to be perfectly elastic at a given (real) wage, a wage that is fixed in terms of Output, the equation of wage to discounted marginal product does not determine the wage, but determines the rate of discount or profit, which is

$$\frac{\text{marginal product of labour} - \text{wage}}{\text{wage}}$$

With these simplifications, the diagram is easy. Labour (input) is measured on the horizontal axis. Output on the vertical. *UM* is the curve of the marginal product of labour, *UA* is the curve of the average product. (I have drawn these curves, in figure 3.1, as straight lines, but I am not assuming that they have this particular form. It is *generally* true that if *UM* slopes downward throughout, *UA* must slope downward throughout.)

When the input of labour is *ON*, the average product of labour is *GN*, the marginal product is *PN*, and the wage is *WN* (*LW* being the horizontal supply curve of labour). Profit per unit of labour is *PW*, and rent per unit of labour is *GP*. The shares of the factors in the product are therefore proportional to *GP*, *PW*, *WN*.

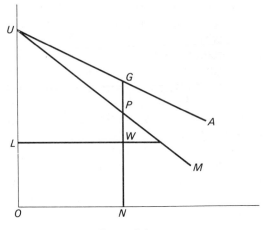

Figure 3.1

It is at once apparent that since *UA* is falling throughout, the share
of wages in total product (*WN/GN*) must be rising. This will be
generally true, whatever the form of the curves. It does not depend
at all on linearity.

As for the rent-share (*GP/GN*) in the case of linearity that is clearly
rising. Ricardo's conclusion that increasing employment of labour
will raise rents is therefore valid, as we should expect, for the linearity
case (arithmetical examples so easily conceal linearity assumptions).
But what if we generalise, not assuming linearity?

This is effectively a two-factor model, so the conventional theory
of distribution in a two-factor model should apply. Labour is variable,
land is fixed. The share of rent in total product should therefore
increase when the input of labour increases *if the elasticity of substitution between the factors is less than unity*, but if the elasticity of
substitution is greater than unity the relative share of rent will move
the other way.[1] This, I think, is effectively what Ricardo's critics
have been saying, and it is not for me to say that it is wrong. It is not
wrong, but it does not quite measure up to Ricardo.

For Ricardo cannot have been thinking in terms of our mathematically defined production functions, with no constraint put upon
them but 'convexity' and homogeneity of the first degree. If one asks

[1] *TW* (1932), ch. 6.

what he is assuming, some of these things are not important; but there are others, on which the mathematical theory does not insist, which are:

On the first settling of a country, in which there is an abundance of rich and fertile land, a very small proportion of which is required to be cultivated for the support of the actual population, or indeed can be cultivated with the capital which the population can command, there will be no rent.

That is what he says (Sraffa edition, p. 69). So the two-factor production function must be such that when land is plentiful relatively to labour, the marginal product of land is zero. I do not find him saying so explicitly that if the input of labour increased indefinitely, relatively to land, the marginal product of labour would fall to zero; this is indeed, on his assumptions, so fanciful a state of affairs that he would have had no occasion to mention it. But I would have thought that no unprejudiced reader of Ricardo could doubt that it is implied. For it is an implication that can only be avoided, consistently with the diminishing returns that are explicitly assumed, by making the marginal product curve converge asymptotically to some horizontal. Of course Ricardo did not bother about that. If anyone had mentioned it to him, one feels sure that he would have dismissed it as just plain silly!

If the production function is restricted by these *two* extra conditions, that the marginal product of land falls to zero when land is sufficiently abundant, and that the marginal product of labour falls to zero when labour is sufficiently abundant, it follows that at the terminal points, where a factor just ceases to be abundant, the elasticity of substitution between the factors *must* be less than unity. It is unnecessary to give a mathematical proof; for it is obvious that when, as a result of an increase in the input of labour, rent rises from zero to a positive quantity, the share of rent must be rising; so the elasticity of substitution must be less than unity. Similarly at the other end.

If the elasticity of substitution were constant, or even approximately constant, along the whole curve, it would follow at once that it must be less than unity everywhere; Ricardo's proposition about the rent share would then be proved. This is a procedure which may appeal to some; I do not care for it myself. 'CES production functions' have been having a vogue; they are mathematically fairly jolly; but what is the empirical reason why the production function should be of this type? I cannot see any.

Nevertheless, if the elasticity of substitution must be less than unity at each end, it can only become greater than unity anywhere if it has a bulge in the middle; and though we must grant that such a bulge could occur, it might fairly be regarded as 'abnormal'. Ricardo is guilty of no more than the omission of a qualification. Are we doing any more than touching up his theory a little when we put it in?

Notice further just what is implied in it. As the input of labour increases, the relative share of rent begins at zero, rises to a positive fraction, perhaps then slips back a bit, but must 'in the end' resume its rise. If a mountaineer starts at sea-level, and finishes the day at the top of his mountain, he must *on the whole* have been climbing; but it is, of course, not excluded that he had to get over a smaller range on the way, and was descending for a while as he came down from it.

Even this is not all − by no means all. For though there are many passages (such as that which I quoted from his *Introduction*) in which Ricardo talks in terms of a three-way distribution, it is a question how far it was this distribution which was ultimately his main concern. So long as one is looking at the three-way distribution, the decline in the profit-share seems to be due as much to the rise in the wage-share (which, as we have seen, occurs without exception) as to the rise in the rent-share, which is subject to the qualification we have just been considering. Why does he put so much emphasis on the rise in the rent-share?

The explanation, I think, is to be found in the chapter on 'Gross and Net Revenue' (XXVI). Wages (subsistence wages) are for Ricardo a cost, a cost which is necessarily incurred in the earning of the surplus (Net Revenue), from which alone the saving which is the source of capital accumulation and therefore of expansion can be derived. Net Revenue is profits + rents; so if the profit share in Net Revenue falls, the rent-share *must* rise, and vice versa.

Now as labour input increases, the wage-share in Gross Revenue (necessarily) rises; so the ratio of Net Revenue to Gross necessarily falls. Thus even if Rent was a constant proportion of Gross Revenue, it would be a rising proportion of Net Revenue. It could even be a falling proportion of Gross, and still be a rising proportion of Net Revenue. Thus when Ricardo is thinking 'net' (as I believe he often is) he can talk of rents gaining at the expense of profits; and though there is still a possible exception (over limited ranges) it has been cut down to a very modest exception.

No doubt it is the fall in the *rate* of profit, diminishing the incentive to save and invest, which is the brake on expansion on which

Ricardo paid greatest weight; this (which figures in the diagram as the ratio PW/WN) is clearly declining, from the downward slope of the marginal productivity curve, *without exception*. But it is reinforced (fairly certainly reinforced) by the transference of net revenue, which is saveable revenue, from a class which looks like having a high propensity to save and invest to one which looks like having a much lower propensity. That they have these propensies is an empirical judgement, but it is not unreasonable. Thus, within the limitations of the model, the retardation is established: securely on the side of incentive, sufficiently on the other.

How much of it remains when we drop the simplifying assumptions – the homogeneous Output and the confinement to circulating capital? So far as the first is concerned, though it bothered Ricardo quite a lot, I do not think it need make any serious difference. While Output remains homogeneous, an expansion in labour input must *necessarily* (as has been seen) imply a rise in the labour share of Gross Revenue; now if (another quite reasonable empirical assumption) labourers spend *relatively* more than other classes on 'food', this shift towards labour will change the 'mix' of Output in such a way as to accentuate the tendency to diminishing returns. The model is harder to set out, but it seems to work in much the same way.

The other assumption (which amounts to making capital-intensity invariable) is much harder to deal with. When we remove it, we make it possible for business to resist the fall in the profit rate by using more capital-intensive methods; but though the decline in the *rate* of profit can be resisted in that way, it cannot be prevented – for it is only because the rate of profit falls that the more capital-intensive methods become profitable. Thus, so far as incentive is concerned, Ricardo's argument still holds; the decline in the rate of profit is slower than it appeared originally, but it is still there – it must be still there. On the distribution side, with which we have been here concerned, there may be more trouble. An increase in capital intensity is a substitution of capital for other factors; the factor for which capital is substituted may be labour, or may be land. If the substitution is heavily for land, it may diminish the share of rent, even the share of rent in the Net Product. Here, therefore, we have another source of exception, more important, I think, than the other.

There are two elements in Ricardo's theory: the empirical assumptions and the analytical structure. The empirical assumptions are of his own time; whether they are right or wrong, for that time, is a matter for historians. But the analytical structure is permanent. It has nothing to do with the landlord and tenant system or with the sleepiness of early nineteenth-century landlords (on whom Ricardo may, or may not, have been too hard); it has nothing to do with his (doubtless oversimplified) supply curve of labour. It should be restated, for our purposes, in much more general terms. It is solely concerned with the impact of capital investment on an economy with some scarce resources, the scarcity of which the investment of capital does not overcome. There can be such resources in any economy; they are not necessarily 'land', they may be labour. There is a revealing footnote of Ricardo's (Sraffa edn, p. 348), in which he contemplates the probability that, already in his time, a part of Net Revenue was going to wages. He has been identifying wages with the 'necessary expenses of production', but then:

Perhaps this is expressed too strongly, as more is generally allotted to the labourer under the name of wages, than the absolutely necessary expenses of production. In that case a part of the net produce of the country is received by the labourer, and may be saved or expended by him; or it may enable him to contribute to the defence of his country.

If Ricardo were writing today, he would have to expand that footnote. But he would not therefore be obliged to change his theory, in its analytical structure.

It must be emphasised (an overwhelmingly important qualification, of which Ricardo in several places, as for instance in the chapter on Machinery, shows himself to be well aware) that his apparatus is based upon the assumption of a given technology; the 'declining rate of profit' is a matter of the exhaustion of the expansion which is permitted by *given* technical opportunities. In a progressive economy, in which improvements are continually being made, there is a force which works the other way. But that, though a tempting form of expression, is not the best way of putting the issue. It is more instructive to think of each invention as setting up what might be called an 'Impulse' – which, if it were not succeeded by other Impulses, would peter out.[2] Ricardo's theory is a theory of the working of the individual Impulse.[3] So interpreted, it remains on its throne – an indispensable part of modern economics.

---

[2] Increasing returns, economies of scale, being treated (so far as they are relevant) as 'inventions'. This is not in fact at all inconvenient.

[3] For a fuller working out of this line of thought, see my Nobel lecture, 'The Mainspring of Economic Growth' (*EP*, 1977).

4

Ricardo and the Moderns

PREFATORY NOTE

This essay was published in the *Quarterly Journal of Economics*, August 1977. It was a joint work by Samuel Hollander and myself. How it came to be written is explained in the dialogue with which it begins.

I still stand by the substance of what we said in it; but I should like it to be read in conjunction with essay 3 above, and with a related passage in my *Causality in Economics* (1979), pp. 48–55. As a result of this later work, I feel, in particular, that the complication that is represented by figure 4.3 had better have been avoided.

The trouble, as so often in economics, is with the concept of equilibrium. One cannot see that Ricardo (or indeed Adam Smith) can have had any other notion of equilibrium except the static, a state of affairs which could go on idefinitely if there were no change in exogenous 'data'. (The distinction between market and natural value, on which so much depends, relies upon this static concept.) Now it follows from the definition of it, just given, that equilibrium is relative to the things that we are prepared to treat as exogenous. Marshall's short-period and long-period equilibria are an example of this, but by no means the only example. So, even though we are being static, we have some liberty of choice about the exogenous.

It is clearly impossible to give a full representation of a growth path, or of any 'dynamic' process, if one can do no more than represent it as a sequence of static equilibria. The behaviour of the economy is going to change, but we have to represent it as unchanging. It may nevertheless be granted that we get some idea of the process by looking at the sequence of static equilibria which most nearly corresponds. That is not good enough, but it is better than nothing. It has now become clear to me that the growth path that is represented on the figures in this essay, cannot be otherwise interpreted than as such a static sequence.

But what kind of an equilibrium should its points represent? I have come to feel that in a circulating capital model, such as is here discussed, it would be odd not to require, as a condition of equilibrium, that *all* processes that are in use should be viable, so that each should give a rate of return that is in excess of our r^*. (This is a point that was originally made by Casarosa; see below.) It has the consequence that positions beyond the 'roof', which appear in figure 4.3, are not acceptable, for they could not be equilibrium positions.

I was led to a different view, at the time when we wrote this essay, since I was thinking that, in a circulating capital model, processes which had been started could still be completed, even though $r < r^*$. That is right. But is not at all obvious that we can define an equilibrium so as to make such an inevitably temporary position an equilibrium position. So, if the path has to be a sequence of equilibria, it cannot go through the roof, but must be repelled by it, as it is by the floor.

One further point concerns that crucial passage in Ricardo's chapter on wages, which we quote and discuss on p. 57 below. We offer a possible interpretation of this passage, which makes it more logical than it appears to be on the surface. It is not suggested that the explanation we give is in Ricardo, nor that it would at all naturally have occurred to those who read him first. One would expect that they would have read him in the light of the corresponding chapter on wages in Adam Smith. Now what Smith says is: 'The money price of labour is necessarily regulated by two circumstances: the demand for labour, and the prices of the necessaries and conveniences of life' (*Wealth of Nations*, Oxford, 1976, p. 103). He does indeed go on to say: 'variations in the price of labour not only do not always correspond with those in the price of provisions, but are frequently quite opposite'. Still he leaves the impression that 'cost of living' has something to do with the matter.

So if the 'cost of living' interpretation was a misinterpretation, Ricardo had certainly laid himself open to it. So it is not surprising to find that this is how he was read, not only by Marx and the Marxians, but much more generally. How else did the Free Traders of the 1840s think that they could invoke the authority of Ricardo for their doctrine that cheaper food would raise the profitability of industry? Ricardo is responsible for 'fixwage', though it is probably not what he meant.

I must make acknowledgements, for the above, to papers by Casarosa and Pasinetti which I heard at a conference at Perugia in 1981 and which have appeared in *Advances in Economic Theory*, edited by Mauro Baranzini (1982).

Introduction

The origin of this paper was a conversation between the authors, which took place when Hollander (S) was visiting Hicks (J) at Oxford. It may be summarised as follows:

S: I am sorry to see from your recent book[1] that, like so many others,[2] you think that Ricardo had what you call a fixwage theory. That is to say, not only did he affirm that in stationary equilibrium (long-run equilibrium) the real wage, or commodity wage, is equal to a fixed level of subsistence – there is no doubt about that – but you make him say that wages are approximately at subsistence level all the time. You construct a model in which the real wage is constant but employment is variable; and you label it Ricardian. But I find many passages[3] in which Ricardo allows that an increase in capital will raise real wages; that is quite inconsistent with your interpretation. All that is necessarily implied by the Malthusian law of population (which Ricardo certainly accepted) is that labour supply will increase when the real wage is above subsistence; only when the wage has come down to the subsistence level will labour supply cease to expand. Ricardo, of course, knew that in his day the population of Britain (and of other countries, such as the United States, in which he was interested) was in fact expanding. One should therefore conclude that he needed to believe that wages in those countries were above subsistence.

J: In spite of what I said, I have no closed mind on the matter; I am open to persuasion that the source of the fixwage theory is Lasalle, or Marx, or von Neumann, not Ricardo. I have myself allowed, in a later pssage in that same book that in Ricardo's view *'it should be possible . . . by steady increase in the demand for labour to keep wages running just a little ahead of subsistence. For though in the long run the supply of labour is elastic . . . it needs a little time to catch up.'*[4] That is quite a step toward your view of Ricardo.

---

[1] *CT*, p. 49.

[2] Leading examples are (1) Nicholas Kaldor: 'The rate of wages is determined by the supply price of labour that Ricardo assumed to be constant in terms of corn', from 'Alternative Theories of Distribution', *Review of Economic Studies*, XXIII (1956), pp. 83–100, reprinted in *Essays on Value and Distribution* (1960), p. 212; (2) Paul Samuelson: 'Though Ricardo had many children, one often wonders whether he knew the biological facts of life, so content is he with the assumption that labour will *soon* adjust to its long-run horizontal wage at the subsistence level'; from 'A Modern Treatment of the Ricardian Theory', *Quarterly Journal of Economics*, LXXIII (1959), p. 224, reprinted in *Collected Papers*, vol. I, p. 415. These downright statements are echoed in the works of several later writers.

[3] See section II, below.

[4] Hicks, *ct*, p. 124.

S: It seems to me that in the light of that you should have removed the former passage.

J: I did not see that there was an inconsistency. I remained of the opinion that fixwage was Ricardo's *formal* theory, though I certainly accepted that he modified it in application, as we all do with our formal theories. What led me to the fixwage interpretation was the famous arithmetical table in the *Essay on Profits*.[5] That table is based upon an assumed technical relation between capital invested and net product, capital invested implying labour invested; no such technical relation makes sense unless the real (commodity) wage is constant. That is why I thought that in his formal theory Ricardo must have assumed the real wage to be fixed.

S: So it was that table! I agree that in the construction of that table Ricardo assumed the real wage to be fixed; in fact, he says so. But he did not assume that it was constant at a subsistence level. He says that he *will assume that capital and labour 'advance in the proper* [i.e. appropriate] *proportion so that the real wages of labour, continue uniformly the same.'*[6] Real wages remain constant, because the capital–labour ratio proceeds suitably. This is a simplifying assumption, made for a particular expository purpose. There is no need to take it more seriously than we take the similar simplifying assumptions that are made (so often!) by modern economists. I stick to my view that Ricardo's general theory was quite different.

That was the substance of our conversation. It presented a challenge. If not fixwage, what was Ricardo's theory? Could one manage to construct a model, which rejected fixwage, but incorporated the rest of Ricardo's assumptions? If one could do that, it would surely throw light upon the issue. It would still be necessary to confront the resulting model with Ricardo's own statements, in order to find out whether one had in fact grasped his meaning. There were these two steps to be taken; we shall try to take them in the two parts of the following paper.

I. The Model

1. *The general model.* We shall allow ourselves, in this part to describe the model in terms that, admittedly, are not Ricardo's but that we

[5] David Ricardo, *Works*, P. Sraffa, ed. (Cambridge, Cambridge University Press, 1951), vol. 4, p. 17. See above, pp. 30, 35.
[6] *ibid.*, p. 12.

think will quickly make it more intelligible to the modern economist. (The translation into Ricardo's language, when we come to it in part II, will not be difficult.) We shall thus, in part I, assume that Product is homogeneous, and we shall use it as a standard of value, so that we can work, in the modern manner, in 'real' terms. We further make the following assumptions.

(i) There is no *fixwage*; but labour supply (L) will increase or diminish according as actual wage (w) is greater or less than subsistence wage (w^*). One would naturally wish to assume that this effect operated only after a lag; but we found it best to proceed without this complication, leaving it to be considered later. This was a fortunate decision, illustrating, we shall see, a fundamental characteristic of Ricardian method.

(ii) There is a similar 'subsistence level' for capital; thus if r is the rate of profit, capital will increase or diminish as r is greater or less than r^*. That is all that we need to specify about the 'supply function' of capital.[7]

(iii) There are diminishing returns throughout.[8]

Now consider figure 4.1, in which w and L are coordinates. The state of the economy, at a particular time, is represented by a point

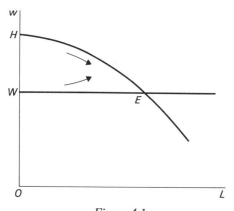

Figure 4.1

[7] It is unnecessary to raise the puzzling question whether it was on the effect on incentive to accumulate, or on the effect on ability to accumulate, that Ricardo relied, or mainly relied. He clearly held that all important savings come out of profits; that being so, each effect will work the same way. (It may be useful, however, to notice that the model would be substantially unaffected if r^* were zero.)

[8] We must assume this, in order to simulate Ricardo in our terms. For what corresponds, in Ricardo's terms, see below, p. 53.

on the diagram (w,L). The horizontal WE is the locus of $w = w^*$. HE is the locus of $r = r^*$; that is to say, for each L the ordinate on HE is the wage that is consistent with a rate of profit equal to r^*. (We shall have much more to say about the genesis of HE, but shall postpone that for the moment. Here we shall indicate merely that it would seem to follow, from the diminishing returns assumption, that HE will be a downward-sloping curve.)

H, we may take it, is above W, since there could otherwise be no capital-using production. Wherever the economy found itself initially, either capital or labour would tend to disappear. There must therefore exist a triangle HEW; it is only from positions within that triangle that both capital and labour will tend to increase.

Suppose that the economy starts from such a position, given arbitrarily. Since $w > w^*$, L must be increasing; so the path of the economy, starting from any such point, must proceed to the *right*. Capital is also increasing; but on whether capital is increasing faster or more slowly than labour nothing is said. So (it appears) w may be rising, or may be falling.

Can we nevertheless prove that there must be a convergence to the equilibrium E, where $w = w^*$ and $r = r^*$? It is at once apparent that, if we could prove that WE and HE (*floor* and *roof* we shall call them) are *barriers*, that job would be done. For at every step on the rightward path, the possible further positions would then be confined within a smaller triangle; the path must therefore converge upon the apex of all these triangles, which is the equilibrium E.

So far as the floor is concerned, it seems pretty clear that it is a barrier. For let us allow ourselves (for the moment) to suppose that a point on WE, to the left of E, has somehow or other been reached. At that point $w = w^*$, so L is constant; but $r > r^*$, so capital is increasing. An increase in capital with constant labour should surely lead to a rise in wages. So on the floor, wages should be rising, and it would seem that in the neighbourhood of such a point wages should be rising. One must conclude that in the working out of a model a point on WE would not be reached; the path of the economy is *repelled* by the floor.

The case of the roof is more tricky. We can, however, deal with it in a similar way. We should now suppose that a point on the roof, between H and E, has somehow or other been reached. Since at that point $r = r^*$, capital is stationary. But since $w > w^*$, L is rising. How is this additional labour to be accommodated without a rise in capital? Only, it would seem, in the same way, by a fall in wages.

However, here that does not settle the matter. For to show that from a point on *HE* the next step must be a fall in wages does not show that the path must stay within the triangle, since at that point the roof also slopes downward. One must show, if one is to show that the path must stay within the triangle, that the fall in wages along the path must be greater than the fall along the roof.

On the path, at a point on *HE*, capital is constant; on the roof, *r* is constant. So we must ask what would have to happen to capital if there were an (imaginary) movement to the right along the roof. If such a movement required the investment of more capital, constant capital would be insufficient to keep the economy on the roof. The path must then turn downward, inside the roof; so the roof, like the floor, will be a barrier. But if it is possible to move rightward along the roof while using less capital, the roof would not be a barrier. The path of the economy might then take a different form, which would have to be separately examined.

We shall show in what follows that empirical assumptions, one of which was made by Ricardo explicitly, and others that would surely have been accepted by him if they had been put to him, are probably sufficient to establish that this exception (as it would then prove to be) can be disregarded. There must then be a regular convergence to equilibrium.

It should be noticed, however, that it does not follow from this convergence that *w* must always be falling as *L* increases. It is entirely possible for a path such as *ABC* in figure 4.2 to be followed. It will be followed if in the initial position (*A*) the wage is low but the rate

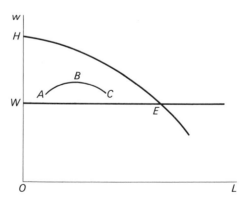

Figure 4.2

of profit is high. There can then be sufficient accumulation to raise wages for a while, before the fall sets in.

The same holds, in principle, for profits. It is conceivable, if the labour response were very rapid (perhaps by immigration), that there might be a phase in which the rate of profit was rising. All that is necessary, if the initial position is one in which both labour and capital are increasing (so that $w > w^*$ and $r > r^*$) is that, sooner or later, there must be a fall in wages *and* a fall in the rate of profit, so as to bring each of them down to its equilibrium value. Either of them, however, may have a rising phase on the way.

What has been presented, so far, is no more than a sketch. It has several weak points, which will probably have been noticed by the reader. They clearly need to be re-examined. But it will be found that in the re-examination we can, for much of the way, keep quite close to Ricardo.

2. *The circulating capital model.* We follow in his footsteps if we begin, as he would surely have done,[9] with the simplest form of circulating capital model.

In this model there is no fixed capital; capital is just 'advances to labour'. The period of production is fixed. With the supply of land also fixed, production is a function of labour supply only. Thus, total product is $F(L)$, with $F'(L)$ positive and $F''(L)$ negative – diminishing returns throughout. The wage is the *discounted* marginal product of labour. Thus, $F'(L) = w(1 + r)$, where w is actual wage and r is actual rate of profit. Capital, here a pure wage-fund, is equal to the wage-bill; so capital $= wL$. Profit is rwL. Rent is $F(L) - LF'(L)$.

Here there is clearly no question that, if L is constant but capital (wL) is increasing, w must be rising. So it is certain that the floor is a barrier. The condition for the roof to be a barrier can be easily worked out.

As we have seen, the condition in general is that, for a rightward movement along the roof, capital must increase. But

$$wL = LF'(L)/(1 + r)$$

and along the roof r is constant; so $LF'(L)$ must increase as L increases. That is to say, the elasticity of the marginal product curve[10] must be greater than 1.

<hr>

[9] For this is the procedure that he adopts in his chapter on 'Value' (ch. 1 of the *Principles*).

[10] Elasticity being measured in the Marshallian manner, with price (or whatever is analogous to price – here the marginal product) being treated as if it were the independent variable.

What can we say about this elasticity? This is not a case where it is useful to think, in the modern manner, in terms of elasticities of substitution. The constant elasticity of substitution assumption, in particular, does not fit Ricardo at all. He himself has told us that:

On the first settling of a country, in which there is an abundance of rich and fertile land, a very small proportion of which is required to be cultivated for the support of the actual population, or indeed can be cultivated with the capital which the population can command, there will be no rent.[11]

Now if, for small L, there is no rent, it would seem to follow that marginal product, over an initial stretch, equals average product.[12] So marginal product must be constant; the marginal product curve must be perfectly elastic. But, on the other hand, if there is any limit to the amount of labour that can be employed productively on the given land (and that there is such a limit is surely implied in any common-sense interpretation of diminishing returns), it follows that for a sufficiently large L, marginal product must fall to zero. The elasticity of the curve (whatever its slope) must then fall to zero. So if this is accepted, the curve must be perfectly elastic at one end and perfectly inelastic at the other. There must therefore (on the average) be a fall in elasticity as one goes along the curve.

If the fall is reasonably regular (and there seems to be no reason why it should not be), there must then be a point on the curve where elasticity equals unity. To the left of that point, the curve will be elastic, to the right, inelastic. We suggest that this is the form of curve that can be most useful for the interpretation of Ricardo.[13]

The roof, it has been shown, is simply a reflection of the marginal product curve (in this circulating capital model). So it must have the same elasticity properties. Let us call M the point where elasticity is unity. The position of M is solely a matter of the shape of the curve (if the curve were a straight line, it would be the mid-point between

[11] *Principles* (Sraffa), p. 69.
[12] But might there not be an increasing returns stretch (as commonly shown in modern textbooks) before the curve turned downward? It would make no substantial difference to the argument if there was; but did Ricardo believe there was? The question is rather intriguing. He had Smith and the division of labour behind him; but it is hard to see that he paid attention to it. There was, however, a passage in the first edition of the *Principles* (note on p. 100 in Sraffa) in which he contemplated the possibility of underpopulation – but not for the Smithian reason. If population is too small, people will not work hard enough – like the Irish! (See also letter to Trower, VII, 48–9.) One fears that he had been talking to 'absentee landlords' in London clubs; it is just their point of view. It is just as well that the passage was suppressed.
[13] This is consistent with what was said, in terms of elasticities of substitution, p. 35 above.

the axes). But the position of E (on the roof) is a matter of the level of w^* (the subsistence level); and that, formally at least, is an entirely independent matter. Thus, if the subsistence level is high enough, E will lie to the left of M; the whole of the roof between H and E will then be a barrier. Only if the subsistence level is too low, so that E lies upon the inelastic part of the roof, will there be a 'hole' in the barrier between M and E; it then becomes possible that the path may go through the roof. It is only in this latter case (if what has been said above on the properties of the curve is accepted) that an *exception* can arise.

3. *The exception.*[14] Ricardo, we fully admit, did not notice the exception (and one may greatly doubt if he would have paid much attention to it if he had). Still, since we have noticed it, we had better attend to it.

Suppose that there is a hole in the roof (M lying to the left of E) and that the path goes through it. What happens? The answer is shown in figure 4.3. The locus of $r = r^*$, to the right of E, now becomes relevant; so it is shown, together with the relevant part of the roof, as MEV.

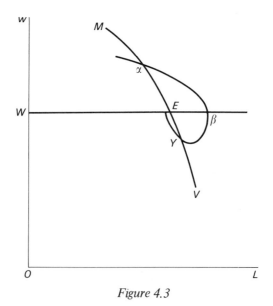

Figure 4.3

[14] I now accept that this exception cannot arise in a circulating capital model, such as is here being discussed. See above, p. 40.

After the roof is passed (at α) $r < r^*$, so that capital (wL) is falling. But since at first $w > w^*$, L is rising. w must therefore be falling; indeed it must be falling quite fast. It is nevertheless impossible (on our assumptions) that the path should again intersect ME between M and E; for the kind of intersection that is possible between M and E is what occurred at α, and at any further intersection between M and E the relation between the slopes of path and roof would be the wrong way round. Thus, w will go on falling, but L will not cease to rise until $w = w^*$ is reached, at a point β, which we have now shown to lie to the right of E. At β we still have $r < r^*$, so capital is still falling; thus though L has now ceased to rise, w will still be falling. But at the next stage L will be falling, so the path begins to turn back towards EV. And here, since L is falling, a second intersection is possible (γ); at γ capital will have ceased to fall, so w must be rising. The minimum of w is reached before γ. It can again be shown in the same way that there can be no further intersection of EV (at this round) between E and γ; so the path will intersect the vertical through E below E, and the floor to the left of E, as shown. Thus, there is a 'cycle' about the equilibrium position.

It is not inevitable that the cycle should repeat. For though when the path 'comes back', the 'hole' is still open, the path, as explained, does not have to go through it. It can in fact be shown (but this does need some mathematics)[15] that there must, in the end but conceivably after several cycles, be a convergence to E.

That is pretty; but, as we have insisted, we make no pretence that it is of any importance.

4. *Fixed capital.* We turn to a matter that is of importance, indeed of great importance. We have begun, as Ricardo would have begun,

[15] It is fairly clear that whatever the supply functions of labour and capital may be (so long as they obey the restrictions with which we have been working) the slope of the path, being the ratio of dw/dt and dL/dt, must be a single-valued function of w and L. It follows that a path, beginning from any specified initial conditions, cannot intersect itself, since at the point of intersection the slope would have two values. That is nearly enough, considering figure 4.3, to show that there must be ultimate convergence, since successive circuits around E must get smaller and smaller. But it is not quite enough, since there remains the possibility that the path might converge, asymptotically, to a fixed circuit around E, never actually reaching E. But this also is ruled out, for a more subtle reason. If there were such a circuit, there would be a 'forbidden zone' around E, which the path could not enter. But though E is a 'singular point' of the path, at which both dw/dt and dL/dt are zero, so that dw/dL is indeterminate, it is clear that at any point indefinitely near to E the slope is determinate and is *real*, in the mathematical sense. So the path can approach indefinitely near to E. There is no 'forbidden zone'.

We owe this last point about the circuit to Nicholas Georgescu-Roegen, and the above way of treating it to Stefano Zamagni.

with a circulating capital model; but Ricardo would not have stopped at that, nor should we.

Whatever the nature of the capital that is employed, a diagram of the type we have been using could in principle still be constructed; for L and w and w^* are all of them representable without any question of the nature of capital arising. Thus we can still use the diagram as a means of separating out the critical issues.

First of all, what is meant, in the general case, by the 'position' (w, L)? As was shown, it is possible, in the circulating capital case, to deduce from given w and L both the quantity of capital and the rate of profit. For capital is wL; and the rate of profit is given by $F'(L) = w(1 + r)$. Thus all the characteristics of the economy that concern us can be deduced from w and L. When we generalise, these convenient deductions fail us. To know (w, L) no longer suffices to determine the characteristics of the economy. With given (w, L) the rate of profit might still be different in so far as the make-up of the initial capital was different; and on that, in the model, nothing is said.

It does not appear that Ricardo ever fully faced the issue; but if he had faced it, what could he have said? He would have had to distinguish between a capital structure that was appropriate (or optimal) with respect to the given w and L, and one that (perhaps because of its history) was inappropriate. That is to say, he would have had to distinguish (in Marshall's manner) between short-period and long-period equilibrium.

In formal theory, it is clear, he does not do that;[16] that was left for Marshall. If one does not do it, what remains? One can hardly get on without allowing oneself the assumption (the dangerous assumption!) that the capital structure is appropriate *all the time*. With that the model can still be saved. With a given structure of capital (the fixed production period of the circulating capital model is one such structure) it will still be true that, given w and L, r will be determined. With different structures, w and L being still given, r will vary. It would be reasonable to suppose (though the conditions for this to be true should of course be worked out) that there would be some structure for which r would be maximised. Suppose that this 'optimum' structure were always selected. Then we should still have r determined when w and L are given; and the quantity of capital, which we should measure, as before, in 'product'-equivalent, would also be determined.

So the model could stand, without (apparently) much amendment. The floor is clearly unaffected by the present generalisation. The

[16] But see below (note 23 to section II).

roof would now indicate the highest wage that could still be paid to each labour force L consistently with a rate of profit not less than r^*. If the wage were lower, with capital still 'optimally' organised, the rate of profit could be higher.

Could one still conclude, in anything like the old way, that floor and roof would be barriers? The question, so far as the floor is concerned, is whether we would still be entitled to argue that an increase in capital must raise wages and lower the rate of profit, L remaining constant. A neo-classical economist would have had no doubts on the matter, but we are not being neo-classical. We are to mean by an increase in capital an increase in value of capital in terms of product, which is not what the neo-classics meant.[17] Modern economics has shown that the matter is not then quite so simple, but we should stray from our theme if we followed up those refinements here. So far as the floor is concerned, we shall therefore take it that the barrier still holds.

We shall not expect, from what has already been said, that the roof will always be a barrier. But we can still conclude (from what was said above about the general model) that the issue reduces to asking whether more capital is necessarily required to employ more labour, the rate of profit remaining unchanged. One's prejudice says that it must be; it is nevertheless of some interest to find that we can carry over to the general model something analogous to the *exception* we have found.

Capital, still in the same sense, is a roundabout way of using labour; but it is also a roundabout way of using land. It would make good sense, and would accord with many known facts,[18] if the latter aspect were realistically quite as important. Thus when land is cheap, the use of natural resources in capital-intensive ways is a rational means of economising in labour. It looks like substitution of capital for labour; but more fundamentally it is a substitution of land for labour by the use of capital. If this is so, the rise in rent, which occurs as a result of population pressure, could diminish the opportunity for profitable (and indeed for productive) investment of capital. (When 'fossil fuels' become sufficiently scarce, man will have to give up his tractors, and 'toil with spade again'.) That could cause a 'hole in the roof' even with generalised capital.

[17] See my paper 'Capital Controversies, Ancient and Modern', (*EP*, 1977, pp. 149ff.).
[18] One thinks not only of our recent experience since the oil crisis of 1973, but also of the historical material presented by Paul David, *Technical Change, Innovation and Economic Growth* (London, Cambridge University Press, 1975).

So much for the 'optimal' or 'long-period' interpretation, which (as will be shown) does appear to give us Ricardo's usual meaning. Of course, in the end it is not good enough. Given time, other things being equal, the structure of capital might become optimal; but at any particular moment (of history) there will not have been time to make the adjustments that are required. Capital is in the wrong form; only as existing equipment wears out, and is replaced, will the structure come right. That is what Ricardo, nearly always, omitted; so if we use our diagram as a means of interpreting him, we must remember that every point on the diagram – every position on the path – is a position of long-period equilibrium, in Marshall's sense. And this means that no way is shown by which the system gets from one point on the path to what follows it! The analysis is inherently static; but the static analysis is carried through consistently. We should think of the same device being used for labour as for capital. The population also has its structure (in particular, its age distribution); but in static analysis that also is in long-period equilibrium. At every point on the path the age distribution must be assumed to be appropriate; that is why, to the astonishment of modern commentators, population is so often supposed to respond *without lag*.

And that is why it was so lucky that we began by allowing ourselves to forget about lags. If we had brought them in from the start, we should have cut ourselves off from an appreciation of the static method of Ricardo.

The simplification that is involved in the static method is indeed drastic. It can be defended only as a first step, suitable perhaps for a very narrow range of problems, but more important as a basis from which further work could proceed. The second line of defence needs no elaboration. This was the first instance of a complicated economic argument, carried through with logical precision; it blazed a trail that all subsequent theory has followed. A word may be said, however, about the first.

Suppose that the theory was just meant as a very long-run theory. For a very long-run theory, the static method, even when carried to the lengths that Ricardo carried it, could be claimed to be not so very inappropriate. We have seen that it would leave it open to him to think of the world of his time (or the Britain of his time) as still in a growing phase, such as is represented by the stretch *AB* in our figure 4.2. Wages would be rising, in what looks like a neo-classical manner, as capital accumulated. But they would still have the shadow of diminishing returns hanging over them, though the point at which that developed into a serious constraint might be quite far away.

We shall now show that this was in fact Ricardo's viewpoint.

II. The Evidence

1. *'Money' wages and real wages.* We are now to start with the hypothesis that what Ricardo had in mind was something equivalent to what has been expressed, in the first part of this paper, by the *HEW* diagram — taking that, of course, in its simpler form, in which the subsistence level (w^*) is high enough for the *exception* not to occur. We would then expect him to think of his economy as being 'now' in a position in which both capital and labour are increasing (for that was surely the position in which he conceived the Britain, or the America, of his time to be). In that position it must be the case, on his principles, that $r > r^*$ (so that capital could be increasing) and that $w > w^*$ (so that the supply of labour could be increasing). In the final equilibrium, which would ultimately be reached in the absence of technical progress, w would have to come *down* to w^*, and r to r^*. Thus over the whole stretch between 'now' and the stationary state, w (the commodity wage) and r (the rate of profit) would *both* have to fall. But this would not be inconsistent with the possibility that there might be stretches in which w was rising and r falling, or stretches in which r was rising and w falling, but w could not rise without r falling, and r could not rise without w falling. In the 'large', however, on the average over the whole stretch between 'now' and 'equilibrium', both would have to fall.

It will be shown, in what follows, that this is precisely what, in substance, we find him saying. We must, however, beware that in one important respect his model is more complex than what we have been using. We have been taking it that 'Product' is homogeneous; but Ricardo's 'Product' is not homogeneous. It is composed of an agricultural segment, produced under diminishing returns, and a non-agricultural segment, produced under constant returns. Even so, it would have been possible for him to use as a standard of value a 'basket' including both sorts of output; such a 'basket', of course, would have been produced under diminishing returns. This is effectively what we have been doing but it is not what Ricardo does. His standard, which he calls 'money', is representative of non-agricultural output; so we may think of him as taking non-agricultural output as his standard of value. Thus if agricultural prices rise relative to non-agricultural prices, while real wages remain the same (in the sense that command over the 'basket' remains the same), Ricardo will say that 'money' wages rise. And it is to the rise in 'money' wages, in this sense, that he attributes the fall in the rate of profit. It is nevertheless the same phenomenon that is being described in his way as in ours.

2. *The main texts from the Principles.* Take first a passage that at first reading looks a bit mysterious, but that on our approach (and in the light of what has just been said) becomes crystal clear. It is the beginning of chapter XXI, 'Effects of Accumulation on Profits and Interest':

From the account which has been given of the profits of stock, it will appear, that no accumulation of capital will permanently lower profits, unless there be some permanent cause for the rise of [money] wages. If the funds for the maintenance of labour were doubled, trebled, or quadrupled, there would not long be any difficulty in procuring the requisite number of hands, to be employed by those funds; but owing to the increasing difficulty of making constant additions to the food of the country, funds of the same value would probably not maintain the same quantity of labour. If the necessaries of the workman could be constantly increased with the same facility, there could be no permanent alteration in the rate of profits or wages, to whatever amount capital might be accumulated.[19]

In this passage Ricardo is opposing Adam Smith, who had said in a passage that he quotes:

The increase of stock which raises wages tends to lower profit. When the stocks of many rich merchants are turned into the same trade, their mutual competition tends to lower its profit; and when there is a like increase of stock in all the different trades carried on in the same society, the same competition must produce the same effect in all.[20]

Ricardo rejoins that the rise in wages, mentioned by Smith, is a temporary rise, which has nothing to do with the long-period tendencies with which he is (and Smith should have been) concerned; while 'competition of capitals' can otherwise be interpreted only as lack of effective demand, and this (again in the long-period sense) he demolishes by an appeal to Say's law. Thus for all that Smith had said, there is no reason why the economy should not persist in a 'steady state', with wages and profits remaining at their initial levels,

[19] *Principles*, p. 289.
[20] *ibid.*

whatever these may have been. (Not, it will be noticed, at subsistence levels, for this is an expanding economy.) But, says Ricardo, there is a reason why (in the absence of technical progress) this cannot happen. It is the downward slope of our *roof* – diminishing returns.

Now look back at the formal enunciation in chapter V, the chapter 'On Wages'. He begins by defining the 'natural price' of labour as that price which will 'enable the labourers, one with another, to subsist and perpetuate their race, without either increase or diminution'.[21] It is a price (we are immediately informed) that is not fixed in terms of 'money' but will vary with 'money' prices of 'food, necessaries and conveniences' (that is to say, it is our w^*). In these terms, we are told, it is fixed, at least by 'habits and customs'.[22]

A sharp distinction is drawn between this subsistence wage and the actual wage, or 'market price'. But 'however much the market price of labour may deviate from its natural price, it has, like commodities, a tendency to conform with it'.[23] Perhaps it is just this word *tendency* that has caused the trouble we are trying to clear up.

A modern economist will often use the word very loosely. A system has a 'tendency to equilibrium', so it may just as well be treated as being in equilibrium all the time. There is no reason why Ricardo should have been using it so loosely. The first meaning of the word *tendency* that is given in the *Oxford Dictionary* (with examples both earlier and later than Ricardo) is 'a constant disposition to move or act in some direction or towards some point, end or purpose'. Surely it is this that is Ricardo's meaning. For he continues:

Notwithstanding the tendency of wages to conform to their natural rate, their market rate may, in an improving society, for an indefinite period be constantly above it; for no sooner may the impulse, which an increased capital gives to a new demand for labour be obeyed, than another increase in capital may produce the same effect; and thus, if the increase in capital be gradual and constant, the demand for labour may give a constant stimulus to an increase of people.[24]

So the actual wage may exceed the subsistence wage 'for an indefinite period'; and it is by no means inconceivable that the excess may increase:

---

[21] *Principles*, p. 93.

[22] 'It is not to be understood that the natural price of labour, estimated even in food and necessaries, is absolutely fixed and constant.... It essentially depends upon the habits and customs of the people' (*Principles*, pp. 96–7).

[23] *Principles*, p. 94.

[24] *Principles*, pp. 94–5.

In different stages of society, the accumulation of capital, or of the means of employing labour, is more or less rapid, and must in all cases depend on the productive powers of labour. The productive powers of labour are generally greatest when there is an abundance of fertile land; at such periods accumulation is often so rapid, that labourers cannot be supplied with the same rapidity as capital.

It has been calculated, that under favourable circumstances population may be doubled in twenty-five years; but under the same favourable circumstances, the whole capital of a country might possibly be doubled in a shorter period. In that case, wages during the whole period would have a tendency to rise, because the demand for labour would increase still faster than the supply.[25]

However, this is no more than a qualification; it corresponds to the *AB* stretch in figure 4.2 above. For he continues:

Although, then, it is probable that under the most favourable circumstances, the power of production is still greater than that of population, it will not long continue so; for the land being limited in quantity, and differing in quality, with every increased portion of capital employed on it, there will be a decreased rate of production, whilst the power of population continues always the same.[26]

Diminishing returns, he is saying, must in the end make themselves felt.

Now this is indeed one of the passages that easily cause trouble. When it is read in its context, it must be interpreted to mean that (as in chapter XXI) a continued expansion, with w in excess of w^*, is not possible, for it is only if that excess wage is maintained that the 'power of population' can 'continue the same'. For it is clear, in the rest of the chapter, that the consequence that is expected from population pressure is a fall in real wages (wages in terms of the 'basket'). As he says himself, the labourer 'will receive more money wages...but his corn wages will be reduced; and not only his command of corn, but his general condition will be deteriorated, by his finding it more difficult to maintain the market rate of wages above their natural rate.'[27] In the former passage he is simply on his way to establishing this conclusion. He is not assuming a fixed wage; he is certainly not assuming a wage that is fixed at a subsistence level, which (in accordance with what he had already said) must check the 'power of population'; he is showing that a fixed wage, at a level above subsistence, cannot in the end be carried through.

[25] *Principles*, p. 98.
[26] *ibid.*
[27] *ibid.*, p. 102.

All this, however, has to be set out in terms of the Ricardian 'money wage'. The issue can best be explained in terms of the circulating capital model. Let w_m be the 'money' wage-rate. Then, in the non-agricultural sector (in the equilibrium Ricardo always assumes) $w_m (1 + r) = $ a constant. In the agricultural sector

$$w_m (1 + r) = p_m F'(L)$$

where p_m is the price of agricultural output in terms of non-agricultural output, that is to say, in terms of 'money'. It follows from these two equations that $p_m F'(L)$ is constant, so that when the marginal product $F'(L)$ falls, p_m must rise. But if p_m rises, while w_m remains constant, real wages ('basket' wages) must fall, since a large part of the wage is spent on agricultural output. But, says Ricardo, they cannot fall to the extent that would be necessary. So 'money' wages must rise:

As population increases, ... necessaries will be constantly rising in price, because more labour will be necessary to produce them. If, then, the money wage of labour should fall, whilst every commodity on which the wages of labour were expended rose, the labourer would be doubly affected, and would be soon totally deprived of subsistence. Instead, therefore, of the money wages of labour falling, they would rise; but they would not rise sufficiently to enable the labourer to purchase as many comforts and necessaries as he did before the rise in price of those commodities.[28]

Without the explanation that we have been giving, the first part of this passage could easily be read as implying that 'money' wages are fixed at the 'money' value of a subsistence basket of commodities – so that wages are adjusted on what we would now call a cost-of-living basis. But this is not what Ricardo means, as his last sentence makes clear. Real wages are *falling*.

'Money' wages are rising (the rate of profit is falling), and real wages are falling, why? It cannot be claimed that in this passage Ricardo gives a clear answer. He is just reading off these results from the model that is in his mind. But if he had been challenged to explain himself, what could he have said?

Consider again the *HEW* diagram. If 'money' wages remained unchanged, and therefore the rate of profit remained unchanged, the whole burden of the adjustment (due to the fall in the marginal product) would fall on labour. But with a fall in the real wage the rate of increase in the labour supply would slow up, while (since the

[28] *ibid.*, pp. 101–2.

rate of profit would be undiminished) the rate of increase of capital would be undiminished; there must therefore, as compared with the position we have just posited, be a tendency for wages to rise. It is what we called the 'path being repelled by the floor'. And similarly, if real wages ('basket' wages) remained unchanged, the rate of profit would fall, so that the increase of capital would be retarded, while the 'power of population' would be unaffected. The path would be 'repelled by the roof'. These are in fact the reasons (within the Ricardian system, the quite logical reasons) why things must work out as he says.

3. *The 'Notes on Malthus'.* The interpretation just given of the 'Wages' chapter is confirmed, and possibly a little deepened, by the comments that were made by Ricardo on Malthus's *Principles* (in 1820). Malthus, after quoting Ricardo's definition of the 'natural price' of labour, says that in his view it is 'a most unnatural price, because in a natural state of things, that is, without great impediments to the progress of wealth and population, such a price could not generally occur for hundreds of years'.[29] Ricardo, in his note on this passage, determinedly sticks to his own terminology; but his reason for doing so is a desire for uniformity of terminology, as between the price of labour and the price of commodities. He does not dispute Malthus's view that the stationary state is remote.[30]

Nor does he dispute the convenience, for less 'secular' purposes, of using a reference path in which there is a 'uniform progress of capital and population', as Malthus calls it. It must, however, be clearly understood that (as he himself had stated in chapter XXI of his *Principles* and as Malthus repeats) uniform progress does not mean 'the same *rate* of progress permanently, which is impossible; but a uniform progress towards the greatest practicable amount, without temporary accelerations or retardations'.[31] 'I agree throughout this section with Mr Malthus in principle', says Ricardo.[32]

4. *Fixed capital.* It is important to recognise that there is not very much about fixed capital in Ricardo's *Principles*. In view of the attention that is paid to fixed capital in the very first chapter 'On Value' (a passage that has had an enormous impact on later economics), this may seem a surprising statement. Yet it is true. There is fixed capital there, and, of course, it also appears in the chapter

[29] *Works*, vol. II, p. 228.
[30] *ibid.*
[31] *ibid.*, p. 256.
[32] *ibid.*, p. 258.

on Machinery (added in the third edition) but in most of the rest of the work it is conspicuous by its absence.[33] It is so far absent that it is tempting to conjecture that the Ricardian system was first worked out in circulating capital terms (more or less as in our own circulating capital model), most of the book being written with that model in mind.[34] The first chapter of a book does not have to be the first that is written; in a theoretical work it is often the last.[35] Thus it would make sense to suppose that what we have from him on fixed capital are no more than the beginnings of a train of thought that is subsequent to the creation of the greater part of his system. The full rethinking, with full allowance for fixed capital, was never made.

Thus it is that the question which has been so important for later economists – what is the effect on the structure of production (or on the fixed capital–circulating capital ratio) when total capital increases *with labour supply constant* – was never seriously considered by Ricardo. What we described as the 'path being repelled by the floor' is indeed, as has been shown, a part of Ricardo's theory; but it is not clear that he ever worked it out in any but circulating capital terms, where the effect is pure arithmetic. It is true that there are passages (added in the 1821 edition) which indicate a substitution of machinery for labour *along the path*, as the rate of profit falls and the 'money' wage rises, or as Ricardo says, 'labour rises': 'The same cause that raises labour, does not raise the value of machines; and therefore, with every augmentation of capital, a greater proportion of it is employed on machinery'.[36] But this is not much to go on. The extension into the field of fixed capital, considered at the end of the first part of this paper, should therefore be regarded as a 'projection' of the Ricardian theory; a projection which we have sufficient evidence to show that Ricardo contemplated, but which in substance he never made.

[33] There is just one other outstanding place where attention is paid to fixed capital, and even to the problems raised by its 'non-malleability'. This is in the chapter on 'Sudden Changes in the Channels of Trade', where he points out that 'it is often impossible to divert the machinery which may have been erected for one manufacture to the purposes of another', while circulating capital (considered as wage-goods) is more easily diverted (p. 266). It should, however, be noticed that this very forward-looking passage appears in a chapter that is essentially a qualification to the main work; it has not been worked into the formal theory.

[34] Notice (1) that the *Essay on Profits* (from which the whole story begins) uses a purely circulating capital model; and (2) the central importance that is attached to the labour theory of value. The latter, as Ricardo explains it, is clearly the result of beginning from a model with no fixed capital and equal periods of production in all industries.

[35] It appears that Ricardo was still at work on chapter I as late as 14 October 1816 (see his letter of that date to James Mill, *Works*, VII, p. 82).

[36] *Principles*, p. 395. (See also p. 41.) 'The same cause that raises labour does not raise the value of machines' because machines are part of non-agricultural output.

5

From Classical to Post-classical: The Work of J. S. Mill

We used to be taught that there were three great names in classical economics: Smith, Ricardo and Mill. There is no question, in more modern times, about the standing of Smith and Ricardo, but Mill, as an economist, seems to have been de-throned. He was, of course, much more than an economist. There is hardly anything in the writings of Ricardo which is not economic; and Smith's other writings are eclipsed by the *Wealth of Nations*. But Mill can keep his reputation as an important, if controversial, social and political philosopher, while his economics are passed over. I shall be solely concerned, in this paper, with those of his writings which are strictly economic; I think I can show that they deserve more attention than they currently receive.

They are all of them contained in two books: *Essays on Unsettled Questions* (1844) and *Principles of Political Economy* (1848). One might thus suppose that they both of them dated from much the same period; but this is a delusion, for he says in the preface to the essays that these were actually written much earlier, in 1829–30. It makes good sense to suppose that they were written for a seminar, on Ricardian economics, which (he tells us in his *Autobiography*) he and his friends used to hold for some years after the death of Ricardo (in 1825). Mill, in those years, was a very young man; he was only nineteen when Ricardo died. But he had been brought up, by his father, to be the intellectual heir of Ricardo. It is very understandable that those young men, at those meetings, should have been puzzling out Ricardo.

These essays, then, represent the first phase of Mill as an economist. Though they are the work of so young a man, they are perhaps the freshest of Mill's economic writings. Anyone who reads Ricardo should read them also.

Practically all of the rest of Mill's economics is in the *Principles*. He says that he wrote this large book during the three or four years before publication. So the publication of the essays may be taken as a signal that he had then begun to go back to economics. For there is very little of economic interest from his pen in the thirties; his main pre-occupation, during those years, must have been his *Logic* (1843). And though he made some changes in later editions of the *Principles*, especially in that of 1852, they are not of major importance. The evidence surely is that after 1848 he again turned away from economics. There is very little about economics in his correspondence, until we come to his last years (he died in 1873). Then there are letters directed to his friend W. T. Thornton, who had written a book entitled *On Labour*. But it seems to me that these letters only show that by that date he had got so far away from economics that he had lost the grip that he had once possessed.

So we may go back to the essays. The first of these, on International Trade, is a major work. Though Ricardo had stated the 'law of comparative cost' it appears no more than incidentally in a chapter (VII of his *Principles*) which is mainly devoted to other matters; its consequences were not fully worked out, and could easily be misunderstood, as did in fact happen. What Mill did in this early work was to work them out. He was particularly concerned with the division of the gain from trade between two trading countries. He made what was then the epoch-making discovery that the relative prices of internationally traded goods could not be determined in terms of cost (as Ricardo had supposed all prices to be determined) but that recourse must be had to 'a principle antecedent to that of cost of production, and from which that law holds as a consequence – the principle of demand and supply'.[1] So international values depended on reciprocal demand, as he himself was later to put it in his *Principles*. This was a first breakthrough to post-classical economics. There is a clear pedigree from this essay of Mill's to his own work on the same subject in his *Principles*; from that to Marshall's *Pure Theory of Foreign Trade* (1879) which is just a re-working of Mill with a better mathematical apparatus; thence to Marshall's *Money, Credit and Commerce* (1923); and thence to some of the writings of James Meade and Harry Johnson, which bring the story up to date. It all goes back to that essay of Mill's.

So that was a first substantial contribution, which has been of permanent importance. It would by itself give Mill a title to fame.

---

[1] *Essays on Unsettled Questions*, 1844 edition, p. 8, Toronto edition, volume 4, p. 237.

The second of the essays, *On the influence of Consumption on Production*, has had no such obvious sequel. It is nevertheless still worth reading, for we have (perhaps) not finished with it yet.

Look at some of the things he says:

Of the capital of a country there is at all times a very large proportion lying idle. The annual produce of a country is never anything approaching in magnitude to what it might be if all the resources devoted to reproduction, if all the capital, in short, of a country, were in full employment.[2]

And again:

This perpetual non-employment of a large proportion of capital is the price we pay for the division of labour. The purchase is worth what it costs; but the price is considerable.[3]

Then on what was already becoming known as Say's Law:

Interchange by means of money is . . . ultimately nothing but barter. But there is the difference – that in the case of barter, the selling and the buying are simultaneously confounded in one operation. . . The effect of the employment of money, and even the utility of it, is that it enables this one act of interchange to be divided into two separate acts or operations. . . Although he who sells really sells only to buy, he needs not buy at the same moment when he sells; and he does not therefore necessarily add to the *immediate* demand for one commodity when he adds to the supply of the other.[4]

Is this the voice of a classical economist, or is it what was to be, one hundred years later, the voice of Keynes? Mill is talking about full employment of capital, Keynes about full employment of labour; but it could hardly have been denied by either of them that the two sorts of underemployment are related. It is nevertheless clear that Mill's essay does not, in the end, go off in a Keynesian direction; and much of what he says on these matters in his *Principles* is not at all Keynesian. The first main object of the present paper will be to show why.[5]

---

[2] *ibid.*, p. 55.
[3] *ibid.*, p. 56.
[4] *ibid.*, p. 70.
[5] I used to think that the change in emphasis, which is surely to be detected between the essay and the *Principles*, was 'politically' motivated; that Mill had become more anxious

One must set these writings in their historical context. The period during which Mill was writing was marked by severe *fluctuations*. There was a famous crisis in 1825, just too late for it to have had any influence on Ricardo's thinking; but when Mill wrote this essay he had this experience behind him – the crisis and the depression which followed. The practical purpose of the essay is to explain that experience, to show that it can be explained in terms of a Say–Ricardo theory, when that is suitably qualified – but it must be qualified! I quote from its concluding paragraphs:

Nothing is more true than that it is produce which constitutes the market for produce, and that every increase in production, if distributed without miscalculation among all kinds of produce in the proportion which private interest would dictate, creates, or rather constitutes, its own demand. . , (This doctrine) only appears a paradox, because it has usually been so expressed as apparently to contradict well-known facts. . . . The essentials of the doctrine are preserved when it is allowed that there cannot be permanent excess of production, or of accumulation; though it be at the same time admitted, that as there may be temporary excess of any one article considered separately, so may there of commodities generally, not in consequence of overproduction, but of a want of commercial confidence.[6]

Before the time of the writing of the *Principles*, there had been further fluctuations – a severe depression in 1840–1, and a boom, which was to lead to the crisis of 1847, during the very time that Mill was working at his book. So he had still to deal with similar experiences. In fact, in the chapter on 'Excess of Supply' (III, 14), which corresponds most closely with the essay, his conclusion is the same as that of the essay – the concluding passages of the essay and of that chapter are strictly comparable. Slumps are

not to provide ammunition for inflationists, such as Attwood and his friends (*CEMT*, p. 163). I have now become convinced that this must be wrong. After all, there is a reference to Attwood in the essay; he is already being opposed (p. 68). I do not now believe that Mill thought that in the two works he was saying anything substantially different. He always thought that there were two sides to the argument. In the essay they appear together; but in the *Principles* they are too widely separated. In III, 14 ('Excess of Supply') both are present; the 'disequilibrium' side is indeed underemphasised, but it should be remembered that this chapter is meant to be read along with the chapter on credit expansion (III, 12) which has just preceded it. What went wrong was the separation of these chapters in the third book from the chapters on capital (I, 4–5) in the first. The reader comes to them first, and can easily take it that they constitute the whole of what Mill had to say on the matter. This was a fault, a most serious fault, in arrangement; but it is not more than that.

[6] *EUQ*, pp. 75–6.

possible, because of a failure of confidence; but that is a failure which in time will right itself. It may well be asked: why does he have such confidence in the inevitability of recovery? There had, in his experience, always been a recovery; but that in itself is no sufficient answer. He is not very explicit, but I think that there is an answer that is implied. Slumps are times of low prices, relatively to some norm; if the norm is firm, that means that the low prices themselves hold out a prospect of recovery, which, sooner or later, must become actual. So there is an underlying stability, provided that the norm remains firm.

So much is common to the essay and the *Principles*; but between the dates of those writings came the 'Currency-Banking' debates, so in the credit chapters of the *Principles* the nature of the norm is considered further. He makes it clear that in his view it is confidence in the maintenance of a Gold Standard (in his days a full Gold Standard, with gold coins in circulation) which is the basis of the required belief that in the long run prices cannot depart very far from normal. He is therefore opposed to the regulation of the Quantity of Money, however defined; the objective of monetary policy should be the maintenance of convertibility. That will not prevent fluctuations, nor could control of Quantity prevent fluctuations; for booms can start with an expansion of trade credit, without the banks themselves being, at that stage, much involved.[7] As the boom develops, it requires to be fortified by more secure forms of credit, so the pressure is carried back from the circumference to the centre of the banking system. It is essential, at that point, that the centre should hold firm; it must protect itself, but only in order to be able to spread security around it. Booms are thus more dangerous than slumps; for a slump will cure itself, while in a boom there is a threat to the convertibility, on which the underlying stability is based. But once it is recognised that there is this threat, wise policy can ward it off.

I would maintain that for the conditions of Mill's lifetime this was good analysis; nothing that happened much before the end of the nineteenth century put it out of date. It is the internationalising of fluctuations, spreading from one industrialised country to another, which has weakened the stabilising power of exchange stability. This, not surprisingly, Mill did not foresee.

---

[7] I here quote a few sentences from my discussion of Mill's monetary theory in *CEMT*, pp. 164-6.

It is unlikely that these monetary doctrines of Mill's had any great influence. It is only in the light of what has happened long afterwards that we can give them, in due historical perspective, the respect they deserve. The other aspects of Mill's teaching (in the *Principles*) to which I shall now be turning, had quicker effects.

Mill had begun by showing (in the First Essay) that there was one major exception to the rule of determination of value by cost, the determination of international values. When he comes back to this matter in the *Principles*, he prefixes to his chapter on international values (III, 18) a brief chapter (III, 16) entitled 'Some peculiar cases of value', in which he recognises that there are other exceptions. These are cases of related goods (complements and substitutes on the supply side). Here also, he recognises, value cannot be explained without reference to demand. He insists that these, like international values, are exceptions; but he has put them next door to one another, so he was tempting someone to ask if there could not be some connection between them. And whether then it would not be possible to build on that common element, so as to construct a more general theory, into which not only Mill's exceptions but also his regular case could be absorbed. That is one way (would it not have been Marshall's way?) by which one could proceed from Mill to more thoroughgoing marginal theory, marginal utility–marginal productivity theory, in which all economic action is reduced to choice at the margin.

Mill had opened the door to it; but one cannot believe that he could possibly have accepted it. There is evidence[8] that Marshall, who did pass through a stage when he was a thoroughgoing marginalist, had passed by the time of the later editions of his *Principles* to a position that was closer to Mill's, to a two-sector model in which average-cost industries and marginal-cost industries were sharply distinguished. He did not kill the uniform model – the Jevons–Walras–Menger model – with its single type of marginal adjustments working throughout; the Mill–Marshall model, with its two sorts of industries, has nevertheless survived. Many of us still find ourselves having to have recourse to it, in one form or another.

I shall be concerned, in the rest of this paper,[9] with what I think was another of Mill's bequests to the next generation of economists. It is a matter of attitude to economic growth. Accumulation and

[8] See review of Whittaker, p. 335 below.
[9] I shall now be borrowing some pages of a paper 'Growth and Anti-Growth' which I published in *OEP*, November 1966, pp. 258–62.

Growth – the relation between them – had been a major issue in the days of Smith and Ricardo, but in the post-classical epoch it almost dropped out of sight. One must not exaggerate. There are two chapters on 'Economic Progress' at the end of Marshall's *Principles*; but there is more of history in them than there is of theory. There is a chapter on Accumulation of Capital at the end of the first volume of Wicksell's *Lectures*, but it is just tacked on to the end of his more important work. And in Walras, Pareto, Böhm-Bawerk, Pigou, there is even less. Not until we come to Schumpeter[10] and Cassel[11] in the early twentieth century is there a change.

Why were the older classical economists interested in growth? If we ask Adam Smith, he will tell us:

It is in the progressive state, when society is advancing to the further acquisition, rather than when it has acquired its full complement of riches, that the condition of the labouring poor, of the great body of the people, seems to be the happiest and most comfortable. It is hard in the stationary, and miserable in the declining state. The progressive state is in reality the cheerful and the hearty state to all the different orders of society. The stationary is dull; the declining melancholy.[12]

Formally, that is, there is a 'natural' or normal level of wages which works very like the normal price of a commodity. If the actual wage is higher than the normal wage, the supply of labour will be tending to increase; if it is lower, the supply of labour will be tending to diminish. But it takes a long time for supply to adjust to demand, so that a condition in which the wage is above the normal level can go on for a long time. In the 'progressive state' the demand for labour is increasing, and in view of the lag this means that wages are, and can for a long time remain, above normal. This, he thinks, and it is easy to agree with him in thinking, is a desirable state of affairs. As for the 'other orders of society', he must surely mean that profits also must be in some sense above normal, or the supply of capital would not be increasing, as it must be if the economy is to be progressive. Capital supply and labour supply are both increasing; growth is unimpeded (just as in the growth models which in the 1960s became so fashionable) by fixity of supply of any factor of production.

---

[10] *Theory of Economic Development*, originally published in German (1911), in English translation (1934).

[11] In his *Nature and Necessity of Interest* (1902) Gustav Cassel advanced an interesting argument, tending to deduce a minimum for the real rate of interest, and consequently of profit, due to the limited length of human life.

[12] *Wealth of Nations* (Oxford edition, 1976, volume 1, p. 99).

Before Ricardo wrote, Malthus had exploded his bombshell; the supply of land is fixed, so indefinite increase of labour and capital, in whatever proportions they are combined, will call forth diminishing returns. But although all that is so important in Ricardo (so that his theory has been labelled 'pessimistic' in contrast with Smith's 'optimism') it is surely the case that in their attitude to growth they are quite close together. For him also it was the progressive which was the 'cheerful and hearty' state: the state which it should be the object of policy to keep going, as long as that could be done at all.

Nevertheless, land is fixed; if the supply of labour goes on increasing, even if capital is increasing with it, the marginal product of the variable factors must diminish – in whatever proportions they are combined. Wages cannot be reduced below their *normal level* without bringing the expansion to a halt; if one sets that constraint on wages, diminishing returns means a falling rate of profit. There is thus some size of population, in any given technical conditions, at which the rate of profit must be reduced to *its* normal level. Once population has reached that point, there can be no more accumulation of capital and no more increase in population, though if Ricardo had heard of the Cobweb Theorem, he could have made our flesh creep by describing a cobweb path to equilibrium, through cycles of pestilence and famine.[13] .

But it is not quite right to take this as a piece of pessimism. His Stationary State is not attractive; but it is a horror that can be put off, by wise policy, by taking good advice, into the almost indefinite future. By developing foreign trade, by the exploitation of the almost limitless resources of the extra-European world, the Ricardian apocalypse is indefinitely, or almost indefinitely, postponable. And what better incentive to virtue than certainty, but indefinitely postponable certainty, of hell fire?

This is where we come to Mill. He disagreed, on this important matter, with Smith and with Ricardo. It was his conviction (and it is evident that the idea occurred to him very early) that this Smith–Ricardo doctrine, of the only decent existence being that of the progressive, growing, economy, in which capital and population are increasing more or less *pari passu* was quite wrong. It was the increase in population that was the Devil; by birth control that could be exorcised. Mill, even in his early years, was a great believer in birth control; he became famous, or notorious, for his birth control propaganda before he had written any of his books.[14] He did that propaganda because he saw the consequence.

If population can once be controlled, there is no need for the economy to go on expanding, in order that wages should be above the subsistence level. Instead of land being the main fixed factor, so that (as in the Ricardian stationary state) surplus production is swallowed up in rent, it is labour that becomes the main fixed factor, so that surplus production can be made to go, at least in large measure, to wages. This is an altogether different, and much more agreeable, picture. The Stationary State is no longer a horror. It becomes an objective at which to aim.

That already followed from which Mill was saying in the 1820s, but by the time he wrote his *Principles* he was evidently going further. He had convinced himself that this objective – if only the growth of population could be limited – would not be far away. So it would soon be unnecessary to go on accumulating; the 'progressive state' that had been beloved by his predecessors could come to an end. He welcomed its demise. Already, in the 1840s, the evils of industrialism, the terrible working conditions, the crowded slums in the industrial towns and so on, were beginning to be recognised. What in earlier days had seemed to be salvation had lost its glamour. There is no doubt that Mill shared this view. The chase of capital after population revolted him, not simply for the Malthusian reason of its effects on the food supply, but for other reasons also. I quote a famous passage:[15]

I cannot regard the stationary state of capital and wealth with the unaffected aversion so generally manifested towards it by political economists of the old school. I am inclined to believe that it would be, on the whole, a very considerable improvement on our present condition. I confess I am not charmed with the ideal of life held by those who think that the normal state of human beings is that of struggling to get on; that the trampling, crushing, elbowing and treading on each other's heels, which form the existing type of social life are the most desirable lot of human kind, or anything but the disagreeable symptoms of one of the phases of industrial progress. The northern and middle states of

---

[14] 'There are two Mr Mills, too, whom those who like reading
What's vastly unreadable, call very clever;
And whereas Mill senior makes war on good breeding
Mill junior makes war on all breeding whatever.'

Tom Moore, the song-writer and satirist, some of whose 'Irish Melodies' are still familiar, appears to have written these lines in 1826.

[15] Mill, *Principles*, (Ashley edition, p. 748, Toronto edition, volume 3, pp. 753–4). I have quoted this passage in its original (1848) form. In the latest edition to which Mill made amendments, after the Civil War in America, it was considerably softened down.

America are a specimen of this stage of civilisation in very favourable circumstances; having, apparently, got rid of all social injustices and inequalities that affect persons of Caucasian race and of the male sex, while the proportion of population to capital and land is such as to secure abundance to every able-bodied member of the community who does not forfeit it by misconduct. They have the six points of Chartism, and they have no poverty; and all that these advantages seem to have done for them is that the life of the whole of one sex is devoted to dollar-hunting, and of the other to breeding dollar-hunters. This is not a kind of social perfection which philanthropists to come will feel any very eager desire to assist in realising.

Though it is only in book IV of the *Principles* that these views become explicit, they influence of the whole structure of the work. What were later to be regarded as 'equilibrium positions' have become more important; the 'path to equilibrium' less important. The designing of the objectives at which one should be aiming moves into the centre of attention. For this one does not need a growth theory; what one needs is a static analysis.

A major thing which follows from this is a new look at distribution. Ricardo had said that he was concerned with distribution, which in his view Smith had neglected. But when one examines how his theory works out, one sees that it is the effect of distributive changes on the growth process which is his concern; he is not concerned with a better distribution as an end in itself. Mill can be, and is. The distribution which occurs at one point in a Ricardian growth process is not particularly important, for it will not last. But the distribution which is attained in Mill's stationary state will last; so it does indeed matter, in a new way.

There are several sorts of intellectual tendencies that are traceable in the next half-century (and longer) that are made more intelligible when they are regarded in these terms. A radical or a socialist who had learned his economics from Mill, or from those who had learned from Mill (at however many removes) would naturally have been more concerned with the static problem, of the workability of a system with a more equal distribution of income *once it had been attained*, than with what he would have considered as mere incidents on the path to his New Jerusalem. That certainly holds for the Fabians, who took their name from not being in a hurry, and for other saints and prophets of the British Labour Movement. It was the division of the cake (as Ramsay MacDonald put it),[16] not the

[16] In his *The Socialist Movement* (1910).

increase in its size, which was their concern. They, like the contemporary economists, belonged to the static epoch.

How far those economists got their statics, even indirectly, from Mill is no doubt disputable. It may be that Mill did no more than dispose of the old growth economics; so that the economists of the next generation were free to take population as an exogenous variable, on the causes of movements in which economics had little to say. This enabled them to turn their attention to static problems which, for the time being, had become more interesting. One can, however, point to the *Economics of Welfare*, coming at the end of the static epoch, but fully maintaining its spirit. Production, how to increase it; distribution, how to improve it; fluctuations, how to diminish them.[17] That is Pigou's framework; it is just what Mill would have thought proper.

This is no place to assess the revival of growth economics in the twentieth century. It is better to conclude with another quotation from Mill — a message from him to present-day environmentalists, who have risen up in opposition to the new growth economics, just as he did to the old.[18]

(There is not) much satisfaction in contemplating the world with nothing left to the spontaneous activity of nature; with every rood of land brought under cultivation, which is capable of growing food for human beings; every flowery waste or natural pasture ploughed up, all quadrupeds or birds which are not domesticated for man's use exterminated as his rivals for food, every hedgerow or superfluous tree rooted out, and scarcely a place where a wild shrub or flower could grow without being eradicated in the name of improved agriculture. If the earth must lose that great portion of its pleasantness which it owes to things that the unlimited increase of capital and population would extirpate from it, for the mere purpose of enabling it to support a larger, but not a better or happier population, I sincerely hope, for the sake of posterity, that they will be content to be stationary, long before necessity compels them to it.

It is interesting to learn from Mill's letters that in his early years, botany had been his principal hobby.

---

[17] There was a section on fluctuation in the first form of Pigou's book (*Wealth and Welfare*, 1912); it was afterwards hived off to make a separate volume (*Industrial Fluctuations*, 1927).

[18] *Principles*, Ashley edition, p. 750, Toronto edition, volume 3, p. 756.

6

Edgeworth, Marshall and the 'Indeterminateness' of Wages

PREFATORY NOTE

The sixty years from 1870 to 1930 were in Britain the time of the rise of the Labour Movement; thus it is not surprising that the British post-classics (Marshall, Edgeworth and Pigou in particular) should have had labour problems very much on their minds. It seemed to them that their marginal utility analysis was well fitted to deal with such problems; nowadays this may seem more doubtful. A paper which comments on some issues they raised in this field may thus fit in here.

It was published in the *Economic Journal* in June 1930; it was my first theoretical paper. I was already working on *Theory of Wages*, to appear two years later. It was in that context that I came to it; only when I submitted it to Keynes (as editor) did he tell me that a section about Dobb, whose 'Sceptical View' had appeared in a recent number,[1] really had to be included. I do not now feel that my section on Dobb added anything useful, so it (together with an exchange with Dobb which appeared in a later issue)[2] is here suppressed. One can now see that both he and I were trying to push on beyond the static approach of the post-classics, but neither of us had got very far. There are just two sentences of my reply to Dobb which I would like to preserve: 'Competition does tend to abolish the exploitation of labour, but it is very slow about it. It is quite slow enough for some interference to be desirable, but what kind is another question.' I wish I had gone on to say that it was improvement in information, on both sides, which my analysis suggested was called for, what had already been begun by the institution of labour exchanges. That should have followed on from the point about 'free communication', which I did regret that Edgeworth had put on one side (p. 74 below). I should not have left it at that.

---

[1] M. H. Dobb, 'A Sceptical View of the Theory of Wages' (*EJ*, December 1929).

[2] *EJ*, March 1931.

For my own later views on these matters, see chapter 4 of *TW* (1932) and pp. 316–19 in the Commentary, which is annexed to the 1963 edition of that book.

Both Edgeworth[3] and Marshall[4] conclude from their investigations (though for different reasons) that there is a degree of indeterminateness, or arbitrariness, about the fixing of wages – even when combination is absent. Such a contention is obviously important, since it seems to imply that (at any rate in the short period) wages might be different from what they are without any effect on the demand or supply of labour, and therefore without any derangement of the economic system.

That combination normally introduces an element of indeterminateness is a generally accepted conclusion; it is not questioned here. This discussion will therefore be confined to conditions where Trade Unionism and Employers' Association are absent.

I

Edgeworth conceived the problem of value as being fundamentally a problem of the determinateness of equilibrium. His answer to the question, 'How far is contract indeterminate?' is the key to a main part of his *Mathematical Psychics.* 'The general answer is, (α) Contract without competition is indeterminate; (β) Contract with *perfect* competition is perfectly determinate; (γ) Contract with more or less perfect competition is less or more indeterminate.' This part is, in fact, taken up with proving this proposition, and with defining the conditions necessary for perfect competition.

But just what did Edgeworth mean by indeterminateness? On this crucial point there has been a great deal of misunderstanding. It was the centre of the great controversy with Marshall, or at any rate it appeared to be. And in other ways it has raised difficulties. Nevertheless, up to a point, the meaning is quite plain. Contract is indeterminate when the general conditions of free exchange – that each party is seeking to better himself by the bargain, and that the terms of the contract are agreed on by the free consent of both parties – do not suffice to determine the terms of the contract and to ensure that one particular rate of exchange will inevitably be arrived at.

[3] *Mathematical Psychics* (1882).
[4] *Principles of Economics* (1890).

Where competition is absent, this is clearly the normal case. If two isolated persons are considering the terms of a bargain to be arranged between them, there will generally be a wide variety of different terms, any one of which would be accepted by both parties in preference to forgoing the transaction altogether. But among these sets of terms, some will be unstable.[5] If by some chance one of these unstable contracts is agreed on (for it could be agreed on, being by definition acceptable to both parties), it will nevertheless be to the interest of both parties to revise it. Suppose that our two persons are an employer and a workman agreeing on the terms of a day's employment. Many different combinations of wages and hours would probably be agreeable to both parties if there seemed no alternative but a breakdown of the contract. But if the terms proposed involved long hours and high wages, it is obvious that a revision in the direction of shorter hours and lower wages might suit both the workman and the employer. Similarly, some combinations of short hours and low wages would be unstable. But although a considerable number of the agreements which appear possible at first sight thus prove unstable, we cannot be sure that any particular set of terms will be the inevitable outcome of the bargaining. If the employer bluffs successfully, he may induce the workman to come at low wages, and to work such long hours that it is not worth his while to offer to work longer as a means to make more. But if his bluff is less successful, hours may be shorter *and* wages higher, while both agreements give a stable equilibrium. The formal conditions of the market do not suffice to establish the terms; they are fixed by 'what has been called the Art of Bargaining – higgling dodges and designing obstinacy, and other incalculable and often disreputable accidents.'[6]

It has been necessary to repeat so much of the familiar theory of bilateral monopoly in order to elucidate the exact meaning given to 'indeterminateness' by Edgeworth. But this is all fairly well accepted doctrine; its application to wage-theory is important in the highest degree. For we have only to substitute combinations for the isolated

[5] It will be noticed that here, and throughout this paper, *instability* is used in a different sense from that which has later become established. I suppose that in 1930 I had not begun to think about unstable *equilibrium.*]

[6] *Mathematical Psychics*, p. 46. It may be observed, as a deduction from this argument, that the possible terms of *stable* equilibrium can be arranged in an ordered sequence. As we proceed along this sequence, the terms become successively less favourable to the employer and more favourable to the workman; or vice versa, for the contrary direction. Therefore, so long as we are concerned with stable agreements, there is a definite relation between wages and hours in a free market. In Edgeworth's terminology, every point of settlement must lie on the 'contract curve'.

bargainers of the above example, and we have the germ of the modern theory of Collective Bargaining.[7] In this precise sense of Edgeworth's, the bargain between Trade Union and Employers' Association is indeterminate; a number of different agreements are possible, each of which is stable and cannot be disturbed by the free action of both parties endeavouring to improve their positions. Only by means of threats and 'bargaining technique' can one party induce the other to agree to a settlement more favourable to it and less favourable to the other. Reasons can, of course be found even in this case, why a particular agreement was arrived at; but an additional set of data is required. From the standpoint of the forces which are sufficient to determine equilibrium in a competitive market, the bargain between two monopolists is indeterminate.

Edgeworth passes on from his discussion of bilateral monopoly to examine the problem of equilibrium under competition. Perfect competition, he holds, in complete agreement with the common view, is perfectly determinate; but the conditions for perfect competition are more complex than is commonly supposed. If any of these conditions is not fulfilled, contract is not perfectly determinate, and there is a range (though often a very narrow range) of different values at any of which the market can reach equilibrium.

The first of these necessary conditions is free communication throughout the market. Edgeworth states this condition, but he says very little about it, rather unfortunately. His reason for preferring special treatment of the other conditions was that they are 'peculiarly favourable to mathematical calculation'. Doubtless true – but it is an omission that must be remembered when applying Edgeworth's conclusions to general theory.

It is the other four conditions to which he draws special attention; and indeed the discussion of them is one of the central parts of the whole book. They are:

(1) The number of buyers and sellers must be indefinitely large.
(2) Each individual must be free to contract with an indefinite number of others at the same time. It follows from this condition that the things exchanged must be divisible to an unlimited extent – a more familiar condition, but one which has not the same range of implication as Edgeworth's.

----

[7] There are, of course, differences. Bargaining associations proceed by way of supply and demand curves, not by 'contract curves' (cf. Bowley, *Mathematical Groundwork*, p. 8). [That, I think, would have been true enough in 1930. In later times it has become less evident.]

(3) There must be no combination, i.e. no individual need seek the consent of other individuals before entering into a contract, but seeks on his own to better himself.

(4) There must be no association whereby groups of persons agree only to enter upon contracts simultaneously.

The third and fourth of these conditions have been excluded from this discussion, but we are concerned with the first and second. The following is the argument by which Edgeworth shows that they are necessary for determinate equilibrium.

He has disposed of the case of a simple monopolistic market, with one buyer and one seller, and he next proceeds to pass over from monopoly to competition by introducing more persons on to the market. The most instructive case is that in which there are two buyers and two sellers. Under these circumstances, how will equilibrium be determined?

In the first place, it is clear that there is sufficient competition to ensure that the same terms of exchange will obtain throughout the market.[8] For if not, 'It will usually be to the interest of the X of one couple and the Y of the other to rush together, leaving their partners in the lurch.' When the terms are not identical, equilibrium is unstable. But although the terms must be identical, they are not necessarily determinate. The range of possible settlements is narrower than in a pure monopolistic market, but it may be appreciable.

Suppose that there are added to the single employer and single workman of our earlier example, another employer and another workman; or suppose that two such couples are brought into contact. Now, if, before communication was opened, the employers had had the better of the higgling and bargaining, and wages were low, then the employers' competition must force them up. But how can it do so? There is only one way. No advantage can be derived by any party from a simple change round, once uniformity of terms has been established. But if wages are very low, an employer may be able to benefit himself by taking on both workmen, and offering terms sufficiently superior to those offered by his competitor to attract the other's workman away. That competitor, 'left in the lurch', will then bid up again in order to recover his unfaithful servant. And this process will go on until it ceases to be advantageous for either employer to take on a second man at terms which the men would

---

[8] If the two employers or the two workmen differ in disposition or circumstances, this requires a little modification. But competition will in any case prevent a wide divergence between the terms.

prefer to those ruling. The terms at which the employers cease to be willing to make such a change will fix the minimum wage at which equilibrium is finally possible in this market.

If the wages ruling before communication was opened were very high, then under suitable technical conditions it may be advantageous for the employers to 'share' a workman. The other workman will therefore be left unemployed, and will reduce his terms sufficiently to persuade one employer to leave this uncomfortable position and re-employ him. This will give the maximum possible wage. The wage cannot be higher than its maximum, because at higher rates it would be advantageous for the employers to share a workman; it cannot be lower than the minimum, because at lower wages it would be advantageous for an employer to take on two. It should be clear that these limits are fixed by different causes, and that therefore there is no reason to suppose that they will normally be represented by the same rate. Normally, there will be a gap between them, over which the rate is still indeterminate.

This argument has been presented in terms of labour contracts, because it is in labour contracts that we are particularly interested. But it will be observed that there is a certain awkwardness in doing so. 'Sharing' a workman is an operation neither familiar nor usually convenient, and it is true that in applying the theory to labour contracts we introduce a complexity at this stage which would be absent if we were dealing with commodity markets. To them the theory applies with less qualification, and it was, of course, in terms of them that the theory was first thought out. But we shall return to this matter later.

As the number of buyers and sellers is increased, the minimum rises and the maximum falls.[9] Thus, in the limit, the range of indeterminateness will tend to disappear, and we have a state of perfect competition with determinate equilibrium. In fact, of course, not many competitors will be required to make the indeterminateness negligible.

The necessity of Edgeworth's second condition has really been established simultaneously with the first. It will have been observed that the only way in which competition can change rates from one level to another (apart from equalising them) is by one buyer entering into contract with two sellers, or vice versa. If this is not possible, then competition is powerless to reduce indeterminateness. Edgeworth illustrates by imagining a market consisting of an equal number of

---

[9] See *Mathematical Psychics*, pp. 37–8.

employers and workmen, and working under the condition that no employer can take on more than one man, nor any man serve two employers. Then, he says, even if there should be a 'sudden influx of wealth into the hands of the masters', equilibrium would not be disturbed. For the employers would be unable to utilise their wealth in increasing their demand for labour.

As a consideration of practical importance in the labour market, this second imperfection is easily disposed of. Edgeworth suggested that it might impede the bidding up of wages by employers in 'many cases of contract for personal service'. These are hard to find; it is not easy to think of a type of 'personal service' where an appreciable number of employers do not demand the services of more than one employee, nor of a case where a 'sudden influx of wealth' would not increase the number of would-be employers on the market. But even if it could be found, the argument would still have no practical significance. For it is really only valid in the special case where the workmen offering their labour are 'equal-natured'.[10] Suppose this is not so; then, if the employers' capacity to pay did increase, they would bid against each other, not to increase the number of their employees (for that is assumed impossible), but to improve the quality of their single attendant. Numbers of employers would seek to secure a servant who was more highly trained, or who possessed some other form of advantage. Previously they could not afford the higher wages which these better men were naturally securing, but now they would bid for them, and try to attract them away from their employers. In this way there would be no obstacle to the bidding up of wages.

This kind of imperfection should theoretically be of greater significance in the opposite case. Edgeworth noticed this, and in an article in the *Giornale degli Economisti* (1891)[11] he observed that the fact that it is much easier for an employer to take on two workmen than for a workman to serve two employers 'constitutes a positive advantage to the workpeople in their dealings with entrepreneurs'. Fortunately he qualified this: 'I do not regard these nice points as more than *curiosa*.' For what does this argument mean in practice? If we are dealing with industrial production, many men being employed by each entrepreneur, the range of indeterminateness involved is only that between the marginal product of n men and $n + 1$. This differ-

---

[10] Edgeworth does extend some of his theoretical analysis to the case of 'different natures'. But, as too often in *Mathematical Psychics*, in the practical illustration such circumstances are overlooked.

[11] Summarised in *Papers*, II, 313.

ence is usually regarded as the atom of economics, into whose recesses we need not pry. But even if the ratio of workmen to employers is small, and the differences do become significant, we can only regard as serious the possibility of the men getting an advantage within the limited range available if we suppose the employers to be 'equal-natured' and equal-circumstanced. Otherwise, different employers will be situated differently with respect to their demand for labour; some will be on the verge of increasing their demand, others on the verge of reducing it. Once we assume a fluid market (i.e. that changes do not in themselves involve costs and inconveniences) we may be certain that a slight change in the situation of employers will inevitably have its reaction on the demand for labour. Even if it is insufficient to cause all employers to change their demand, it will influence some. Edgeworth's second imperfection naturally produces '*curiosa*'; it is a problem of discontinuity, and the effects of discontinuity are usually reduced to vanishing point when we have individuals of varying capacities on the market.[12]

To the first imperfection (limitation of numbers in the market) Edgeworth pays little attention. He tells us that it 'applies to Monopolies', and leaves it at that. In fact, of course, there can be little doubt that it is very much more important than the second imperfection.

This may perhaps suffice as an abridged statement of Edgeworth's argument and criticism of its details. The more important question of its relation to actual labour problems will be postponed until we have examined the rival theory of Marshall.

II

The passage in which Marshall suggests the existence of a range over which wages may be indeterminate is to be found at the end of his chapter on Market Price. 'When a workman is in fear of hunger, his need of money (its marginal utility to him) is very great; and if at starting he gets the worst of the bargaining, and is employed at low wages, it remains great, and he may go on selling his labour at a low rate. This is all the more probable because, while the advantage in bargaining is likely to be pretty well distributed between the two sides of a market for commodities, it is more often on the side of the

---

[12] To complete this argument, the case of a class of labour where total numbers are very limited should formally be included. This is the case, of course, where the rule that 'no man can serve two masters' most commonly breaks down.

buyers than on that of the sellers in a market for labour.'[13] The opposition between this doctrine and Edgeworth's is apparent; but so is its extreme convenience as a basis for the defence of Trade Unions. It is not surprising that it has raised considerable controversy, especially as consideration shows that Marshall's meaning is extremely obscure. He himself declared that 'the practical importance of this consideration is not very great'; but others do not seem to have agreed with him. In order to appreciate his meaning, and evaluate its importance, it still seems necessary to examine what he said more carefully than has been done up to the present.[14]

At first sight, Marshall is maintaining that there is an arbitrary element in the determination of wages, arising from the simple fact that wages are low. In consequence of this, it is impossible in the case of labour to make the simplifying assumption which he found so useful in his general value theory, that the marginal utility of one of the commodities exchanged remains constant throughout the transaction. The same difficulty arises in the labour market as in a market where barter is practised. 'The real distinction between the theory of buying and selling and that of barter is that in the former it generally is, and in the latter it generally is not, right to assume that the stock of one of the things which is in the market and ready to be exchanged for the other is very large and in many hands, and that therefore its marginal utility is practically constant.'[15] It was barter that Marshall particularly analysed, and if we are to throw light upon the case of wages, the celebrated 'nuts and apples' example by which he illustrated the problem of barter must first be considered.

Throughout his theory of market price, Marshall treats of groups of buyers and sellers who have *stocks* of commodities which they wish to exchange. He imagines the sale to proceed by stages, a fresh bargain being struck as each dose of a commodity is sold. Under these circumstances he has no difficulty in showing that:

(1) Even in a position of bilateral monopoly, with one buyer and one seller, the *final* rate of exchange will be determinate if one

---

[13] *Principles*, 8th edition, p. 335.

[14] The first criticism of this passage was naturally made by Edgeworth. In his *Giornale* article he pointed out the divergence, but unfortunately fell at the same time into a misapprehension about Marshall's use of the term 'Rate of Exchange'. This was pointed out by Berry. In replying, Edgeworth did not make it as clear as was perhaps desirable that his main criticism stood. Neither the note on this controversy in Marshall's *Principles* (later editions), nor Edgeworth's summary in the *Papers* are as illuminating as the original articles. (See *Giornale degli Economisti*, 1891, March and October (Edgeworth), June (Berry). Also Edgeworth, *Papers*, II, 313, and Marshall, *Principles*, note xii *bis*.)

[15] *Principles*, Appendix F. [It will be noticed that 'barter' is used by Marshall in a sense quite peculiar to himself.]

of the commodities exchanged has a constant marginal utility to both parties.

(2) Even in a state of competition, where there are many competing buyers and sellers, the *final* rate of exchange will not be determinate unless the constancy of one marginal utility is given.

(1) If the stock of one of the commodities (A) held by both parties is sufficiently large for the transaction to make no appreciable difference to its marginal utility to either of them, then the rates at which they will be prepared to exchange the other commodity (B) will depend simply on its (B's) marginal utilities to them. If an extensive transaction is to take place, then there will have to be a considerable gap between the marginal utilities of the first unit to buyer and seller (between demand-price and supply-price). Exchange can take place at any rate between the two. But whatever is the rate of exchange, it will make no difference to the demand-price and supply-price of a second unit. These will depend on the marginal utilities of that unit, and so are *ex hypothesi* unaffected by the rate at which the first unit has been exchanged. It is therefore evident that B will go on being exchanged until its marginal utilities to both parties are equal. This must happen after a determinate number of units of B have been exchanged (determinate in the sense that it is independent of the terms on which the earlier units were exchanged); and the rate at which the last unit is exchanged is also determinate, since it is proportional to the marginal utility of the last unit.

But once this assumption of constant marginal utility is dropped, the rates at which earlier units were exchanged begins to have a very significant effect on the demand and supply prices of later units. Equilibrium will be reached sooner or later according as the earlier stages of the bargain favour one party or the other.

(2) The multiplicity of buyers and sellers makes no essential difference to this argument. There is less likelihood of a wide divergence in bargaining technique between the two sides when they are composed of many individuals; and consequently 'the mean of the bargains would not be so likely to differ very widely from' the final equilibrium rate 'as in the case of barter between two people'.[16] Nevertheless, if there is any divergence, it will affect the demand and supply prices for subsequent units, and thus affect the position of final equilibrium.

How far can this argument be applied to the case of labour? The only situation in the labour market which can possibly correspond

---

[16] *Principles*, Appendix F, p. 792.

exactly to the problem of barter is a bargain between employer and workman for a single day's, or a single week's, work. (This is the only case in which the problem can possibly be treated as one of *stocks*.) It does not seriously distort this case if we suppose the workman to sell his labour piecemeal, hour by hour. Then all that the barter argument can prove is that, in single contracts of this kind, superior bargaining capacity could have no effect on the length of the working day if the marginal utility of money to the workman were constant. In fact it is not constant; and so, if wages are low, as a result of the employers' superiority in bargaining skill, the workmen will be prepared to work long hours. This conclusion is certainly correct; but it can hardly be called profound.

Now there is a strong reason for supposing that this is not what was in Marshall's mind. He adduces as a second source of employers' advantage in bargaining 'the fact that each seller of labour has only one unit of labour to dispose of', and he cannot have done this unless he was thinking of the amount of labour the workman offers as fixed. This seems to preclude any attainment of equilibrium by dosing, and leaves us with the alternative, but not much more satisfactory view, that Marshall *was* thinking, in this case, of a continuous market, and not of an exchange of stocks, although every other example in the chapter in question is concerned with exchange of stocks.

Once we assume a continuous market, with production and consumption going on all the time, with contracts being made afresh at regular intervals, then it is true that Marshall's statement would, under certain conditions, be formally justified. In a single contract (for a single week's work, say) the lowest rate which the labourer will be prepared to take will be largely governed by the marginal utility of money to him; and since that marginal utility will be high, the rate will be low. When recontracts take place in subsequent weeks, the low wages earned will have done no more than satisfy the labourer's most immediate wants, and will have left him without any reserve on the basis of which to refuse the bad terms offered. He will 'go on selling his labour at a low rate', for the marginal utility of money to him is no less than it was before.

But if this is a correct interpretation of what Marshall meant, the argument seems curiously out of place where it occurs, for it is subject to an important qualification from which the arguments that surround it are free. In a continuous market, the question of competition or monopoly *is* significant. If we suppose a single workman serving a single employer – both in isolation – and the first week's work is done on terms disadvantageous to the workman, then he is likely to go on selling his labour at the same low rate, for he will have no lever to get the contract revised in his favour. But if we suppose multiplicity of employers and workmen, free communication and a competitive market, terms which were fixed in the first week to the workmen's disadvantage will be subsequently modified by the employers' mutual competition, by some employers endeavouring to take on more men. Wages will thereby be bid up to the normal value of the labourers' marginal net product, and the first disadvantageous contract will have no effect in depressing them. It is quite true that in the case of barter, with the assumptions Marshall made, competition is ruled out. But if his doctrine about wages is to make any sense, competition is relevant.

III

It seems to follow from the foregoing discussion that the only 'imperfection' that is likely to have any durable effect on the determination of wages is monopoly and limitation of the market. Edgeworth's second imperfection is seen to be altogether negligible when we take into account differences in efficiency between labourers; and Marshall's 'varying marginal utility' can have only transitory effects, unless there are impediments to the action of competition. It remains for us to examine what is the significance of these impediments in the real world.

There are two possible cases of monopoly that seem worth consideration. The first – and it is clearly this that was in Marshall's mind – is where a single labourer comes to an employer and offers himself for a vacancy, the only vacancy that he knows of within the area that he can reach with his limited means. This is clearly a case of bilateral monopoly (however transitory the monopoly may be), and in consequence it is supposed that the employer, sizing the man up from his tattered appearance, offers a wage near to the lowest that he thinks the man will take, even although it is far below that which he would be willing to pay under other circumstances. No doubt, odd men seeking casual jobs are sometimes engaged in this way; but it is unlikely that it has ever been the general rule throughout industry. Pushed to its logical extreme, it would mean that employers engaged labour by a process of discriminating monopoly – a thing which no employer who was not a fool, and who wanted to get good work out of his men, would do. In an industry of small firms, each employing only a few workmen, it would no doubt be commoner than in large capitalistic enterprise. But at no time is it likely to have made much difference to the general level of wages; as industry develops, this slight effect must inevitably tend to disappear.

It is, of course, very difficult to verify this conclusion by a study of English industry today, with its minimum wages and Trade Union control. But it is significant that thirty years ago Mr and Mrs Webb reached by observation the same conclusion: 'The most autocratic and unfettered employer spontaneously adopts standard rates for classes of workmen, just as the large shopkeeper fixes his prices, not according to the higgling capacity of particular customers, but by a definite percentage on cost.'[17]

It is much more possible for an employer to exercise simple monopoly on a large scale. Technically, this is not a case of indeterminateness, since it is obviously to the interest of a monopolist employer to push wages down to the lowest point which is consistent with his retaining the labour of a requisite number of workmen, and this raises no analytical problem. But the cases are so closely connected that it may fairly be considered here. When other employment of anything like the same kind is completely outside the reach of his employees, an employer may easily exercise great monopoly power.[18] Where, as in the more common case, the labourers can secure other employment, but only with varying degrees of difficulty, the conclusion is less certain. On the whole it would appear probable that partial monopoly of the ordinary kind does not have much effect in depressing wages; though it is perhaps partly responsible for some districts lagging behind others when there is a general rise of wages to meet rising prices.

For it must be remembered that the influence of competition on wage-fixing is rarely exercised directly. Competition governs wages, as the law keeps order, by readiness to step in, not by continual interference. Particularly is this the case in a country like England, where labour turnover is generally small. In the majority of cases, a man gets higher wages by persuading his employer that he could get them somewhere else, not by actually changing round. Such changes would cause inconvenience to employers as well as to workmen;

[17] *Industrial Democracy*, p. 281.
[18] Some of the most striking and conclusive instances of this are to be found when a large country is being developed by a few alien capitalists. There have been instances where wages have remained for years unaffected by a considerable rise in the price-level. [I was thinking of the gold mines in South Africa. I had just returned from my first visit to that country when I wrote this paper (see below, p. 357).]

wages can well move without them. It is natural, therefore, that wage-changes in one firm should roughly follow another, even if actual transferences of labour were to be a matter of some difficulty.

But considerations of this kind open up wider perspectives. Once we go forth into the actual world, we must take into account a host of other circumstances which are properly excluded from an extension of the pure theory of value. Some of these actually simplify the problem; the fact that in a large works, the hours worked by different labourers must be the same (or at any rate bear a relationship determined by technical considerations), means that in some labour problems the variability of hours, which so complicates the pure theory, can be left out of account. But the existence of large capital investment has other consequences less favourable to a simple theory of wages. A change in demand for the finished product will be met by employers in a different way according as they expect it to be temporary or permanent; this expectation will affect their demand for labour and so will affect wages. An increased demand which is expected to be brief will not lead to any extension of plant; it will be met by working overtime, only to a slight extent by taking on more labour. At a later stage, if the increased demand continues, it will usually be necessary to carry out a more thorough reorganisation, which is likely to be accompanied by a more considerable expansion of the labour force; but direct raising of wages is not the only way in which an increased supply of labour can be secured. Up to a point, much can be done by advertisement, or by the engagement of rather inferior workmen. Wage-rates will only be raised if other resources are exhausted and if the employers are convinced that the good times are likely to be of fair duration. Similarly, in the case of a reduction in the demand for his product, an employer may decide to make for stock, or to discharge those workmen who are least essential to him, without reducing wages and so causing bad feeling, if he considers the depression is likely to be short.

Such matters can be only suggested here, not worked out properly; but it is rather surprising that the phenomenon of the 'wage-lag' to which they point has not received more attention in relation to the problem of indeterminateness. They are indeed strong reasons for supposing that wages do not in practice correspond with the marginal net product of labour at all precisely. If there is any considerable tendency for wages under free competition to fall below marginal net product, it is far more likely to be due to the characteristics of the trade cycle[19] than to any 'bargaining advantage'.

[19 That is to say, to more 'dynamic' elements.]

7

Léon Walras

I suppose that this paper, which appeared in *Econometrica* in October 1934 (only the second year that journal had existed) was intended as an introduction of Walras[1] to econometrists. It is strange to think that there was a time when that could have seemed to be necessary. I was (and am) no econometrist myself, and I don't think I did the job at all well. There is too much about the relation of Walras to Marshall, who naturally bulked large in the circles in which I was moving; and there is nothing about Cassel, who would have been more to the point. I was wholly ignorant, at the time I was writing, of the important work, arising out of the Cassel version of Walras, which was then going on at Vienna (this is discussed in my survey of *Linear Theory*, pp. 250ff. below). I was thinking of Walras in the terms of what I myself had got from him – the inspiration he had been to me – the foundations on which *VC* was to be built, in the years which followed.

I had already, when I wrote, made the acquaintance of that great Walras scholar, W. Jaffé; he had helped me on some biographical points, and had shown me the beginnings of his great collection of letters. But the work which Patinkin was to do on Walras's theory of money lay far in the future; I could not have dismissed the money theory so lightly if I had known what Patinkin was to make of it. (Still I don't think I really like it; I remain, on Money, much more Wicksellian than Walrasian.)[2]

The letter which Keynes wrote me about this paper is quoted on pp. 296-7 of the second volume of this collection.

---

[1] Born at Evreux, 1834; in 1870, after ten years of journalism, business, and other miscellaneous activities, he became Professor of Political Economy at Lausanne, a position which he held until 1892. His *Eléments d'Economie Politique Pure* appeared in two parts: the theory of exchange in 1874, the theory of production in 1877. (Second edition 1889, 3rd 1896, 4th 1900.) He died in 1910.

[2] See essays 19(IV), 21 and 23 of volume II.

I

Like John Stuart Mill and John Maynard Keynes, Léon Walras was the son of an economist. His father, Auguste Walras, was one of those excellent people (they seem to have existed since very near the dawn of history) who taught the true but unhelpful doctrine that value depends on scarcity (*rareté*);[3] the son followed the father's teaching, but added to it something which lifts it on to another plane of precision. He defined *rareté* as *l'intensité du dernier besoin satisfait par une quantité consommée de marchandise*;[4] scarcity equals marginal utility.

His position with Jevons and Menger as one of the independent discoverers of the Marginal Utility principle is generally regarded as Léon Walras' chief title to fame; and this no doubt justly enough. But anyone who comes a little closer to these writers cannot help feeling a little resentment at the habit of classifying them together, even for the joint receipt of such an honorable title. For each of them made contributions to economics which are peculiarly his own, and it is for these special contributions that they are still worth reading today.

Indeed, the modern reader of Walras' *Eléments d'Economie Politique Pure* is struck by its affinity, not with the work of Jevons or Menger, but with that of Marshall. For a quite considerable part of the way Walras and Marshall go together; and when they separate, it is a difference of interests, rather than of technique, that divides them. While Walras was seeking for the general principles which underlie the working of an exchange economy, Marshall forged an analytical instrument capable of easier application to particular problems of history or experience. Yet, since the followers of Walras cannot always afford to be pure philosophers, and Marshallians have their moments of reflection, the two systems have inevitably tended to grow back into one another as the years pass by.

This affinity between two writers of different upbringing and obviously very different mental outlook – their simultaneous development of what was then a very new line of thought – looks at first sight surprising, and one feels almost obliged to explain it by the intrinsic excellence of the path they followed: 'it seems no honest heart can stray'. Yet in fact there is a clear historical reason for it,

---

[3] A. A. Walras, *De la nature de la richesse et de l'origine de la valeur* (1832).
[4] *Eléments d'Economie Politique Pure*, p. 76. All references to the *Eléments* will be to the *Edition définitive*, i.e. fourth and subsequent editions.

one decisive influence we know to have been felt by both. Each of them had read Cournot.

Now although each makes a specific acknowledgement to Cournot, it is in each case couched in very general terms.[5] They each tell us that Cournot showed them how to use the differential calculus in economics, and this may mean much or little. But it is at least striking that certain very significant elements of Cournot's mathematical economics, going far beyond the mere idea of using mathematical methods, appear in Walras and appear in Marshall.

One of these is of course the demand curve itself (which already implies a resolution to treat economic quantities as if they are continuous variables). But more important, and less obvious, is the conception of perfect competition. Cournot's analysis, it will be remembered, passed from Monopoly to Duopoly (or Limited Competition), and from Duopoly to Unlimited Competition, which he defined as a state of affairs in which no single producer is able to influence appreciably the prices of the market. It was this last conception (applied to the theory of exchange value generally) which enabled Walras and Marshall to overcome the difficulties which had baffled Jevons, those difficulties which arise from the differences in the wants of different buyers of a particular commodity.[6] In the hands of Walras, the conception of perfect competition was converted into a special technique of using prices as economic parameters. Although of course this technique was

[5] Walras, *Eléments*, Preface, p. viii. Marshall, *Principles*, Preface to the first edition, pp. ix–x.

[6] Cf. Jevons's ugly and unsatisfactory device of 'trading bodies', which smudges over the distinction between monopoly and competition.

The relation between Jevons's work and that of Cournot is curious. When he wrote the first edition of his *Theory* Jevons had not read Cournot; but he had read Lardner's *Railway Economy*, 'which treats certain questions of Political Economy in a highly scientific and mathematical spirit. Thus the relation of the rate of fares to the gross receipts and net profits of a railway company is beautifully demonstrated in pp. 286–293 by means of a diagram. It is proved that the maximum profit occurs at the point where the curve of gross receipts becomes parallel to the curve of expenses of conveyance' (*Theory of Political Economy*, 1st edition, pp. 17–18). Lardner thus plotted total receipts and total costs against price – a peculiar way of putting it, to our ideas; but it is obvious that in so doing he adopted the most direct way possible of expressing the fifth chapter of Cournot's *Recherches* in geometrical form. Whether this is really what happened, I am unable to say; all that can be said is that it is definitely possible. For at the time Lardner wrote his book (1850) he was living in Paris, and so was Cournot; and there was at least this link between them, that in 1835, three years before he wrote the *Recherches*, Cournot had translated a book on Mechanics by Lardner into French.

But if we cannot prove the filiation, so much at least is clear: Jevons started from a theory of monopoly substantially identical with Cournot's. Where Walras and Marshall had the advantage over him was in their possession, not only of Cournot's theory of monopoly, but also of his theory of Unlimited Competition.

used by Marshall as well, its very consistent employment is highly characteristic of Walras's work.[7]

With this equipment, it was fairly easy to give an adequate analysis of the simple exchange of two commodities under competitive conditions. (Cournot had confined himself to the selling of products by producers, and did not examine the logically prior problem.) Accordingly, we find Walras beginning his *Eléments* in this way (1874), and Marshall following with a substantially equivalent analysis, hidden under the guise of a theory of International Values (1879).[8]

Walras's treatment fails of complete generality in only one respect; the downward slope of the demand curve is not quite so inevitable an assumption as he thought it. But he was well aware that the downward slope of the demand curve does not necessarily imply that the supply curve derived from it is upward sloping. If a person is buying X, and giving Y in exchange, then, if his demand for X becomes inelastic, his supply curve of Y will turn back towards the price-axis. In this case it becomes possible that the demand and supply curves for Y may cut several times; but some of these intersections will be points of unstable equilibrium.

Faced with this difficulty of multiple intersections, Marshall cut the knot by his distinction between the 'theory of International Values' and the 'theory of Domestic Values'. In 'International Values', the possibility of negatively inclined supply curves is serious; but they are unlikely to be particularly important in practice, because the competition of domestic industry generally suffices to keep a country's demand for imports in terms of exports fairly elastic.[9] In the theory of 'Domestic Values', we may take commodities to be usually sold by producers or dealers who have themselves no direct demand for what they sell. Negatively-inclined supply curves can then only arise from increasing returns.

Apart from the reference to increasing returns (a problem he never seriously examined), this reliance on sale by producers, whose reser-

---

[7] I should now like to emphasise that it is *not* a characteristic of Marshall's. He did use it sometimes, but he much preferred to use quantities as parameters, even when he was coming nearest to Walras.]

[8] *The Pure Theory of Foreign Trade.* There is, I think, no question that Marshall's analysis is quite independent of Walras's. Yet they differ in only two ways: (1) Marshall uses aggregate curves, instead of the simple price-quantity curves used by Walras; (2) Marshall's 'Increasing Returns' complication has of course no counterpart in Walras's simpler problem.

[9] This is, indeed, to interpret the early Marshall by the late (*Money, Credit, and Commerce*, pp. 351-2).

vation demand is negligible, was Walras's way out also.[10] But before coming to that point, he widened the problem by a consideration of multiple exchange, where more than two commodities enter into the picture. In order to treat this question, he supposed one of the n commodities to be chosen as a standard of value (*numéraire*), in which prices are reckoned, but which is itself subject to no demand other than that which arises from its ordinary properties as a commodity.[11] There thus remained $n - 1$ prices to determine. From the conditions of given stocks at the commencement of trading, and equalisation of the marginal utilities of expenditure in all directions, he derived each individual's demand (or supply) for each commodity. Then the ordinary equations of supply and demand in each market give the conditions of equilibrium. They are n in number, but that in the market for the *numéraire* is superfluous, as it follows from the rest. There are thus $n - 1$ equations and $n - 1$ unknowns; a set of prices must therefore exist which satisfies the conditions of equilibrium.

Here, for the first time, we have a characteristically Walrasian doctrine. What is it worth? On our estimation of it our view of Walras's individual contribution to economics must largely depend.

Now it is, of course, quite clear that, even when they are applied to this pure problem of exchange, the equations are far too complicated to be of much use in analysing any actual situation. But that is surely not their function. Where they are supremely useful is in elucidating the general way the price-system works, and in giving us a classification of those factors which may be relevant to any particular case. In practice we have to select out of that over-long list those which are most important for each special problem. When that selection is performed, we may get a result which conforms to the simpler scheme employed by Marshall; but on the other hand we may not.

The types of equations used by Walras in determining exchange equilibrium are two; those which express the dependence of the

---

[10] *Eléments*, p. 163. It may be questioned whether Walras had as much right to it as Marshall (often) had.

[11] 'Nous supposons ici les achats et reventes de (A) comme intermédiaire s'effectuant de manière à n'influer en rien sur le prix propre de cette marchandise. Dans la réalité, les choses se passent tout autrement. Chaque échangeur a par devers lui un approvisionnement de monnaie en vue de l'échange et, dans ces conditions, l'emploi d'une marchandise comme monnaie, a sur sa valeur une influence que nous étudierons plus loin' (*Eléments*, p. 156). Recent economic thought has suffered, I think, by its neglect of this valuable device. The *numéraire* is a fanciful notion, perhaps; but it is the only logical way by which we can suppose exchange (or lending) to take place *in natura*.

amounts demanded and supplied by particular individuals on the system of market prices, and those which express the equality of demand and supply in particular markets. These two classes stand on very different footings. So far as the first class is concerned, they have become the essential foundation for the whole branch of economics to which they refer. On them is based, and had to be based, all the work in the field of demand and of related goods, which has been carried out by Edgeworth, Pareto, and others. In the process of development Walras's conception of utility has been much refined; but we still work with Walras's equations, however differently we write them.

The second class, which expresses the equation of supply and demand in the different markets, seems much more simple and obvious; yet it has proved much more open to criticism, for it is on this class that the meaning of Walras's system of general equilibrium depends, and by far the most important divergence between Walras and Marshall turns on this point.[12]

Walras's own account of the nature of equilibrium is this. Persons come on to the market with certain stocks of commodities, and certain dispositions to trade ('dispositions à l'enchère') and a particular set of prices is proposed. If at these prices supplies and demands are equal, then there is equilibrium straight away. But if demands and supplies are not equal, prices will be changed until equilibrium is reached.

What, however, Walras does not make really clear is whether any exchanges do or do not actually take place at the prices originally proposed, when those prices are not equilibrium prices.[13] If there is no actual exchange until the equilibrium prices are reached by bidding, then Walras's argument is beyond reproach on the score of logical consistency, though it may be called unrealistic. (The market then proceeds under Edgeworth's principle of 'recontract', or provisional contract.) But if such exchanges do take place, then, in general, the final equilibrium prices will be affected by them.

Marshall's way out of this dilemma was to concentrate on a particular market, where he could show that if the marginal utility of one of the commodities exchanged could be treated as constant,

---

[12] Cf. Edgeworth's review of Walras in *Nature* (1889) and his controversy with Bortkiewicz in the *Revue d'Economie Politique* (1890-91). Also his comment in *Papers*, II, 311.

[13] 'Les marchés les mieux organisés sous le rapport de la concurrence sont ceux où les ventes et achats se font à la criée, par l'intermédiaire d'agents tels qu' agents de change, courtiers de commerce, crieurs, qui les centralisent, de telle sorte qu'aucun échange ait lieu sans que les conditions en soient annoncées et connues et sans que les vendeurs puissent aller au rabais et les acheteurs à l'enchère' (*Eléments*, p. 44). This remains ambiguous.

then the final rate of interchange would be independent of the path followed to reach it.[14] But this solution – which is, after all, only a very particular solution – is usually not available in the case of General Equilibrium.

Neither Walras nor Pareto faced up to this difficulty; when we do so, it is impossible to avoid the conclusion that the 'Lausanne equations' are of rather less significance than they imagined. The equations of Walras are not by any means a complete solution of the problem of exchange; but they remain a very significant step towards such a solution. For Walras's system of prices will be reached, either if contracts are made provisionally or (a more important case) if people come on to the market on successive 'days' with the same dispositions to trade, and there is no carry-over of stocks (or a constant carry-over) from one day to the next. When it is understood in the last sense, the theory of static equilibrium of exchange takes its place as a step towards the development of a complete theory with which future exposition is unlikely to dispense.

II

From the General Equilibrium of Exchange, Walras passed to the General Equilibrium of Production. For him, as for the Austrians, the problem of production fell into two parts: one relating to the pricing of factors of production, which are only used in combination with one another; the other relating to the rôle of time in production – the theory of capital.

The first of these problems (which corresponds to the Austrian theory of imputation) is really no more than an extension of the theory of value: it studies one particular kind of interrelation of prices. In this field Walras's original work was chiefly confined to a consideration of that problem which from his point of view is the simplest (though the Austrians naturally found it the hardest from their standpoint); the case where the 'coefficients of production' are fixed, so that the quantities of all factors needed to produce a unit of each kind of finished product are technically given.

With fixed coefficients, and with perfect competition, the equilibrium prices of the products must depend on the prices of the factors; thus, given the prices of the factors, the whole price-system (of products and factors) can be derived by simple process of addition. But, given this whole price-system, the demands for products

---

[14] Marshall, *Principles*, Book v, ch. 2; also the Appendix on Barter.

and the supply of factors can be determined from the tastes and abilities of the individuals composing the economy. Again, once the demands for the products are determined, the demands for the factors can be technically deduced. We can thus write both the demands for the factors and the supplies of the factors as functions of the set of factor-prices; and determine equilibrium in the factor markets as before. The equilibrium prices in the factor markets now determine the equilibrium prices of the products.

This solution is of course valid only under the assumption of fixed coefficients; but Walras was quite aware that it could easily be extended to the more realistic case of variable coefficients.[15] One cannot help thinking it to be a great pity that he did not trouble to work out this hint, for it would have led directly to the general law of marginal productivity.

Nevertheless, even as it is, this part of Walras's work has great merits. The particular relation which it exhibits has quite general significance, and could hardly have been discovered in any other way than this. Even when the coefficients of production are variable, so that a rise in the price of one particular factor influences the demand for it mainly by encouraging a substitution of other factors within industries, there will still be present this further tendency: that the factors which co-operate with this first factor will find it more profitable to devote themselves to the production of products for which relatively little (or none at all) of the first factor is required.

Again, we have here an excellent illustration of the value of Walras's work for the clearing up of questions of principle – the sort of question which Marshall so frequently left rather confused. Walras's equations give the most exact version that has ever been given in the 'opportunity cost' element in value; and at the same time they preserve the essence of the 'real cost' principle for which Edgeworth and Marshall contended. They exhibit the supplies of the factors as variable, but as determined by the system of prices in

[15] 'Nous supposons, comme on voit, les coefficients ... déterminés *a priori.* En réalité ils ne le sont pas: on peut employer, dans la confection d'un produit, plus ou moins de tels ou tels services producteurs, par exemple, plus ou moins de rente, à la condition d'y employer moins ou plus de tels ou tels autres services producteurs, par exemple, moins ou plus de profit ou de travail. Les quantités respectives de chacun des services producteurs qui entrent ainsi dans la confection d'une de chacun des produits sont déterminés en même temps que les prix des services producteurs, par la condition que le prix de revient des produits soit minimum' (*Eléments*, p. 212). This passage first appeared in 1877. (The condition of minimum cost follows from that of maximum profit – under conditions of perfect competition.) For Walras's later work on Marginal Productivity, see particularly his 'Note sur la réfutation de la Théorie anglaise de fermage de M. Wicksteed', which appeared as an appendix to the third (1896) edition of the *Eléments*, but was subsequently omitted.

fundamentally the same way as the demands for commodities, with which they are interdependent.

It is hardly necessary, at this date, to discuss at any length that one of Walras's conditions which was so vehemently attacked by Edgeworth[16] – the condition that prices equal costs of production, so that the entrepreneur makes 'neither profit nor loss'. For this device, in spite of its paradoxical appearance, is nothing else than the reckoning of 'normal profits' (the profits which the entrepreneur could earn in other activities) into costs; and similar forms of definition are now adopted for their extreme convenience by many economists who would acknowledge no direct debt to Walras.[17] It may indeed be questioned whether the full implications of this method of statement have been explored – particularly with respect to its application to dynamic conditions. But the device itself needs no defence nowadays.

III

Those parts of Walras's doctrine which we have hitherto considered are on the whole uncontroversial; it is true that they raise difficult problems of interpretation, but no one seems to doubt that in some sense they are valid enough. It is these parts which have passed into the body of economic teaching; and when we want to study them we are inclined to go, not to Walras's own works, but to the rather more elegantly stated versions of his successors, such as Pareto or Wicksell.

Walras's theory of capital, however, has not reached this happy position. By Pareto it was simply ignored; by Wicksell it was attacked.[18] It has therefore not passed into any recognised 'Lausanne' tradition, and is liable to be dismissed as something of an aberration. In spite of this, it has its merits; though there can be no question that it needs a good deal of repair in details before it can become a usable theory.

[16] Edgeworth, *Papers*, I, 25.

[17] e.g. Robinson, *Economics of Imperfect Competition*; Keynes, *Treatise on Money*.

[18] Wicksell, *Uber Wert, Kapital und Rente*, pp. 142-3. Barone ('Sopra un libro di Wicksell' – *Giornale degli Economisti*, 1895) replied to some of Wicksell's criticisms, and apparently convinced him that he had overstated his case. Wicksell's comments in his *Lectures* (English edition, I, p. 171) are appreciably milder; while in his late paper 'Professor Cassel's Economic System' (reprinted in the English edition of the *Lectures*, p. 236) he takes what I should consider a very balanced view.

If a reader who is acquainted with the work of Böhm-Bawerk[19] and Wicksell approaches Walras's theory of capital, the first thing which will strike him is that it is purely a theory of fixed capital. Walras begins from a discussion of the capital value of income-yielding goods. He shows that the ratio of capital value to net income yielded (after allowance for depreciation and insurance) must tend to equality for all such goods; otherwise people would sell the more expensive (relatively to yield) and buy the cheaper. Thus there emerges a 'rate of net yield' (*taux du revenue net*), which, in equilibrium, must be equal for all capital goods.

How is the 'rate of net yield' determined? By the condition that the prices of new capital goods must equal their costs of production. Granted that a certain amount of new saving is coming forward, this saving will give the demand for new capital goods.[20] The saving has then to be divided among the various capital goods that can be produced in such a way as to maximise the rate of net yield.

Substantially, that is Walras's theory; it is a theory, which, if taken literally, is open to very serious objections.

For one thing, as Wicksell pointed out, it determines the rate of interest on the market for new capital; and is therefore apparently inapplicable to stationary conditions, when no net addition to the capital equipment of the community is being made. Further, as Walras would have realised if it had not been for his confusion about the exact meaning of equilibrium,[21] it is only a stationary state that we can get any sensible sort of equilibrium, so long as people expect the prices of products to remain unchanged in the future (as Walras tacitly assumes they do). This dilemma is fatal to the theory as Walras presents it.

But it is not necessarily fatal to the whole method of approach. For once we assume that the reinvestment of depreciation allowances is not technically given (in the way Walras supposed), but that these funds are reinvested according to the best prospects open for them at the moment of reinvestment; then the 'new capital goods' become not only net additions to the capital stock, but also replacements, and the demand for these goods is no longer confined to new savings, but consists of depreciation allowances as well. With this slight exten-

[19] Walras's theory is, of course, earlier in date than Böhm-Bawerk's; it was substantially complete by 1877.

[20] Savings are of course also a function of the rate of net yield, which now enters into the determination of expenditure on the same footing as the prices of commodities. It must be remembered that savings are expressed in *numéraire*.

[21] The confusion we discussed above. It gets palpably worse in the later part of Walras's work. See, for example, the rather pathetic passage on pp. 214–15 of the *Eléments*.

sion, Walras's system becomes immune from Wicksell's criticisms; the capital market does not disappear in the stationary state.[22]

Walras did not make this amendment, but its possibility deserves attention; for it shows the essential rightness of his method, which survives the imperfect way in which he used it. Once the amendment is made, Walras's theory of capital becomes as good as Wicksell's, and better than Böhm-Bawerk's. It is still subject to the static limitations within which their theories are also confined, but it is as good a basis for extension in a dynamic direction as theirs — and in some ways it is perhaps better.[23]

IV

Walras's work on the theory of money,[24] and his relatively uninteresting writings on applied Economics, cannot detain us here. It was in pure economics that his real interest lay, and the discovery of the conditions of static equilibrium under perfect competition was his central achievement. Like many pioneers, he was a little vague about the exact meaning of some of his results, and was perhaps inclined to claim for them more than they are actually worth. Yet our consciousness of its limitations should not blind us to the greatness of his achievement. Static equilibrium is far from being the whole of economics, but it is an indispensable foundation; and the greater part of that foundation was laid by Cournot and Walras. There are very few economists who have contributed so much to the permanent body of established truth as Walras did.

---

[22] It is interesting to observe that, once this amendment is made, the limitation due to Walras's concentration on fixed capital disappears. For the method of reducing fixed capital to circulating, introduced by Jevons and Böhm-Bawerk, works both ways. If a machine is economically identical with a collection of half-finished goods which will be ready at different dates, so is a collection of half-finished goods economically identical with a machine. [This was running on much too fast, as was generally done in those days. Von Neumann, already in 1934, knew better; I must have discovered this point, quite independently, before I wrote chapter XVII of *VC*. See below, pp. 98–9.]

[23] The 'original factors' of the Austrians, being largely 'bygones', are a thorough nuisance in economic dynamics.

[24] See Marget, 'Léon Walras and the Cash-Balance approach to the Problem of the Value of Money' (*Journal of Political Economy*, 1931). In this field Walras did at least make a serious attempt to integrate monetary theory with the rest of economics; he did something to prepare the way for Wicksell.

8

The Austrian Theory of Capital and its Re-birth in Modern Economics

This is a paper which was given at a meeting, in Vienna in 1971, to mark the centenary of the publication of Menger's *Grundsätze*, the book which is commonly, and rightly, regarded as the beginning of what was to be the 'Austrian school'. Together with other papers given on that occasion, it was published in a volume entitled *Carl Menger and the Austrian School of Economics*, edited by J. R. Hicks and W. Weber (Oxford University Press, 1973). Though we were supposed to be celebrating Menger, I would not refrain from choosing a subject which had more relevance to the work of later 'Austrians', such as Böhm-Bawerk and the early Hayek; for I was at that time at work on *Capital and Time*, and had indeed published a first sketch of its argument in the *EJ* a year before. I have not included that sketch in this collection, since the book which followed it so completely superseded it. I was at one time inclined to think that on the same ground the present paper should be excluded; but there is a good deal more here than there is in the book about the relation between my neo-Austrian theory (the correct use of neo- in this description should be noticed) and the work of the Austrian school, properly so called. Besides, it is a good introduction to the book, as the *EJ* article hardly was. Some misapprehensions about the book might well have been avoided if more that is in this paper had gone into the book.

There have been two occasions during the last hundred years, when the Austrian theory of capital has made a particular impact. One was in the 1880s and 1890s, the days of Böhm-Bawerk; the other was in the 1930s, when the flag was raised again by Professor Hayek. The controversies that arose on those occasions have never been wholly stilled. They have continued, sometimes in the old form, but more often in quite new forms, right up to the present time. Indeed, as I hope to show, much of the main modern controversy about capital is just the old controversy in a new guise. If the modern controversy is to be settled, its relation to the old is one of the things that will have to be understood.

Though the origins of the Austrian theory of capital are in Menger (and I yield to no one in the honour I give to Menger), I am not going back to Menger;[1] I have too much to say on what has happened later. I shall take the theory in the form Böhm-Bawerk gave it; or perhaps I should say, in the form I learned it myself from Professor Hayek. There were four years, 1931–5, when I was myself a member of his seminar in London; it has left a deep mark upon my thinking. In much of my work it has been overladen by other influences, but it has survived. The present paper, I hope, will be proof of that.

At the end of the discussions in that seminar – I speak of those in which I myself took part – we were, I believe, on the point of taking what now seems to me to be a decisive step. I was, at least, on the point of taking it myself. There is evidence for that, in my *Value and Capital*, much of the groundwork for which was done before I left London; though what I say on the Austrian theory in that book[2] seems to me now to be put the wrong way round. Schumpeter, in his *History*,[3] says it is 'not in Böhm-Bawerk's spirit'; and in the way it is put he is doubtless right. It is presented as criticism, when it could have been new construction. I appeared to be closing a door, when I should have been opening it. I shall try to present it here, when I come to it, in a form which to the shade of Schumpeter (and even to that of Böhm) might be more appealing.

I

There are different theories of capital, because there are varieties of capital. The capital, the *real* capital, of any economy extends the whole way from very durable instruments – almost land, and some would say that land itself should be included – to goods that are *in the pipeline*, goods in process of production. It is no easy task to achieve a theory that is equally competent all round. There are some theories that start at the fixed-capital end, and are very weak when they come to working capital (circulating capital). There are others that start from working capital, on which they are strong, but when they come to fixed capital they tend to lose

[1] Except on one point; see note 8 below.
[2] *VC*, ch. XVII, esp. pp. 222–4.
[3] *History of Economic Analysis* (New York, 1954), p. 909.

grip. We can distinguish these types among the 'older' economists – and again among the constructions that are advanced by our own contemporaries.

The purest proponents of the *fixed-capital* theory, in Böhm's generation, were Clark and Walras; they were so oblivious of the problems of working capital that it is tempting to call them the 'quasi-land' school. (It would be unfair to Marshall to group him with them; he was more aware of working capital than they were; but it remains that he did not deal with working capital very well. His *short period* is conceived much too much in fixed-capital terms.)[4] Böhm's, in terms of this classification, is quite clearly a working-capital theory.

Now from whichever end of the spectrum one starts, there are things that belong to that end that one can see clearly; but those that are more visible from the other end may be left rather dark, or very dark. That there are some things that can be done, and quite successfully done, if one starts from the 'quasi-land' end, I feel no call to deny. For it is this school, under its modern name of the *Production Function* school, which is the dominant school in much of contemporary economics, and I am willing to recognise that it has substantial achievements to its credit. In production function theory, as usually presented, working capital seems to drop out. That does not matter for some purposes; but there are other purposes for which it does matter.

The 'Austrians', of course, did not forget about fixed capital, as the others so often forgot about working capital; but they did not really know how to deal with it. They thought (or hoped) that there was some way in which fixed capital could be 'reduced' to working capital; but it has now become quite clear that this cannot be done. We were already feeling (in the Hayek seminar to which I referred) that there was an obstacle; but we did not know what the obstacle was. Now we know. It has come up in many forms – in Sraffa's *Production of Commodities by means of Commodities*, in the work of the Linear Programmers, in the discussions that have been based on von Neumann. It has been hidden in mathematical complexities[5] but it is really very simple. Goods that are produced by the use of fixed capital are *jointly* supplied. It is the same capital good which is the source of the whole stream of outputs – outputs at different dates. So it is impossible to deal with fixed capital, *and also to deal*

---

[4] As I have explained in *CG*, pp. 51–2.
[5] For a brief statement of the mathematical reason why joint supply is such a difficulty, see *CG*, p. 324.

with working capital, unless one faces up to the joint-supply complication. And it is a complication. It is really quite formidable.

It is a complication (it is useful to notice) that appears, not only here, but elsewhere in economics. It was already encountered by J. S. Mill, who introduced joint cost as a 'peculiar case of value'.[6] If it were not for joint supply, we could, on the whole, get on very well with a cost-of-production theory of value. So it is here. If it were not for the joint supply that is implied in the use of fixed capital, we could get on very well with the Böhm-Bawerk model, in which there is associated with every unit of final output a sequence of previous inputs which have 'led to' that output, or are responsible for that output; so that the cost of the final product is representable as the sum of the costs of the associated inputs, accumulated for each by interest for the appropriate length of time. In an economy which uses fixed capital such imputation is not possible.[7]

It follows, for this reason alone, that there is much of the traditional Böhm-Bawerk construction that must be abandoned.[8] There is no *period of production*; there is no *roundaboutness*; these are at home in a working-capital model, but in a model that is to extend to fixed capital they do not fit. These are drastic excisions. If we perform such surgery, is there anything left? The chief things, I am going to maintain, are left.

[6] *Principles*, book 3, ch. 16. It is curious to reflect how different would have been the development of economics if this chapter of Mill's had been put in its proper place, as a continuation of chapter 6 of the same book. The famous 'theory of the subject is complete' must then have been withdrawn; for Mill himself was showing that it was not complete. [See above, p. 65.]

[7] The point, it may be remarked in passing, is well understood by the intelligent accountant. He is well aware that in the case of products that are jointly supplied, the allocation of overhead costs is arbitrary; and he is also aware that the depreciation allowances which he makes are arbitrary, for they similarly involve an allocation of common costs to the jointly produced outputs of different dates.

[8] One must distinguish between the 'no joint production' assumption, which is all (!) that is necessary for Böhm-Bawerk's imputation to be possible, and the stronger assumption of non-circularity (as one may call it) which already appears in Menger's classification of goods into 'higher' and 'lower' orders. Though the non-circularity assumption is explicit in Menger, it seems to me that it is implicit in the work, or perhaps in most of the work, of the classical economists. I cannot believe that they thought of the economic system, in what has become the regular input–output manner, as a *network* of industries selling to one another; it is more natural to suppose that they thought of 'high-order' industries selling to 'lower-order' industries, which sold (ultimately) to the final consumer, along a one-directional *chain*. For the relatively simple economies with which they were concerned, the one-directional chain was surely a good approximation. I wonder how far it is the case that the input–output *network* came into the consciousness of economists before the 1920s. I doubt if it is in Walras; I suspect that it does not emerge until people like Sraffa and Leontief began to work on Walras in the light of what they found in *modern* censuses of production.

What we must not abandon are Böhm-Bawerk's (and Menger's) true insights – the things that are the strength of the 'Austrian' approach. Production is a process, a process in time. Though there are degenerate forms (such as the pure service, the *unproductive labour* of Adam Smith, which 'perishes in the very instant of its performance') the characteristic form of production is a sequence, in which inputs are followed by outputs.[9] Capital is an expression of sequential production. Production has a time-structure, so capital has a time-structure. All these things stand; they are not affected. But what is to take the place of the things we reject?

II

A production process must now be defined as a *stream* of inputs, giving rise to a *stream* of outputs. It may consist, for instance, of the building of a factory, or the construction of a machine, followed by a stage during which the machine (or plant) is worked. But that is just an illustration; a process can take many forms. What, in general, are the conditions that must be satisfied in order that a process should be *viable*?

If we allow ourselves to think in market terms, a part of the answer is easy. The process must yield more than the market rate of interest; or, more strictly, the value of the stream of outputs, capitalised at the market rate of interest, must cover the cost of the stream of inputs, similarly capitalised. But if we do no more than apply this test to the beginning of the process, we have not done enough. It is not sufficient to reckon the capitalised value of the process, in this manner, at the beginning; for a process has a capital value, not at the beginning only, but throughout its course. It is a necessary condition for viability, of the process as a whole, that its capital value should be positive (or, more strictly, non-negative) *throughout*. For at every stage in the life of a process the question may be raised whether it should be continued. The continuation of a process is an investment decision, like the beginning of the process; the remainder of the process, at the point of decision, is

---

[9] It is only the purest of pure services that are an exception. The 'service industries' which play so important a part in the modern economy are rarely pure services in the sense required. The distributive trades are no more than stages in a process which extends far beyond them and of which the temporal character is unmistakable. Most professional services require some sort of equipment, which must be produced before they can be performed. Even the 'speech of the orator', when delivered today, finds few listeners if it is not broadcast on the radio.

like a new process; it will not be undertaken, so the original process will not be continued, unless the remainder is profitable. So the condition for viability is that capital value should be non-negative over the whole of the course.[10]

The rule is valid (it will be noticed) whether we think of the typical process as having a finite length, or as continuing indefinitely. It will not be continued indefinitely if at any point its capital value becomes negative. If that happens, at any stage, the process will be cut short; it will be *truncated*, to use the convenient term that has lately been introduced by Professor Arrow.[11] The finite length is accordingly the more general case; so I find it convenient to think of the typical economy as being composed of a number of processes of finite length. Each particular process extends for a finite time; at the end of that time it is abandoned, as its capital value has fallen to zero.

How 'good' this model is can only be shown by experience. It may yet be claimed for it that it accommodates both fixed and working capital with equal ease; it is competent to deal with both.

Let us go back to the beginning of the process, which needs some further attention. At the beginning, when the process is only a project, when nothing has actually been done, we should like to say that its capital value is zero – for nothing, as yet, has been invested. But if we value capital in a forward-looking manner, as we have hitherto been doing, the initial value is not zero, or not necessarily zero; a profitable undertaking may be expected to have a value, here also, that is positive. But that depends upon the rate of interest that is used for discounting. It can be shown (and I shall show in a moment) that a viable process has a rate of interest that reduces its forward-looking value, at the start, to zero. This is the rate of interest that 'belongs' to the process; it is the *yield* of the process; it is the 'internal rate of return'.

If capitalisation is performed *throughout* at this rate, the initial value will be zero; it will subsequently become positive, rising to a peak (or perhaps to a series of peaks) and then falling again to zero at the end. And it is easy to show that when capitalisation is performed at this rate, equality between backward and forward measures of capital will be maintained – not at the beginning only,

---

[10] I do not think one need make any exception to this principle, if one applies it *ex-ante*, to the planning of the process; and this is in fact the main way in which it is to be taken. It may indeed happen, in execution, that capital value becomes negative unexpectedly; and that the process has nevertheless to be carried on for a while in order to meet long-term contracts. In a fuller statement this would have to be fitted in.

[11] See the note by Arrow and Levhari, *EJ*, 79 (1969), pp. 560–6.

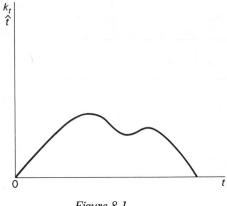

Figure 8.1

but throughout. The forward valuation (by discounting future surpluses) and the backward valuation (by accumulating past 'investments') will be the same.

A viable process must therefore have a capital value (when the rate of interest that belongs to the process is used for discounting) that has a time-profile such as is shown in figure 8.1. It begins at zero, rises through positive values, and then falls to zero; as soon as it falls to zero the process is terminated. This includes, it will be noticed, the pure working capital case, beloved of the older Austrians; when the process is that of maturing wine, or growing trees, there is a long rising part of the curve, and a very short falling part (when the wine or the timber is sold); but that fits in. It also includes the pure fixed capital case, the plant that 'works itself' — even when the plant is purchased initially in full working order; the plant then comes in as an initial input, so the curve is humped the other way; but that fits in too. Every sort of production (every sort, at least, that has a time-pattern) is of this same general type. This is the sense in which 'inputs coming before outputs' still survives; the curve must have a rising portion before it can have a fall.

III

We are now in a position to prove, very quickly, a fundamental theorem.

Divide the whole 'life' of the process into 'weeks', numbered $0, 1, 2, \ldots, n$. Suppose that inputs and outputs occur at the *beginnings* of the weeks. (The output which we mark by this convention as the output 'of' week t might more naturally be regarded as the output of week $t-1$; but I find it more convenient to attach it to week t – this is simply a matter of labelling.) I write *as* for inputs, *bs* for outputs, *in value terms*. I write k_t for the capital value of the process at the beginning of week t, before the inputs and outputs which (on this convention) are associated with week t have been accounted for. I write $R = 1 + r$, where r is the one-week rate of interest. Then

$$k_t = b_t - a_t + R^{-1}k_{t+1}$$

The capital value at the beginning of the week equals the value of the output of the week (which accrues immediately) *minus* the cost of the inputs of the week (which is incurred immediately) *plus* the discounted value of the capital at the end of the week. This holds for every week ($t = 0, 1, 2, \ldots, n$).

Now suppose that the *as* and *bs* remain unchanged (it is still the same process which we are considering) but that there is a fall in the rate of interest. r falls, so R^{-1} rises. It is immediately apparent from the above equation, that k_t will necessarily be increased, so long as k_{t+1} is positive, *and* so long as k_{t+1} is *not reduced* by the fall in interest. But it follows, in the same way, that k_{t+1} must be increased, so long as k_{t+2} is positive, and so long as k_{t+2} is not reduced. And so on, to the end of the process. But, for week n,

$$k_n = b_n - a_n + R^{-1}k_{n+1}$$

and *if the length of the process is unaffected by the change in the rate of interest*, k_{n+1} is zero and remains at zero. So k_n is unaffected by the change in the interest rate. Thus k_{n-1} must rise, and therefore k_{n-2} must rise, and so on. For the sequence of ks to be positive (which we have seen to be a condition for a viable process) is sufficient to establish the theorem, that every k_t rises, when r falls, *for a process of given length*.

The qualification about the length of the process being given can readily be removed. For since every k_t ($t = 0$ to n) will be raised, when the process is kept to the same length, no k_t which was formerly positive can cease to be positive; so there can be no reason for shortening. All that is possible is that the process may be lengthened. It will be lengthened if k_{n+1}, which was zero at the higher rate of interest (so that the process was cut short after week

n), becomes positive at the lower rate; but if that happens, the intermediate ks must be raised, *a fortiori*. So it is generally true that a fall in the rate of interest will raise the capital value of any viable process, at every stage of it.

Since the 'week' may clearly be taken as short as we like, the theorem is not dependent upon our peculiar assumption of the inputs and outputs being placed at the beginnings of the weeks. This was nothing more than a device to simplify the statement of the proof.

I think I may claim that I already had the theorem in *Value and Capital*, with the outline of a proof which is substantially the same as that just given.[12] But I put it in a peculiar way, as a property of an 'Average Period of Production', which was artificially constructed so as to maintain continuity with the Böhm-Bawerk tradition. I do not now feel that this was helpful. It is much better to state the theorem in the more straightforward form I am here giving to it. For it is much easier, when it is stated in this form, to set it to work.

A first corollary that follows from the theorem is the *uniqueness of the internal rate of return*. For the theorem applies to k_0, as to the other k_t. If we start from a rate of interest which is such that k_0 is zero (the other ks being positive), any reduction in the rate of interest must increase k_0. So k_0 cannot be zero again at any lower rate of interest. The internal rate of return is unique.[13]

As is well known, there are many ways of proving a proposition corresponding to this, in other models.[14] But I know no way which is equally simple, nor so clear in its economic sense and its economic implications. It is a very good way with which to start.

---

[12] *VC*, pp. 201, 186.

[13] While the above argument proves uniqueness, given existence, it does not prove existence (in the mathematical sense). But it can readily be shown that any process that is viable at any rate of interest must have an internal rate of return — with one exception. For such a process must clearly be viable at zero interest; if its inputs and outputs are undiscounted, its k_0 must either be zero (in which case $r = 0$ is its internal rate of return) or it must be positive. But in the latter case, if the rate of interest rises (the truncations which are induced by the rise in interest being regularly performed) k_0 will steadily diminish, and must finally be reduced to zero — save in one special case. This is the case when $b_0 - a_0$ is positive (or zero). For if $b_0 - a_0$ is negative, and k_1 is positive (as it must then be if k_0 is not to be negative), it is inevitable that

$$k_0 = b_0 - a_0 + R^{-1}k_1$$

should ultimately be reduced to zero by a rise in the rate of interest.

Thus the only exception is the degenerate case of the process that is *instantaneously* viable, so that $b_0 >$ or $= a_0$ *by itself*. This, we may agree with Böhm, is production without capital.

[14] See, for instance, my *CG*, ch. 14.

It is, of course, only a start. From this point (I am sure) many roads diverge. I can do no more, in this paper, than take a few steps along one or two of them.

IV

There is one that starts by asking an obvious question. I have said that inputs and outputs are to be taken in value terms; what determines those values? One does not want to go far into that question in a theory of capital (though Böhm did find that he had to include a theory of value in his theory of capital); but one cannot leave it altogether on one side. If one does so, one is taking too much for granted.

I shall confine attention (here) to the simplest case. Suppose that production is *fully integrated* – so that the *process* extends the whole way from 'original factor' to final product.[15] There is just one original factor, to be called labour, and one final product, which I shall call 'corn'.[16] So all the inputs are inputs of labour, all the outputs are outputs of corn. (The labour may, of course, be making ploughs, or harvesters, or fertilizers; but all that is *inside* the process.) Either labour or corn may be taken as standard of value; I find it more natural to choose corn. Thus the wage of labour is expressed in terms of corn; the rate of interest is reckoned in terms of corn; and capital values are calculated in terms of corn.

The process of production may now be treated as a *technique* – a technical method by which labour is converted into corn, over time. a_t and b_t are then to be interpreted as *quantities* of labour input and corn output which are associated with week t from the start of the process, the process being taken to be of unit size.[17] Since we are taking corn as standard of value, b_t can also be interpreted as the value of the output; but the value of the input is wa_t, where w is the corn-wage of labour. Only if w is given are the values of inputs and outputs determined; but for any w we can establish an internal rate of return on the given process, a rate of interest r that 'belongs' to it.

---

[15] So in this application, but not (I think) more generally, I am assuming 'non-circularity' (see note 8, above).

[16] It is not implied, by this conventional description, that the product is something material. If it were not that it must be a possible object of exchange, I might have called it 'utility'

[17] 'Constant returns to scale', it will be noticed, here creeping in.

If w is raised, all k_ts will be diminished; so the capital-value curve can only be restored to its *proper* form, with $k_0 = 0$ and later ks positive, by a fall in the rate of interest. It follows from what has been said that there is a particular fall in interest which will bring this about. Thus there is a rate of interest which corresponds to each particular w (for the given technique). We can draw it out as a curve, and we have proved that it must be a downward-sloping curve.

The expression of a given technique by a (w, r) curve such as this is a useful feature of modern growth models; but it can hardly be said to be a discovery of modern growth theorists, since something very like it is already in Ricardo. There is nothing specially 'Austrian' about it. It may, however, be claimed that to reach it in this way is to reach it by a rather expeditious route. Having reached it in this way, we can use it in the conventional ways; but we shall find, before we have done, that we can also use it in interesting ways that are less conventional.

One of the conventional ways in which we may use it is to turn it into a theory of *choice of techniques.* If a number of different techniques (for converting labour into corn) are available, each will have a (w, r) curve of its own. At any particular level of wages (w) there is likely to be some particular technique which is the most profitable (having the highest rate of return); but as w changes, the particular technique which is the most profitable may well change. Thus there is a *frontier*, or envelope curve, consisting of the outer portions of the particular technique curves. It indicates the most favourable r for given w (and, by implication, the most favourable w for given r) that is available 'within the technology'. All this, however, is so well understood, and has been so much discussed, that I do not need to enlarge upon it further.[18]

Another of the conventional applications is to the construction of a model of a *steady state*.

In a steady state, with given technology, the rate of wages (w) remains unchanged over time; so the technique which is chosen remains unchanged over time, and the length of time for which it

[18] I suppose I shall get into trouble if I do not mention the possibility of *re-switching*; and duly affirm that in the present construction, as in others, it is not ruled out. There is no reason why the particular technique curves should be linear, or should be convertible into a linear form by some transformation; so it is perfectly possible that a pair of particular curves may have multiple intersections. It should, however, be noticed that a rise in w, even though r is adjusted to compensate, will commonly alter the *length of time* for which it pays to carry on a 'given' process; so that even if the same process 'comes back' at a different w, it is likely that it will not be the same process in all respects. Even though the same 'machine' is used, the date at which it is scrapped may very well be different.

is carried on remains unchanged over time. It is required, in such a model, for equilibrium in the capital market, that the rate of interest should equal the rate of return on that technique; so there is a relation between the wage and the rate of interest which can be written explicitly, as

$$k_0 = \sum_0^n (b_t - wa_t) R^{-t} = 0, \quad \text{or} \quad w = \sum b_t R^{-t} / \sum a_t R^{-t}$$

with $R = 1 + r$, as before.

The economy consists of a collection of processes of this standard type. Each process is of finite length, so the time will come, for any process, when it 'dies'. Thus it is necessary, for the continuance of the economy, that there should be 'births', or 'starts', as well as 'deaths'. In a stationary economy the births (and deaths) will be constant; in a steadily expanding economy (the form of steady state that figures so much in modern discussion) they will be increasing at a constant rate. Then if x_T is the number of starts in week T (T is calendar time),

$$x_T = x_0(1 + g)^T$$

where g is the constant growth rate. I shall write this $x_0 G^T$, putting $G = 1 + g$, as with r.

The employment of labour in week T, in the processes that were started t weeks ago, is $a_i x_{T-t}$; so that the total employment of labour in week T is

$$A_T = \sum_0^n a_i x_{T-t} = \sum a_i x_0 G^{T-t} = x_0 G^T \sum a_i G^{-t}$$

The total final output of week T may be similarly expressed as

$$B_T = x_0 G^T \sum b_t G^{-t}$$

so that product per unit of labour

$$(B_T / A_T) = \sum b_t G^{-t} \sum a_t G^{-t}$$

which is independent of T, as it should be.

Thus we find (as is found in other steady-state models) that B/A is the same function of g as w is of r. The same curve (figure 8.2) can be used to express both relations. If OR is the rate of interest, RP is the corresponding rate of wages; if OG is the growth rate, Gp is product per unit of labour in the steady state (B/A).

Now if K_T is the total value of capital (in terms, of course, of 'corn'), rK_T is total profits and gK_T is net investment. Then, from

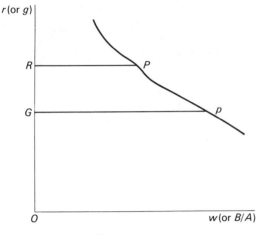

Figure 8.2

the Social Accounting 'Identity' (which can be shown to hold in this model, as elsewhere)

$$\text{Wages} + \text{Profits} = wA_T + rK_T = B_T + gK_T$$

$$= \text{Consumption} + \text{Net Investment}$$

we find that if $r > g$, $B > wA$; so there is a surplus of final product over what is needed to pay wages.[19]

All that then remains to be done is to introduce some hypothesis about saving, sufficient to give a further relation between B and wA; as soon as we have that, the steady-state model is *closed*. There are several alternative hypotheses which will do this for us; I do not know that one is more sensible than another.

[19] Thus it is necessary, for the consistency of the model, that the curve in figure 8.2 should be downward-sloping; or, more strictly, that the straight line Pp (whether or not it coincides with the curve) should be downward-sloping. Now it has already been shown (as a consequence of the fundamental theorem) that the (w, r) curve, as formerly defined, is downward-sloping; but in the proof of that, we assumed the duration of the process to be variable, and to be varied (when w varies) so as to maximise the rate of return. Along the curve of figure 8.2, the duration of the process is kept constant; it is a *restricted* (w, r) curve. It does not follow, from our previous argument, that the restricted curve is downward-sloping; all we know is that the restricted curve lies within the unrestricted curve, and is tangential to it at P. What would happen if the restricted curve were such that p lay to the left of P (while still below P)? This is a possibility which, for anything that has been said, is not ruled out, or not entirely ruled out. The answer must be that a steady state, with wage RP, would not be possible. That there are conditions in which steady-state equilibrium is not possible, should not be at all surprising.

This is an elegant construction; since it emerges in very nearly the same form in many versions of growth theory, it, and the uses that can be made of it, are becoming familiar. It is very conveniently set out on a diagram such as figure 8.2, which can be developed quite a long way. I shall not develop it here, for I am very sceptical of the importance of such 'steady state' theory. The real world (perhaps fortunately) is not, and never is, in a steady state;[20] it has adventures which are much more interesting. I have only given this much attention to the steady state, in order to show that these tricks can be performed by the 'Austrian' method, just as well as by any other. I hasten to pass to my more important contention, that there are more relevant things which it can do distinctly better.

V

A 'steady state' theory is out of time; but an 'Austrian' theory is in time. It is in time that it belongs. It can have time and change taken out of it, as was done by Wicksell, in his 'stationary state' version, and as was done in the 'steady state' version that I have just been giving; but if we treat it in that manner we deprive it of its strength, for we are stating it in a form in which it loses its peculiar virtues. A steady-state theory works in terms of reciprocal determination; but a theory which belongs in time should not be operating with the third of Kant's categories. It should be working in terms of the second – in terms of cause and effect.

A causal analysis, at least of economic problems, must take the following form. We take our stand at a base date (call it $T = 0$). Everything that has happened before that date, *in the past*, is taken as given. We compare two alternative paths that extend into the future. Along one of those paths some new 'cause' is not operating; along the other it is. The difference between the paths is the effect of that cause. The difference itself extends over time, so that there are 'short-run' and 'long-run' effects. But merely to distinguish between short-run and long-run is not sufficient; it is the *whole* of the difference between the paths which is the effect of the cause.

The Austrian theory (especially, perhaps, in its revised form) is very well adapted for the study of causal problems, in this sense. There is a wide variety of such problems that can be studied with its aid. I can do no more, here, than give an example.

---

[20] Not even in that more sophisticated 'steady state' that accommodates 'neutral' technical progress.

Let the cause, the effect of which we are to study, be an invention. The paths which are to be compared are that followed by the economy when the invention has occurred, and that which would have been followed if it had not occurred. (Since the second of these paths is inevitably a theoretical construction, causal analysis of this type is bound to be, at least in part, theoretical.)[21] The base date, from which we operate, is that at which the invention is *adopted.* I shall retain my former simplifications, of the single input (labour) and the single output (corn). The invention consists in the discovery of a new *process* for converting labour into corn. It is an addition to the former technology.

We do not need to suppose that the economy, at the base date, is in a steady state. But it is operating under the old technology; so there will be some technique, within the old technology, which (at the rate of wages ruling at the base date) will be more profitable than any other within that technology, so it is *dominant.* The new processes – those started just before the base date – will be using this 'old-dominant' technique, as we may call it. But there is no reason to suppose that all the processes which are 'alive' at the base date will be using the old-dominant technique. There may well be processes, started at still earlier dates, when technology was still more primitive, or when the rate of wages was different; yet they still survive. The techniques they use were dominant, at the time when they were started; but at $T = 0$ they have ceased to be dominant. Yet there may still be positive capital value left in these old processes (positive, that is, at the wages and interest of $T = 0$); so long as they have a positive capital value they can still be carried on.

What happens at $T = 0$, as the immediate result of the invention, is the replacement of the old-dominant technique by a new-dominant technique. The rate of return on the new-dominant must be higher than that on the old-dominant (or it would not be adopted); it must be higher at the rate of wages of $T = 0$ (which, it can be shown, is unlikely to change *immediately* as a result of the invention). So we may take it that the regular immediate result of the invention is to raise the rate of interest, while leaving the rate of wages unchanged.

As a result of the rise in interest, some of the old processes may be truncated; that can be allowed for. The more this happens, the greater the amount of the truncation, the more labour will be released for the starting of new processes of the new-dominant sort; so the passage to a position in which the new-dominant tech-

[21] These ideas were subsequently much elaborated in my *CE* (1979).

nique has been generally adopted will be by so much the more rapid. But, excepting in the special case in which the supply of labour is perfectly elastic, there must, after the first phase, be a reaction on wages. This reaction may itself have the result of causing a different technique, within the new technology, to become dominant; that is a possibility which must not be left out of account. It is, however, rather well allowed for in conventional theories; what is less well understood is the course of wages, as it will be if the same new-dominant technique continues to be dominant. But that is one of the things we need to understand.

It would take too long to discuss that issue here, even to the extent to which I am at present able to discuss it. But there is just one point, highly relevant to the history of Austrian theory, which I should like to make.

Much will depend upon the characters of the two techniques, old-dominant and new-dominant, which are adopted for new operations under the old and the new technology. Each of them will have a time-pattern, expressible as a series of inputs and outputs (a_t, b_t). All we know is that the rate of return, on the new-dominant technique, must be greater than that on the old-dominant – at the initial rate of wages. But this condition is consistent with all sorts of differences in the time-patterns; the effects on wages, on the course of wages over time, will be markedly different according as the time-patterns differ in one way or another. Some of these differences can be accommodated within the conventional classification of inventions into labour-saving and capital-saving; but by no means all. It is strongly suggested that the conventional classification is not good enough. It requires, at the least, to be further qualified.

There is one of these qualifications which in the present gathering I surely ought to mention. There is no reason at all why the time-pattern of *output*, in new-dominant and old-dominant, should be the same. It is for instance perfectly possible that the start of the outputs should be deferred to a later date, to a later stage in the process, on the new technique than on the old. This deferment is a cost, but it may be offset by some other saving. Suppose that on the old technique there is a constructional phase (with no final output) lasting for one year; but on the new technique, with the same man-hours of labour being employed in total, it lasts for two years. The additional cost, reckoned at the date when the 'machine' is ready, could well be offset by a reduction, from then on, in the cost of operating labour. Such a technical change will ultimately be more productive; but there will be an awkward stage, on the way, when final output is *reduced* below what it would have been without the technical change, the stage at which the new machine is not ready. It is not difficult to conceive of circumstances in which this temporary reduction in final output will be quite hard to accommodate.

This is the kind of point which stands out when one works with an 'Austrian' model, even of the old type; but when one works with a Production Function, it is quite obscured. Professor Hayek, who (I think) was the first to notice it,[22] probably made too much of it; but it has its place in a properly general theory. It is one of the (quite various) things that can happen.

[22] *Prices and Production* (London, 1931).

9

Is Interest the Price of a Factor of Production?

PREFATORY NOTE

I must first explain how this paper came to be written. Ludwig von Mises, whom I had been taught to reckon as the leading representative of the third generation of 'Austrians' (Menger, *Grundsätze*, 1871; Böhm-Bawerk, *Positive Theory*, 1890; Mises, *Theory of Money*, 1912) went like others into exile in the thirties and spent the rest of his long life in New York, where he died in 1973 at the age of 92. During most of those years he was teaching at New York University. He gathered round him quite a body of followers, who like to think of themselves as the true heirs of the old 'Austrian school'. They were provoked by my *Capital and Time* to ask me to address them. This is the paper I gave them, in January 1978, which was later published in *Time, Uncertainty and Disequilibrium*, edited by M. J. Rizzo (Lexington Books, 1979).

It does not have much to do with *Capital and Time*; for when I wrote it, I was already working on *Causality*, to appear the next year. Some of the leading ideas of that book already appear in this paper. Chief of these is the contention that in order to explain a historical process, we have to confront what actually happened with what we think would have happened if something had been different. Thus we cannot explain (at least in economics) without the use of a 'counter-factual' model. I maintain that in such a model the economy (in a suitably broad sense) must be in *equilibrium*.

We know that the actual experience was not an equilibrium experience; there were surprises, and unforeseen changes of course. But it is hardly possible that the hypothetical experience should not be an equilibrium experience, for it is under our control, so there can be no surprises in it.[1]

In the book, as in the recent *IS–LM* paper (volume II, essay 23) which is related, I treat the Keynes Multiplier theory (not the Kahn version) as a typical example of this kind of analysis; but there is

---

[1] p. 120 below.

nothing at all necessarily Keynesian about it. I could even give it an 'Austrian' pedigree; for it goes back, in my own thinking, to the perfect foresight inter-temporal equilibrium, which I got from Hayek.[2] The step forward from that, which makes all the difference to empirical relevance, came with the realisation that perfect foresight, even in 'equilibrium', need not go on for ever; it can be confined within the period that is under discussion. We need no more of it than that.

The acceptance of this notion has, I now realise, been made more difficult by confusion (a very natural confusion) between this sense of equilibrium and the old static sense – in which an economy is supposed to settle down into an equilibrium when 'data' remain unchanged over a sufficient time. I do discuss that in the book,[3] where it belongs, with the Classics. To the slowly changing economy, with which they may well have thought they were dealing, it would not be without relevance. But I cannot see that in our day one would often have occasion to make use of it.

The question on which I am to speak would be thought by many to be a nonsense question; maybe we shall decide, in the end, that it is. I must admit that I have chosen it, not for its own sake, but as a peg on which to hang something much wider, not much short of a confession of faith of an economic theorist – which may begin, not inappropriately, with a personal story.

I was brought up as a Baptist. At that time there were (in England at least) two sorts of Baptists: Particular Baptists and Open Baptists. It used to be said of the Particular Baptists that when they went to Heaven (there was no doubt that they would go to Heaven) they would be put into a little corner with a curtain round it, so that they should not know that there was anyone else in Heaven! My parents, I am glad to say, were Open Baptists. When I began to grow up, I read a book in which it was said that the poet John Milton had been reported to be an 'irregular and defective' Baptist; that, I thought, was just the kind of Baptist for me. Now, at the other end of my life, I find myself addressing a congregation of rather Particular Austrians, while I myself am no more than an 'irregular and defective' Austrian. I have ventured to give the description 'neo-Austrian' to the theory which has been developed in one of my books, and it has been stamped on for heresy. So I know that I have got to defend myself.

[2] Volume II, p. 7.
[3] *CE*, ch. 4.

It seems to me that Austrian economics has two distinctive doctrines. The first (I accept that Particular Austrians regard it as much the more important) may be described as the Supremacy of Demand, or, better perhaps, the Supremacy of Marginal Utility. This is opposed not only to the Classical (or Marxist, or even sometimes Keynesian) determination of value by cost, but also to the Marshallian half-way house, in which both Utility and Cost play a part, like the blades of a pair of scissors, as Marshall said. The second Austrian doctrine, not at all the same as the first, is insistence on the nature of production as a process in time, with the temporal relations between inputs and outputs occupying a similarly commanding position. There are relations between these two doctrines, but they are separate. It is possible to hold to one without attaching much importance to the other.

In the days when I learned my Austrian economics, when I was working with Hayek in London in the early thirties, it was the second which appeared to our group to be the characteristic Austrian doctrine; I am sure that the same would have held, at that date, for Hayek himself. Later on, we know, he has changed his emphasis. I myself have continued to be more interested in the second doctrine; it is an approach which, on some occasions at least, I still find myself wanting to use. It appears both in *Value and Capital* (1939) and in *Capital and Time* (1973). The latter book I would claim to be evidence that the two doctrines really are separate. For while it is truly 'neo-Austrian' in the sense of the second doctrine, the simplifying assumptions (of the single final good and the homogeneous labour) which it maintains, almost throughout, enable it to avoid, almost completely, any reference to the first.

I do however recognise that the two doctrines have something in common; a relation to time. The reason why such stress is laid upon valuation by utility, not cost, is because it is held that utilities are future, though often very near future, while costs are past. Bygones are bygones; decision-making refers to the future. The goods that are in the shops, even the unfinished goods that are in the pipeline, would not have been produced unless it had been thought that it would pay to produce them; but now they are there, the value that is set upon them now reflects their utility now. Even when the decision to produce them was taken, it was taken with an eye to their saleability, and hence to their utility, in what was *then* the future. Since it was then future, the producers did not know it; we know it, but they did not.

All that is obvious. One need not be an 'Austrian' to see it, even to attach importance to it. I am sure that Marshall attached importance to it; and so, surely, did Keynes. Where the 'Austrian' diverges comes later.

Though, at the time the decision to produce was taken, the future was not known, something must have been presumed about it. If nothing was presumed, the choice of things to produce must have been entirely random; it is obvious that in the real world it is not entirely random. It is not sufficient to suppose, as some would do, that production to be undertaken must be covered by forward contracts; they do of course help, but surely much production is in fact undertaken which is not so covered. Further, why should anyone enter into a contract for future delivery? He will only do so if he has some expectation of what his wants will be at the delivery date. So, whether or not there are forward contracts, production will not be undertaken unless expectations are formed, and they must have been formed in some way. Just how are expectations formed?

All, I think, would agree that expectations must be formed from past experience. (That is where the past, after all, does come in.) Past experience may well be very various, and the distillation of expectations from a complex past must itself be a complex matter. (Think of all the projectors, econometrists and others, who are nowadays engaged upon it.) Nevertheless, however complex and sophisticated the methods of projection that are used, there is something rather simple which is common to them. The only way of making the projection that is needed is to look for some pattern that has been *normal* in the past, and then to assume that it will continue to be normal in the future, for as far ahead as it is necessary to look. This does not mean that it is assumed that the projection *will* be realised; it will not, after all, have been true that the past experience was always normal. All that is needed is the assumption that future experience, on which some view has to be taken in initiating production, will not differ, very much, from what is projected.

What does one mean by 'very much'? The answer, I think, is mainly as follows. If what actually happens does not differ *very much* from what is projected, the addition of the new information, which comes from the realised experience, does not alter the norm which has been distilled from past experience; if it does differ *very much*, the norm is altered. It is of course true that if we are thinking in terms of very short time-units, days or weeks, an extremely favourable, or extremely unfavourable outcome on some particular day, or in some particular week, is unlikely to affect the norm; the divergent outcome must continue for some time before the norm is affected. That can be granted and yet the principle still holds.

All that, I hope and indeed believe, is substantially common ground; it is at the next step after that that we come to the parting of the ways. A non-Austrian economist (of almost whatever 'school') would hold that it is of the greatest importance to distinguish between a condition in which norms are unchanging (so that they are not being upset by current experience) and a condition in which they are being upset. The former he would describe as a condition of *equilibrium*.

I admit that when equilibrium is defined in that way, it is wider than many of the equilibria that are found in economic writings. It does not have to be a stationary equilibrium, in which inputs and outputs are unchanging; nor does it have to be a non-inflationary equilibrium, in which prices are unchanging, or some index of prices is unchanging; it could even be a fluctuating equilibrium, with a built-in cycle, such as is beloved by market analysts. All these, however, are special cases of the general concept; and I believe that it is the general concept itself which is at issue. It is the general concept itself which, even as a tool of analysis, the 'Austrian' rejects.

I have a good deal of sympathy with his allergy about it. I have myself become quite critical of equilibrium economics, especially when that is taken in the way so many economists take it. Of course we know that the real world is not an equilibrium system; plans do go wrong, expectations are cheated − but how much easier it would be to understand it if that were not the case! So how tempting it is to suppose that the system studied is in equilibrium, no doubt only approximately, but approximately enough. Then we can go straight ahead, setting our mathematical engines to work on it, churning it out.

It will be noticed that in equilibrium, since what happens now (and will happen in the future if equilibrium is maintained) is similar to what has happened in the past, we can in a sense dispense with time. One period of time is just like another. I fully agree that that is very dangerous.

Nevertheless, I do not believe that we can dispense with equilibrium, though we must be careful not to overuse it. It has practical uses, which we cannot afford to be without.

Some of these concern projections, or predictions of the future, if one is bold enough so to call them. As I have explained, these can be no more than extrapolations, predictions of the path that will be followed on some hypothesis; that is to say, they are extrapolations of some assumed normality, hence of some assumed equilibrium. I do not think that such projections are useless, even though they so often go astray. It is necessary, for current decisions, to peer into the future; it is rational to do so with any means that are at our disposal. I shall nevertheless not discuss that use further here. For I think that there is another use, which is perhaps less controversial. It seems to me to be more revealing.

Business decisions are directed towards the future; but not all of the work of the economist (and here I mean the *applied* economist) is directed towards the future – though if he specialises in that direction he will no doubt be of more direct use to business and will earn a larger salary! There is a part of the economist's job which is similar to that of the historian – understanding the past. It could indeed be said that when he works in that way he is being a historian; for there does not seem to be any *logical* difference between the tasks of explaining the causes of the American Civil War, or of the English Civil War, and of explaining the causes of the abortive boom of 1972-3. There are of course differences, vast differences, in the material available for study, so that different techniques are required for its analysis; in that respect the work of the historian and the work of the economist are different from one another. Each, however, is looking for explanations. The meaning of explanation, in the one field and in the other, cannot be very different. I much doubt if it is different at all.

I must not indulge myself in a disquisition on the nature of historical explanation; but there are some things about it which need to be said. If one asserts that A was the cause of B, where A is some event occurring at some time, while B is some event (or sequence of events) occurring at some later time, one must at the minimum be asserting four things. First, that A existed, and secondly, that B existed. Thirdly, that a state of affairs in which A did not exist, but other things contemporaneous with A did exist (so that we can give a meaning to *ceteris paribus*) is conceivable. Fourthly, that if that state of affairs (with A not existing) had been realised, B would not have existed. Though this last assertion is crucial, it has no meaning unless we can make the others.

Of these four statements the first two are, or can be, purely factual (one can indeed think of instances in which A and B are so stated that their existence is questionably factual, since they themselves are some kind of generalisation, but let that pass). The third and the fourth, however, are clearly not factual. They imply some kind of theoretical construction, which may fairly be described as a model. The model must be such that *within it* A can be treated as an independent variable; and the consequences of its presence or absence, again within the model, must be predictable.

The demands which are made upon a model, if it is to be used in this way, are evidently severe; so it may be well to take a sceptical view, holding that we have no more than a few simple models which have any hope of meeting these requirements. If the Austrian position is interpreted as expressing this scepticism, I have a good deal of sympathy with it. I would nevertheless observe that similar scepticism can be found in the work of at least some others, who would not usually be labelled 'Austrian'. Marshall himself, with his preference for application to relatively simple problems of industrial structure, may be taken as an example. It is indeed true that there are many modern economists, Keynesians, but not only Keynesians, who are more ambitious. It does no harm to remind them, now and then, how fragile are the foundations on which they build their high towers.

All the same, we cannot dispense with models. All of our concepts, even those which the most orthodox follower of Menger or Mises must insist on retaining, are dependent on models, though they may indeed be rudimentary models. It is meaningless, for instance, to associate market value with marginal valuation, unless something is implied about the valuation of a quantity greater or less than the quantity actually taken. Any such valuation is a theoretical construction. Just the same holds for it as for points on *IS* or *LM* curves, points other than that which is supposed to be actual. All alike are theoretical, or hypothetical, constructions; all alike refer to models.

Nevertheless, though the models are hypothetical, they need to refer to reality; and that means that they must have a time-reference, or at least an implicit time-reference. The timeless, or static, models which abound in our text books are at the best unfinished business; they are not complete models, capable of being used in comparisons such as I have been describing; they can be no more than the stuff out of which complete models can be made. The historical application is in this respect clarifying. Any actual experience, which we seek to explain, will be set in history; it will be a story with a beginning and an end. The beginning must be in the past, and it is best to think of the end, also, as being in the past, though it is of course in principle possible for the story to be taken right up to the present day. But I have often reminded my students, who have wanted to do just that, that the present goes on moving while the research continues. Now if this is the standard form of the actual experience, the hypothetical, which is to be compared with it, should take the same form. One can in fact use an equilibrium model much more safely if one keeps firmly in mind that it also is to refer to a particular time-period, with a beginning and end.

Suppose that the period, which is under examination, is the year 1970. The actual events of the year are recorded; we may suppose, for the present purpose, that we know all the facts about them that we need to know. We then confront this actual experience with a hypothetical experience, in which something, which we are at liberty to choose, has been changed. Now we know that the actual experience was not an equilibrium experience; there were surprises, and unforeseen changes of course. But it is hardly possible that the hypothetical experience should not be an equilibrium experience, for it is under *our* control, so there can be no surprises in it. If then we compare the actual experience, which is *not* an equilibrium experience, with a hypothetical experience, which is, we are cheating; so to make the comparison fair we are bound to doctor the actual, suppressing the surprises, even though we admit that they are important. This, I suppose, is what the 'Austrian' cannot take. I would answer that if he takes that line, he must confine himself to description. He cannot proceed to the further step, of finding explanations, even of searching for explanations. I am myself not prepared to refuse the task of looking for explanations, even though I am well aware how dangerous it is. I hope that what I have said has made it clear that I do not underestimate those dangers. I think that one should be always on the look-out for ways of taking precautions against them.

If one accepts that we should always be talking about a period, or year, with beginning and end, the standard schema of an economic process, in a closed system, within a year, is ready for use. We shall need it in what follows, so, elementary as it is, it will be well to set it out.

The year begins with a stock of goods carried over from the past; to this, during the year, a flow of services is applied. As a result a flow of outputs emerges. There remains at the end of the year a stock of goods to be carried over to the next. So, looking at the year by itself, there is a stock input and a flow input; there is a flow output and a stock output. That, I believe, is the best way of classifying; it is certainly the safest.

It does indeed have its inconveniences. It is not very convenient to have two sorts of inputs — stock inputs and flow inputs; how much handier it would be if they could be reduced to one! Therefore some people have sought to replace the initial stock by a flow of services derived from it, and others have sought to replace the flow of labour by a stock of 'human capital'. Neither device, however, is necessary; I feel myself, rather strongly, that much more is gained by distinguishing.

Much also is gained, much more than symmetry, by following von Neumann in treating the *whole* terminal stock as part of output. Additions to the stock are of course to be considered as part of output – investment output; but if investment is taken net, usings-up of the initial stock have to be deducted. Even if investment is taken gross, usings-up of working capital have to be deducted. It follows that either, if taken in value terms, is a difference between one total and another; even if we take the items separately, some are positive and some negative. When we come to making comparisons, comparing what was with what might have been, it is awkward to work with negative items. That can be avoided if we adopt the von Neumann convention.

My preliminaries are now completed. I can turn – at last – to my title question.

You will have noticed that my question falls, almost grammatically, into halves; for there is a middle term that is missing. For the moment I shall not fill it in; I shall just call it Blank. 'Is interest the price of Blank?' is the first sub-question; 'Is Blank a factor of production?' is the second. If the title question is to be answered in the affirmative, we must find a meaning for Blank which will enable us to marry the sub-questions, answering each in the affirmative.

It is the second sub-question which turns out to be the more tricky; it forces us to decide how we define a factor of production. Economists, in general, have just enumerated. The factors of production are Land, Labour and Capital; or just Labour and Land; or just Labour and Capital; or just Labour. Enumeration however is not definition; the variety of enumerations itself shows that definition is called for. With the aid of the period-schema which I have been setting out, we can, I think, get a general definition. It would run as follows.

A factor of production is anything which can serve as an input into the productive process when that is taken as a whole. This sounds harmless, but there are three items in it which need notes.

(1) *Input.* It is one of the advantages which we get from the period-schema, and from the von Neumann convention which I have associated with it, that the distinction between inputs and outputs is clear-cut. There are no negative outputs, so input has a clear meaning.

(2) *Taken as a whole.* 'Factor' is a macroeconomic concept. Since it refers to the economy as a whole (a closed economy), it is not to be interpreted in terms of transactions within the economy. So it is not necessary, in order that a thing should be a factor, that it should have

a price. In order that a thing should have a price, it must be appropriable, but it is not necessary that a thing should be appropriable for it to be a factor of production. What is necessary is that it should make a contribution to production, in the sense that if it were removed, production (or output) would be diminished. Or, more usefully, if a part of it were to be removed, production would be diminished. Which comes to the same thing as saying that the factor must have a marginal product. (The marginal product need not be taken in terms of an index of production in general; it is sufficient to take it in terms of some particular product, or collection of products, which has value.)

(3) *Can serve as an input.* It is not necessary, in order that a thing should be a factor, that it should *actually* be producing; what is necessary is that it should be producing in some of the hypothetical alternatives that are being considered. Take for instance the case of unemployed labour. If in actuality some labour is unemployed, we do not have to deny the title of factor to that labour, so long as conditions in which it would be employed are among the alternatives that are contemplated. Only the (so-called) labour which would not be employed, or used, in any such circumstances would not be a factor.

With these understandings, I think that the definition holds.

Now I can turn to fill in, or to try to fill in, my Blank. There are several candidates. Let us call them in for examination.

It is unlucky, and can be confusing, even extremely confusing, that so many of them have the same name — Capital. It will be essential to distinguish. But for the present, I shall just call them Capital I, II, III and so on.

Capital I is the original meaning, the business sense of the principal of a loan. There is no doubt that interest is the price of Capital I. But Capital I is not a macroeconomic concept, so it cannot be a factor of production. It falls flat on the second sub-question.

Capital II, which surely is a factor of production (as appears from the period-schema) is the initial stock of goods having value, which is inherited by the current period from the past. Capital II does have a marginal product; if there had been more of it, more of any scarce constituents of it, production could have been increased; if there had been less of it, production must have been diminished. (Remember that the terminal stock is part of production.) But interest is certainly not the price of Capital II. Capital II does have a price which can at least be imputed to it, at its own date, the starting date; this is what we call its capital value in terms of something, presumably money. It also has another price, the annual value that is attributed to it; and the rate of interest does play a part in associating this annual value with the capital value. Even so, it cannot be true that the rate of interest is the price of Capital II, considered as annual value. The annual value of Capital II, or of any piece of equipment which enters into it, is its annual earnings, a rent or quasi-rent as Marshall called it. So Capital II, though it passes my second sub-question, falls down on the first.

Capital III is still the initial stock, but it is to be taken, now, in value terms. If what we call the price of this capital is its annual value, then its price, per unit, is the rate of interest. So Capital III may perhaps be said to pass on sub-question 1. There are indeed some qualifications to that which are rather obvious; but I shall not pause to consider them here.

The trouble with Capital III, in my view, is on the other side; is it a factor of production? Many economists, including some Austrians, have wished so to regard it; but I cannot believe that that is right. The test of a factor of production, it has been shown, is that it has a marginal product; that is to say, a change in its quantity must be conceivable, *as* a change in an independent variable; an effect of that change on production must be conceivable. Now it is of course true that if Capital II is changed, and the prices at which it is valued are unchanged, Capital III will be changed; but why should those prices be unchanged? We would expect them to be changed, in consequence of the change in Capital II. They may also change in consequence of other changes, which themselves could indeed be regarded as primary changes. Suppose, for instance, that the (flow) supply of labour is increased. We should expect that this would increase production; that is all right; labour is a factor of production; no question about that. But among the consequences of the labour change are likely to be some changes in the values of the capital goods in the initial stock, so that even if Capital II is unchanged, Capital III is changed. Since Capital III is subject, must be subject, to these induced changes, it cannot be treated as an independent variable, and hence as a factor of production.

I am, of course, assuming that Capital III is being valued in what Austrians (and not only Austrians) would hold to be the correct manner; that is to say, in terms of its future productivity. That of course is not the value that 'stands in the books' of the proprietors, at the opening date. Every student of economics knows that this book value should be rejected, but I think it will be useful to keep it on our list, as Capital IV.

The ratio between the annual value of a capital good and its Capital IV value is not a rate of interest, but a rate of profit, perhaps not even a 'true' rate of profit. And Capital IV cannot be a factor of production *of the period*, if it is valued at historical cost, which has nothing to do with the values, or even with the events, of the period. Could it, however, be restored (it has in effect so often been asked) if replacement cost values are used, in place of historic cost values? That is quite an interesting question; if we try to answer it, in our terms, the result is rather revealing.

I begin with the obvious objections to replacement cost. How does one replace, within the 'year', a ten-year-old machine? We have only got one year to 'age' it in. And what do we do if the manufacture of similar machines has been discontinued? The 'real' cost (whatever that is) of replacing it now may be far in excess of its original 'real' cost; to the actual events of this year that must be quite irrelevant. These objections are in practice insuperable, but in theory they could perhaps be avoided. Suppose that we allow ourselves to assume that the system has been in equilibrium (in one of the senses previously outlined) during the *whole life* of the machines in question, right back to the date of their original construction. If such an assumption could be granted, it could be true that the forward-looking value (Capital III sense) would be equal to the replacement value (Capital IV), so that the 'annual' price of Capital IV would be the rate of interest. Capital IV, in equilibrium with Capital III, would have won through.

It will be clear, from what I have said already, why in my view that cannot be granted. I have (I think) shown that, so far as hypothetical constructions are concerned, the economy, during the period (or year) must be supposed to be in equilibrium. We cannot manage it otherwise. But to go on from that to suppose that it has *always* been in equilibrium is quite a different matter. It is a 'relapse into statics', as I have called it in another place,[4] a relapse into timelessness. It must surely be avoided.

Where then are we left? Do all candidates fail? Can Blank not be filled in? Perhaps there are some other candidates.

One, for whose appearance you may well have been waiting, does not properly come into sight until the period-schema has been elaborated a little further. I have said that the inputs of the period should comprise both stocks and flows; and that the outputs should

[4] *EP*, pp. vii–viii.

comprise both stocks and flows. Now a stock, with reference to time, is quite determinate; the value of that stock is what mathematicians would call a scalar quantity. If we are measuring it in money, it is just so many dollars.

A flow, however, even in value terms, is not a scalar; it is not sufficiently described by its total over the period, or by its average over the period. It must have a distribution over time, which cannot be adequately specified by a single number. It must have a time-shape.

The time-shape of the flows (of input and of output) is chiefly relevant to our problem when the period considered is rather long. Suppose we make it quite long, say ten years; that is quite as long a period as it is sensible to take. The lengthening increases the size of the flow output (regarding it as a total) relatively to the terminal stock; but it also makes the time-shape of the flow output more variable. That is to say, it increases the variety of time-shapes that can usefully be introduced into our hypothetical constructions. In particular, a flow output which starts low and rises rapidly, as against a flow output which starts higher but rises less rapidly, are effective alternatives. It could be that the initial stock is the same in each, that the flow input of labour (including its time-shape) is the same in each, even that the terminal stock is the same in each; nevertheless, especially if the period is long enough, the time-shape of the flow output, within the period, could be different. We have then to consider how we should describe the change from the one time-shape to the other.

It could happen that on the faster growing path, the total of output (which we must assume to be measurable in some invariable standard), when it is taken over the whole period, is greater than it is on the slower path. The faster path, therefore, by sacrificing some earlier outputs, has substituted later outputs which are larger. So, looking at the total of production over the whole period, there is on the faster path an increase in production; an increase which is not to be attributed to increase in the initial stock, nor to increase in the flow of labour. To what is it to be attributed? We have to invent a factor of production to which to attribute it. There has been no agreement on the name of that factor. Senior called it Abstinence; Marshall and Cassel called it Waiting; Böhm-Bawerk Roundaboutness; Barone and Wicksell just Time. It is quite hard to resist calling it Saving! But since all these terms are so 'loaded', I shall refrain from using any of them. I shall just call it ITSO, for Intertemporal Switch in Output. I dare say that that will be sufficiently mysterious!

ITSO, then, can be a factor of production, under suitable conditions, if the switch is in the right direction. But it is only at the margin, in the comparison of one hypothetical path with another, that we can find a place for it. It is not like Labour, or like Capital II, which can be thought of as responsible for the whole of production, so that if they were removed (either of them, indeed, were removed) production would be zero. It is essentially comparative. (This is where Böhm-Bawerk, with his Subsistence Fund, and the early Hayek, with his Average Period, went wrong.) It does nevertheless satisfy what we have seen to be the crucial test. It does have a marginal product.

Still thinking in terms of hypothetical constructions, we can say that its price is the rate of interest. Any such hypothetical path, as we have seen, must be an equilibrium; that is to say, it must proceed as if there were perfect foresight *within the period.* In that equilibrium, the marginal product of ITSO and the rate of interest (in competitive conditions, if we allow ourselves to suppose them) will come together. So, perhaps, after all it is ITSO who is the successful candidate. But what a rummy candidate he is!

He cannot put in an appearance unless the period that is under consideration is fairly long. For his switch, when we look at it in detail, involves first the transference of some elements of the labour flow and of the initial stock, from the production of current flow output to the production of instruments; and secondly the use of the instruments to produce additional flow output, all to be accomplished *within the period.* (It will be noticed that the *whole* of the additional flow has to be realised within the period.) On the other hand, the longer the period, the harder it is to tolerate the assumption of equilibrium over the period, the assumption on which (as we have seen) he relies. For remember what I said before about historical comparisons. We have to compare the actual sequence of events, over what is now to be a long period, say 1965–75, with a hypothetical process which is in equilibrium. If the comparison is to be at all fair, we have to assume that the actual experience does not differ *very much* from what it would have been if it was to be in equilibrium. Over a short period, that may be tolerable; but over ten years? Ugh!

So if we give ITSO a pass mark, we do not congratulate him upon it. Indeed there are many who would throw mud at him for it. I think I can hear them making a noise outside. You will recognise them; they are a crowd of Keynesians. We must attend to them, for they have a candidate of their own.

They have of course been jumping to the conclusion that I have been saying that Saving is a Factor of Production; and that, in their view, is terrible. But I have been careful to talk about ITSO, not about Saving. One can certainly recognise that there are models in which an increase in Saving will not result in an increase of output at a later date, but will just result in a fall in current employment, that is to say, in current flow input. And that is certainly not productive! Our increase in ITSO, with other things equal, must imply that there is no change in current flow input; so in their terms it is an increase in Saving which is matched by an increase in Investment. Perhaps that will keep them quiet!

We still have to examine their candidate. His name is Liquidity. To say, as Keynes did, that the rate of interest depends on Liquidity Preference, and to say that rate of interest is the price of Liquidity, may be accepted to be much the same thing. So they may claim to have their master's authority for giving Liquidity a pass on my sub-question 1. Keynes did not say that Liquidity is a Factor of Production, for he did not use that language; but on our definition of Factor is that not implied in what he did say? He would certainly have said that in conditions of 'involuntary unemployment' an increase in Liquidity would increase production. So it would seem that in Keynesian terms, Liquidity passes, on both counts.

It would be wrong to attempt, at the end of this paper, any serious statement of my own view of Keynesian economics. I think I may be excused it, for I have done it elsewhere at some length: in my *Crisis in Keynesian Economics* (1974) and in *Economic Perspectives* (1977). All I will say in this place is just this.

I still have the greatest admiration for many parts of Keynes's construction, but there are two critical points on which he invited misunderstanding, or perhaps one should say that they are qualifications which are indeed present in his work — they are formally stated by him — but which, no doubt because of the time at which he was writing, during the Great Depression of the thirties, he did not feel called on to stress to the extent which (we can now see) they deserve.

The first is concealed by that unfortunate phrase *involuntary unemployment*, which does not, in Keynes, carry at all the same meaning as the ordinary man (including so many economists) would naturally attribute to it. We would now do much better to call it *Keynesian unemployment*, defining it by the consequence which he drew from its existence. Keynesian unemployment is unemployment which can be reduced by an increase in Liquidity.

The second concerns Liquidity itself. It is not the case, as a casual reading of the *General Theory* might suggest, that Liquidity can always be increased by an increase in the supply of money. Keynes is really quite clear on that. In formal statement, Liquidity is defined as money supply measured in 'wage-units', that is to say, money supply deflated by a wage-index. Whether that is the correct adjustment to make, I shall not pause to consider. But we have Keynes's own authority for saying that some adjustment is necessary. It is confirmed by our own inflationary experience that circumstances are possible in which an increase in the supply of money does not increase Liquidity. Mises, you will no doubt be wanting to remind me, knew that long ago, but he was not good on Keynes's case, as Keynes (I recognise) was not good on his. *Now* we need both.

Dennis Robertson, one of whose gambits I have been imitating in the structure of this paper, had a favourite quotation from *Alice* — 'everyone has won, and all must have prizes'. I have been distributing prizes, but also a few slaps. You will, I fear, feel in the end that I am too Open to be an Austrian; for I am an Open Marshallian, and Ricardian, and Keynesian, perhaps even Lausannian, as well. I put perhaps to the last, for I think I have shown why I now rate Walras and Pareto, who were my first loves, so much below Menger. I hope I have shown how much I have got from him, and from thinking about him.

Part II
Competition and the Firm

10

The Theory of Monopoly:
A Survey

PREFATORY NOTE

This was published in *Econometrica* in January 1935, by which date what have remained the most famous works on its subject had already appeared. They had received important reviews; but there does not seem to be any other writing of that time where they are looked at together. I do not think, even now, that there is much that is wrong with my survey, so far as it goes. The device of 'conjectural variations', of which much is made, has not caught on; but as it is used here, as a means of classifying the particular solutions to the problem of duopoly, which had been advanced by the first explorers of that question, it still has something to be said for it. The thing which is most seriously missing is any consideration of the 'welfare' aspects. As I have said elsewhere,[1] I was at that time a disbeliever in welfare economics; so I had no means of judging the relative efficiency of the market forms I was discussing.

After I had done my main work on welfare economics and consumers' surplus (essays 2, 4 and 5 of volume I of this collection) all this became much clearer — clearer, I think, not only to me but also clearer than it had been to those whose work I had been discussing. It is worth observing, for instance, that when one has the consumers' surplus technique at one's disposal, the assumption of the single-product firm can be dropped without any difficulty. The issue is one of products, not of firms — or of firms only in so far as they represent bundles of products. One can grant that an increase in product differentiation enables the wants of some consumers to be satisfied better; the question is whether that gain is worth a loss in economies of scale. It is in much the same way that the issue appears in the book by Scitovsky, my 1952 review of which here follows. My own approach, to a conclusion that is similar to his, is spelt out in the prefatory note to that paper.

[1] p. xii in volume I of this collection.

All that, in 1935, was absent. I was just thinking of the question whether the new theories (as they then were) had made a contribution to *positive* economics; it seemed to me that they had not made much. (That was why I could at that time still be happy with the perfect competition model of *Value and Capital*, on which in 1935 I was beginning to work.) Modern analysis of what I have called *fixprice* markets ('customer' markets as Okun called them, 'oligopolistic' with Sylos Labini) which lays great stress on uncertainty and imperfect knowledge still lay a long way ahead. It is far from sufficient, nowadays, to go back to Marshall, as I was tempted to do in the concluding passage of this survey.

The last five or six years have seen the appearance of at least four important works specially devoted to the subject of monopoly – those of Dr Zeuthen, Dr Schneider, Professor Chamberlin, and Mrs Robinson;[2] while there is, I think, no theoretical subject which has received more attention in the recent volumes of most of the chief economic journals than the theory of monopoly and imperfect competition. To most of these articles I shall refer as we proceed; but the names of Mr Harrod, Mr Shove, Dr v. Stackelberg, and Professor Hotelling, cannot be omitted from even a preliminary bibliography.[3]

The preoccupation of contemporary theorists with problems of monopoly does not appear to be due, as might perhaps be expected, to their consciousness of the increased urgency of these problems in the modern world. It may very well be that monopoly is more important today than it was fifty years ago, though it is not so obvious as it appears at first sight. It is certain, however, that the phenomena of monopolistic competition to which attention has so particularly been directed are not new phenomena; they were observed and analysed, however imperfectly, by older economists, by Cairnes and Wicksell, if by no others.[4]

The widespread interest in monopoly theory is much easier to account for on grounds inherent in the development of economic

---

[2] F. Zeuthen, *Problems of Monopoly and Economic Warfare*, London 1930; Schneider, *Reine Theorie monopolistischer Wirtschaftsformen*, Tübingen 1932; E. H. Chamberlin, *Theory of Monopolistic Competition*, Harvard 1933; J. Robinson, *Economics of Imperfect Competition*, London 1933.

[3] R. F. Harrod, 'Notes on Supply', *EJ*, 1930; 'Law of Decreasing Costs', *EJ*, 1931; 'Doctrines of Imperfect Competition', *QJE*, 1934; G. F. Shove, 'The Imperfection of the Market', *EJ*, 1933; H. Hotelling, 'Stability in Competition', *EJ*, 1929.

[4] Cairnes, *Political Economy*, pp. 115–16 (quoted Chamberlin, *op. cit.*, p. 106); Wicksell, *Lectures on Political Economy*, 1, pp. 87–8.

theory itself, though here an element of coincidence is present. On the one hand, the generally increased interest in mathematical economics during the last few years has naturally turned attention back to the work of Cournot, the great founder of the subject, and still one of its best teachers. It was Cournot's creation of elementary monopoly theory which was the first great triumph of mathematical economics; yet Cournot had left much undone, and it is not surprising that the endeavour to complete his work should have been an attractive occupation for his successors.

But if some modern monopoly theorists have been seeking to fill the gaps in Cournot, others have been more concerned with the gaps in the work of Marshall. These gaps were more skilfully pasted over, and it was not until after many years' criticism that they were clearly discerned. But the controversy on the 'Laws of Returns', begun by Mr Sraffa in 1926, and carried on more or less continuously in the *Economic Journal* for some years afterwards,[5] made it increasingly evident to the most convinced Marshallians that the device of 'external economies', by which Marshall sought to reconcile the postulate of perfect competition with the observed facts of increasing returns, would not bear the weight that had been imposed upon it. A tendency therefore developed away from the postulate of perfect competition. The participants in the discussion began to assume as the normal case that a firm can influence to some extent the prices at which it sells, that it is confronted with a downward sloping demand curve for its products, though this demand curve may have a high elasticity. With this assumption, the cardinal difficulty of increasing returns disappeared, since a firm might still be in equilibrium under conditions of diminishing cost. But numerous other difficulties started up, and it became necessary for these writers, like those mentioned before, to make a detailed examination of the theory of monopoly.

From each line of approach a substantially similar theory has emerged, though there are important points which still remain controversial. It remains convenient for us to discuss the modern theory under the old headings: (1) *Simple monopoly*, where the individual firm is confronted with given demand functions for its products, and given supply functions for its factors; (2) *Monopolistic Competition*, the relations of a group of firms producing similar products, i.e. an industry; (3) *Bilateral Monopoly*, where one firm is selling to another.

[5] See bibliography in *EJ*, 1930, p. 79.

I. Simple Monopoly

As far as simple monopoly is concerned, the improvement on Cournot is mainly a matter of exposition, although there has been some further enquiry into the effect of monopoly on the demand for factors of production.

1. If the prices at which the monopolist hires his factors are fixed, his cost of production can be taken as a simple function of output. Let $\phi(x)$ be the total cost of producing an output x.

If the monopolist's selling price is p, and $p = f(x)$ is the demand curve confronting him, his profit on selling an output x will be

$$xf(x) - \phi(x)$$

which is maximised when

$$xf'(x) + f(x) = \phi'(x)$$

So much has been familiar since Cournot; the principal recent innovation has been to give the expression on the left of the last equation a name 'Marginal Revenue'.[6] The equation can then be written

Marginal Revenue = Marginal Cost

which is certainly a convenient way of expressing the first condition of monopolistic equilibrium.

Since the elasticity of the demand curve

$$= \eta = -\frac{f(x)}{xf'(x)}$$

$$\text{marginal revenue} = \text{price}\left(1 - \frac{1}{\eta}\right)$$

The second condition of maximum profits is that

$$\frac{\mathrm{d}}{\mathrm{d}x}\{xf'(x) + f(x) - \phi'(x)\}$$

should be negative. This can be written

$$\frac{\mathrm{d}}{\mathrm{d}x}(MR) < \frac{\mathrm{d}}{\mathrm{d}x}(MC)$$

---

[6] So Mrs Robinson. It seems the most convenient of the names which have been suggested.

Monopolistic equilibrium is therefore stable, so long as the marginal revenue curve slopes downwards more steeply than the marginal cost curve. All cases where the marginal revenue curve slopes downwards and the marginal cost curve upwards are therefore stable, but instability may occur if either of these conditions is not fulfilled. Upward sloping marginal revenue curves, though possible, are unlikely to be very important, since the demand curve from which a marginal revenue curve is derived may be taken to be always downward sloping. Much more important is the fact that stable equilibrium with a downward sloping marginal cost curve is possible, so long as the downward slope is less than that of the marginal revenue curve, and so long, also, as total receipts exceed total costs by an amount sufficient to keep the monopolist in business.

The question of stability once settled, it becomes possible to apply the apparatus in the ordinary manner, familiar in elementary theory, to simple problems of change. A rise in the marginal cost curve will reduce output, a rise in the marginal revenue curve will increase it; but a rise in the demand (average revenue) curve may not increase output, unless it is such as to cause a rise in the marginal revenue curve. Similarly a rise in average costs will not contract output, unless it is associated with a rise in marginal costs, or is otherwise large enough to drive the monopolist out of business.

2. *The monopolist and the factors of production.*[7] It is convenient, for the analysis of this problem, to conceive of the monopolist as owning certain factors of production (his *private factors*, we may call them) and hiring others. If he is unable to vary the supply of these private factors, then it is strictly correct to suppose him endeavouring to maximise his profits, that is to say, to maximise the net earnings of these private factors. If this assumption cannot be made, difficulties emerge, which had better be examined later.

If the quantities of factors hired are $a, b, c, \ldots$, their prices are π_a, π_b, π_c, $\ldots$, and their supply curves to the monopolist are given, then

$$\text{Monopoly profit} = xp - a\pi_a - b\pi_b - c\pi_c - \cdots$$

This is maximised when

$$\left(p + x\,\frac{dp}{dx}\right) dx - \left(\pi_a + a\,\frac{d\pi_a}{da}\right) da - \left(\pi_b + b\,\frac{d\pi_b}{db}\right) db - \cdots = 0$$

---

[7] Robinson, *EIC*, Books VII–IX; Schneider, 'Bemerkungen zur Grenzproductivitätstheorie', *Zeitschrift für Nationalökonomie*, 1933. See also Dr Schneider's *Theorie der Produktion* (1934); pp. 57, 76.

which becomes

$$MR \, \mathrm{d}x - MC_a \, \mathrm{d}a - MC_b \, \mathrm{d}b - \cdots = 0$$

if we write MC_a for $\pi_a + a(\mathrm{d}\pi_a/\mathrm{d}a)$, and so on.

Taking $x = \phi(a, b, c, \ldots)$ as the production function, technically given, then

$$\mathrm{d}x = \frac{\partial x}{\partial a} \, \mathrm{d}a + \frac{\partial x}{\partial b} \, \mathrm{d}b + \cdots$$

Substituting in the above, we have

$$\left(MR \, \frac{\partial x}{\partial a} - MC_a\right) \mathrm{d}a + \left(MR \, \frac{\partial x}{\partial b} - MC_b\right) \mathrm{d}b + \cdots = 0$$

Since this equation must hold for all values of $\mathrm{d}a, \mathrm{d}b, \ldots$, it follows that

$$MR \, \frac{\partial x}{\partial a} = MC_a, \quad MR \, \frac{\partial x}{\partial b} = MC_b, \cdots$$

for all factors.

$MC_a, MC_b, \ldots$, are the *marginal costs to the monopolist* of hiring an additional unit of the factors, $a, b, \ldots$. If the supply curves of the factors slope upwards, these marginal costs will exceed the prices of the factors by $a(\mathrm{d}\pi_a/\mathrm{d}a)$ etc., respectively; that is to say, by the additional amounts which have to be paid on earlier units in order to keep their prices on a level with that of the marginal unit of the factor. $MR(\partial x/\partial a)$ is conveniently described as the 'marginal value product' of the factor a; it is the increment in the total value of the product which results from the application of an additional unit of a. The condition of factor equilibrium is thus that the marginal value product of a factor should equal its marginal cost.

The stability conditions for factor equilibrium do not appear to have been fully investigated; but a cursory examination suggests that there are several ways in which the presence of monopoly brings into the possible range of stable equilibria positions which would not be stable under perfect competition.

If the supply curve of any factor to the monopolist is horizontal, so that the monopolist is unable to affect the price of that factor, then even so his demand for that factor will be reduced below what it might have been, if the product demand curve confronting him is imperfectly elastic. Monopolistic exploitation of the consumer therefore brings about a directly consequent reduction in the demand for factors. And if a number of monopolists are employing a particular factor, they may each be unable by isolated action to influence the price of the factor; and yet, in their efforts to exploit the consumer, they will each reduce their demand for the factor, and the price of the factor may, in consequence, be reduced. But this is a different thing from the additional reduction in demand which comes about if a monopolist is able to influence the price of a factor directly, so that he takes into account the saving on other units which he gets by reducing his demand at the margin. The first type of reduction would be called by Mrs Robinson 'monopolistic exploitation' of the factor, while she has invented the term 'monopsonistic' to describe exploitation of the second type.

3. *Simple monopoly and joint production.* Nearly all the writers here discussed have confined their analysis of simple monopoly to the case where the monopolist produces only one product.[8] For reasons which will appear later, this limitation seems rather unfortunate. A brief but illuminating discussion of the problem has, however, been given by Dr von Stackelberg, which we may here reproduce.[9]

It is convenient, in order to isolate the problem, to assume that the prices of the factors are now given to the monopolist; we can then introduce a cost function expressing the total cost of production of quantities $x_1, x_2, \ldots,$ of the different products. Let $\phi(x_1, x_2, \ldots)$ be the cost function.

Then Monopoly profit $= p_1 x_1 + p_2 x_2 + p_3 x_3 + \ldots - \phi(x_1, x_2, \ldots)$.

If we assume that the demand curves for the various products are independent, so that p_1 depends upon x_1 only, not on $x_2, x_3, \ldots,$ then the conditions of equilibrium are

$$\frac{d}{dx_1}(p_1 x_1) = \frac{\partial \phi}{\partial x_1}, \quad \frac{d}{dx_2}(p_2 x_2) = \frac{\partial \phi}{\partial x_2}, \ldots$$

The ordinary 'marginal revenue marginal cost' condition still holds.

If, however, the demand curves are not independent, then the conditions become

$$p_1 + x_1 \frac{\partial p_1}{\partial x_1} + x_2 \frac{\partial p_2}{\partial x_1} + \cdots = \frac{\partial \phi}{\partial x_1}$$

$$p_2 + x_1 \frac{\partial p_1}{\partial x_2} + x_2 \frac{\partial p_2}{\partial x_2} + \cdots = \frac{\partial \phi}{\partial x_2}$$

---

[8] Professor Chamberlin gives us an interesting account of the factors which determine what that one product shall be (*Theory of Monopolistic Competition*, chs. 4 and 5).

[9] H. von Stackelberg, *Grundlagen einer reinen Kostentheorie* (Vienna 1932), p. 68. See also Hotelling, 'Edgeworth's Taxation Paradox', *Journal of Political Economy*, 1932.

and so on. That is to say, the monopolist has to take into account, when fixing the output of any particular product, not only the reaction of an increased supply upon the price of that product, but also its reaction upon the prices of all other products which he is selling. If the cross-coefficients $(\partial p_2/\partial x_1$ etc.) are negative (roughly speaking, the case when the different products are competitive in consumption),[10] these reactions will lower the marginal revenue curve for any particular product, and so tend to restrict output. But in the opposite case, when the cross-coefficients are positive, the marginal revenue curve will be raised; so that here the restriction of output under monopoly will be less than we should have at first expected.

If $x_2(\partial p_2/\partial x_1) + x_3(\partial p_3/\partial x_1) + \ldots$ is positive, and greater than $\partial \phi/\partial x_1$, it may pay the monopolist to produce a finite output of x_1, even if he has to give it away. And such a phenomenon is surely not uncommon; a very considerable part of what are usually described as 'selling costs' comes very conveniently under this head. The subject of selling costs has been analysed at considerable length and with much insight by Professor Chamberlin, who maintains, however, the single-product firm as the foundation of his analysis. It may be suggested that the subject could be further illuminated, and brought closer into relation with fundamentally analogous cases where the 'bait' is not actually given away, if a start had been made from Dr von Stackelberg's more general case.[11]

4. *Discrimination.* From one point of view, discrimination is a limiting case of joint production. When we say that a single commodity is sold by a monopolist at various different prices, the singleness of the commodity consists solely in its various units being perfect substitutes on the supply side. We can introduce this condition of being perfect substitutes in production, and so go over from joint production to discrimination.

But this line of approach, although it has conveniences, and brings discrimination into a very satisfactory relation with general monopoly theory, is not that which has traditionally been adopted. Of recent writers, Mrs Robinson is the only one who had added anything substantial to the traditional theory of discrimination. She has

[10] I say 'roughly speaking', for it is becoming apparent that the terms *competitive* and *complementary* conceal a great many ambiguities. (See Hicks and Allen, 'A Reconsideration of the Theory of Value', *Economica*, 1934 [reprinted in vol. I of this collection. Now see also essay 22 below.])

[11] The same foundation might be used for an analysis of monopolistic exploitation by 'compulsory joint supply'.

devoted to it what is probably the best, as it is certainly the most ingenious, part of her book; there can be no question that these chapters will find their place along with Dupuit and Pigou on the very select bibliography of discrimination theory.

5. *The 'private' factors.* Most modern writing on monopoly, as we have said, has been content to assume a monopolist simply seeking to maximise his profits, that is to say, it neglects possible changes in the supply of private factors. This omission seems to me unfortunate, though it must be confessed that the subject presents grave difficulties.[12] On the one hand, unless we assume that the marginal utility of money to the monopolist is constant, we cannot unambiguously express in monetary terms the subjective cost to the monopolist of producing additional units of output; we are therefore unable to introduce the private factors into the 'marginal revenue = marginal cost' equation, and are obliged to fall back upon Paretian indifference curves, more cumbrous, and in this case decidedly less informative. The second difficulty is even more formidable. Under conditions of monopoly, there is no reason to suppose any particular connection between subjective cost and *output*, since it is probable that a considerable part of the monopolist's efforts and sacrifices will be devoted, not to increasing his output, but finding to what precise point he should restrict it. Now, as Professor Bowley[13] and others have pointed out, the variation in monopoly profit for some way on either side of the highest profit output may often be small (in the general case, it will depend on the difference between the slopes of the marginal revenue and marginal cost curves); and if this is so, the subjective costs involved in securing a close adaptation to the most profitable output may well outweigh the meagre gains offered. It seems not at all unlikely that people in monopolistic positions will very often be people with sharply rising subjective costs; if this is so, they are likely to exploit their advantage much more by not bothering to get very near the position of maximum profit, than by straining themselves to get very close to it. The best of all monopoly profits is a quiet life.

II. Monopolistic Competition

1. We come now to the 'group problem', the equilibrium of a group of firms producing similar but not identical products. The treatment

[12] Cf. Robinson, 'Euler's Theorem and the Problem of Distribution', *EJ*, 1934.
[13] *Mathematical Groundwork of Economics*, pp. 25, 60.

of this problem by Professor Chamberlin and by Mrs Robinson (the same applies, though with some qualification, to Mr Harrod) is based upon a very neat geometrical proposition.[14] Since the products of the various firms are not identical, the demand curve which confronts each individual firm will not be horizontal, but will slope downwards.[15] On the other hand, if entry into the industry is free, it will be impossible for the firms in the industry to earn more than 'normal profits'. On the basis of the first assumption, it is concluded that the output of each firm will have to satisfy the condition of monopolistic equilibrium, marginal revenue = marginal cost. On the basis of the second, it is concluded that the price of each product will have to equal average cost, when average cost is calculated in such a way as to include 'normal profits'.

If then we write π_x = average cost (in the above sense) of producing an output x, and p_x = the price at which the firm can sell that output, the second condition gives us

$$p_x = \pi_x \qquad (1)$$

while we have from the first condition

$$\frac{\mathrm{d}}{\mathrm{d}x}(xp_x) = \frac{\mathrm{d}}{\mathrm{d}x}(x\pi_x)$$

$$\therefore \quad p_x + x\,\frac{\mathrm{d}p_x}{\mathrm{d}x} = \pi_x + x\,\frac{\mathrm{d}\pi_x}{\mathrm{d}x}$$

$$\therefore \text{ from (1)},\ \frac{\mathrm{d}p_x}{\mathrm{d}x} = \frac{\mathrm{d}\pi_x}{\mathrm{d}x} \qquad (2)$$

From (1) and (2) it follows that the demand curve and the average cost curve must touch at a point of equilibrium.

Since the demand curve is downward sloping, the average cost curve must also be downward sloping at the equilibrium point. Equilibrium under monopolistic competition is only possible when average costs are diminishing; that is to say, the equilibrium output of a firm will be less than the output which would give minimum average costs – the output which would actually be reached under conditions of perfect competition. From this Professor Chamberlin proceeds to the conclusion that analysis based on perfect competi-

---

[14] Chamberlin, *Theory of Monopolistic Competition*, p. 84; Robinson, pp. 94–5; Harrod, 'Doctrines of Imperfect Competition', *QJE*, 1934, p. 457.

[15] Professor Chamberlin constructs this individual demand curve on the assumption that the prices of the rival commodities remain unchanged (p. 75). Mrs Robinson's formulation seems distinctly ambiguous (p. 21).

tion makes 'the price always too low, the cost of production too low, the scale of production too large, and the number of producers too small'.

In order for us to estimate the importance of this result, we must begin by examining the premises on which it is based. To take first the 'average cost curve'. When Walras and Pareto reckoned profits into costs, they were thinking of conditions of perfect competition, and their conclusion that price = average cost, so that the entre- preneur makes '*ni bénéfice ni perte*', meant nothing else than that the private factors of the entrepreneur could get no other return in the static equilibrium of perfect competition than would have accrued to them if they had been directly hired out on the market. But is it possible to transfer this conception to the theory of mono- polistic competition? So far as the private factors are to some extent unique, so that there are no perfect substitutes for them (and this seems the most likely case in which monopolistic competition might arise), they can have no market price which is not to some extent monopolistically determined. If there are perfect substitutes for them, why are those perfect substitutes not being employed in making perfect substitutes for the product?

There is only one way out of this dilemma, and I can only suppose that it is this which the writers in question have in mind. The factors of production, private or hired, may be sufficiently divisible, and sufficiently scattered in ownership, to ensure that there is a perfect market for them, or something sufficiently perfect for the imper- fections to be negligible. But there may still be a range of increasing returns in the production of any particular product, due to indi- visibilities in the production function, not in the factors themselves.[16] If this is the case, substantially homogeneous factors may be put together by a limited number of firms into a limited number of different products, each of which is unique, and the demand curve for each of which is downward sloping.

This is the only state of affairs of which the Chamberlin–Robinson apparatus seems to be an exact description; it is probable that it does correspond with a certain region of reality. But I cannot help feeling that the application of the apparatus is implicitly much exaggerated. This is only partly because of the actual heterogeneity of factors – both writers accept this difficulty, and at the worst it only means that the technical apparatus is over-rigid. They can still claim to have

---

[16] Kaldor, 'The Equilibrium of the Firm', *EJ*, March 1934, p. 65n. On the general question of indivisibilities and costs, see also the appendix to Mrs Robinson's book; also Schneider, *Theorie der Produktion*, ch. 1.

shown that monopolistic restriction of output is compatible with earnings in no way out of the ordinary. A much more serious objection arises from the variability of the product.

There are two relevant sorts of product variation. One, the only kind which has been much discussed, is where each firm produces a single product, but the nature of that product is capable of being changed. This problem has been dealt with mostly in terms of location; a product available in a different place is economically a different product, and a change in the location of the firm is one of the ways of varying the product. (Professor Chamberlin's discussion of location is, however, reinforced by a discussion of the same problem in more general terms.)

In his paper, 'Stability in Competition',[17] Professor Hotelling had demonstrated that there is a tendency, when two firms are competing for a given market, for them to get together in the centre of the market. This tendency in itself would thus be favourable to the establishment of conditions of approximately perfect competition, if it could be shown to hold for more firms than two.

Unfortunately, as Professor Chamberlin shows, this is not so.[18] Once there are more than two firms in the market, they will tend to scatter, since any firm will try to avoid being caught between a pair of others. It seems evident that this general tendency to dispersion will be present when it is a question of quality competition as well as of competition in location, though of course the possible kinds of variation are even more complex.

Thus, so long as we retain the 'one firm one product' assumption, variability of the product is not sufficient to prevent an appreciable degree of imperfection in the elasticity of the demand curve confronting any particular firm. The position seems, however, to be different once we drop this assumption.

In fact, when 'product' is interpreted in the strict economic sense of a collection of articles that are to the consumer perfect substitutes, almost every firm does produce a considerable range of different products. It does so largely because there are economies to be got from producing them together,[19] and these economies consist largely in the fact that the different products require much the same overheads. Further, at any time the products it is actually producing will probably not exhaust the list of products it could produce from approximately the same plant. Thus it will have various potential

---

[17] *EJ*, 1929. See also Zeuthen, 'Theoretical Remarks on Price Policy', *QJE*, 1933.

[18] *Theory of Monopolistic Competition*, Appendix C.

[19] In the sense that it costs less to produce outputs x_1 and x_2 in a single firm, than it would cost (in total) to produce output x_1 in one firm and output x_2 in another.

products which it could produce in small quantities at quite a low marginal cost.

Now when other producers are able to supply small quantities of highly competitive products at low prices, this is at last an effective force tending to keep the demand curve for a particular product of a particular firm very highly elastic. Of course, it will probably not be perfectly elastic; for in fact any degree of specialisation on a particular line offers a *prima facie* case that the specialising firm has some particular facilities for that line, and it may be able to carry out a certain degree of restriction before it tempts other firms to follow it. Further, a firm is always likely to be on the lookout for a line in which it is relatively safe from such competition. Nevertheless, this consideration does seem to go a good way to justify the traditional practice of economists in treating the assumption of perfect competition as a satisfactory approximation over a very wide field.[20]

A considerable degree of the sort of market imperfection we have been discussing seems likely to arise in two cases only: (1) where the producer has command of some specialised 'factor', such as patent, legal privilege, site, or business capacity, for which no clear substitute is available; (2) where economies of scale are narrowly specialised, so that it would be impossible for another firm to produce commodities highly competitive with these produced by the first firm excepting at much greater marginal cost. There is no doubt that such conditions as these are fairly frequent, but they are, after all, precisely the cases which have been traditionally treated under the heading of monopoly.

2. *Duopoly.* There is, however, one further difficulty of great importance. We have suggested that the demand curve for a particular product of a particular firm will usually be kept highly elastic by the incursion of other producers selling small quantities of highly competitive products, if the first firm raises its price. But if they do so, will not the first firm retaliate on them?

Two cases have thus to be distinguished. The first is when the other potential producers are fairly numerous. In this case, they are not likely to be much deterred by the fear of retaliation. For although the first firm may find it profitable to turn its attention to some other product if it meets with competition in the line it had first chosen, the chance of that other product being highly competitive with the products of any particular other producer is small.

---

[20] Cf. Shove, 'The Imperfection of the Market', *EJ*, 1933, pp. 115–16.

In the other case, when the other potential producers are few, the fear of retaliation is likely to be more serious, and it may very well stop poaching.

The difficult problem which arises from the relations of a very small number of competing firms has been much studied in recent years, but there has not yet developed any very close agreement on the solution. Largely owing to the difficulty of the problem, it has been chiefly studied in its most simple case, that of two firms producing an identical product – duopoly.[21]

The theory of duopoly has a long history; and here we can do no more than allude to the classical theory of Cournot, and the displacement of Cournot's theory by the criticisms of Bertrand and Edgeworth, which form the ancient history of the subject. Edgeworth's solution, based on 'the characteristic freedom of the monopolist to vary price', involved such peculiar assumptions about costs that it could hardly have held the field forever. The post-war period therefore saw a renaissance of Cournotism, led by Amoroso and Wicksell;[22] this movement is represented also by the chapter on 'Mehrfaches Monopol' in Dr Schneider's book.[23] In the next stage, criticisms of both the Cournot and Edgeworth solutions were offered by Dr Zeuthen and by Professor Chamberlin;[24] it then became clear that each of the rivals had pointed the way towards a possible solution, but that even together they did not exhaust the list.

A very convenient line of approach, which sets these alternative solutions in their places, and so opens a path towards a general theory, can be developed from a hint given in Professor Bowley's *Mathematical Groundwork*.[25] It is this approach which appears to be gaining ground at present. Its main principle can be expressed as follows.[26]

The marginal revenue, which a duopolist endeavours to equate to his marginal cost,

$$= \frac{d}{dx_1}(px_1)$$

where x_1 is his output, and $p = f(x_1 + x_2)$, x_2 being the output of

[21] Chamberlin, however, has made at any rate a preliminary investigation of the more complex cases where several firms are involved. See his sections on 'oligopoly' (*Theory*, pp. 100, 170).

[22] Amoroso, *Lezioni d'economia matematica*; Wicksell, Review of Bowley's *Mathematical Groundwork*, *Archiv für Sozialwissenschaft*, 1927.

[23] Schneider, *Reine Theorie*, ch. 4.

[24] Zeuthen, *Problems of Monopoly*, ch. 2; Chamberlin, *Theory*, ch. 3, which substantially reproduces his article on 'Duopoly', *QJE*, 1929.

[25] p. 38.

[26] The following owes much to some unpublished work by Mr W. M. Allen, of Balliol College, Oxford.

his rival. Thus

$$MR_1 = \frac{d}{dx_1}(px_1) = p + x_1 f'(x_1 + x_2) + x_1 f'(x_1 + x_2)\frac{\delta x_2}{\delta x_1}$$

The marginal revenue curve which confronts the duopolist is thus in part dependent upon a quantity $\delta x_2/\delta x_1$, which we can only interpret as the degree to which the duopolist expects his rival to expand (or contract) output, if he himself expands his output by an increment dx_1. Since $f'(x_1 + x_2)$ is negative, a negative value of $\delta x_2/\delta x_1$ will raise the adjusted marginal revenue curve of the duopolist, and thus be favourable to an expansion of output; a positive value will favour a contraction.

The conception of these 'conjectural variations', $\delta x_2/\delta x_1$ etc., has been analysed in very general terms by Professor Frisch.[27] There is, in the short period, no need for any particular degree of consistency between the conjecture of the first duopolist $\delta x_2/\delta x_1$, and that of the second $\delta x_1/\delta x_2$.

The equation of marginal revenue and marginal cost thus determines the output of the first duopolist, once the output of the second duopolist, and the first duopolist's conjecture as to the variation of this output are given. For any particular type of conjecture, we can thus construct a 'reaction curve', similar to that employed by Cournot, giving the preferred output of the first duopolist, corresponding to each possible output of the second. A similar reaction curve can be constructed for the second duopolist, and the intersection of the two will give the point of equilibrium.

In the majority of cases, these reaction curves will be negatively inclined,[28] and in the majority of these cases, the inclination will be

[27] 'Monopole – Polypole – La Notion de Force dans l'économie', *Nationaløkonomisk Tidsskrift*, 1933.

[28] The condition for negative inclination is that

$$1 + \frac{hx_1}{x}\left(1 + \frac{\delta x_2}{\delta x_1}\right)$$

should be positive; where h is the 'adjusted concavity' of the market demand curve. (That is to say,

$$h = \frac{(x_1 + x_2)f''(x_1 + x_2)}{f'(x_1 + x_2)}$$

Cf. Robinson, *Economics of Imperfect Competition*, p. 40.) Since we may assume that in all sensible cases, $1 + (\delta x_2/\delta x_1)$ is positive, it follows that the reaction curve will be negatively inclined in all cases when h is positive (when the demand curve is convex upwards) and also for a considerable number of cases when h is negative. It has been further shown by Mr Allen that in such cases of negative inclination, the slope of the reaction curve will also (for reasons of stability) be numerically less than 1, excepting when there is a high degree of asymmetry between the positions of the two duopolists. 'Normal cases' are defined as satisfying these two conditions, so that dx_1/dx_2, taken along the reaction curve of the first duopolist, lies between 0 and -1.

146 The Theory of Monopoly

such that an increased output by the other duopolist will react on the first in such a way as to increase the total output of both together. If we confine our attention to these *normal* cases, which are much the most likely to yield stable solutions, the more interesting assumptions about conjectures which have been made by recent writers fall into their places very simply.

(1) If the conjectural variations are both zero, we have of course the Cournot case. (2) If one of the conjectural variations is zero, but the other duopolist takes as his conjectural variation the actual slope of the reaction curve of his rival, we have the case of an 'active' policy by one duopolist.[29] In *normal* conditions, this will make the conjectural variation of the active duopolist negative; thus, as compared with the Cournot case, it will raise his marginal revenue curve, increase his output, and (again in normal conditions) lead to an increased total output, and so a lower price. (3) If both duopolists act in this manner, each calculating conjectural variations from the other's Cournotian reaction curve, we have a curious case which has been investigated by Dr von Stackelberg and Mr Harrod.[30] In normal conditions, once more, this will lead to a further expansion of total output, and a further fall in price. (4) There does not seem to be any reason why we should stop here. One duopolist may become doubly 'active', and calculate a conjectural variation from the reaction curve of his rival on the assumption that the rival is active. In most, though not (it appears) quite all, *normal* cases, this would lead to a further fall in price. The process becomes similar to one of price-cutting.

But once we are on the road of competitive price-cutting, it is reasonable to suppose that, sooner or later, one duopolist or the other would perceive that his conjecture that an increase in his output was leading to a contraction of his rival's was proving wrong. Once he acted on this, and constructed a conjectural variation based on this experience (and consequently a *positive* variation) the whole situation would be transformed. Price-cutting would give place to 'tacit combination'; positive conjectures, again in normal conditions, would give a higher price than that given by the Cournot equilibrium.[31]

---

[29] v. Stackelberg, 'Sulla teoria del duopolio e del polipolio', *Rivista italiana di statistica*, June 1933. This article also contains an important and ingenious extension of the theory to the case of several producers.

[30] v. Stackelberg, *ibid*. Harrod, 'The Equilibrium of Duopoly', *EJ*, June 1934.

[31] Nicoll, 'Professor Chamberlin's Theory of Limited Competition', *QJE*, February 1934. Mr Nicoll's case of tacit combination emerges if we write

$$\frac{\delta x_2}{\delta x_1} = \frac{x_2}{x_1}, \quad \frac{\delta x_1}{\delta x_2} = \frac{x_1}{x_2}.$$

The method just described is capable of extension to the case where the product of one duopolist is not a perfect substitute for that of the other. We have only to write $p_1 = f_1(x_1, x_2)$, $p_2 = f_2(x_1, x_2)$; the two sellers will now of course usually sell at different prices. We then have

Adjusted marginal revenue of first seller

$$= \frac{d}{dx_1}(p_1 x_1) = p_1 + x_1 \frac{\partial p_1}{\partial x_1} + x_1 \frac{\partial p_1}{\partial x_2}\left(\frac{\delta x_2}{\delta x_1}\right)$$

from which we proceed much as before. This highly general solution can be applied whatever is the relation between the demands for the products; it can thus be applied to cases where the products are complementary instead of competitive.[32] Here $\partial p_1/\partial x_2$ will probably be positive, so that it is an anticipated consequential expansion of the other's output which will raise the marginal revenue curve of the first duopolist, and vice versa.[33]

III. Bilateral Monopoly

'Bilateral Monopoly' is a phrase which has been applied to two different problems, and it is well to keep them distinct. The first is the case of isolated exchange, or of exchange between a group of buyers and a group of sellers, each acting in combination. Now so far as this problem is concerned, when the exchange is studied *in vacuo*, without reference to other people (outside the two groups) who may be indirectly concerned, I think one may say that there is complete agreement among economists. It has been evident since the days of Edgeworth that isolated exchange leads to 'undecidable opposition of interests',[34] and that therefore the problem is indeterminate, in the sense that the mere condition of each party seeking its maximum advantage is not sufficient to define an equilibrium.

The second problem is a more complex one. It arises when the commodity sold is a raw material or factor of production; so that we have also to take into account the relation of the buyer of the raw material to another market – that in which he sells his finished

---

[32] Cf. Edgeworth, 'The Pure Theory of Monopoly', *Papers*, vol. II, 122–6.

[33] See further, on the subject of duopoly, Professor Divisia's paper to the Leyden meeting of the Econometric Society, summarised in *Econometrica*, June 1934, and also in the *Revue d'Economie politique*, May 1934.

[34] *Mathematical Psychics*, p. 29. [See pp. 73–4 above.]

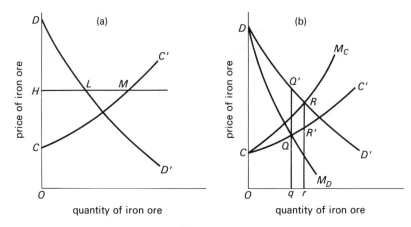

Figure 10.1

product. For this problem there existed a solution alternative to
Edgeworth's, that of Cournot; Cournot had concluded that this
more general problem is determinate. Here, as in the question of
duopoly, Cournot has his modern followers; his position is defended
by Dr Schneider, and also, though with considerable qualifications,
by Dr Zeuthen.[35]

It must be confessed, however, that the reader of their works finds
it very difficult to see just how the presence of a consumers' market
makes any difference to the opposition of interests deduced by Edgeworth; and we have the authority of Professor Bowley in support of
the view that there is indeterminateness also in the more general
case.[36] Personally, I find myself in agreement with Professor Bowley;
but I think it may be worth while to restate Professor Bowley's
argument in terms of the *marginal revenue* concept, since this seems
to make the crux of the dispute clearer than it has been made up to
the present.

A, a monopolist producer of raw material (iron ore), is selling to
B, a monopolist producer of finished product (steel). Now, as we
have seen, B's demand curve for iron ore (DD') is given by the
marginal value product of iron ore (i.e. marginal physical product of
iron ore in steel production × marginal revenue from the sale of
steel); while A's supply curve of iron ore will be given by his ordinary
marginal cost curve (CC'). That is to say, if a particular price OH is

[35] Schneider, *Reine Theorie*, ch. 2; Zeuthen, *Problems of Monopoly*, pp. 65ff.
[36] 'Bilateral Monopoly', *EJ*, 1928.

fixed by some external authority, A would be willing to supply HM units, B would be willing to take HL units; the amount actually sold will be whichever of these is the less. Now, within limits, the higher the price fixed, the greater will be A's profits, the lower the price fixed, the greater will be the profit of B. There is thus an opposition of interests. But this only within limits; for after a point it would not pay A to push up the price any further. The output which maximises A's profits will be given by the intersection of the curve marginal to DD' with CC'. DD' is the demand curve confronting A; we can draw a marginal revenue curve (DM_D) corresponding to it, to cut CC' at Q. A vertical line through Q cuts the horizontal axis in q, and DD' in Q'. Then the most profitable position for A is when his output is Oq and his price $Q'q$.

If on the other hand, B can fix the price, what is the point where his profits are maximised? This is found by drawing a curve marginal to CC' (CM_C), to intersect DD' in R. Draw $RR'r$ perpendicular to the horizontal axis. The output most favourable to B will then be Or, and the price $R'r$.

Thus there does seem to be an 'opposition of interests'; how did Cournot and his followers come to an opposite view? They would hold that there is an equilibrium with the price at $Q'q$, for in this case both producers are earning a maximum monopoly profit, B from the consumers of steel, A from B. That is perfectly true; no monopoly action by A can stop B earning a monopoly profit from the consumers. But A is not only a monopoly seller with regard to the consumers; he is also a monopoly buyer with respect to A. If he is allowed to do so, he will also extract a monopsony profit from A; it was this that Cournot left out of account.

As we have said, this indeterminateness does not mean that the law of causality is suspended; it only means that the static assumptions of fixed demand and cost curves do not suffice to determine the price. Attempts have been made by Dr Zeuthen and myself to reach a determinate solution by introducing more 'dynamic' factors.[37] Dr Zeuthen's solution proceeds by examining the probability of each side breaking off relations, which correspond to each set of terms; mine by considering the length of time for which either party would be willing to 'strike' in order to get any particular price. The two methods appear to be complementary.

[37] Zeuthen, *Problems of Monopoly*, ch. 4; 'du Monopole Bilatéral', *Revue d'Economie politique*, 1933; Hicks, *TW*, ch. 7. A treatment somewhat similar to Dr Zeuthen's is to be found in G. di Nardi, 'L'Indeterminazione nel Monopolio bilaterale', *Archivo Scientifico*, Bari, 1934.

IV. Conclusion

I have so far confined my remarks to the purely formal aspect of
recent work on monopoly; but in conclusion something ought to be
said about the applicability of this now well-developed technique.
It is evidently the opinion of some of the writers under discussion
that the modern theory of monopoly is not only capable of throwing
considerable light on the general principles underlying an individual-
istic economic structure, but that it is also capable of extensive use in
the analysis of particular practical economic problems, that is to say,
in applied economics. Personally, I cannot but feel sceptical about
this.

We have already seen, in the case of duopoly, that the marginal
revenue of a duopolist depends upon a term which can properly be
called 'conjectural'. It is not the actual degree to which the second
seller's output would change — it is the estimate of this degree on the
part of the first seller. But once we have seen this, why mark this
term only as conjectural? Is not the slope of the individual demand
curve confronting a simple monopolist conjectural too? There does
not seem to be any reason why a monopolist should not make a
mistake in estimating the slope of the demand curve confronting
him, and should maintain a certain output, thinking it was the
position which maximised his profit, although he could actually have
increased his profit by expanding or contracting.[38]

It is this subjective character of the individual demand curve which
leads one to scepticism about the applicability of the apparatus. For
what are the objective grounds from which we can deduce the
existence of a significant degree of imperfect competition? It may be
said that as soon as we find firms concerning themselves with a price
policy, or undertaking selling costs, some degree of imperfect competition must be present. This may be granted;[39] but what degree?
Is it important or negligible? There is no means of finding out but
to ask the monopolist, and it will be kind of him to tell us.

Whether competition is perfect or imperfect, the expansion of the
individual firm will be stopped by factors which are purely subjective

---

[38] This argument is fortified if the demand curve is interpreted (as for most purposes
it probably ought to be) as a fairly 'long-period' demand curve.

[39] Professor W. H. Hutt, 'Economic Method and the Concept of Competition', *Economic
Journal of South Africa*, June 1934, disputes this as far as selling costs are concerned. His
argument would appear to be valid so long as advertisement and product are sold in fixed
proportions, but it ceases to be so if the 'coefficients of consumption' are variable.

estimates; in the one case by rising subjective costs or costs of organisation;[40] in the other by an estimated downward slope of the marginal revenue curve. Objective facts give us no means of distinguishing between them.

The new theories seem to make little difference to the laws of change as they are exhibited in the traditional analysis; usually they do no more than suggest new reasons why we should get certain familiar effects, and there is very little means of distinguishing between the new reasons and the old. Whether an industry is monopolised, or duopolised, or polypolised, or operates under conditions of perfect competition, we shall expect a rise in demand to lead to a rise in output (though in all cases there are possible, but highly improbable, exceptions); and it is still likely that the rise in demand will be accompanied either by no change in price, or by a rise. New reasons are indeed adduced why a rise in output may be accompanied by a fall in price; it may be due to a rise in the elasticity of demand to the individual firm, rather than to economies of the Marshallian type. But the new explanation is not overwhelmingly convincing, and does not drive the Marshallian from the field.[41]

It does indeed now become possible that a rise in supply — if it takes the form of an influx of new firms — may actually lead to a rise in price, as would not be possible under perfect competition. Yet the conditions for this to happen, that the influx of firms should make the demand curve confronting each firm in the industry *less elastic*, is so peculiar, that it is hard to attach very much importance to this case — at least, as analysed.

It is therefore hard to see that the new analysis does much to displace Marshallian methods. Marshall's assumptions are simpler, and if we are unable to tell which of two hypotheses is more appropriate, the simpler has the obvious claim to be chosen. But of course

[40] Cf. E. A. G. Robinson, 'The problem of management and the size of firms', *EJ*, June 1934, and the same author's *Structure of Competitive Industry*. Also Kaldor, 'The Equilibrium of the Firm', *EJ*, March 1934.

[41] It is tempting to propose a rehabilitation of Marshall on the basis of these recent developments. Since it has become clear that 'increasing returns' are mainly a matter of indivisibilities and discontinuities, it is very possible that a firm may be in perfect competitive equilibrium with its (conjectured) demand curve horizontal, at the point of equilibrium, although it knows that a considerable increase in output would enable it to diminish average costs (of hired factors) considerably. But it is uncertain whether so large an increase in sales could be brought about without a considerable reduction in price, and refrains from expansion because it is unwilling to take the risk. This seems at least as plausible a construction as the other, and better suited to a world of very imperfect knowledge.

On the general question of discontinuity in cost, see M. Joseph, 'A Discontinuous Cost Curve', *EJ*, Sept. 1933.

this is not to say that in strong cases — cases, for example, where discrimination is practised — we are not obliged to assume monopoly conditions, and to make what use we can of the elaborations here described.

From this point of view, substantial gains have certainly been made; we are now in the possession of a much more complete theory of monopoly than was the case a very few years ago. If, when we have it, it seems less use than had been hoped, this is not an uncommon experience in the history of human thought.

11

Scitovsky on Competition

PREFATORY NOTE

This was a review of Tibor Scitovsky: *Welfare and Competition* (1951). It was published in *American Economic Review*, September 1952.
Though the other reviews which are included in this volume are grouped together in part V, this particular review belongs with the other papers in part II so I have placed it here, as I would like it to be read with them. But it also has a relation with several of the 'welfare' papers in volume I, so there is a good deal about it which needs to be explained.

By the time I was writing, and by the time he was writing, we had the developments of the forties in welfare economics behind us; each of us had contributed to them, so I was hoping that he would have begun with a statement of those principles. But in spite of the word *welfare* in his title, he did not do that. It was my feeling, and still is my feeling, that if he had done so, his approach would have been clarified.

For I was already of the opinion that it is, in general, impossible to use the perfect competition model as a standard, in the way that he did (apart from the reservations to which I drew attention). In an economy where scale economies are important (and I myself, at least since 1939, have never denied that they are important)[1] the organisation of production on a perfect competition basis is just not feasible. But an optimum, any sort of an optimum, must be feasible; so the perfect competition model − whatever its uses in other respects − will not do as a representation of an optimum organisation.[2] What is there that will do? I am afraid there is nothing. But this does not mean that welfare economics is futile; far from it. We can still use it as a basis for the *criticism* of existing organisations;

---

[1] 'Foundations of Welfare Economics' (essay 2 in volume I).
[2] This is made most explicit in essay 12 of volume I ('Optimisation and Specialisation') which, of course, was not available to Scitovsky.

suggesting other *feasible* organisations which may be compared with it, and endeavouring to assess the gains and losses, which might accrue to those affected if there was a change to any of these alternatives. That is the 'more fertile country' to which I alluded at the end of my review. I wish I had been more explicit.

From this point of view (to which I think I had come before I read Scitovsky's book) it is cost–benefit analysis, based on consumer's surplus theory,[3] which becomes central. So far I disagreed with him; but from that point onwards, I had much to learn from Scitovsky. I was, and am, much impressed by the distinction he draws between the well-informed and the ill-informed market. He is thinking of goods that are sold to final consumers; so it is the degree of information possessed by those consumers on which his distinction depends. I would agree that it is to the well-informed market that consumers' surplus most comfortably applies. It is only in the well-informed market that we have a right to assume that consumers, by their choices, are 'revealing their preferences'; so to analyse their choices in terms of traditional utility (or preference) theory makes good sense. Into the ill-informed market comes the purveyor of information, who stands between the consumer's preferences and the choices he makes. And the party who has a natural advantage in the provision of that information is the producer himself.[4] The costs of providing it, and of getting it attended to, are, in Scitovsky's view, a main cause of restriction of entry and so of competition.

It may be that Scitovsky lays too much stress on this; there surely exist many other costs of entry, and one can readily think of cases where these other costs must be more important (the iron and steel industry, so much studied by later writers on oligopoly, is an obvious example). He was nevertheless quite right, from the point of view of welfare theory, to lay his main stress on the information point. I would go farther than he does in that direction. I would say that there is no reason why an informed market, with free (or better *easy*) entry, should not be optimally organised. Even though the condition of price equalling marginal cost is not satisfied, average cost exceeding marginal cost, and average cost (for variations in output) therefore not being minimised, the more fundamental criterion that there would be no clear gain from a reduction in the number of firms (or varieties of product) can still be satisfied. Of course it is not true that it is necessarily satisfied; the gains from

---

[3] Rehabitation of Consumers' Surplus (essay 4 of volume I).
[4] Note on Advertisement, appended to essay 6 in volume I.

standardisation may be so great as to outweigh the loss from failing to cater for particular tastes.

But how right he is to emphasise that the replacement of the varieties by the standardised product leaves the welfare problem wide open. It is now the producer who decides on what variety to standardise; and though while he is in the process of establishing his monopoly (or oligopoly)[5] he must pay attention to what is acceptable, or what he can make acceptable, he is under no such compulsion once his position is established. He can adjust the quality of what he sells to suit his own convenience (including the convenience of quiet relations with those whom he employs). The danger of sagging quality when competition is restricted may often be more important than exploitation by price.

Professor Scitovsky's contributions to modern welfare theory have been so outstanding that a book on that subject from his pen would be an event. This is not that book. It is a very important book, but in spite of the two words in its title, it is a book about Competition, not a book about Welfare. It is not a book of the Pigou type, which builds up a theory of Welfare Economics, and then applies that theory (among other applications) to the study of Monopoly and Competition. It is a book of the Chamberlin-Robinson type, which is primarily concerned with Monopoly and Competition; though it wisely goes back to Pigou in its use of the technique of Welfare Economics as a source of principles by which the various market-forms which it studies can be judged. The judgement which emerges is, on the whole, a very balanced judgement; Professor Scitovsky has helped us a great deal to get this difficult and controversial problem into proper focus.

Instead of beginning, as I myself would rather wish he had begun, with an outline of the Welfare principles which are going to be applied, Scitovsky starts with a classification of market forms.

[5] I myself remain unconvinced that duopoly – in the sense of two quite independent firms dividing the market for a nearly identical product fairly equally between them – is possible, in the longer run, without some degree of understanding, or collusion. But indeed in the shorter run nearly anything can happen.

I remember once talking with Geoffrey Heyworth, who had worked his way up through the firm to become, in the end, the chairman of Unilever, about the apparently arm's length duopoly between the two Dutch margarine firms, as described in the second volume of Charles Wilson's *History of Unilever*. It lasted for nearly twenty years (at the beginning of this century) and only ended when the legal charges, of the actions which the two parties had taken against each other, became insupportable. How could that happen? 'Ah' he said to me 'you should have seen those chaps'.

Leaving on one side the case of the undeveloped market (characterised by isolated or only partly competitive bargaining) and the
case of the controlled market (characterised by trade at prescribed
prices) we are left with three main types, to the study of which
almost the whole of the book is devoted. These are (1) *perfect
competition*, in which both buyer and seller are 'price-takers' (to
use the elegant term which Scitovsky borrows from Lerner, to
mean the same thing as the 'quantity-adjusters' of Frisch); (2) *free
competition*, as Scitovsky calls it, being the *imperfect competition
with free entry* of Mrs Robinson; (3) *restricted competition*, or
imperfect competition without free entry. It is of course admitted
that actual markets do not always fit very exactly into these types,
and that markets which approximate to one type co-exist with
markets which approximate to another. Nevertheless, Scitovsky
chooses to concentrate on his types, and to get out his main results
in the form of comparisons between model economies, in which
the one type of market or the other is established more or less
throughout.

The case of perfect competition is studied at considerable length,
but (except towards the end) nothing that is very new seems to
emerge. The main purpose of the discussion is to show that the
perfect competition model satisfies the static efficiency tests of
welfare economies, which are introduced at this point, so that there
is not much room to give them the general justification which they
surely still require. It is fully admitted that the perfectly competitive
economy is a theoretical construction, which has never, even approximately, existed. Its theoretical function is to serve as a standard of
reference, by which the other forms that are nearer to the actual
can be judged.

This is the attitude to perfect competition theory which Scitovsky
usually takes; but he does not always hold to it. There is another
strand in his thought, which is related to an alternative conception
of perfect competition. 'At the beginning of the nineteenth century,'
he tells us, 'these markets [the perfectly competitive markets for
materials and staple foodstuffs] were the only exceptions to the then
almost universal rule of competitive bargaining; this fact led many
economists of the time to expect competition to become more
perfect and the number of perfectly competitive markets to increase
with the passage of time' (p. 19). In fact, this has not happened;
but supposing it had happened, would it have meant that the welfare
optimum would have been attained, so that the wants of consumers
would have been satisfied as well as they could have been from

available resources? It hardly seems probable. The doubts thus raised lead Professor Scitovsky to append to his static analysis of perfect competition, in which perfect competition is a standard of reference, a dynamic analysis (chs. IX and X), in which perfect competition has ceased to be a standard of reference, but is itself found wanting by some further (unspecified) criterion.

The chief deficiencies which are discussed in these chapters are two. One is imperfect foresight ('cobwebs' and such like) which are shown to be more damaging in perfectly competitive markets than in markets where producers take more direct account of the behaviour of their competitors. This, it may be accepted, is a genuine deficiency of perfect competition as usually defined; Scitovsky has done well to emphasise its importance and to bring it into some relation with his static theory. The other is concerned with the supply of capital to the individual firm. In effect, what is here contended is that though other markets may conceivably be perfect, the capital market, by its very nature, cannot be perfect; so that the only 'perfect competition model' which could conceivably come near to being realised in practice is one in which the firm's supply of capital is strictly limited – this limitation providing the explanation why the firm cannot grow to an immoderate size. The substance of these contentions may be granted, yet it remains inconvenient to admit an imperfectly competitive capital market into a model which is still called perfectly competitive. It proves inconvenient as a matter of exposition; for since the imperfect capital market has to be studied before any general technique for the study of imperfect markets has been developed, Scitovsky finds himself obliged to concentrate attention on the special case in which the supply of capital to the individual firm is *fixed*. This is an interesting special case, but surely it is a special case, with rather peculiar properties. It is a pity that these peculiar properties are given, as a result of the classification adopted, more attention than they deserve. My own feeling is that the imperfect capital market belongs to the theory of free competition, not to that of perfect competition; there would have been less trouble if Scitovsky could have brought himself to deal with it in that place.

One would indeed be glad to think of ways of transferring subjects from part II (Perfect Competition) to part III (Free Competition); for if part II is rather long, and not (at this time of day) very original, part III is novel and exciting. This is partly because no less than four of its six chapters are devoted to a special study of the firm under imperfect competition – 'the Price-Maker's Behaviour' – which succeeds in making a remarkably fresh approach to a well-worn subject. One suspects that these chapters form the part of the book about which, for a while at least, most will be heard.

The essence of these chapters may perhaps be summarised in the following way. Anyone who has thought at all about the matter will agree that the choices which confront an actual entrepreneur are exceedingly complex; though it is not difficult to write down (at least in symbolic language) a general description of them, the resulting maximisation problem is so difficult as to be quite unmanageable. It is unmanageable by the economist; and it is also unmanageable, in these terms, by the entrepreneur himself. Some simplification is therefore necessary. The economist, confronted with this problem of simplification, naturally proceeds by the method which he has found useful in other cases; he simply leaves out those aspects which he cannot conveniently handle, and reduces the problem to manageable terms by a process of exclusion. But this procedure is not open to the business man himself, who cannot abdicate his responsibility in this way. He has to seek an alternative means of simplification. If, therefore, economists and business men are to become mutually intelligible, as they must do if economists are to be able to use business data and to have worthwhile views on business problems, a bridge between the business man's simplifications and the language of economic analysis has got to be built. To the building of this bridge Scitovsky has made a notable contribution.

He begins from the economist's end, with the familiar equation of marginal revenue and marginal cost. But, since he intends to go on at once to consider variations in the non-price ingredients in the seller's offer (quality, advertising and so on), he proceeds at once to re-formulate the equation in a new way. He uses the term price-variation cost to mean the difference between price and marginal revenue; that is to say, price-variation cost is the cost of selling a marginal unit of output by the route of diminishing price. The classic equation can then be written in the form

Price Variation Cost = Price − Marginal Production Cost

or

Price Variation Cost = Profit Margin.

The advantage of this reformulation is that it can so readily be extended to deal with the non-price ingredients. It can readily be shown that quality improvement, selling expenditure and the rest will each of them be carried to the point where their variation costs (similarly defined) will be made equal to the profit margin. The simplest way of envisaging the *whole* problem of selling policy is to think of each type of variation being carried up to the point where its (marginal) variation cost equals the profit margin. The central importance of the profit margin for the entrepreneur's own conception of his problem is, by this simple device, made abundantly clear.

It is further suggested that in most cases we shall expect the entrepreneur to begin by setting a profit margin, which will mainly depend on his estimation of the competitiveness of the market confronting him, and to proceed subsequently by adjusting all the other variables to it. Logically, he ought to reconsider his profit margin everytime he makes an adjustment in another variable; but there will generally be insufficient information available to him to make such reconsideration worthwhile. Indeed, since the problem is one of simplification, it is practically less dangerous to simplify by assuming variables to be independent, and demand functions to be linear (or iso-elastic), than to simplify (as economists are tempted to do) by leaving variables out of account.

To this brilliant analysis of the role of the profit margin (the full range of which cannot be more than suggested here), Scitovsky adds – what has hitherto been very badly needed – a complementary study of time-factors in selling policy. What period of time should the business man take into consideration when fixing prices or when determining the other variables? Brushing aside such trivialities as customers' annoyance at frequently changing prices, which have received too much attention in the literature, Scitovsky deals at length with three specifically economic factors, which can be used as the basis for a remarkably coherent theory. These are (1) the costs of making a change, sometimes (but not always) small in the case of price-changes, nearly always considerable in other cases; (2) certain indivisibilities; (3) the reaction-time of consumers, called by Scitovsky (not I think very happily) the 'turn-over period.' About the last of these, in particular, quite a number of important things can be said. All three factors usually work against frequent changes in selling policy, though they have other more special effects in addition. Thus, for instance, slow reaction-times work in favour of stability, but they are also inclined to set greater obstacles in the way of price-reductions than of price-increases. Even in a competitive market (so long as it is not perfectly competitive) prices must usually be expected to come down more slowly than they go up.

We are now three-quarter way through the book, but the most important things which Professor Scitovsky has to say still lie ahead. These are chiefly to be found in the remaining chapters (XV–XVI) of part III, which deal with the Conditions of Free Competition, and the Efficiency of Free Competition, respectively. In these chapters the corresponding problems of Restricted Competition are already covered by implication; little therefore remains to be done in part IV except to make some of the consequences of chapters XV–XVI more explicit.

Many of the Conditions of Free Competition are familiar enough. There must be a 'competitive spirit'; the technical economies of large scale must not be too overwhelming; and so on. To these familiar considerations Scitovsky adds another, which is much more interesting though it may prove more controversial. Free Competition is most easily maintained in an *informed market*. An informed market is one in which buyers either are, or think themselves to be, good judges of the quality of the goods offered. Uninformed markets, in which the consumer is a prey to the advertiser, most easily fall into a state of Restricted Competition.

For this distinction two main reasons are offered. In the first place, it is relatively easy for a new firm to enter an informed market. There will usually be little difficulty in devising a variety of product which will satisfy the special tastes of some consumers; in an informed market these consumers can readily and quickly be drawn to the new product when it is offered, so that the new firm has no great difficulty in making a start. The heavy advertising expenses, needed before a foothold can be established in an uninformed market, are a formidable barrier to the entry of new firms. The second reason is more subtle. In an uninformed market, a sufficient volume of advertising expenditure will usually enable a firm to hold its existing customers; this means that one of the limits to size which has been most stressed by economists – the limitation of entrepreneurial capacity – is relatively inoperative. Limited entrepreneurial capacity may limit the *rate of growth* of a firm in an uninformed market, but does not limit its absolute size. But in an informed market, much entrepreneurial capacity is taken up with the mere holding of existing customers; this both limits the size to which the individual firm can expand, and it also limits the life of many firms. Thus the population of firms tends to be a floating population, for which 'free entry to the industry' is not merely potential but actual. Though the other, more technological, factors must not be forgotten, there is, in Scitovsky's view, a distinct correlation between the degree of informedness of a market and the freedom of competition in it.

The reader who accepts this argument (for my own part I think I would accept it, though I am not quite sure how far it should be carried) has already, even before reaching the crucial stage of the debate, been got into a state of divided sympathies. Which do we like better – the world of Free Competition, with its intelligent consumers, each of them a little entrepreneur in his own affairs, or the world of Restricted Competition, in which all save an élite of entrepreneurs are progressively stultified, but which can use the Law of Increasing Returns to attain material wealth quite outside the other's reach? This is indeed the dilemma with which Scitovsky confronts us. The use of welfare criteria to discuss the 'Efficiency of Free Competition' simply drives it home.

Free Competition is not Perfect Competition; it gets worse marks than Perfect Competition from the standpoint of the static welfare tests. The discrepancy between price and marginal cost, made explicit by the existence of the profit margin, has (in Scitovsky's view) received exaggerated attention as a direct cause of departure from the welfare optimum. In a genuinely free market, profit margins (properly measured) cannot be very wide, and cannot prevent the attainment of an approximately correct relation of marginal costs between competing firms. There are two indirect consequences of the discrepancy which are more important. One is the tendency to an excessive number of firms (the Chamberlin–Robinson 'excess capacity' which Scitovsky fully admits); the other is a bias against roundabout methods which involve purchase of materials from other firms, the cost of which is exaggerated by 'pyramiding' of profit margins. In both of these ways the Freely Competitive Market takes less than full advantage of the economies of scale which are technologically open to it.

In these particular respects Restricted Competition is likely to do better. But Scitovsky owes it to his approach that he is in no danger of exaggerating these virtues – of falling into the adulation of Restricted (or rather of Controlled and Restricted) Competition which has been implicit in the work of too many of his predecessors. Though Free Competition has the defects which have been stated, it does at least ensure that a given output is produced by each firm as efficiently as possible (apart from the 'pyramiding' point). Restricted Competition does not even give us that assurance. It is always unlikely that in an uninformed market consumers' wants will be satisfied particularly well. Economies of large scale and capital-using technology are bought at a great price.

This, more or less, is where Scitovsky's argument takes us. But, having got there, is there not another thing, which Scitovsky does not say, which needs to be said? If anything of this sort is true – and it seems to me that in general, though not perhaps in every particular, the case is proved — is it not time that economists abandoned the discussion of these problems in terms of *general* models, Perfect Competition, Free Competition, Restricted Competition and the like? The conclusion which has emerged from the study of these models is negative. In a world of large-scale production and scientific technology (whatever may have been the case in a simpler world, but the same conclusion probably holds there too), there is no practicable market form which could be made to exist at all generally, and which does not have great disadvantages to match its advantages. The search for the ideal is therefore a will-of-the-wisp. It is time that we ceased to conduct these discussions on so general a basis. What is now needed is not a general theory of market forms but a technique by which we can most accurately and usefully assess the advantages and disadvantages of change — of practicable change — in particular cases. What we need is a theory — it must, I think, be a continuation of our theory of welfare economics — which will enable us to treat each particular problem, each particular proposal, on its merits.

This reflection is in no way a criticism of the great service which Scitovsky has performed. It is no criticism of the guide who has helped us over the brow of a hill that he has not yet also led us into the more fertile country which now lies in front.

12

Stickers and Snatchers

This essay appeared in *Oxford Economic Papers* in February 1954, under the title (not nowadays very explanatory) of 'The Process of Imperfect Competition'. As is indicated, it arose out of discussions which were prompted by a new paper in Harrod's *Economic Essays* (1952), in which Mrs Margaret Paul (see her 'Note on Excess Capacity' in the same number of *OEP*) also took part.

It was Harrod who had directed our attention to the question of the way in which an imperfectly competitive model — that is to say, a model of an industry with rather easy entry — could be supposed to work. The study of static equilibrium conditions is not enough; one must look at the situation from the point of view of a prospective entrant, considering the policies (*over time*) that can be open to him. That was what Harrod was trying to do; I was carrying on from his work. Ours has not been a line of approach which has much appealed to subsequent writers; but it still seems to me that for a complete theory of a market with easy entry (what Baumol in *AER* (1982) has lately called a 'contestable' market) something of this sort is required.

That there are social losses from short-run 'snatching' is here rather taken for granted. The point still seems to me to be often valid, but it needs more careful statement than it here receives.

I

The purpose of this paper is to discuss certain aspects of the relation between the theory of imperfect competition and the Marshallian doctrine of the short and long periods. Consulting the Scriptures, one finds that this is a matter which hardly arose on the approach adopted by Chamberlin; while Mrs Robinson, though she was undoubtedly alive to the problem, said nothing about it that was very consecutive.

Thus it was left to Harrod, in his 1934 paper,[1] to give what long remained the classical analysis. Nearly all economists who have been teaching this subject during the following twenty years have taught what they had learned from that paper; certainly I have done it myself. This prop and stay is now taken from us. For in the new paper[2] which is added to the old one in *Economic Essays*, Harrod goes a long way in retreat from his former position. It is, I think, impossible to defend the old theory from some of the criticisms which its author now brings against it. It has to be replaced by something different. I do not, however, feel that Harrod has completed the construction of the new theory which his latest work causes us to envisage. Some essential elements seem still to be missing. It is in the hope that I may be able to provide some of these elements that I have written the present paper.

I propose, quite deliberately, to be rather formal. For what I am looking for is a model which will provide a skeleton for the new theory, just as the familiar cost and demand curves (with their derivatives) did for the old. I shall not be much concerned with the clothing of the skeleton. All I am seeking to do is to construct a model that is usable, and that will start us thinking in sensible directions.

II

Consider the position of a firm which is proposing to set up a new plant. Time, as it stretches forward from the date of decision, will be treated as divisible into three *periods*. The first is the *construction period*, in which output will in any case be zero. The second I shall provisionally call the *close period*; during this period the plant, if built, will be completed and in action, but competitors will not have had time to get similar plants into action. The third, which may similarly be called the *open period* (both because it is of indefinite length and because the market is now open to competitors), begins at the date when competitors will have had time to get similar plants into action, if circumstances are such that it is to their interest to do so. For simplicity I shall assume that a single price-and-output policy has to be chosen for the close period and a single price-and-output policy for the open period. In other words, variations in price within the close period or within the open period (though they may of

---

[1] 'Doctrines of Imperfect Competition', *QJE* (1934); reprinted in *Economic Essays*, p. 111.

[2] 'Theory of Imperfect Competition Revised', *Economic Essays*, p. 139.

course occur as a result of unexpected changes in the market situation, when the time comes) are not envisaged at the time the plan is drawn up. I hope that the reader will be able to accept these as reasonable simplifications.

I shall (as is the common practice) assume that factors can be hired (or acquired) on the market at constant prices, so that cost functions are determinate. I shall then proceed to identify these cost-functions with the Marshallian cost-functions of the *short* and the *long* period. This is admittedly a drastic simplification; but I think it should be acceptable, at least for many applications if not for all, on the following ground.

It is reasonable to assume that the plant which is being put up will be fairly durable – of a durability which is long in relation to the length of the close period. The technical necessities of production by modern techniques will ordinarily ensure that this is the case. It follows that the size of the plant which must be constructed will be related to the output which is planned for production in the *open* period. The output (per week) in the open period will then play the same part in our theory as Marshall's long-period output, while the output (per week) in the close period, being produced from a plant which is not necessarily in perfect adaptation to it, will be a short-period output in Marshall's sense. I shall accordingly allow myself to use the familiar terms 'short-period output' and 'long-period output' for the outputs per week of the close and open periods respectively. Thus in our theory, as in the old theory, the significant variables may be described as short-period output and long-period output; it is these which determine the production plan of the enterprise.[3] But we must be very careful to distinguish cases in which expectations of future market conditions are formed in one way or another.

III

On this approach, the Harrod 1934 theory of imperfect competition appears as the particular case in which the market conditions con-

[3] It is not meant to be implied by this framework of assumptions that the output of the firm is necessarily homogeneous. A considerable degree of heterogeneity can be allowed for by supposing the figure which represents the *output* of the firm to be an *index* of output, and by assuming that the composition of the output which corresponds to any given value of the index is determined independently of the considerations which are our present concern. This simplification is of course quite out of the question when we are specially concerned with problems of the composition of output; but for present purposes, when we are solely concerned with *scale*, there does not seem to be any harm in it. It is, I think, a great mistake to conclude that the *theory* of the single-product firm is made inapplicable to reality by the empirical fact that most firms produce a variety of different products.

fronting the firm are expected to be the same in the open as in the closed period – the simplest case out of a variety of alternatives. If we were to adopt Lange's terminology,[4] we should call it the case of static expectations; but for reasons which will appear later I should prefer to say that in this case expectations are *simple.* I need not repeat the well-known argument which shows that on this assumption short-period output (determined from the condition that short-period marginal revenue equals short-period marginal cost) and long-period output (determined by the corresponding long-period condition) are equal. I shall indeed be coming back to that argument in a different connection. Here we may merely note that simple expectations engender a flow of output which is itself stationary.

The theory of market equilibrium which is based upon this type of behaviour by the firm will then run as follows. It is assumed (for there is no advantage in assuming the contrary) that actual demand during the close period coincides with expected demand. Nothing will therefore happen, during the close period, to impede the realisation of the plan. During the (realised) close period there does therefore exist that *static* form of excess capacity which is represented by the downward slope of the average cost curve[5] – a downward slope which is established by the tangency between that short-period average cost curve and the long-period average cost curve, so long as the latter is taken to be downward sloping. Such static excess capacity as this is fully compatible with equilibrium.

Before going farther it is necessary to distinguish between the case of the marginal and that of the intramarginal firm. If our firm is a marginal firm, it will not make significantly more than normal profits during its close period, so that there will be no reason why it should have to face additional competition when the market becomes open. Thus there is no reason why the expectation of unchanged demand in the open period should not be verified. The close period situation will maintain itself in the open period. The same output will continue to be produced, and the static excess capacity will remain.

If our firm is an intramarginal firm, its profits (during the close period) will be in excess of normal, and it is therefore to be assumed that the commencement of the open period will be attended by the arrival of competitors. The demand curve for our firm will shift to

---

[4] O. Lange, *Price Flexibility and Employment*, p. 1.

[5] Average total cost, in Harrod's terminology. But I cannot refrain from a word of protest against this term, which I have long disliked. Total cost is usually employed to mean average cost multiplied by output; it is a thorough nuisance to have to use it in another sense. Could we not agree to say 'average inclusive cost', which is clear and unambiguous?

the left, so that the output which it will produce will be less than that which it had initially planned for the open period. Output is thus still smaller, in relation to the capacity of the plant, than it would otherwise have been. But the excess capacity which arises from this cause must be sharply distinguished from the other. That was a static, but this is a dynamic phenomenon – it arises from a discrepancy between actual demand conditions and those which were planned for. It is a phenomenon of miscalculation and disequilibrium.

I suppose that the story would then be continued as follows. As time goes on, the industry will 'fill up'; the point will ultimately be reached when no further profit is to be got from entry by a new firm. When this point is first reached the industry will consist of (1) the latest arrivals, which are approximately marginal, (2) the old firms, which were intramarginal. So far as the marginal firms are concerned, they are in equilibrium, with static excess capacity, but no dynamic excess capacity, straight off. So far as the older firms are concerned, they must continue with their dynamic excess capacity until their plant wears out; when it does so, they replace it with new plant, more appropriate to their now reduced circumstances. In effect, when they do so, they convert themselves into marginal firms; they abolish their dynamic excess capacity, but their static excess capacity remains with them. It is in this way that the industry is supposed to settle into its *long-period equilibrium*.

IV

This, I think, is the old story; it is this story which Harrod now seeks to modify – by abandoning the assumption of simple expectations. It must at once be granted that this assumption is a particularly weak link in the preceding argument. It does not need much imagination to realise that entrepreneurs are much more sensitive to the danger of potential competition – which affects the anticipated long-period demand for their products – than they are to the elasticity of short-period demand. I find myself in hearty agreement over the need for abandoning this particular assumption.

But when we abandon it, what do we put in its place? There is only one sort of simple expectation, but the varieties of complex expectation are many. It is not possible to analyse any of these varieties properly without a formal extension of the existing theory of the firm. For as soon as the assumption of simple expectations is abandoned we lose the power of determining short-period output and long-period output separately; they have to be jointly determined. We need a theory of this joint determination before we can get any farther.

V

As a first step in the construction of that theory we have to face the old riddle: what does the entrepreneur maximise? Corresponding to any choice of the two key variables there will be a particular short-period profit, and a particular long-period profit, that can be expected: how does he weigh one of these against the other? It seems to me that we ought to think of him as maximising a certain combination of these two profits. Thus if g is the amount (per week) of short-period profit, and G is the amount (per week) of long-period profit, he maximises $lg + mG$, where l, m are *weights*. If we remember that price and output are taken to be constant *within* each of the two periods, and apply the ordinary rule of maximising the present value of the stream of profits, this is in fact the result which we get. (On this derivation, we implicitly assume a perfect capital market; but it is not evident that the assumption of an imperfect capital market would make any difference to the result.)

The weights l, m may then be taken to be governed by such things as the lengths of time for which the close (short) and open (long) periods are expected to last, the rate of time-preference, and the willingness to bear risks. Such subjective factors (and capital-market factors) may well, on occasion, be of great importance. The entrepreneur who is mainly interested in seizing a quick profit (I shall call him the *Snatcher*) will have a high l relatively to his m; the one who is mainly interested in building up a steady business (I shall call him the *Sticker*) will have a high m relatively to his l.[6] Such types of psychology are, I think, readily recognisable in the pages of business history. I shall simplify by treating these weights as permanent characteristics of particular firms, so that they can be reckoned as constants; but it must of course be noticed that to do so is to make a drastic simplification.

I shall continue to use small letters for short-period magnitudes and capitals for long-period magnitudes. Thus x and X will be short-period and long-period output respectively. r and R will be the (total)

---

[6] I acknowledge the debt which I owe, for this distinction, to reflection upon Mrs Paul's paper, which appeared in the same number of *OEP*.

revenue per week expected from selling these outputs; c and C will be the (total) costs per week, assumed capable of allocation between periods. Thus what the entrepreneur maximises is

$$lg + mG = l(r - c) + m(R - C).$$

In order that this should be a maximum, its partial derivatives with respect to x and X must be zero. Using the suffix notation for partial derivatives, this gives us two equations

$$l(r_x - c_x) + m(R_x - C_x) = 0$$

$$l(r_X - c_X) + m(R_X - C_X) = 0$$

to determine the two key variables x and X.

This is the complete generalisation of the 'marginal revenue marginal cost' equation; but it is usually capable of some simplification. In the first place, since the firm is under no compulsion to disclose its open-period price-policy during the close period, the effect of the planned long-period output on short-period revenue can ordinarily be taken to be zero. Thus $r_X = 0$. Further, since we are making the usual Marshallian assumption that the size of plant is determined by long-period output only, short-period output will have no effect upon long-period cost. Thus $C_x = 0$. The equations accordingly reduce to what I shall regard as their standard form

$$l(r_x - c_x) + mR_x = 0$$

$$l(-c_X) + m(R_X - C_X) = 0.$$

The 'straight' parts of these equations (the term in l in the first, and that in m in the second) correspond to the ordinary relations of marginal revenue and marginal cost; the 'cross' parts are the qualifications which need to be inserted in the present, more general, case. It will be noticed, as a convenient feature of the model with which we are working, that no more than one 'cross marginal revenue' and one 'cross marginal cost' survives in the standard form of the equations, so that these terms can be used for R_x and c_X without ambiguity (though also without symmetry).

These equations have now to be interpreted in the light of the familiar relations (already utilised) between short-period and long-period cost. For the purpose of the present analysis these relations would be presented in the following way. We have seen that c (short-period total cost) is a function of x and X, while C (long-period total cost) is a function of X only. But we know that if X is chosen in such a manner as to make c a minimum for given x, x and X will be equal, while c will then be equal to C. Thus if $x = X$, $c_X = 0$ (since c is minimum) and $c = C$. Now C_X (long-period marginal cost) is the derivative of total cost against a change in X, x being kept equal to X, and c_X being therefore equal to zero throughout. Thus $C_X = (dc/dX)$ (the *total* derivative) when $x = X$. But

$$\frac{dc}{dX} = \frac{\partial c}{\partial X} + \frac{\partial c}{\partial x}\frac{dx}{dX}$$

(by the usual rule for a total derivative). Here, when $x = X$, $(\partial c/\partial X) = 0$, $(dx/dX) = 1$. Thus $C_X = (dc/dX) = (\partial c/\partial x) = c_x$. Thus we have the additional information that when x and X are equal, short-period and long-period marginal cost are equal ($c_x = C_X$); while the cross marginal cost (c_X) is zero.

VI

As a first step in the application of this model, we may verify the classical Harrod analysis for the case of simple expectations. The characteristics of this case are (1) that R_x is zero, since long-period demand is unaffected by short-period output (or price-policy); (2) that if $x = X$, $R = r$. The cross-term in the first of our standard equations drops out in the light of the first of these conditions; that equation accordingly reduces to the familiar equation of short-period marginal revenue and short-period marginal cost. The second equation is then satisfied by $x = X$. For if $x = X$, the cross-term in the second equation drops out (as we have just seen), while the remaining terms become identical with their short-period counterparts. $C_X = c_x$ (as just established); $R_X = r_x$ (by the assumption of simple expectations). Thus if $x = X$, and either of the two standard equations is satisfied by the common value, the other will be satisfied also. But so far we have offered no more than an algebraic proof of what was well known already.

We now strike out into less well-charted seas. The next assumption which I should like to examine is that in which the entrepreneur's expectations remain static, so far as the general state of demand, for the products of the industry of which he is a part, is concerned; but in which he expects the arrival of competitors in the open period — competitors who will arrive independently of anything which he can do by his short-period policy. This is not one of the hypotheses to which Harrod particularly desires to draw our attention (in his 1953 paper). He is (very naturally) anxious to rush on to the discussion of *growth*; and so far as he will admit the case of expectations that are in any way static, he is mainly interested in the possibility that the firm may seek, by its short-period price-policy, to keep out competitors. Now conditions in which the firm is able, by its short-period price-policy, to influence the behaviour of competitors, to keep them out of (or let them into) its own particular market, seem to me to have a distinct flavour of oligopoly about them. I shall therefore call that case the case of *oligopolistic expectations*. The present case, which comes before it in our present procedure of generalising the old Harrod theory of imperfect competition, I shall call the case of *polypolistic expectations*.

VII

With polypolistic expectations, long-period revenue remains unaffected by short-period policy, so that it is still true that the cross marginal revenue is zero. The cross-term in the first equation still drops out. The first equation still reduces to the familiar equation of short-period marginal revenue and short-period marginal cost. But the second equation cannot be relied upon to simplify similarly. It will, however, simplify approximately, if our firm is very much of a Sticker, with m large relatively to l; the cross-term in the second equation will then be small, and the second equation can be represented, to a sufficient approximation, by the equation of long-period marginal revenue and long-period marginal cost. Both R and C are now functions of X only, so that this equation suffices to determine X (and with it the size of plant) directly. But since the firm expects a smaller demand for its product in the open period than in the close period, the size of plant will be smaller than it would have been apart from the expectation of future competition. Polypolistic expectations make for smaller plants, which draw less of the economies of large scale, than would be put up if expectations were simple.

The size of plant being determined, the first equation (of short-period marginal revenue and short-period marginal cost) remains to determine short-period output. x and X are now so far independent that we can think of the two equations being represented, in the usual manner, on the same diagram. Short-period demand being greater than the expected long-period demand, short-period marginal revenue (for a given output) will be greater than long-period marginal revenue. Short-period output will accordingly be greater than the planned long-period output. Though the firm will still be planning for a situation in which it will have static excess capacity in the long period, it is not inevitable that such excess capacity should exist in the short period. Short-period output may well be in excess of that which would minimise cost from the chosen plant.

If, however, our firm is less of a Sticker, the size of plant which it installs may be influenced by the fact that it does not propose to produce its short-period output from the plant which is best suited for producing that output. The term $l(-c_X)$ may then become appreciable. Now if $X < x$, c_X must be negative; an increase in the scale of the plant will lower short-period total cost. It follows that if any attention is paid to this element, it will work in the direction of increasing the scale of plant chosen. It will thus do something to offset the tendencies described in the previous paragraph, but it seems most unlikely that it will go so far as to offset them altogether.

VIII

What is the theory of market equilibrium which corresponds to this case of polypolistic expectations? Once again it is necessary to distinguish between the marginal and the intramarginal firms; but it is no longer possible to define a marginal firm as one which expects to make no more than a normal profit. For each sort of firm will expect to make a larger profit in its close period than it will be confident of making in its open period. Thus those expectations which will just induce a firm to come in will be for a *more than normal* profit in the close period just offsetting a *less than normal* profit in the open period. On that basis it is just worth while to come in; but it will be more tempting to come in on that basis if one is a Snatcher, being specially interested in short-period profit. Marginal firms are thus very likely to be Snatchers. I think that this conclusion accords very well with experience, which finds a very common characteristic of an industry with genuinely free entry to be a rapid turnover of marginal firms.

This rapid turnover is not necessarily a wasteful process; but I think we are justified in regarding it as being, in general, a source of waste. But the wastes which are associated with it are not such as can be analysed in terms of static excess capacity. So long as these firms can produce profitably there is no reason why they should not produce more or less up to capacity; once they cease to be able to do so, they are heading for disaster.

So far as the intramarginal (and comparatively stable) firms are concerned, their expectation of future competition will prevent them from over-expanding their plants in the way they were supposed to do in the 'simple' theory. In their close period (immediately after their plant is put up) there is no reason why they should not produce up to capacity; later on, when their competitors have arrived, they will (if they have calculated aright) be producing no more than the output for which their plant was planned, so that the usual excess capacity of the static kind is, formally at least, present. But it should be noticed that all that has happened at this stage is that the dynamic excess capacity of the simple expectations case has been transmuted into a static excess capacity. And this, indeed, is not the end of the story. When such firms come to replace their plants, they will still (so we may suppose) have polypolistic expectations, which will cause them to reduce their plants to that size which would be appropriate to them if they were marginal firms. The 'static' excess capacity accordingly disappears; it turns out to have been 'dynamic' after all!

We must, I think, conclude that the real evils of this sort of industrial organisation (and industrial psychology) are very inadequately expressed in terms of static excess capacity. The real wastes, which we should expect to find in practice, are much more obvious, much less highbrow. They consist in the turnover of marginal firms, and in the inability of the steady firms to expand their plants to such a size as will enable them to take full advantage of the economies of large-scale production.

IX

I now turn to the case of *oligopolistic expectations*, where the firm considers that the amount of competition which it has to expect in the open period is a function of its own close-period price-policy. This gets us nearer to the field in which Harrod is interested though it should be noticed that we are still retaining the assumption that the general state of demand, for the products of the industry as a whole, is expected to remain static.

As before, we commence our study by a consideration of the standard equations.

The cross-term in the first equation is now no longer negligible; an increase in short-period output (a reduction in short-period price) may now suffice to deter competitors, and may therefore increase the demand for the firm's product in the open period. The cross marginal revenue will then be positive. This means that the classical equation of short-period marginal revenue to short-period marginal cost is liable to under-estimate the short-period output which it will be profitable to produce. But there is more to be said on the matter than that.

It is possible, if our firm is very much of a Sticker, that it may be largely uninfluenced by the straight terms in its first equation; its short-period output may be mainly determined by the effect of that output on long-period sales. We can even think of an extreme case (that of the *Perfect Sticker*) in which short-period output will be solely determined by the condition $R_x = 0$.

What would be the practical meaning of the equation in this limiting form? It is not to be supposed that the firm could go on expanding the long-period demand for its product by indefinite increases in short-period output. There will be some short-period price which will be so low that it does all that can be done in the way of deterring competitors; once short-period output is greater than the output corresponding to this critical price, the cross marginal revenue is *necessarily* zero. Thus the condition $R_x = 0$ merely implies that short-period output must be kept greater than this critical output; but it does not tell us how much greater. To that extent short-period output appears to be indeterminate. Yet there is in fact no point in reducing price below the critical price; so that it seems fair to think of the Perfect Sticker as fixing a price which is low enough, in his view, to deter competitors, and then selling what he can sell at that price. Now this is a kind of behaviour which begins to look, in a certain sense, familiar. One begins to ask whether it is not the case that the firms which have been interviewed by Andrews[7] are firms which are (or think themselves to be) Perfect Stickers?

It is entirely consistent with the present theory that most firms should be Perfect Stickers; whether or not that is so is an empirical question. But theory can nevertheless insist that the Perfect Sticker is a theoretically extreme case; that for anyone who gives any weight at all to the *l* terms in his equations the costs of the policy we have been describing may be very formidable. There is nothing inconsistent in being a Snatcher and having oligopolistic expectations; an entrepreneur who gives fair weight to both short-period and long-period considerations may well decide, on occasion, that the output needed to deter competitors will be, in the short run, too expensive

---

[7] The reference is to P. W. S. Andrews, *Manufacturing Business* (1949).

to produce. He must then resign himself to the probable appearance of competitors; in spite of the chance which he had of acting otherwise, he will in fact act as if his expectations were polypolistic.

X

Let us return to the Perfect Sticker and look at his second equation. He is doing all he can to put off potential competitors, and the long-period demand which he expects must be established on that basis. Since he neglects l terms, he will determine the size of his plant solely on the basis of long-period marginal revenue (which is now a function of long-period output only) and long-period marginal cost. His equations have accordingly reduced to the limiting form

$$R_x = 0, \qquad R_X = C_X.$$

The behaviour which is represented by these equations is worth a little consideration.

It may conceivably happen that the firm believes in its ability, by keeping price sufficiently low, to keep out competitors altogether. If so, it will follow that the choice of a short-period output which is consistent with the first equation will cause the long-period demand curve confronting the firm to be the same as the short-period demand curve. That is to say, though its expectations would not have been simple if it had acted differently, it has got itself into a position which is such that it can allow itself to have simple expectations. The complete position which it will take up will therefore be the same as that which it would have taken up if its expectations had been simple. It will plan for an equal output in the close period and in the open period; in consequence, *though it does not know that it is doing it (or anything equivalent)* it will in fact act in such a way as to make short-period marginal revenue equal to short-period marginal cost. Thus, provided that short-period output is greater than the critical output, it does not after all matter whether the firm is a Sticker or a Snatcher; it will act the same way in either case. And the way in which it will act is precisely that which emerged from our study of simple expectations. If the firm were a marginal firm, it would then follow that it was in a state of static excess capacity; but a firm which was in the situation we have just been describing does not look much like a marginal firm – its position is hardly distinguishable from that of the textbook monopolist!

The somewhat paradoxical conclusions which we have just reached are indeed to be attributed to the fact that we have been examining an extreme case. It is very extreme to assume that our firm can get into such a position, by its low price policy, that it can be *sure* of excluding competitors. The most we should expect, in an industry which in any way deserved the name of competitive, is that it would feel that it had a good chance of keeping them out. If so, it could not attain to the position we have been supposing, in which it could be treated as having *simple* expectations; the most which could be expected would be that its expectations would be mildly polypolistic. It would then work on the assumption that long-period demand would be somewhat less than short-period demand, but perhaps not so very much less. It would then follow (applying our analysis of the polypolistic case) that its short-period output would be somewhat in excess of its planned long-period output; and that excess might be quite sufficient to abolish its static excess capacity.

XI

All this assumes that a short-period output in excess of the critical output can profitably be chosen. A Perfect Sticker will (as we have seen) always choose such an output; but if the short-period costs of producing an output as large as this are high, it is hardly conceivable that the firm will behave as a Perfect Sticker. If such an entrepreneur pays any attention at all to short-period costs, he will always be looking over his shoulder to see if this *strong* policy is worth while. Now it is most unlikely that it will be worth while unless it can be maintained and carried through; thus it will not be worth while unless the long-period output which is being planned for is itself greater than the critical output. In the case of a firm which is operating under strongly diminishing costs, this latter condition is perhaps not unlikely to be satisfied — so that the balance is likely to swing in favour of a *strong* policy. But when costs are falling less steeply, or when the firm has more of the Snatcher mentality, the balance may swing the other way.

But whichever way the balance swings, the general results of our study of oligopolistic expectations go far to confirm those which we got in the polypolistic case. Such firms as are Stickers by disposition and such as have strongly diminishing costs are likely to have a bias in favour of a *strong* policy of excluding competitors; they will accordingly act as if their expectations were no more than mildly polypolistic. Firms whose costs are falling less steeply will be unable to afford so strong a policy; if they are Snatchers by disposition, they will not care to attempt it, even if they could afford it. They will thus act as if their expectations were strongly polypolistic. We are thus brought to a classification of firms which appears very similar to that which we reached in the polypolistic case. For firms which belong to the second of these types will behave in a manner which is broadly similar to that which we associated with the marginal firms of our former model; while the first type has the same sort of correspondence with the steady intramarginal firms.

XII

I have so far maintained the assumption that the general state of demand for the products of the industry remains stationary, and is expected to remain stationary, throughout the whole story; the various states of expectation which we have been considering differ solely with respect to the expected intensity of competition. There would, I think, be no difficulty in superimposing upon this analysis the consequences of alternative hypotheses about the growth, and expectations of the growth, of this general demand. But most of what has to be said under that head is no way specially concerned with the structure of the market under consideration; it is not at all specially concerned with *imperfect* competition. If entrepreneurs expect a future expansion of demand, they will install larger plants than they need in the short run; and during the short run these plants will not be used to capacity. In a complete statement of the theory here adumbrated places would have to be found for a number of elementary points of this sort. But I do not think that I need trouble to lay them out here at the tail of this article.

There is, however, one matter which is excluded by the 'static' assumptions which we have maintained, and which does unquestionably belong to the problems we have been discussing. We have been obliged, by our assumption of a stationary state of demand for the products of the industry, to imply that the demand which the firm can expect in the open period is never greater than the demand which it can expect in the closed period – that the one differs from the other solely because of the (possible) arrival of competitors in the latter case. This is evidently unrealistic.[8] Now this point is not fully met by the admission that the theory needs to be extended to meet the case of a general growth in demand. For there remains the possibility (which links on to our discussion of oligopolistic expecta-

---

[8] As Harrod rightly insisted when he saw a first draft of this paper.

tions) that the firm itself may not merely carry a *strong* policy to the point of maintaining its close-period market in the open period, but may endeavour to build up its goodwill (by moderation in price-fixing, and also by advertisement and other selling expenditure) to the extent of expanding its market in the further future beyond what it can attain in the near future. Evidently this may happen without an expansion in the *volume* or *scale* of demand for the products of the industry; but it does imply that the firm can influence the *character* of the demand with which it is faced. If such influence is possible (goes on being possible), and if costs are falling in such a way as to make the strong policy possible also, then the firm which is most successful in pursuing the strong policy must come to dominate the industry, so long as the volume of demand for the product as a whole is not increasing. This, however, is in its turn a trite conclusion; I mention it merely in order to show how it links up with the general discussion of this paper.

What I have tried to discuss in this paper is the old story of Imperfect Competition with Free Entry; not Monopoly, nor the Tendency to Monopoly. Some would hold that Imperfect Competition, in this sense, is almost a thing of the past; but even if that were so, it would remain worth study, because it is more nearly an effective alternative to existing forms of industrial organisation than the Perfect Competition which preceded it as a theoretical model. The view of it which I get is related to that put forward (in 1953) by Harrod (and of course owes its origin to Harrod's work); but it is not identically the same. I agree with Harrod that there has been too much fuss about static excess capacity; while dynamic excess capacity (very real trouble though it often is) has nothing special to do with imperfect competition. Yet, having said that, I must add that more seems to me to be left of the old doctrine about the 'wastes of competition' than he seems to have come to allow. Where I still find such wastes are in the disincentive to large-scale investment in an unassured market, and in the incentive to small-scale 'snatching' – not in anything which could be detectable in the regular organisation of the ordinary successful, or moderately successful, firm. But these wastes are quite genuine wastes; the fact they have been so generally noticed by practical men does not mean that they are beneath the attention of economic theorists.

Whether these evils are greater than the evils of monopoly, or near-monopoly, is a question on which it is still permissible to have more than one opinion. Personally, I do have more than one opinion. Circumstances alter cases.

13

Limited Liability:
Pros and Cons

This essay was written for a conference, organised by the Acton Society, which was held at the Certosa di Pontignano, Siena, in September 1979. It was published in the proceedings of that conference, *Limited Liability and the Corporation*, edited by Tony Orhnial (Croom Helm, 1982).

The shareholder in a company with limited liability is an anomalous animal. He has rights of ownership, without the responsibilities of ownership. His admission was a major departure from the age-old principles of property and contract on which the growth of trade and industry, up to the time of his appearance, had depended. What were the reasons for his admission? And what have been its consequences?

There is not much doubt why he had to be admitted. If there were no provision for limited liability, every firm (in a private enterprise economy) must have just one owner, or it must have a small group of owners. It would have to be a small group of owners when each was liable for the debts of the firm, if it ever came to be wound up, to the full extent of his wealth, his personal wealth. So it would be most unwise to invest in a firm, as part-owner, unless one was prepared to keep in close touch with its affairs, so as to see that one was not ruined by the mistakes that it made. To be a 'sleeping partner', without limited liability, would be exceedingly dangerous.

Thus the capital that was used by a firm would inevitably be limited by what its proprietor, or the small group of proprietors, could personally put up, and by what they could borrow. But the amount they could borrow would itself be limited by the security they could offer; that would depend upon what they themselves had put up, and ultimately, upon their personal wealth. Even in such conditions a firm might become large, by earning large profits and reinvesting them. But it could not start large; and the development of such industries as need to make large investments of capital in order to produce at all would be severely hampered. Indeed, if there were no limited liability, such investments could hardly be made at all, except in the public sector. Thus it is not surprising that the building of railways was historically connected with the coming of limited liability.

In so far as one associates economic progress with economies of scale (and though there are disputes among economists about the degree of the association, it can hardly be denied that there is some association) it must be regarded as a major achievement of limited liability that it has made much of our economic progress possible. There may be other forms of organisation which would have had the same effect; but this is the form which has been used in most 'capitalist' countries.

Looking then at this original use of limited liability, as a means of enabling entrepreneurs to get control of more capital than they could put up themselves, or could borrow on bonds or debentures, it is already apparent that the 'ownership' of the company by the shareholders, who are introduced for this purpose, is little more than nominal. The shareholders, by law, have the right to elect the directors; but in practice, when an issue is made, the directors are in place before the shares are issued; those who subscribe to the issue show by subscribing that they have no desire to turn those directors out. Thus, whatever the legal position, the fact is that capital is being provided by shareholders, just as it would be provided by bondholders – only on different terms. While the bondholder is promised a fixed rate of interest the shareholder is promised a share in profits. The shareholder is much more like a bondholder than he appears to be in legal theory. That this is the right way of looking at the matter is shown by the fact that the terms of an equity issue can be varied, just as interest offered to bondholders can be varied, by adjusting the capital that the proprietors, becoming directors, are supposed to be putting up, and of course in other ways. There are qualifications to this in the field of takeover bids (to which I shall be coming later) but usually it is nearer to reality to think of the shareholder as a peculiar kind of bondholder than to think of him as part-owner of the company.[1]

Now how has it been possible to raise capital on these peculiar terms – capital which, it must be supposed, could not be raised, or could not be so advantageously raised, by borrowing at fixed interest? This is a key question; it will be convenient, when attempting to

[1] See my early essay on 'Uncertainty and Profit' reprinted as volume II, essay 2 in this collection.

answer it, to take it in two stages, beginning with the case in which the shares are not freely transferable, and going on to the more important case when they are. The former is quite a real case; it extends beyond the case of the private company, or non-quoted company, where there are legal restrictions on transferability; for there may be *de facto* restrictions, as when the new shareholders are no more than a moderate extension of the small group, who have direct knowledge of the business, to people who have personal knowledge of the directors, or some personal relation with them. It will be useful to begin by considering this private company case, since it brings out, by contrast, how important is the matter of transferability.

Already in the case of non-transferable shares, we have to consider the matter from the two points of view, that of the investor who is to buy the shares, and that of the company, as represented by the directors, which is issuing them. Take first the investor's position. Why should he buy shares, when he could have invested in bonds? That the equity investment may be looked on as a hedge against inflation is an argument in its favour which in some recent years may well have been of much importance; but it may be disregarded here for, at the time when limited liability first prospered, it cannot have been significant. It must have been another advantage which was the attraction.

One may look at the matter in terms of the probabilities of return that are offered on the two alternatives. All that has to be considered, when the share is to be non-transferable, is the annual return which is to be expected, in some (representative) future year. If the capital were raised on a bond, it could only have been raised on the bond if there were a high probability that the interest agreed would be paid; there would nevertheless be a (usually small) probability that the borrower would be unable to pay, so that a part (or the whole) of the capital that had been invested would be lost. In the case of the share, it will be useful to suppose that there is some *most probable return*,[2] which plays much the same part as the agreed return on the bond. The maximum that can be lost (when there is limited liability) is the same as with the bond − total loss of all that has been invested. The probability of total loss is however greater, since the claims of bondholders must be met before there can be anything to distribute on the shares. The probability of partial loss

---

[2] *Most probable* is to be understood as it would be understood in a discussion of this sort in practice. The reader must put out of his head the concepts of mathematical probability theory, which do not apply, since the decision in question is unique.

(a return which is significantly less than that which appeared the most probable) is clearly much greater in the case of the share. Both of these are disincentives to investing in shares. What is there to be set against them? It might seem, at first sight, that all that there is to set against them is the probability of a return which is greater than the most probable return; this is zero in the case of the bond, but in the case of the share may well be substantial. One, at least, of the attractions of shareholding, as against bondholding, is the possibility of what one might call extra gains.

I do not believe, as I shall be explaining in a moment, that the possibility of extra gains is the only attraction which is normally offered to potential shareholders. If it were to be a major attraction, the investor would have to be a bit of a gambler — who is characteristically willing to swap a high probability of a moderate loss against a low probability of a gain that is large in comparison. It is indeed very likely, as we shall be seeing, that a propensity to gamble is one of the things that contribute to explain the growth of equity investment. But the extra gains that are possible from investing in a share with restricted transferability can rarely be enough to arouse the propensity to gamble. There must be something else.

What that is emerges as soon as we consider the alternatives from the company's point of view. When saying that the agreed return on the bond and the most probable return on the share were comparable, it was not implied that they will be equal. There is a good reason why the return on the share should be higher. It is to the interest of the company (that is to say, of the former proprietors) to offer a prospect of a higher return on the share, because (so long as the question of control does not arise) finance by share-issue diminishes risk.

Interest would have to be paid in good and bad times alike; but in bad times the dividend would be reduced, so the burden of finance by shares would be less. It is true that it would be expected that in good times the dividend would be increased; but it is precisely in such times that an increased out-payment can most easily be borne. The firm would be insuring itself, to some extent, against a strain which in difficult conditions could be serious, at the cost of an increased payment in conditions when it would be easy to meet it. It is in this sense that the riskiness of its position would be diminished.

It would be worth its while to pay a premium to secure this reduction in risk; it would thus be worth its while to offer a (most probable) higher return on the share.

This assumes, it will be noticed, that the firm is itself what economists would call *risk-averse*, while it has been allowed that the investor may possibly have a tendency the other way, having a positive liking for some sorts of risks. What happens if (as in our case of the non-transferable share is really more likely) the investor also is a risk averter? Financing by shares transfers a risk from the firm to the investor. If the investor himself is a risk averter, he will not accept the transfer without exacting a premium; but, as has just been shown, it will be to the firm's interest to offer it, up to a point. The premium will have to be higher (so equity financing will be less attractive to the firm) if potential investors are risk averters than if they are gamblers. But the existence of risk aversion among potential investors does not necessarily cut off equity investment.

Such an analysis, when applied to a real case, would be altogether too sketchy. Far too many things have been left out. All the same, it should start us thinking on the right lines.

One of the things which has been left out was concealed in the use that was made of 'most probable return'. Most probable to whom? It is almost inevitable that the 'insiders' who are raising the capital have more information about the prospects of the firm than 'outside' investors can have (though this does not necessarily mean that the insiders have better judgement of it). Investors may be, and often have been, misled into buying shares which they would not have bought if they had had more information, information that was somewhere available. A major objective of company law has been the removal, or at least the reduction, of some of the chief sources of inequality in information; in so far as that endeavour is successful – it can never be wholly successful – it must be favourable, at least in the long run, to the growth of equity investment. For a widespread awareness of gross inequalities in information must increase the risks, to the investor, of investment in shares. And that, if he is a risk averter (and perhaps not only if he is a risk averter), must make it harder to persuade him to 'bite'.

For this reason, and not only for this reason, the circle of investors who can be tempted in, as shareholders, on terms that are profitable to the issuing firm, must be expected to be rather narrow – so long as the condition of restricted transferability is maintained. Even a modest injection of share capital may nevertheless help, if only because it will improve the firm's credit and thus make it easier to raise loan capital also. But if the additional capital that is required is large, not enough can be done in this way. Much more can be done if the restriction on transferability is removed. The situation of all parties is then transformed.

There can, in the first place, be a much stronger appeal to the propensity to gamble. When transferability is restricted, the investor must expect to wait quite a time for the possibility of extra gains; and when they appear (if they do appear) they can hardly be 'glittering prizes'. But when the share is transferable, there is a chance that it will be possible to sell it at a profit, even in the quite short run. I put this in the first place for historical reasons. Big issues of shares have always been most easily placed when there is a bull market, when the market most resembles what Keynes called it, a 'casino'. The South Sea Bubble, and the Mississippi adventure of John Law, its French contemporary, are, of course, the classical examples.

What these examples also show is that the association of share issue with a bull market is one that goes both ways. This is because the transferable share, carrying limited liability, is a liquid asset. It is not as liquid as cash, or as the closer substitutes for cash; but it is liquid in the sense that it can be turned into cash, at short notice, whenever cash is required. So the successful speculator can take his profit, whenever it seems good to him to take it. Even if he does not sell, he has an asset against the security of which he can borrow, then, perhaps, using the proceeds of the loan to buy more shares. Thus a speculative boom is built up. Where does the money come from? The answer, as economists are by now well aware (but it took them much trouble to find it) is that the market as a whole (meaning by that the total of those who are dealing on the market), because it is regarding the share as a liquid asset, is willing to hold a smaller proportion of its assets in monetary form than it was before the boom started. New shares, the dazzling prospects of which have been well advertised, are ideal as a speculative counter. Ways of controlling speculative booms have indeed been developed, far beyond anything that was contemplated in the eighteenth century; but the potentiality of such booms is still present, when anything occurs to light it up.

Now though it is in a bull market that shares are most easily placed (and therefore, from the point of view of the issuing firm, most cheaply placed) they will have to be held in the end; and at that stage those who hold them must surely be risk averters. Even so there are advantages, to the investor, of transferability. One of them, still, is the liquidity advantage. The share can still be disposed of, at a price, if the shareholder changes his mind about the prospects of the company, or if he wishes to sell for any other reason. Another, which comes from the combination of limited liability with transferability, but which is not fully effective until the market in shares is generally well developed, is that the investor can reduce his risks by diversifying his portfolio. Under limited liability, as we have seen, the shareholder is made more like a bondholder, in that he cannot lose more than he has put in; so he can imitate the age-old practice of lenders at fixed interest, diminishing his risks by spreading them. It is only the risk of loss on his portfolio, as a whole, which matters to him. If the securities in which he invests are different, being subject, at least to some extent, to different risks, the risk of loss, on the portfolio as a whole, must be less than the risk on any single investment. Without limited liability this could not be done, since investment even in a second enterprise would increase the investor's risks; but with limited liability it can be. It is this, combined with the liquidity advantage, which explains why it is possible to issue shares at no more than a modest 'premium', when there is limited liability and transferability, even though investors are risk averters.

But let us now look at some of the consequences. It is inherent in these advantages, both in the liquidity advantage and in the practice of risk spreading, that the individual shareholder, in a fully developed limited liability system, must tend to lose contact, other than a purely financial contact, with the companies of which he is legally part owner. His right to elect directors must then become, in most circumstances, a mere formality. There are special cases in which this does not happen; but let us begin by considering the more usual case when it does.

The firm is now (we will take it) well established; it has been well established for some considerable time. Who controls it? and on what principles should we expect them to control it? The first of these questions takes time to come up, for (as we have seen) the original directors are in place at the beginning. But the time will come when they have to be replaced; successors, on occasion, will have to be found. When provision for the election of directors by shareholders has become ineffective, the directors themselves must make provision for succession. It is however by no means evident that the method of providing successors by co-option is any less effective, economically, than that which has to be used in the private business, or partnership. It should indeed be more effective, since in the latter case the choice is likely to be confined to members of a few families, while the directors of a company are not so confined. The company is ruled by what, in political terms, would be called an oligarchy; but experience seems to show that 'open' oligarchies, which recruit themselves from wider circles, are more efficient, and more durable, than those where recruitment is narrower.

One may approach the other question by thinking of that which is familiar in examination papers in economics: what does the entrepreneur maximise? So long as one can think of a single entrepreneur in command of a business that belongs to him, there is no doubt what he should be expected to maximise – the discounted value of expected net returns (discounted at his individual rate of 'time-preference'). Allowance will have to be made for risk, and perhaps for the toil and trouble involved; but all that is well understood. In the formation of the limited liability company the same principle, as we have indeed been seeing, will apply. The entrepreneur, at this stage, is the former proprietor, or proprietors, as directors; it is the prospective net return, accruing to them, which they will naturally seek to maximise. But after formation it should correspondingly be the prospective net return to the shareholders as a whole which is maximised. That is surely the legal theory; but when one goes on to our late stage, when there is a new generation of directors, and the shareholders have lost touch with the company, can that legal theory still be realistic? One can more easily imagine the directors seeing it to be their duty to do their best, not for the shareholders, but for the company. But what is the company?

It is tempting to answer this question in terms of idealism, idealism in the philosophical sense. The company is an entity, to which those who work for it owe allegiance, as one owes allegiance to the state, to one's church, or to one's trade union. But to extend these rather high-falutin' ideas to a company whose business it is to make (say) biscuits must surely make it (as Shakespeare would say) 'a little o'er-parted'. Cannot the company, whose interests are to be served, be given a more concrete meaning? One can see several meanings which might, on occasion, be given to it.

In each of these meanings the company would be identified with people; for it is people, some people, whose interests must ultimately be served. But the core of people whose interests are served may be narrowly or widely defined. It may just consist of the directors (or perhaps of no more than the managing director); it may consist of the management as a whole. Or sometimes of the management plus a nucleus of the work force. And why not of the work force as a whole? To this last alternative, in spite of the political pressures behind it, there are obvious objections. On the one hand the inclusion of the whole work force implies a high degree of rigidity in employment, which in times of technological change can be very cramping. On the other, much of the work force is (normally nowadays) separately organised; it cannot, in view of its own allegiances, allow itself to be too closely identified with the company for which it works.

What is common to all these alternatives is that the shareholders are excluded from the core. They must be given their legal rights; but it is only if the company goes into liquidation that their legal rights become effective. They have no right to a continuing dividend; what dividend they are paid is whatever best suits the interests of the core.

That is not to say that the dividend may not be substantial. It is to the interest of the core to pay a dividend, and a dividend that is thought to be a reasonable one, because a failure to pay a reasonable dividend must diminish the market value of the shares. And it is to the interest of the core to keep up the market value of the shares — for two reasons.

The first, the traditional reason, is that a high value of existing shares makes it easier to raise more capital — either as share capital or as loan capital — if more capital is required. That can be important, though it should be noticed that it may cut both ways. By paying out less in dividends, retaining more capital in the business, there will be less need to raise capital outside.

The other, which in later times may have come to be of more importance, concerns takeovers and mergers. A takeover bid, in the light of what has been said, may be considered as a counter-attack by shareholders who, in the course of the process that has been described, have been so nearly pushed out. Although a 'change of government', shareholders turning out directors by direct election, is not more practicable than it was, the market has provided an alternative. The prices at which a company's shares are normally valued are based upon the expectation that the company will continue under the same management; for the sale of a few shares by one individual and their purchase by another cannot normally affect any voting. If, however, a company's policy is such that an outsider can feel sure that it is not doing its best for its shareholders, it will become worth his while to offer higher prices for large blocks of shares, in order to acquire enough voting power to change the management, either in person or in policy. Having brought about this revolution, the shares can be sold again, and if the prospects of the company, as assessed by the market, then seem to be sufficiently improved they can be sold at a profit. When directors have got themselves into the state of mind (the origins of which have been explained) of thinking that they are working for the interest of the 'company' or even of the 'public', or for anything other than the interests of their shareholders, they may, in accordance with the legal position, lay themselves open to a flank attack on these lines.

The outsider, who makes the bid, will itself, in most cases, be a company; and it will be easier for it to make the bid if its own shares are strong. For, on the one hand, it will then be possible to offer shareholders in the weak company shares in the strong company in exchange; and, on the other, if cash has to be offered, the cash can more readily be borrowed. Thus it is not only weak companies which have an interest to see that the value of their shares is maintained, for defensive reasons; it is also strong companies who have a corresponding incentive, so as to make it easier for them to expand by acquisitions. When the two incentives are taken together, they cover a good part of the ground; so the position of the shareholder is stronger than might appear at first sight.

The takeover sanction has a good reputation among economists; and there is no doubt that, in the case of a management that has gone sleepy, or has forgotten to keep its eye on profitability, it is a sanction that has an economic function. But what facilitates such takeovers also facilitates mergers and conglomerates; these are regarded with more suspicion. But perhaps we should always be suspicious. Both are dependent upon the fact that the (transferable) share is a liquid asset; and as such, it has a value which is much dependent upon what that value is expected to be in the quite near future. The market in shares has quite a short time-horizon. Those who control businesses, industrial businesses in particular, must look further forward. It is not necessarily to the social advantage that control should be tossed about, in pursuit of short-term financial gains.

We have seen that it is transferability, as well as limited liability, which gives the typical share its peculiar character. It is the combination which has enabled ownership to become anonymous. There is in that one great advantage, one probably overriding advantage, in that it has made large enterprise, which is also free enterprise, possible. But the divorce of ownership from responsibility for control is not in itself an advantage.

It may therefore be observed, in conclusion, that there is something to be said for the system, which seems to be evolving under the pressure of taxation, in which the shares of large companies are held, in large blocks, by institutions – banks, pension funds and so on – which have a sufficient stake in the company to have an incentive to keep in close touch with its affairs, just as the holder of a non-transferable share has an incentive to do. Such a system could indeed be regarded as that of the private company writ large. It would indeed lose something, perhaps much, in flexibility; but it could offer gains in other ways.

14

The Concept of Business Income

This was written for a conference of the International Institute of Public Finance, held at Taormina, Sicily, in September 1979. It was published in the proceedings of that conference; a version also appeared in the *Greek Economic Review*, December 1979. The full title, originally given, was 'The Concept of Income in relation to Taxation and Business Management'.

I think that in this paper the concept of 'capital gains' is greatly cleared up. It turns out that there are *two* distinguishable interpretations: what I call external gains and what I call exceptional gains. Endless confusion, with serious practical consequences, has resulted from their being superposed.

The subject of this paper is one with which I have been concerned on two quite separate occasions during my life as an economist. On each occasion I have had to think about it, but I have had to think about it in quite different ways. One was when I was writing the chapter on Income in my *Value and Capital* (1939), a chapter which has since been regarded, at least in some circles, as a rather standard presentation of the theory of the matter; the other was when I was a member of the British Royal Commission on the Taxation of Profits and Income (1950–53). What I mainly learned on the latter occasion was the remarkable difference between the meaning (or meanings) of income, as the notion appears to the economic theorist, and the meaning which is given to it, which indeed, as I shall be explaining, has to be given to it, when income is considered as an object of taxation. Nevertheless, though the meanings are different, they are related. Thus when the fiscal concept gets into difficulties, as it notoriously does in times of inflation, these difficulties raise issues which take one back to the theoretical concept. For it is something much nearer to the theoretical concept which, for his own purposes, the business man requires.

It is revealing to look at the issue historically. I think it is generally agreed that the ancestor of all modern income taxes is that which was imposed, in England in 1799, for the financing of the war against the French Revolution. It has often been said that this was a combination of five separate taxes, the 'schedules' which have been a formal feature of the British income tax ever since. The point was that incomes of different sorts had to be reached in different ways. It was easy to tax the interest on government debt, for the facts of that were directly known to the government; taxes on income from land were familiar, and could continue to be assessed in the old way; contractual salaries also were fairly easily assessable, by reference to the contracts by which they were paid. Where a difficulty arose was in Schedule D, business income. What was the income of a business man, say the owners of a cotton mill? (I take what would have been a leading case in the England of the time in question.) All that could be done, to begin with, would be to get him to state it himself ('self-assessment'), with just a hope that he could be shown up, from some sort of common knowledge, if what he declared seemed too outrageous.

For the fact was, at that stage, that one could not even be sure that the business man himself would know what his income was. When he was bidden to declare his income, he might well reply: what do you mean? And what answer could be given to him? Could anything be done but to refer to the old principle – already, at that date, an old principle – of the desirability of 'living within one's income'; if one spent more than one's income, one's prospect for the future would be damaged. So, on this line of thought, the income derived from a business would be the *maximum* that could be *safely* taken out of the business, for personal expenditure or for the payment of taxes, without damaging the prospects of the business. But that, it is clear, would be a matter of judgement; just how much is *safe*? The tax-collector would be in no position to form much of a judgement on the matter; so would have to rely, very largely, upon the taxpayer's judgement, who could not be prevented making a judgement very much in his own favour.

It was therefore inevitable, so long as this situation persisted, that income tax would bear less heavily upon the profits of business, than upon other incomes which could be more objectively assessed. It just could not reach profits in the way it could reach other incomes. An income tax with this deficiency could not be regarded as a fair way of taxing; and it is clear from the evidence that it was not regarded as fair. Later on, in England at least, but I suspect that the same story has been repeated in other countries, there has been a change.

I believe that the main cause of the change has been the development of the limited liability company, or corporation. A shareholder in such a company is nominally a part-owner of the company; but his situation is more realistically described if he is thought of as one who has lent money to the company, not on the promise of a fixed payment of interest on the loan, but on the promise of a share of profits. When the usual method of raising capital is by borrowing at fixed interest, no more need be required by the lender than that he should be assured of the general 'soundness' of the borrower; it is not necessary for him that the profit which is to be earned by the borrower should be exactly assessable. But if what is promised is a share in profits, the prospective shareholder has the right to enquire: what profits? So the growth of the company form of organisation required the development of company law, including regulations for the ascertainment of profits, in what could at least be made to appear to be an objective manner. This put the tax-collector in a much better position, for he now had an ally. There was the shareholder, with another interest in the ascertainment of profits, who came to his assistance.

At this point the accountant enters. He has now to be given a regular place in the ascertainment of profit – a duty to provide a fair account of the performance of the business, for the benefit, in the first place, of the shareholders; but the work which has been done for the benefit of shareholders can also be used for the assessment of tax. He will naturally desire to be as objective as possible, in order to minimise disputes between the (several) parties that are now concerned. But this means that he cannot measure profit, or income, in the former sense, of the maximum that can be *safely* taken out of the business, for on that there can be endless argument. He must seek to measure profit in some other way. It was fortunate, for him, that there was another way to which he was already accustomed.

One does not need to have much detailed knowledge of the history of accounting to see that its origins must go back to a time when industry was rudimentary; so that the main kind of activity for which accounts were required was merchanting. There are several ways in which the terminology of accounting bears traces of its mercantile origin. 'It is characteristic[1] of the business of the mer-

---

[1] I am borrowing this passage from a paper of my own on *Capital Controversies: ancient and modern*, where I had to make use of this analysis of accounting procedure for another purpose. (The paper is reprinted in *EP*; the passage in question is on pp. 157–8.)

chant that it is divisible into separate units. Every bale of cotton or pound of cheese which ever forms part of his stock is acquired at a particular date and sold at a particular date: purchase, retention and sale constitute a separable transaction. (Complete separation is of course not attained in practice, since there are overheads which have to be allocated; but it is so nearly attained that it sets the pattern.) So the accounts of the merchant may be regarded as a bundle of separate accounts. Purchases and sales are indeed going on continuously, so that if they are set out in a time-sequence, the separate accounts will overlap; it is only if an account were prepared for the whole history of the business, from first setting-up to final closing-down, that a record of purchases and sales would tell the whole story. In any annual period there must be transactions which have started before the beginning of the year but are completed within the year; there must similarly be transactions which are begun within the year but are not completed at the end. But these in the case of a mercantile business cause the minimum of trouble. They can be dealt with by the accepted rule of never taking a profit on any transaction before it is completed. The initial stock of the year will then be brought in *at cost*; and the final stock will be valued at cost in the same manner.

Now what was to be done, on these principles, with plant and machinery? The use of land, being regarded as a permanency, could be brought in as a regular charge; but the plant and machinery is not expected to last indefinitely, though its use is spread over a time which is longer than the accounting period. It is important to observe that it is the extension of the use to a duration which is longer than the accounting period which creates the difficulty. There would be no difficulty, here as in the mercantile case, if the account were drawn up for the whole life of the business, from first setting-up to final closing-down. It is for the annual account that there is the problem. The cost of the machine has to be set against a series of sales, the sales of the outputs to which it contributes, but some of these sales are sales of the present year, some are later, and some, maybe, earlier. There is thus a problem of imputation; how much is to be reckoned into the costs of this year, and how much into the costs of other years? It is the same problem as the allocation of overheads, and to that, as is well known, there is no firm *economic* solution.

Neither has the accountant found a solution – only a name and a set of, essentially arbitrary, rules. The 'depreciation quotas' must add to unity, but that is all that is known, at all firmly, about them.

The form of the account is preserved, but only by bringing in, as the capital which is supposed to be invested in the machine at the beginning of the year, that part which has not been absorbed (by being allocated as a cost to the outputs of preceding years) and by reckoning as the capital invested at the end of the year that part which has not been absorbed in those years not in this year – so that it is left to be carried forward to the future. This is in fact what accountants did, probably what they had to do, as soon as they were confronted with the problem. It was what they still do, even to this day.'

That the distribution of the accountant's depreciation quotas is essentially arbitrary is fairly well accepted nowadays; thus it has been discovered that it is open to the taxing authority to impose a different rule, for the assessment of profits that are liable to tax. (Accelerated depreciation, and so on.) There is thus no reason why there should be any simple rule which would cause the profits that are calculated by its use to have any correspondence with the income that would be assessed by the criterion with which we began – the maximum that can be *safely* taken out of the business. If we call the depreciation which would fall to be deducted from the receipts of the year, on this criterion, the *true* depreciation, the accountant's depreciation is at best a proxy for it. But, as we have seen, the true depreciation is a matter of judgement, so it provides no firm figure. Yet the question still arises – if the true depreciation could be assessed objectively, what relation to the accountant's depreciation would it have? This, we shall find, is by no means a nonsense question. There are some quite interesting things to be said about it.

It will be useful, for this purpose, to write out the accounts of the business in formal terms. Let R be the current receipts of the business during the year, E current expenses, C capital expenses. All these, we may take it, are quite objective. (There is indeed a question of what expenses are to be reckoned as capital expenses, but I shall come to that later.) In contrast with these 'firm' items, stand the initial capital, the final capital, and the depreciation, all of which are determined by the accountant in accordance with his accounting conventions. So I shall mark them with stars. K_0^* will thus be the initial capital, as it 'stands in the books', K_1^* the final capital and D^* the depreciation.

Then what the accountant presents are

(1) a current account, which could be written

$$\text{Current profit} = R - E - D^*$$

(2) a capital account, which would be written

$$K_0^* + C - D^* = K_1^*$$

From the capital account, given K_0^* and K_1^*, D^* follows; and then, from the current account, current profit is determined.

Now how is one to construct a 'true' set of accounts, with which this conventional account could be compared? In general, as I have insisted, it cannot be done, since what would have to replace K_0^* and K_1^* are no more than subjective estimates. There is, however, an exceptional case, an improbable case, but nevertheless a possible case, in which it could be done. This is the case of the business which had changed hands at the beginning of the year, having been purchased for a price which we will call K_0 (unstarred, since there is nothing conventional about it); and which is then sold again at the end of the year, for a price which we may similarly call K_1. I shall make a good deal of use of this 'double take-over' model, which I find to be a convenient tool to bring out principles.

There can, I think, be little doubt that an accountant, who was asked to do the accounts of a business with this peculiar history, would refuse to do them in terms of K_0 and K_1; he would insist in doing them in terms of K_0^* and K_1^*, the values which 'stand in the books'. The economist, however, would find K_0 and K_1 much more interesting. He would want to start from K_0 and K_1 (doctoring them, maybe, for changes in the value of money, but that again I shall come to later); it would be these *market values* which he would want to take as representing the initial and final capital.

With a double take-over, K_0 and K_1 would be values that would be available to the accountant; what could he make of them? Though he refused to use them for the construction of a capital account *of the business*, he could not refuse to use them for a capital account *of the proprietors*, the temporary proprietors, the proprietors during the year. But in that account, if K_1 stood on one side, and $K_0 + C - D^*$ on the other, it is unlikely that there would be a balance. There would be a difference, which he would reckon as a capital profit, a capital gain (or loss).

It will be noticed that the sum of current profit and capital profit is

$$(R - E - D^*) + K_1 - (K_0 + C - D^*)$$

$$= R - E - C + K_1 - K_0$$

from which all starred items have disappeared. The distinction between C and E (current expenses and capital expenses) has also become immaterial.

If we denote the 'economist's' depreciation by D (suppressing the star), the depreciation, that is, which would be calculated by using K_0 and K_1 as initial and final capital, his capital account would have K_1 on one side and $K_0 + C - D$ on the other, which would balance, since D had been chosen to make it balance. So he would show no capital gain; the whole of what the accountant reckoned as current profit + capital gain would appear as (undifferentiated) profit.

Now it is surely a question whether it is not a weakness of the procedure which has just been attributed to the economist, that it can make no distinction between current profit and capital profit. It is not just that such a distinction is commonly required by legislation; if it had not been the usual practice to pay attention to it, legislators and lawyers would not have paid attention to it – so we must look for a further reason. The events of the year, even from the point of view of the temporary properties have been of two kinds. There has been (1) the regular running of the business and (2) the double take-over. It is not mere curiosity to wish to know how much of the total profit to be attributed to each.

So one is brought back to the underlying question: why should anyone (apart from tax law and company law) want to have a *current* account of a business? At the time when it is drawn up, it relates to the past; nothing can now be done about the past: 'bygones are bygones'. The only purpose of having an account of the past is the guidance one hopes to get from it about future performance. The future is unknown, but action about it has to be taken, action that needs to be based on some evidence. The purpose of the current account is clarified when we look on it as a way of presenting some of that evidence.

This is the reason why the separation of current profit from capital profit is important. It is the current profit which has been earned in the past which is relevant to the future; the capital profit is *necessarily* irrelevant. That can readily be seen in the case of our two take-overs. Those who purchase the business in the second take-over will have wanted to look at the current profit, as part of the information on which to base their decision on how much to offer. A capital profit, accruing to the temporary proprietors (those of the year) would depend on what they in their turn had paid for the business in the past; but that, from the point of view of those to whom they sell, does not signify. What concerns them is the value of the business now, not its value at a date some time ago.

The current profit, when it is looked at from this point of view, should be an index of the performance of the business during the year to which it refers; elements which refer to its activity in previous years should in principle be excluded. The accountant's proxies, as is now notorious, do not succeed in excluding them. The $D*$ which he uses for depreciation is not an estimate, based in some way or other on the actual performance of the business during the year in question; it is derived, by conventional rules, from figures that are given to him, firm figures indeed, but figures of previous expenditure, which do not belong to the year for which the account is being made. In stationary conditions, when one year is much like another, that may not much matter; but in non-stationary conditions it is bound to be misleading.

Is there any way of cutting out this reference to the past, and still identifying a *current* profit? Keynes sought to do it by substituting 'user cost' for depreciation; but it is hard to see that user cost can ever be more than a subjective estimate. It does not make contact with the accountant's problems and therefore with tax problems, so it is not much help to us here.

Much more help can be got from the ingenious analysis of Erik Lindahl, published[2] as long ago as 1933. It may be translated into terms of our double take-over model as follows.

We start from the capital account (of the 'proprietors')

$$\text{Capital profit} = K_1 - (K_0 + C - D^{**})$$

in which I write D^{**} for D^*, as a sign that the accountant's way of measuring depreciation is no longer to be taken for granted. The first question to be decided, on Lindahl's approach, is to find a way of defining D^{**}, or rather $C - D^{**}$ (the *net investment* of the economist) so as to make the new capital account as meaningful as possible.

Let us re-arrange this capital account, writing it

$$K_1 - K_0 = (C - D^{**}) + \text{capital profit}$$

This shows at once that the problem is one of dividing $K_1 - K_0$, deciding how much is to be allocated to $(C - D^{**})$ and how much to capital profit.

K_0 has been defined as the price that was paid for the business at the beginning of the year. It may thus be regarded, in the manner that has become familiar, as the capitalised value of expected future returns, in what we are regarding as the current year *and afterwards*. K_1 is also a capitalised value but it relates to a different future. The future, for K_0, includes the activity of the year, but from

[2] See E. Lindahl, *The Concept of Income*, (1933), in *Economic Essays in Honour of Gustav Cassel*, (1935), pp. 399–418.

the future for K_1 that is excluded. This is one difference, but there is another – a difference of information. In the course of the year new information about the prospects of the business after the year is likely to have become available.

The account is drawn up, as is obviously necessary, after the end of the year; it is reasonable to take it that it is the prospect as it appears at the end of the year which is the last to be relevant. At that date the information implied in K_1 is already available. So K_1 is in a double sense a firm figure. It is not just given (by our double take-over assumption); it is also based upon the information available at the exact time at which (or for which) the computation is being made. But when this aspect is taken into consideration, it becomes apparent that K_0 is not a firm figure in this second sense. At the time when K_0 was established, some of the information on which K_1 is based was not yet available.

Consequently, if there is to be parity of information (and the account it to refer to information as it is at the end of the year) K_0 needs to be doctored. We have to consider what K_0 *would have been* if the information available at the end of the year had been available to it. This information includes (1) the actual performance of the business during the year, and (2) K_1 itself. At the end of the year these are known, so K_0^{**}, as I shall call the new substitute, is what K_0 would have been if the actuals of the year (R, E and C) had all been known, and K_1 had also been known. Though at time O these are all in the future, they must all be supposed to be known, with no uncertainty about them. Thus K_0^{**} is just what would be paid, at time O, for the right to receive R during the year and K_1 at the end of the year, on condition that E and C, during the year, are paid out. The contract in these terms is quite precise, with no uncertainty about it.

The introduction of K_0^{**} enables the capital account, as written above, to be divided into two parts

$$K_1 - K_0 = (K_1 - K_0^{**}) + (K_0^{**} - K_0)$$

Can we identify these two parts with the two parts of our former division, making $C - D^{**} = K_1 - K_0^{**}$ and $K_0^{**} - K_0$ the capital profit?

To interpret the capital profit in this way, making it simply a measure of the gain (or of course loss) due to change of information between time O and time 1, seems quite agreeable. One does want to think of it as a revaluation, due to new information, and that is what is shown. But the consequence, on the side of current profit, is, at least at first sight, surprising.

For the 'contract', as explained, is precise; it is so precise that it is possible to calculate $K_0{}^{**}$. We have only to introduce a rate of interest (r), which must be supposed to be established outside the business, and perform the discounting. Since the contract is certain, a gilt-edged rate of interest, with no risk-premium in it, will do. All that then remain to be specified are the dates, within the year, at which R accrues, and at which E and C are paid out. Nevertheless, because of the given rate of interest, these can all be accumulated, or discounted, to a single date, and we may suppose that that has been done. So let them be represented by their values at the *end* of the year. Then

$$R - E - C + K_1$$

is the value of the contract, at the end of the year; and this is to equal

$$(1 + r) K_0{}^{**}$$

Now see what happens when we put $C - D^{**} = K_1 - K_0{}^{**}$

$$\text{Current profit} = R - E - D^{**} = R - E - C + K_1 - K_0{}^{**}$$

$$= (1 + r) K_0{}^{**} - K_0{}^{**} = rK_0{}^{**}$$

So current profit is just the interest on the calculated value of the initial capital — interest that has accrued during the year.

Lindahl himself was well aware that this was the consequence of his proceeding; but what are we to make of it? We have been looking for a definition of current profit which, so far as possible, should register the performance of the business within the year, excluding what has happened before and what is to come after. But

$$rK_0{}^{**} = \left(\frac{r}{1 + r}\right) (R - E - C + K_1)$$

so that K_1, which is the capitalised value of expected net receipts *after* the year, would appear to have a large part, even, in many cases, the dominant part, in determining the *current* profit. So the Lindahl definition, when it is looked at in this manner, seems still to be infected by the future, having little to do with the performance of the current period.

There is, however, another way of looking at it. We are still defining current profit as $R - E - D^{**}$; and it follows from the definition of D^{**} that if it were to be the case that $C = D^{**}$, $K_0{}^{**}$ would equal K_1. Thus we can alternatively define D^{**} as the capital expenditure which would have to be incurred if capital were to be maintained intact, in the sense that the prospect of the business was as good at the end of the year as it was at the beginning, *as we can now see with hindsight that it was at the beginning.* That does look like a formulation which belongs to the current period, as rK_0^{**}, which we have seen to be equivalent, apparently does not.

It will be noticed that in this case, if $C = D^{**}$, and so $K_0^{**} = K_1$, current profit $= rK_0^{**} = rK_1$. So if $C = D^{**}$, so that capital is (just) 'maintained intact', the business can look forward, on the basis of information as at the end of the year, to earning in future years a current profit which is equal to that which it has earned in the current year. Indeed, if a sum of money equal to K_0^{**} had been invested in a security with no terminal date, yielding a fixed rate of interest r, rK_0^{**} would be the income that would be derived from that security *in each year.* So rK_0^{**} is the income, constant over time, which is equivalent, in terms of capital value, to that which could have been expected from the business, if what happened during the year had been foreseen at the commencement, and if the knowledge of its further prospects, which is present at the end of the year, had been available at the beginning. This is effectively what Friedman would call the *permanent income* derived from the business. It is to a concept of permanent income that the Lindahl analysis seems finally to come.

If a permanent income is to be derived from a business, it must surely be a continuing business; this is confirmed by what may well appear at first sight as a paradoxical consequence of the Lindahl definition. For suppose we apply it to the case of what is not a continuing business, a business that is set up at (or after) the beginning of the year and closed down at (or before) its ending. Receipts and expenses may be accumulated to the end of the year, as before; so the total net profit, in the notation we have been using, is $R - E$. (Since there is no sense in capital expenditure for the benefit of future production, when there is to be no future production, we may take it that $C = 0$.) How much is current profit, and how much is capital profit? The accountant would surely say that all of $R - E$ is current profit; there is no carry-over from the past, so his D^* must be zero. Keynes, I think, would take the same view; since there is no carry-over to the future, there can be no user cost. But that would not be Lindahl's view. He would say that since the venture is terminated, $K_1 = 0$; and as we have seen, $C = 0$. But K_0^{**} would not be zero; with K_1 and C both zero, K_0^{**} would be equal to the discounted value of $R - E$. Current profit would be interest on this; the remainder (with moderate interest much the greater part) would be capital profit.

This follows, inevitably, from the identification of current profit with permanent income. The only way in which a permanent income can be got from a non-permanent venture is by investing the proceeds at interest.

To this, one may be sure, the accountant would protest: the income in question is not an income of the business since it arises outside the business. It is, at the most, an income of the proprietors. As we have ourselves seen, there are reasons why it is important, for accounting purposes, to ascertain an income *of the business*; we must accept that by the Lindahl method this has not been done. Yet I do not think that what I have said about the Lindahl method has been in vain.

For it has enabled us to distinguish, more sharply than could be done in any simpler manner, between the two different distinctions which are hidden away in what purports to be a single distinction – that between current profit and capital profit. There is (1) the distinction between profit that is earned within the business and that which is earned, is some sense, outside it; let us call this the distinction between *internal* and *external* profit. There is (2) the distinction between *normal* profits and *exceptional* profit, which is so sharply identified in Lindahl's analysis. These two distinctions are entirely different. It may happen that an external profit is exceptional: it may happen that an exceptional profit is external; but there is no reason of principle why the two distinctions should coincide.

When a machine, only part of the capital cost of which has been written off, is sold by the business that has been using it for a price which is greater than that at which it 'stands in the books', the difference is reckoned by the accountant as a capital profit. He has a reason for doing this. He regards the profit as external; the firm is not in business to sell used machines. Gains that have been made in this way are irrelevant to the valuation of the firm as a 'going concern'. Once we have grasped the distinction between external and exceptional, we can understand that there is sense in the accountant's convention.

The economist, however, who is not particularly concerned with whether the profit is earned inside or outside, is, again quite properly, more interested in the normal-exceptional distinction. For the business itself, both are important; but one would think that it is the normal-exceptional distinction which is the more important. For it is this latter which corresponds most nearly to the subjective notion with which we began – of what can safely be taken out of the business for personal expenditure (or distribution of dividends) and for payment of taxes. A company is usually restrained by law from paying dividends 'out of capital'; so it is common practice to accumulate a reserve fund, or dividend equalisation fund, from which is can pay a 'normal' dividend even in years when profits have been *exceptionally* low. The fact that this is so commonly done is evidence that the conception of a normal profit, in the temporal sense that here is relevant, does play a part in business policy.

Now what is the bearing of all this on Taxation? I will be bold to say that I see no case for the treatment of external gains, for tax purposes, any differently from internal gains. The purpose for which they are so treated, by the accountant, seems to be irrelevant to the question of tax. This holds, not only for the taxation of companies, but also for the taxation of persons. In the British income tax, gains from betting, or from prizes (such as a Nobel prize) are excluded from tax, essentially on the ground that they are external, not being derived from the business from which the taxpayer earns his living. Gains from stock exchange speculation are taxed separately, essentially on the same ground. When I say that the internal–external distinction is irrelevant, I imply that all these should be taxed as income. And so – an even more startling conclusion – should gains from bequests.

Any widening of the scope of income tax, in this direction, must, however, make more critical the question of exceptional gains. For though the distinctions are different, there can be no doubt that in practice there are many external gains which do cause income (in the inclusive sense including external gains) to become *very* abnormal. If bequests – to take the leading example – were taxed as income, the income of the taxpayer, in the year in which the bequests were received, might well be many times his normal income, even his normal income after he had received the bequest. If income tax were proportional, imposed at the same rate whatever the income, this might not much matter. But no income tax is ever completely proportional; there is always an exemption limit and there usually is progression above it. To tax a large *exceptional* gain, accruing in one year only, having little or no relation to the taxpayer's normal circumstances, on a progressive scale, would surely be monstrous. A widening of the tax base to include external gains, if it were to be at all comprehensive, would therefore have to be accompanied by special treatment of exceptional gains.

That could not, I think, be an easy matter. One can think out schemes for doing it, but they get into great difficulties if they are carried very far. It would be inappropriate, when concluding this paper, to dilate upon them. Instead, I shall make two general points.

First, I am not meaning to suggest that a simple way, which may be thought to be suggested by the formal analysis I have taken from Lindahl, is in fact a solution. If 'true' income is interest on capital, as Lindahl appears to say, and if the rate of interest which is to be applied can be assumed to be given objectively, would not a tax on capital value be the best way of taxing income from capital? If it were to be a continuing tax, it would have to be applied at a rate which was less than the assumed rate of interest; thus if the rate of interest were 10%, a capital tax of 3 per cent would be equivalent to an income tax at 30 per cent per annum. Replacement of tax on income from capital by a capital tax is a project which naturally appeals to economists; but I would not wish to be thought to be recommending it myself. It is not just that the cost of repeated revaluations would be enormous; the principal objection is that the capital value of assets, which are not currently being sold, is a matter of judgement, or of opinion. The accountant's conventional way of measuring income, though (as we have seen) it has elements in it that are arbitrary, is largely based upon actual transactions, those which we have been symbolising by R and E. It would not be an improvement to replace this relatively firm assessment by one that in practice must even more, even much more, be arbitrary.

I avoided this difficulty in my model, by assuming that the business, the profit of which was being assessed, did actually change hands, in a take-over. When that occurs, it gives a *true* capital value; but (fortunately) it does not often occur. The mere purchase and sale of shares, which do not carry control with them, does not establish a capital value in the relevant sense.

The other point I want to make concerns inflation. If income from capital could be taxed by taxing capital, the tax, at least in principle, would be inflation-proof; for the assessment would be made, and the tax would be paid, in money of the same value. (I am of course abstracting from lags in the machinery of assessment and collection.) A conventional income-tax, as we know so well nowadays, is not inflation-proof, since the values that 'stand in the books' are based on costs that were incurred in earlier years, when money did not have the same value. It would be out of place, at the end of this paper, to say anything much about the proposals, now so widely canvassed, for mending this distortion. I will merely observe that the conventional accountant's method, even when it is applied in conditions of fairly stable prices (of final products) aims to do no more than to identify the surplus, above what is needed to maintain capital intact, when capital is interpreted as money capital; but this implies that if, with economic progress, the prices of 'machines' are falling, relatively to the prices of finished products, more will be deducted, on the accountant's method, than is necessary to keep the business in working order as a going concern. Perhaps it is just as well that that is so; it gives an incentive to take advantage of technical improvements. It follows, however, that if, in times of inflation, all that is desired is to give depreciation allowances which will have the same effect as those which were given in times of constant prices, the answer should be to write up the values carried forward by a *general* price-index. Yet it seems inevitable that when it is proposed to make corrections to the conventional allowances, to adjust to inflation, the question of whether the conventional allowances were appropriate, even in absence of inflation, is bound to be raised. So one comes back to the subjective assessment — how much can be *safely* taken out of the business — from which the accountant's procedure had been thought to be an escape. There are many things which inflation throws into the melting-pot, and this is one of them.

Part III
International Trade

15

Productivity and Trade

This is taken from my Inaugural Lecture, as Drummond Professor of Political Economy in Oxford, that was given in May 1953. A complete text of that lecture was published in *OEP* for June of that year. What appeared in my *Essays in World Economics* (1959) excluded an introductory section, on the history of the Chair I was occupying; it was then entitled 'The Long-term dollar problem'. I have here thought it proper to shorten it yet further. What had appeared to be the 'dollar problem' in 1953 was still appearing to be such in 1958, though it was on the point of abruptly changing its character. In later years all this topical part has dated very badly. But the core of my argument, the general issue which I raised, has not dated; it started discussions which have gone on, in one form or another, ever since. So it is better now to let it stand by itself.

What is the correct theory of the effects on international trade of disparate increases in productivity, between one country and another? I am thinking of the disparity as a long-run phenomenon, so the theory I am looking for must be a long-run theory. Since the disparate increases in productivity are to be thought of as going on all the time, there can be no state of equilibrium; but since we are to be interested in the process as a whole, not in particular incidents of the process, we need pay no attention to effects that are bound to be episodic. In practice, when a country experiences adverse trading conditions, it begins by running a deficit on its balance of payments — a deficit which is covered by loss of reserves (whether held in gold or in some other form) or in some other temporary way. But the extent to which such temporary expedients can be used is always limited; they can therefore do no more than provide breathing-time, without affording any permanent means of adjustment to an enduring difficulty. We are here to be concerned with permanent adjustments; we may therefore look across all such temporary expedients, and make it a rule that the balance of payments of every country goes on being balanced – somehow. The only countries which can export gold, so long as this rule holds, are the gold-producers; import of gold can only take place to the extent of the gold-producers' exports. Balance of payments deficits and surpluses also (for one country's surplus spells another's deficit) are otherwise ruled out.

This assumption of continuous balance is undoubtedly the right approach to the problem before us; it is justified in itself, but it is at the same time an immense convenience. It enables us to cut straight through a vast tangle of complications, which in practice occupies the whole foreground, and may easily prevent us from seeing the real issues. And it is not the only simplification which we are at liberty to make. Since our inquiry is concerned with the effect of productivity changes, we can also cut out the 'geometrical' complications which bothered the generation of Marshall and Edgeworth; we can go straight back to the basic simplicities of Ricardo and Senior.

The distinguishing assumption of the Ricardian theory was the hypothesis of *constant cost* – that all commodities (or at least all manufactured commodities) are produced at a cost per unit which is independent of the amount produced. Dubious as this assumption may be in many connections, in this place it is a very harmless simplification. For what makes cost curves slope upwards or downwards is changes in productivity *induced* by changes in the scale of output; in this inquiry, where we are concerned with the *effects* of changes in productivity, we should give ourselves unnecessary trouble if we bothered to sort out the spontaneous and induced changes into separate boxes. The assumption of constant cost merely enables us to treat all changes in productivity as spontaneous – and in the present context that does no harm at all.

I therefore assert with some confidence the perfect applicability of Ricardian theory to the problem which I have undertaken to examine. We can, indeed, not merely make Ricardo's assumptions, we can also ask some of Ricardo's questions. In particular, we must still distinguish between the real (or barter) effects of productivity changes and the monetary effects by which they are in practice so greatly complicated.

What I mean by barter effects are those which persist whatever the course of money incomes – those which remain even if we suppose that money incomes in the various countries can be changed in whatever way is necessary to make adjustment as simple as possible. By monetary effects I mean those which arise out of difficulties in the adjustment of money incomes. Nineteenth-century economists studied these monetary effects in terms of a particular 'monetary mechanism'; we are nowadays obliged to take a different view. But the changed approach to monetary problems does not prevent the distinction between real and monetary effects from holding good; it is, indeed, of crucial importance. For monetary difficulties are in principle capable of being eased, if not wholly dissipated, by appropriate institutions. Thus if the difficulty which we find is purely monetary, it ought to be possible to find a means of doing something about it; but if the monetary problem hides a real problem, no monetary wizardry can conjure it away.

The decks are now cleared, and we can get to work. I shall begin by setting out my analysis in rather formal terms.

Let us consider two countries, A and B, which are trading together, and which are such that productivity in A is increasing more rapidly than productivity in B. It will, I think, make little difference to the essence of the argument (and will certainly facilitate its exposition) if we neglect the expansion of productivity in B, and simply assume that productivity in A is increasing while that in B remains constant. We begin from a position in which the balance of payments between the two countries is in balance, as we are bound to do by our assumptions; but it does not matter how the balance has been brought about. It may be due to the classical forces which were thought to operate under free trade, or to changes in the volume of employment, or to import restrictions. On any of these suppositions the argument would be substantially unaffected.

I begin by laying down a proposition of central (though in relation to practical problems rather limited) significance. If productivity in A is increasing *uniformly* – at the same rate in all of A's industries – the barter effects of the development are most unlikely to be harmful to B. The simplest way of proving this proposition is to see what would happen if money incomes in B remained unchanged, while money incomes in A rose to the full extent of the rise in productivity. Then the cheapening of A-products would be wiped out by the rise in A-incomes, so that the prices of A-products would be unchanged. The prices of B-products are of course unchanged, so that all prices are unchanged. Money income in B is unchanged, so that there is no reason why B should buy any more or less of A-exports than before. But A-income has risen, and this will affect A's demand for B-exports. Though it is possible to construct weird cases in which the conclusion would not follow, we can surely be confident that in practice a rise in A-incomes, with all prices constant, would cause A's demand for B-exports to *rise*. This means that if A-incomes rose to the full extent of the rise in A-productivity, the balance of payments would turn in B's favour. If it is not to turn in B's favour, but to remain in balance, the rise in A-incomes must accordingly be less than the rise in productivity. But if A-incomes rise by less than the rise in productivity, there will be some reduction (however small it may be) in the prices of A-exports. Money income in B can remain constant, and the prices of B-products can remain constant; nevertheless the balance of payments can remain balanced, while B gets her imports from A rather more cheaply than before. The real income of the B-population must be somewhat improved.

Thus, so far as barter effects are concerned, a *uniform* increase in productivity in A is almost certain to redound to B's advantage. So far, the classical optimism is justified; some part of the improvement in A will slop over to B.

What, however, of the monetary effect? It is an essential element in the story we have been telling that A-incomes rise relatively to B-incomes. There is a fall in the prices of A-products relatively to B-products, so that the commodity terms of trade (what are ordinarily called the terms of trade) move in B's favour. But the factorial terms of trade (to use Professor Viner's convenient expression for the ratio of money incomes, which is the relative value of A's factors of production and B's factors of production) move in favour of A. Now a strong movement of the factorial terms in A's favour – and it will be a strong movement, if the change in productivity is considerable – is only consistent with a steady level of money incomes in B if money incomes in A are rising rapidly. So far we have simply assumed that A-incomes do rise sufficiently rapidly; but though it is possible that the requisite rise in A-incomes may come about from some extraneous cause, it is difficult to think of any automatic mechanism which will have the desired effect. The classical mechanism of gold flows has been discredited, not only by modern theory but directly by modern experience; yet even if one believed in that mechanism, it could only do the job which is here in question to quite a limited extent. Deflation in B would only be prevented if there was a sufficient output of new gold to support the requisite rise in A-incomes; otherwise, the 'inflation' in A would have to be matched by a deflation in B. Even on the basis of this now outmoded theory, it would be expected that money income in B would decline, unless indeed there were a sufficient output of newly mined gold to come to the rescue.

A more modern approach would, in substance, confirm the same conclusion, though the qualifications which it would introduce would be different. We should now expect that an employer would be constrained to raise the weekly wages of his employees to some extent when they (or he) achieved greater productivity; but the initial gain which accrues to the employer from the introduction of more productive methods would be wiped out if he could not expect to secure a substantial net reduction in money cost from the improvement. It is further to be expected that when costs are reduced, then (by one or other competitive or semi-competitive mechanism) prices will soon follow. In the course of this adjustment there will be effects on saving (which are fairly clear) and effects on investment (which are not). I shall not attempt to discuss these in detail, but shall merely conclude (as I think most economists would do) that while there may be some 'natural' increase in money incomes in A, in consequence of the rise in A-productivity, it is most unlikely (in the absence of extraneous factors) that this increase will be sufficient to prevent the appearance of a downward pressure upon the level of money incomes in B.

It has therefore to be expected, if the rate of increase in productivity in A is rapid (or rapid relatively to the increase in productivity in B), that there will be a deflationary effect on B, assuming that there is a stable rate of exchange between A's and B's currency, and that B takes no special measures to counteract the deflation. This is what has to be expected if the level of money incomes in A moves in what we may call a 'natural' manner. It is of course perfectly possible that special causes, such as rearmament, or a flood of specially capital-using inventions, may cause money incomes in A to rise more rapidly than has been assumed. If so, the monetary pressure on B would be relieved. But no reason has been advanced which would justify us in regarding such relief as anything more than a temporary exception to a general rule.

It does nevertheless remain true, under the assumptions that we have been making, that the only reason why B gets into trouble is that A-incomes fail to rise with sufficient rapidity. There will, we may say, be some *appropriate* rate of rise in A-incomes (less, but perhaps not much less, than the rate of increase in productivity) which will keep trade between the two countries in balance, even though the level of B-incomes remains in money terms completely unchanged. If A-incomes do rise at this appropriate rate, there need be no deflation in B, while B is actually benefited by a certain change in the commodity terms of trade in its favour. It is only when A-incomes rise at less than the appropriate rate that B gets into difficulties.

Now, at this point, instead of tracing out consequences any farther, I want to ask you to stand back from the picture I have been drawing, and ask: Is it right? Does it in fact describe the kind of thing we have been experiencing? Surely the answer is that it does not.

I have nevertheless chosen to draw it out in some detail, both because it is a useful basis for further investigation and because it has so evidently been in the minds of many people who have given advice on economic policy during these last years. I think that this was especially the case just after the war. One remembers very well how we used to be told (even by Lord Keynes[1]) that inflation in America was a very good thing from the point of view of this country – that it would help to get us out of our difficulties. It might not last for ever, but it would be a help to us so long as it lasted. Now if America and Britain were the A and B of our example, and if our picture was drawn correctly, that would be true. All that would have been neces- sary would have been that we should have stopped our wages from rising, while American wages continued to rise; we should then have been freed from balance of payments troubles, while we could have continued to enjoy our own modest rate of real economic progress. All we should have needed to do would have been to control our own inflation; in the conditions supposed, that should not have been particularly difficult. That is the story we used to be told; but after the experiences we have had, it can hardly go on being told to us any longer.

What is it that has gone wrong? Not, I think, that the whole theory is wrong – though that is a conclusion to which people are only too ready to jump when they find a discrepancy between theory and fact. All that has happened is that a little assumption has crept in – an assumption which (unlike most writers on the subject) I have made explicit. It is the assumption that productivity in A is increas- ing *uniformly* in all industries.

No one, of course, has ever supposed that productivity does ever increase at a uniform rate in all industries; what has been implied is that differences between industries in this respect do not matter. There are indeed some sorts of differences which would not much matter; if the non-uniformity was quite random, it would certainly make little difference to the preceding argument. But it makes a very

---

[1] I refer to Keynes's posthumous article, 'The Balance of Payments of the United States', *EJ*, 1946.

great difference if the non-uniformity is biased, so that the improvement in productivity is concentrated upon industries that have a special relation to foreign trade. There are two sorts of bias which come into question here, of which one is much more relevant to present discontents than the other. But we need to consider both sorts in order to get a balanced picture.

Let us accordingly take as our next subject of study the case in which the improvement in productivity is concentrated upon the goods which A exports; or, as we shall find it convenient to say, when the improvement is export-biased. In order to simplify the argument, let us say that there is a uniform improvement in productivity in A's export industries, but no improvement at all elsewhere. This, we shall find, is a case which is extremely favourable for B. For suppose that incomes remain constant in both countries; the prices of B-exports will then remain constant (for there has been no change in productivity in B), while the prices of A-exports are reduced. There is not much reason why the quantity of B-exports to A (and therefore their value, since their prices are constant) should be much affected; the quantity of A-exports to B must increase, but since their prices are reduced, it is by no means certain that their total value will rise. With suitable (and quite possible) demand conditions in B, it is perfectly possible that trade will continue to balance at unchanged money incomes in both countries – that is to say, at unchanged factorial terms of trade. Thus in this case there may be no monetary difficulty; and even if there is some, it will be fairly small. The commodity terms of trade must, however, turn in favour of B, so that in this case there is bound to be a real gain to B, which is greater than the gain which occurs in the case of all-round uniformity.

This, you may say, is a sweet story; but it is matched by the ugliness of what happens in the corresponding case of an improvement that is 'import-biased' – one, that is, that is concentrated upon the A-industries which compete most closely with B-exports. In this case it is certain that the factorial terms of trade must turn against B (so that there are the same monetary difficulties as in the case of uniformity); but B is now afflicted with a *real* (or barter) loss as well. We can show this in the same manner as before. If incomes in both countries remained constant, the prices of A-products which competed with B-exports would fall, so that A's demand for B-exports would decline; and this would itself be enough to cause a deficit in B's balance of payments, for there would be no reason why B's demand for A-exports should be affected. Thus in order to maintain a trade balance there must be a rise in A-incomes relatively to B-incomes; the factorial terms of trade must turn adversely to B. Further, since there has been no improvement in productivity in A's export industries, a rise in A-incomes implies a rise in the prices of A-exports, so that the commodity terms of trade must turn adversely to B. Whatever are the monetary arrangements, whatever the course of money incomes, an improvement in A-productivity that is *import-biased* must make B worse off.

A balanced view of the matter we are discussing would therefore distinguish three cases: (1) that in which the improvement is export-biased, which is the least likely to lead to monetary difficulties, the least favourable from the point of view of the improving country, and the most favourable for the foreigner; (2) that in which the improvement is more or less uniformly distributed, when there may well be monetary difficulties, but in which (if the monetary difficulties can be overcome) some part of the gain goes to the foreigner; (3) that in which the improvement is import-biased, when there are monetary difficulties as in the second case, and a real loss for the foreigner as well. This is a pure classification of cases; but it is a natural common-sense classification, with nothing academic or artificial about it. It is the kind of classification which one would expect to be able to use for the analysis of historical and contemporary experience.

It is, indeed, tempting to hazard the guess that it can be translated, rather directly, into terms of historical categories. Those periods of history which have seen a great growth of *trade* must nearly always have been periods in which productivity, in some sense, was increasing; it is much easier to see how improvements in productivity should lead to a growth of *trade* if the improvements that are taking place are export-biased. Export-biased improvements increase the advantages of foreign trade relatively to those of domestic production; the growth of trade is thereby directly stimulated. It is, indeed, possible to argue that any great growth of trade, which is not purely due to geographical exploration, must be due to export-biased improvements; for it should be noticed that improvements in transport and in the art of merchanting reckon as export-biased on our classification. But it is, of course, not necessary that the rate of improvement should be very different in the various countries that are trading together – though it would be surprising if such disparities were not in practice a pretty general rule.

We should further expect to find that the improvements which *start* a process of development will be export-biased. This is little more than a deduction from the general principle of the division of labour. Countries, like people, are most likely to make their improvements in those sorts of production which they already do relatively well than in those they do relatively badly; though not an infallible rule, it is one that is likely to hold unless there is special reason to the contrary. Since it is the things which they make relatively well which they will be exporting, or on the point of exporting, improvements in these industries will be export-biased. But all this means is that the first stage in a process of development is very likely to be export-biased. It is a stage which will be marked by growth of trade, by growth in the international division of labour. Though the division of labour will be limited, in Adam Smith's famous phrase, by the extent of the market – or, as we should say, by the inelasticity of foreign demand – such relative inelasticity is at this stage a stabilising factor. It prevents the advancing countries from advancing too rapidly in relation to the rest, and thus from upsetting the international equilibrium.

But if our analysis is right, this will, in general, be no more than the first stage of the process. The very improvements upon which the expansion is based set up forces which tend to change its character. Even though the improvements are likely to be made, in the first place, in those countries which already have a comparative advantage for the industries mainly affected, the mere fact that improvements have been made, that the techniques and organisation of production have been altered, sets up forces which tend to change the pattern of comparative advantages. It is certainly true that the change which then ensues may take a long time to declare itself fully. Even though the ideal location of production, from the point of view of such things as natural resources and transport costs, has shifted away from the old centres – so that if the whole production system had to be started anew it would no longer be sensible to specialise in the old way – nevertheless the old centres still retain their accumulated skill, and may be able to retain a lead on that basis, even when the geographical factors have turned against them. But once this point is reached, the position of the old centres has become very vulnerable. It has to be expected that some of the countries which were formerly their customers, but which possess the right natural resources for home production of the things they used to import, when production is organised according to the new methods, will in time acquire the skills which will enable them to compete. When this happens on a large scale, the process passes into its second stage – notice that it is still a stage of development for the world economy, taken as a whole – in which the lead is taken by new centres, which are now making improvements that are import-biased. Thus when our analysis is put into an historical dress, it suggests as a normal sequence the succession of an export-biased by an import-biased phase.

I am no historical determinist; and it is no part of my intention to suggest that historical phenomena will ever fit very neatly into any such logical pattern. But I do think that we see the shadows of such patterns across the face of history. Western Europe is not the first metropolis of trade and industry which has suffered from the competition of the new lands which it has itself developed; there was, I fancy, an element of this same process in the decline of ancient Greece; we ourselves in this island grew great in the fifteenth century and later at the expense of the Flemish and Italian centres on which we had formerly depended. But though such historical examples warn us that the process under discussion is not at all uncommon, they also indicate that there is nothing inevitable about its denouement. After the general expansion of the first phase has given place to the expansion here, contraction there, of the second, it may happen that the troubles of the contracting countries lay so heavy a burden upon the whole international economy that its general progress is brought to a halt. It may happen that the contraction remains localised, and that the expanding centres of the second phase establish a new leadership. It may happen that the centres which have lost their old comparative advantages develop new ones and begin a new expansion of their own. If Professor Postan is right,[2] the history of the Netherlands in the fifteenth and sixteenth centuries affords a remarkable example of this happier outcome.[3]

---

[2] *Cambridge Economic History of Europe*, vol. ii, ch. 4, especially pp. 251–6. The somewhat different version of the story which is told by Miss Carus-Wilson in ch. 6 of the same volume will also repay attention.

[3] I have thought it well to leave this final paragraph, though it is very tentative, since it leads on to one of the themes of my *TEH*, esp. pp. 54 ff.

16

Import Bias:
A Reply to Critics

This is the major part of what appeared as Note B in *Essays in World Economics* (Oxford University Press, 1959). Having decided to cut out the topical part of the preceding paper, the paper that was being criticised, it seems proper to make a corresponding excision here. So I confine attention to the theoretical issues. The chief of the critics to whom I was referring was Harry Johnson; see footnote on p. 222 below.

I must begin my reply by insisting on the purpose of the exercise. I was trying to illustrate the way in which simplified models, though they can never tell us the whole truth about any situation or process, can enable us to see things which we should not see if we kept our analysis more faithful, at all stages, to the immense complexity of fact. It seemed suitable for this purpose to take a model of established authority, and to show that it can still say something to us, when it is applied to a modern problem. This was an answer to the oft-repeated call for a 'simpler economics'. I have some sympathy with that call, though I should be the first to admit that it is impossible to be simple and yet to speak the whole truth on any economic problem of major importance.

The classical 'constant cost' assumption has the quality, as is well-known, that it enables us to study prices independently of the conditions of demand. Alternatively (as indeed is illustrated in the Keynesian theory) it enables us to study income-formation independently of the variation of prices (relative prices). It is a drastic simplification, which is bound to get one into trouble if one pursues it very far; but it may still be true that by beginning with such a simplification, and subsequently modifying it in the proper way, we can get to the heart of a problem in the quickest manner that is open to us.

The crucial point in which my analysis appears to have got into trouble by its simplifications (the point on which my critics have mainly fastened) concerns the so-called 'central' proposition – that an 'unbiased' increase in productivity, in one country alone, must tend (in the final equilibrium) to confer some net benefit on the rest of the world, considered as another 'country'. The significance of this proposition depends, of course, on the meaning, which one gives to 'unbiased'. Within my Ricardian model, unbiased has a clear meaning; and within that model my proposition (as I think is generally admitted) is true. If one drops the Ricardian assumptions, the meaning of 'unbiased' must be reconsidered; I shall be maintaining in what follows that there is a proper generalisation of the definition to meet the conditions in which my critics are interested, but it is (perhaps) not a very obvious generalisation. In any case, most of those who have written on the subject appear to have missed it.

I had better begin by repeating my original argument. Under the *constant cost* assumption, the goods which are produced in a particular country (A) must either be export goods (in which A has a comparative advantage) or they must be 'Home' goods, as I shall call them, which are prevented from entering into international trade by natural immobility or by costs of transport. Goods which are imported into A must be goods of distinctive type, being such that in their production A is at a comparative disadvantage. Some of the home goods, or even some of the export goods, may 'compete with imports' in the sense that they would be used for the purposes for which the imports are used, if they were a little cheaper. When we talk about 'import-competing goods', in the Ricardian model, we must be using the term in that sense.

Granted these assumptions, a uniform increase in productivity in A is a uniform reduction in the real costs of those products in which A has a comparative advantage; if factor prices rise in A to the precise extent which is necessary to offset the reduction, all money costs in A will be unchanged. At unchanged money costs, A will be unable to expand exports; while any expansion in A's total money income will lead to an expansion in imports (unless her imports are inferior goods). Accordingly, if employment is to be maintained (without controls and interferences that are here irrelevant), factor prices in A must rise by *less* than the rise in productivity. The terms of trade are then turned in a direction that is unfavourable to A, or favourable to B (taken to represent the 'rest of the world').

All this assumes constant costs. But under constant costs, as we have seen, it is necessary that the goods imported into A should be *different* in type from any of those produced in A; it is not possible for any of A's imports to be identical in character with any of the goods produced at home. This is an unrealistic restriction; what happens if we drop it? We must (effectively) then assume that some, at least, of A's products are produced under increasing costs. But as soon as we do that, the change in productivity, or in real cost, as between one situation and another, becomes ambiguous; an actual change will be partly due to the 'technical' change, which was all that we formerly considered, and partly to the change in output which has occurred. We cannot talk about changes in cost, pure and simple, without some reference to output changes.

It is tempting (and this is the line which several of my critics have adopted) to say, at this point, that productivity changes must henceforward be measured purely in output terms. A uniform expansion in productivity would then be taken to mean that (initially, before factors have shifted) the outputs of all goods produced in A are increased in equal proportion. Suppose that there is this expansion in output, and that (corresponding to my income assumption) factor prices are at the same time so raised as to prevent product prices from falling. It has been made abundantly clear that there is then no reason (as there was under my assumption) why the balance of payments should be affected unfavourably. For it is necessary, now, to take the expansion in demand for importables,[1] setting against it the expansion in the home supply of importables; and, indeed, to take the expansion in the supply of exportables, setting against it the expansion in the home demand for exportables. There may be taken to be an expansion under all four heads (no 'inferior goods'); but that does not show that the *differences*, which are imports and exports, will move in any determinate manner. It all depends on the way in which the increments of demand are distributed. Cases can be constructed in which the balance of payments goes my way, and cases can be constructed in which it goes the other way. There is no firm standard of reference, such as I appeared to get in my argument.

All this must be granted; but I must still insist that this definition by outputs is only one possible definition of an unbiased expansion. If this will not do, we can still look about for another.

I do not think that it is a promising alternative to take the actual change in costs, between the new equilibrium and the old, as our criterion. For suppose that in some particular line there is both some import and some home production, both before and after the change in productivity and in incomes. Then, if the import price is the same, the money cost of production must be the same; if factor prices

---

[1] Imports plus home products that compete with imports.

have risen, 'productivity' must have adjusted itself so as to keep the cost of production in line with the price of the import. This must be so, whatever has happened to productivity (in any autonomous or 'technical' sense) in the industry in question. If the industry has not been able to improve its efficiency, in that sense, its output will fall; it will reduce its costs by abandoning marginal units. If it has been able to improve its efficiency, it will be spared that contraction; but how are we to say whether its improvement in efficiency is the *same* as that which has been attained in other industries? We can get no answer to this question if we look at costs alone.

The only alternative that remains (as far as I can see) is to measure the improvement in productivity by the change in costs (at unchanged factor prices) which *would* occur at an unchanged output. I am going to maintain that it is this which is the *right* generalisation. Suppose that there is a uniform increase in productivity, in this sense, and that factor prices are adjusted so as to leave money costs, for the un-changed outputs, the same as they were before. There is then no reason why exports should increase (whether the export industries are constant cost or increasing cost industries); and there is *also* no reason why the outputs of import-competing industries should increase, for they also are no better able to compete with imports than they were before. Consequently, under these assumptions, the country will remain in equilibrium at its previous output. It is, of course, a Keynesian under-employment equilibrium; but it is an equilibrium in the Keynesian sense, for any expansion of output would mean an increase in imports with no expansion in exports, so that there would be an adverse movement of the balance of pay-ments. In order to absorb the additional productive power that has been generated, there must be a *smaller* rise in factor-prices than we have just been supposing; for tariffs, and such like interferences, are of course once again irrelevant to the argument. But a reduction in factor prices, which will enable the internationally competing indus-tries to expand, will cause the terms of trade to move unfavourably.

It will be noticed, of course, that I am taking it for granted that conditions are such that a cut in factor prices will work in the direc-tion of improving the trade balance; or, in other words, that elastici-ties are such as to exclude the 'perverse case' of devaluation theory. This is, at bottom, the same exception as that which we put on one side when we excluded 'inferior goods'. I think it is now admitted that this exception is unimportant in relation to the long-period problems with which the present argument − in fact, if not in form − is concerned.

It accordingly appears that my central proposition can stand, after all, so long as the 'unbiased' improvement is properly interpreted; and I think it can be shown that 'biased' improvements also will work out, more or less, as I said. Take the case of an export-biased improvement. Suppose that there is a 10 per cent improvement in productivity in the export industries, the improvement being interpreted in the sense just defined, but that productivity in the import-competing industries only improves by 5 per cent. If factor prices rise by 10 per cent, there can be no expansion in exports; while since the money costs of the import-competing industries are raised, those industries are liable to lose ground in the home market. 'Perverse' possibilities apart, this involves a contraction of output, and an adverse movement in the balance of payments; the position is by so much the worse than it was in our 'unbiased' case, when there was merely a failure of output to expand, so as to take advantage of the potential improvement in productivity. 'Other things being equal', it would seem fair to say that there must be a larger cut in factor prices, and a larger cut in export prices, in consequence, than would have been necessary if we had started with an unbiased improvement of 10 per cent all round.

Now take the case of an improvement that is import-biased. Say, now, that export productivity rises by 5 per cent while in the import-competing industries it rises by 10 per cent. If factor prices rise by 5 per cent, exports will be unchanged; but the money costs of import-competing goods are now lowered, so that there will be a tendency for imports to be pushed out. There will thus be an expansion of output, and a favourable movement of the balance of payments (which may persist, even when the increased imports, which are demanded out of increased incomes, are allowed for). But there are then two cases, according as balance of payments equilibrium is restored, given these factor prices, at a level of output which is short of full absorption,[2] or whether it is not. In the former case, we again come to a Keynesian equilibrium, with the 5 per cent rise in factor prices, exports unchanged (because their money costs are unaltered), imports unchanged (because the expansion in the demand for importables has just offset the increase in their supply), while the increase in capacity is not yet wholly absorbed. In order that it should be absorbed, it will be necessary (as when the improvement is unbiased, or export-biased) that there should be a reduction in factor prices, involving a change in the terms of trade in favour of the rest

---

[2] I say 'full absorption' not 'full employment' since labour is by no means the only factor to be absorbed.

of the world; but of course ('other things being equal') it will be a smaller change in the terms of trade than in the cases which we have previously examined.

If, on the other hand, the expansion (arising from the increased competitive power of the import-competing industries) is directly sufficient to absorb the new capacity, so that full absorption is reached (with a 5 per cent rise in factor prices) *before* the balance of payments has returned to equilibrium, it will be a rise in factor prices *beyond* the 5 per cent level which will become necessary. Then (this is the full 'import bias' case[3] which I had in mind) export prices must rise, the terms of trade must turn adversely to the rest of the world, so that the rest of the world will lose by the improvement in A's productivity.

All this part of my argument can therefore, I would claim, be rehabilitated; but beyond that point I have many concessions, or retractions, to make.

I am, of course, not pretending that in 1953 I could see what has just been set out, anything like as clearly as I now see it; I was at that time living within my Ricardian model; the possibility of extending it was no more than a 'hunch'. There were in consequence many loose-nesses of expression, which (I think) the reader is now in a position to correct. I do not need to refer to them in detail; there are two, however, which should be mentioned.

One is that I was too inclined to talk as if *any* import-biased improvement must have the effects which, as is now quite clear, are to be associated with the second and more extreme kind of import bias only. This is indeed an error which could be checked up from what I did say; for I had maintained (correctly) that an unbiased improvement must tend to the advantage of the rest of the world, and it is obvious that there is then room for an improvement which is only slightly import-biased to have the same effect.

The other is that I jumped too quickly from the theoretical case, in which A is developing while B (the rest of the world) is stationary, to the practical application in which both A and B must be taken to be developing, though at different rates. It should have been set out,

---

[3] Our 'ultra-import-bias' as Professor Johnson called it in his *Manchester School* (1955) article. The revised version of his analysis (in chapter III of *International Trade and Economic Growth*) where the 'ultra-import-bias' has become an 'ultra-anti-trade-bias', seems to diverge a good deal further from mine.

For the possibility of an 'ultra-export-bias', such that a cost-reduction involves so violent an adverse movement of the terms of trade that it is net disadvantage to the improving country, see J. Bhagwati on 'Immiserising Growth' (*Review of Economic Studies*, June 1958).

more explicitly, that in the latter case we must superimpose the effects of B's expansion upon those of A's; and that the net result of the super-position does not only depend upon the direction of the effects (export or import-bias) but also on their size. It is perfectly possible that B may be gaining little (or even losing) from its share in the indirect effects of A's expansion, and yet that it may be doing quite well, by virtue of the direct effects of its own.

17

The Factor Price Equalisation Theorem

This originally appeared as Note C in *Essays in World Economics* (Oxford University Press, 1959). It has not received much attention but I still think it has something to say.

The first part is a mere checking through of Samuelson's argument, keeping his own assumptions. This does no more than express it in a form which facilitates the use I am going to make of it. My own contribution, to which I would still attach some importance, is in the second part.

The first part of this note contains some comments on the meaning of Samuelson's theorem[1] under its own assumptions: perfect competition, constant returns to scale, no factor movements, but free (costless) movement of goods, identical technical knowledge and identical 'quality' of the factors of production between the countries considered. I shall be confirming that under these assumptions the theorem is strictly correct. But since the assumptions are in themselves so obviously unrealistic, it is a question how much bearing the theorem can have on what goes on in the real world. I shall nevertheless be contending, in the second part, that it does have some bearing; though the practical conclusions that are to be drawn from it are rather different from what might be expected, at least at first sight.

I

Suppose that we have two countries, A and B, which are economically identical. All the Samuelson conditions are satisfied, but in

---

[1] P. A. Samuelson, 'International Trade and the Equalization of Factor Prices' (*EJ*, June 1948); 'International Factor Price Equalization Once Again' (*EJ*, June 1949).

addition there is identity of tastes, and identical supplies of the factors of production. (It will be sufficient to take these to be two in number, 'labour' and 'capital'.) It is reasonable to expect that the same prices (of factors and of products) will rule in each country; and that (whether or not there are facilities for trade) there will in fact be no trade between them.

Now suppose that in country A, alone, there is an increase in the supply of one factor: say capital. If there are no facilities for trade, the effects of that increase are well known. There will be a fall in the price of capital in A relatively to that of labour, and this will set up a double substitution in favour of capital; (1) a tendency for technical methods to be changed in the direction of using more capital and less labour; (2) a relative fall in the costs of more capital-using products, so that consumers will tend to substitute these more capital-using products for those which are more labour-using. Partly along one of these routes, partly along the other, the demand for capital will increase and the increased supply of capital will be absorbed.

That is what happens if country A is completely isolated; but it is worth observing that essentially the same kind of thing will happen if there is a removal, not only of the obstacles to trade, but also of the obstacles to factor movement. For the two economies then become virtually one economy, so that the processes just described will take place throughout the whole combined economy, in country B no less than in country A. In between these we have the case with which we are chiefly concerned, in which there is mobility of products but no mobility of factors. It is Samuelson's contention that the same effects will follow in this case as in the case where there is factor mobility — up to the point where factor endowments become so different that complete specialisation, or rather what we shall later call 'almost complete specialisation' occurs.

In the absence of trade, the increased supply of capital in A would change the relative prices of A's products, to something different from what they were, and therefore to something different from what B's now are. But this, once trade is permitted, cannot be a position of equilibrium. A will start exporting to B those more capital-using products in which A's costs have become relatively lower, and importing from B those more labour-using products in which B's costs have become relatively lower. This process will go on until there is a sufficient amount of trade to establish equality of product prices between the two countries. But that cannot happen, for moderate differences in factor endowments, until equality of factor prices has been established as well.

It is indeed clear that the increased demand for B's more labour-using products (for export to A) and diminished demand for B's more capital-using products (by the competition of imports from A), must tend to raise the price of labour in B relatively to the price of capital in B (for the quantities of both factors, available in B, are assumed to be unchanged). There must therefore be some tendency for B's factor-price ratio to be moved in the same direction as A's. The full Samuelson result, that the expansion of trade must generally proceed to such a point as will establish a complete equalisation of factor prices, requires, however, a further step which is crucial.

Let us look at a pair of commodities (1) and (2) each of which is still to be produced in each country in the final equilibrium. It will be necessary, in order that there should be equilibrium, that the unit cost of production of each commodity should be the same in the one country as in the other. This will generally show that the factor prices must be the same. Suppose, first of all, that the same coefficients of production (the quantities of factors needed to make a unit of product) are used in each country; that this is true for product (1) and for product (2). Let these labour coefficients be l_1 and l_2 for the two products, and let the capital coefficients be c_1 and c_2. Let w, w' and r, r' be the prices of the factors in the two countries. Then we have, from the first product

$$l_1 w + c_1 r = l_1 w' + c_1 r'$$

and

$$l_2 w + c_2 r = l_2 w' + c_2 r'$$

from the second. It follows that

$$r' - r = (l_1/c_1)(w - w') = (l_2/c_2)(w - w')$$

But these last equations cannot hold, if the capital intensities (l/c) for the two commodities are different, unless $w = w'$ and therefore $r = r'$.

There will thus be a stage, while the factor endowments of the two countries are only moderately different, when A's extra capital is accommodated by A taking over more and more of the more capital-using industries; but so long as there are any 'overlapping industries' (in which there is some production in both countries), this process can go on without the factor prices in the two countries having to diverge. It is indeed true that as the supply of capital expands (in A) its price will fall relatively to the price of labour; what is being maintained is that the same fall will be occurring in both countries. Since capital is becoming relatively cheaper, there will be a tendency to substitute capital for labour; methods of pro-duction will be changed in that direction. But since there is the same relative cheapening in both countries, there will be the same substitution in both countries; B-methods will still be the same as A-methods, for each commodity. It is by taking over the relatively more capital-using industries that A accommodates its relatively more abundant supply of capital; B is driven out of these relatively more capital-using industries, and is obliged to concentrate on those which are relatively more labour-using (but in the process of doing so capital in B is set free, which may permit of some substitution of capital for labour in these nevertheless more labour-using industries).

All this while there is no reason why the factor prices should be differentiated from one another. But how long can this process continue? It has its limit at the point when the process of A taking over the more capital-using industries is finished: when differences in the capital-intensities of the industries, which are still conducted both in A and in B, have disappeared.

This, it is important to notice, need not be a point of 'complete' specialisation. There may still be overlapping industries, but (at the point where the break comes) the capital intensities in the over-lapping industries must be the same. At that point, there is nothing left to tie the factor-price ratios in the two countries together. Further expansion in the supply of capital in A will reduce the price of capital in A relatively to the price of labour; but that further reduction need not be echoed in B. B may still remain able to compete, in the overlapping industries, because its higher price of capital can be offset by a lower price of labour.

Here, however, it is necessary (as previously it was not necessary) to allow for the possibility of differences between the coefficients of production, for the same industry, between the two countries. So far, though there has been a substitution of capital for labour in each industry, it has been the same substitution in both countries (for, under constant returns to scale, the coefficients of production depend on the factor-price ratio, and on that alone). But at the point we have now reached, the factor-price ratios have begun to diverge, and the coefficients of production may therefore begin to diverge. What difference is made by this possibility?

It seems often to be supposed that the variability of coefficients makes it easier to have a variety of overlapping industries, when factor-prices are different. I much doubt whether that is the case. For, as we have just seen, it would be perfectly possible, in a world of fixed coefficients, to have a group of overlapping industries, with the same capital intensities; though the factor-price ratios were different in the two countries, the differences in factor prices might so offset one another that costs were equalised between the two countries for the whole of the group. (The position might be described as one of 'almost complete specialisation', since in a sense there would only be one overlapping 'commodity'; but this 'commodity' would be made up of several physical commodities, which were merely behaving as one commodity since their technical coefficients were the same.) When, however, we allow for the variability of coefficients, it seems probable that a group of this kind would tend to break up.

Suppose, for instance, that there is only one of the formerly overlapping industries in which coefficients are variable; in the rest they are to be supposed to be fixed, as before. Then, with a relative fall in the price of capital in A, there will be a relative increase in capital intensity in the variable-coefficient industry. It will accordingly pass out of the class in which costs are equalised, and enter that in which A's costs are lower. If B is still able to compete in the fixed-coefficient industries, it will not be able to compete in the variable-coefficient industry. The range of overlapping industries will be narrowed.

It is at first sight tempting to suppose that as the number of variable-coefficient industries was increased, there would of necessity be a continuance of this process; the group of overlapping industries would be rapidly broken up, so that the system would proceed at once from a condition in which factor prices were equalised to one in which the overlap was reduced to a single physical product. I am myself inclined to maintain that it is precisely this which, save in special cases, would be likely to happen. But there are special cases; they have received a great deal of attention (more, perhaps, than they deserve) so that something must be said about them.[2]

In the first place, it might happen that all the overlapping industries were variable-coefficient industries, but that a given shift in the factor-price ratio brought about the *same* substitution of capital for labour in each of the industries.[3] It would then be possible that costs of production should continue to be equalised between the two countries, for the whole group, even though the factor-price

---

[2] I am referring to Sir Roy Harrod's article (*EJ*, June 1958); and to the first chapter in Professor Johnson's previously cited book.

[3] That is to say, the elasticity of substitution, of capital for labour, in each of the overlapping industries was the same.

ratio had become different in the two countries. The various products in the group would still be 'behaving like a single product'.

Otherwise, if the rates of substitution were different, the group would tend to break up; but this is not the end of the story. For it is possible that though this group broke up, another might form. The relative fall (in A) of the r/w ratio may not only cause a relative fall in A's cost of production of those goods already produced in A; it will also affect the costs at which A *could* produce the goods which in the former position had been more labour-intensive, so that in the former position it had abandoned their production to B. It may so happen that there are some of these goods for which the relative fall in A's r/w ratio leads to so great a (potential) substitution of capital for labour, that in the new position they do a 'leap-frog' and fall into the more capital-intensive group, so that A takes them over. This is perfectly possible, and one would expect that there would be cases in which it would occur. It is further possible, within that first possibility, that some of the 'leap-frogging' industries might happen to reduce their costs to exactly the same extent as some of the former overlapping industries, so that a new overlapping group would be formed from these diverse sources. But it is evident, when one looks at the matter in this way, that it would be very much a matter of chance whether there were any substitutions which happened to come out in just this way, for any particular pair of factor-price ratios. I cannot see that the overlapping which arises in this manner, for all the attention that has been given to it, can be anything more than a fluke.

II

These are the reasons why I would maintain that Samuelson's theorem is true, on its own assumptions, without exception that is of any significance. Granted these assumptions, there are two possible conditions – one in which factor prices are equalised, and there are overlapping industries – the other in which factor prices are not equalised, but there is 'almost complete' specialisation. But the assumptions on which these results are based are very narrow; how much bearing can they have on anything that actually happens?

I do not myself believe that they have much direct bearing; they cannot do much to explain the international inequality of incomes, either now, or in the past, or at any particular future date. For it is by no means the case that countries only differ from one another, in reality, by differences in the quantity of capital (per head of labour) that is at their disposal. It is one of the great drawbacks of the method of international trade analysis that descends from Ohlin (for it was Ohlin[4] who originally taught us to think in terms of the kind of simplification which is used in Samuelson's theorem) that it treats the factors of production in different countries as being identical in quality (so much 'capital' and so much 'labour'); whereas, when the factors are not mobile, it is the *products* which are compared, by being traded against one another. There is no direct means of knowing whether the 'same' factor, in different countries, is really the same factor or not. (In this respect, the comparative cost theory, in terms of opportunity cost, is a much more *suitable* apparatus for the study of international trade.)

As things are in fact, at any particular time, the capital stock of any country is by no means an undifferentiated stock of productive power; it is embodied in a wide variety of useful things of high specificity. Nor is the labour force an undifferentiated mass; the skills and abilities that are possessed are themselves also highly specific. There is nothing surprising, in a world of this sort, in the discovery that there are great international inequalities in factor prices, and yet that it is common for countries to import particular goods, of which they also produce some quantities at home. What must be implied (what is of course implied if the home industry is not protected) is that their supply of specific factors is such as to give them a comparative advantage for a limited output, but not for a larger one. They must be producing under increasing costs, of a kind which is ruled out in Samuelson's world.[2]

But is that the whole story? If it were the whole story, we should have to conclude that the theorem we have been examining is a mere curiosity; the sooner we leave it, and go back to something more sensible, the better. I do not believe that that is quite right. There are problems of international economics for which Samuelson's assumptions, or something nearer to those assumptions, may be more appropriate. Instead of asking what explains the things which happen now, suppose we ask the more hypothetical, but nevertheless exceedingly interesting, question: suppose that there was a régime of universal free trade, without factor movements, how should we expect that things, in the very long run, would work themselves out? There are many specificities (due to natural resources and climatic

---

[4] Bertil Ohlin, *International and Interregional Trade.*
[5] So far, then, and on this side of the matter, I agree with Harrod.

differences) which would not disappear, even in the very long run; to that extent the Samuelson model is not perfectly appropriate, even to the problem to which we have now come. But it is not un-reasonable to suppose that in this long run, capital stocks (so far as they are man-made) could be transformed into whatever form was most appropriate; many specificities in the capital stock can there-fore be taken to disappear. And whatever differences at present exist in the capacities of the labour forces of different nations, may also (I think) be neglected in this very long run. Partly this is a matter of the question we are putting – it is interesting to ask what would happen if these differences could be neglected; partly because it is reasonable to assume that the differences are in large part a conse-quence of environment – if environment became such that Indians or Africans could earn European incomes if they had European efficiency, then (it is plausible to maintain) their efficiency would rise, at least in the long run, to the higher level.

To the problem thus posed the Samuelson model does seem to be appropriate – not perfectly appropriate, but as appropriate as any simple model is likely to be. It is significant that under the assumptions we are now making, there are two possible sorts of equilibrium – one in which factor prices are the same, and there is (or may be) much 'overlapping'; the other in which factor prices differ, but specialisation is complete, or 'almost' complete. If differences in capital endowment are small, the first type of situation is the more probable; if large, the second. It does not seem at all unreasonable to suppose that the long-run equilibrium of a free trade world would be of this character; but if so, it is quite important to realise it.

There is indeed one important consideration which is left out of Samuelson's model, but which turns out to tend in the same or more or less the same direction. Samuelson's products are all produced under conditions of constant returns to scale; double all factors, and you double the product. This is a very convenient assumption for some sorts of theoretical analysis, but there is a tendency for it to be over-employed.[6] That there is a general tendency to increasing returns to scale would seem to be nearer the facts – and it is an assumption which gives very intelligible results in the field of inter-national trade theory.[7]

[6] This may partly be due to the popularity of Linear Programming, and suchlike techniques, which are very dependent on the 'constant returns to scale' assumption.
[7] It should be said, in defence of Ohlin, that the tendency to economies of scale was one of the complications which he did take into account.

It is reasonable to suppose (and commonly is supposed) that there is a close connection between increasing returns and high capitalisation; expansion of production is much more likely to call forth increasing returns when a product is much capital-using (or when it is shifted over to a technique which is much capital-using) than when it is not. Accordingly, when we rework our former exercise with this addition, we must allow that A (the capital-wealthier country) will develop economies of scale in the industries where its output is expanding; consequently, even though (for the present) factor prices are equalised, A's costs, for these products, will become lower than B's costs, and B will be more rapidly obliged to withdraw from these industries by A's competition. The tendency towards complete specialisation will accordingly be greater than in the Samuelson model; it will not merely be the probable solution when factor endowments are very different; it becomes a very probable solution in the case when they are similar, as well.

So far as the economies of scale are specific to particular industries, this conclusion is (I think) correct; the tendency to complete specialisation in such a world, under universal free trade, would be very strong. It may, however, be suggested that many of the economies of large scale are less specific; once a country has built up a large manufacturing outfit, with the auxiliary services and the technical skills that are needed to support it, its ability to secure economies of scale (in the long run) over quite a large range of different products will be very high. Consequently, though there will be a stronger tendency to complete specialisation, even among equally endowed countries, than there is in the Samuelson model, that part of his structure may not wholly disappear. Similarly well-endowed countries will still be geared together by the possibility of adjusting the kinds of things they produce to the nature of their resources; the gap between them and the less well-endowed countries will nevertheless remain.

Long run forces, if they are real forces, should be observable, in the actual world, as tendencies; it can, I think, be maintained that a tendency of the sort which has just been described is indeed to be observed. When we allow for the wide margin of error which does undoubtedly exist in our statistics, when they are regarded as measures of real income standards, the existence of a tendency to equalisation, among the more 'advanced' or 'industrialised' countries, is by no means difficult to swallow. Such long-run inequalities as exist among such countries, are plausibly to be ascribed, in the main, not to immobility of factors, but to (artificial or natural) impediments to trade.

But when we compare these developed countries with the non-industrialised countries, the case is very different. There is no tendency to equalisation, either between the industrialised and non-industrialised, or (what is also very significant) among the non-industrialised themselves. They may. be rich or poor, according to their endowment with natural resources. Those which are rich in natural resources can industralise themselves, if they choose; it is easy for them to accumulate the necessary capital. But they may not choose; for they may do as well (or better) by employing their labour in the way which most directly offers. But those which are poor in natural resources have no hope save in industrialisation – and here is their dilemma. A small industrial sector does not develop sufficient economies to make it competitive; a large industrial sector requires so much capital as to be out of reach.

So understood, the analysis which emerges does not sound to me so unrealistic. It sounds to me like ringing true.

Part IV

Mathematical Economics

18

A Note on the Elasticity of Supply

The original version of this note appeared in the *Review of Economic Studies* in October 1934; it made no claim to be more than an exercise. My first inclination, when preparing this volume, was to suppress it. But then I was told that there are still some people who find it useful; so I thought I should look at it again. I was appalled, when I did so, at the crudity of the mathematical proofs that were given of my propositions; I could not let the note appear again without rewriting them in a more elegant form. The result of that (as it would be) was that I found some consequences I could have drawn in 1934, but had missed.

Thus what appears here is in three parts. The first is a simple reprint of the first part of the old note. The first paragraph of this is of some historical interest, as indicating the grounds on which (at LSE in 1934) we thought that, in spite of the rumours coming from Cambridge, there was still a case for going on working at the old-fashioned full-employment economics. The rest is a statement of the results to which, on the assumptions stated, I still think I quite correctly came.

The second part is a re-statement of the mathematical argument. The third contains some comments, which I now feel to be called for.

I

1. Of all the difficulties presented by Marshall's *Principles*, not the least is a certain asymmetry which appears to exist between his demand curve and his supply curve. The demand curve, we are definitely told, is drawn up under the assumption that the prices of rival commodities – that is to say, of finished goods – remain unchanged;[1] about the supply curve no exactly corresponding in-

[1] p. 100.

formation appears to be provided, but Marshall has been generally understood to mean that the prices of such factors of production as are not specific to the industry are to be taken as given, while of course those factors which are specific to the industry have independently given supply curves. If this interpretation is correct, how far is the construction justified? How far is the assumption of given commodity prices (lying behind the demand curve) consistent with the assumption of given prices for transferable factors (lying behind the supply curve)? They are consistent, it is fairly evident, in two cases only: (1) where the industry employs so small a quantity of these transferable factors, that a moderate expansion in its output will have a negligible influence on the total demand for them; (2) where there exist unemployed reserves of the transferable factors, their price having thus been fixed by monopolistic or quasi-monopolistic decisions.

There can be no doubt that it was the first of these cases which was in Marshall's mind, so that it was this which he would have invoked as a justification of his procedure. But today one hears more stress laid upon the second. It is the existence of unemployed resources which is held to justify the use of Marshallian constructions, and to justify them, very often, in places where one can hardly suppose that Marshall himself would have cared to use them. And one cannot help feeling that the foundation on which such imposing erections are often reared, is rather fragile. It is true that with labour we do have a factor of which there often (but very far from always) exist reserves, unemployed in the precise sense required here; but labour is not the only factor of production in the sense needed by the argument under discussion. Stocks of raw materials may well be much in excess of 'normal', but they are not 'unemployed' for the purpose of this argument; a change in demand may easily have a very considerable effect on their price.

Economic arguments which make the provisional assumption of full employment – in this sense – are therefore not by any means futile; it does seem worth while to investigate the precise relation between a supply curve which assumes the prices of transferable factors given (the *supposed* Marshallian curve), and a supply curve which assumes prices of other finished commodities to be given; although for there to be any difference between the two, we must assume that some transferable factors, at least, are fully employed.

2. I shall confine myself in what follows to a very simple case – that of a closed community in which there are only two industries. I

shall assume further that in each industry only two factors are employed. This case is almost ridiculously simple, but, as we shall see, it is not a very easy matter to elucidate the position fully even in such a very simple case; and even this case does seem to bring out certain points of importance.

Within these assumptions, I shall examine two sub-cases: *I. Where only one factor is transferable between the industries, so that each industry employs one specific and one non-specific factor. II. Where both factors are transferable.* I shall assume conditions of perfect competition throughout, that the total supplies of the factors are given, and that both factors are fully employed.

I. If only one factor is transferable, an increase in the output of industry X will raise the supply price of its product: (1) in so far as extension of output involves increasing marginal costs in terms of the transferable factor, (2) in so far as withdrawal of that transferable factor from the other industry tends to raise its price. Normally, therefore, the consequential change in the price of the transferable factor will make the supply-curve of industry X slope upwards more steeply than it would otherwise have done, i.e., the elasticity of supply of industry X will be reduced. The extent to which it will be reduced depends upon the steepness of the marginal cost curve of the other industry (in terms of the transferable factor); and also upon the relative importance of the two industries. If e_x is the elasticity of supply of industry X (assuming the price of Y to be fixed), ϵ_x, ϵ_y the elasticities of the marginal cost curves of X and Y (in terms of the transferable factor), k_x, k_y the proportions of the total social income spent upon X and Y respectively, then the exact mathematical relation is

$$\frac{1}{e_x} = \frac{1}{\epsilon_x} + \frac{k_x}{k_y} \frac{1}{\epsilon_y} \tag{1}$$

A proof of this formula will be given below.

If k_x is negligible relatively to k_y, it will be seen that e_x can be taken as equivalent to ϵ_x (Marshall's case). But if k_x is not negligible, e_x will be less than ϵ_x.

II. If both factors are transferable, and if (as it is probably correct to assume here) the production functions are linear and homogeneous, then the elasticity of supply, calculated on the assumption of constant factor prices, is necessarily infinite for each industry.[2] But this does not mean that the elasticity of supply,

---

[2] Cf. Sraffa, 'The Laws of Returns under Competitive Conditions', *EJ*, 1926.

calculated on the assumption of a constant selling price in the other industry, is necessarily infinite. It may be infinite; for if in the two industries the technical coefficients happen to be in the same ratio, it will be possible for industry X to expand without disturbing the ratio in which the factors are employed in industry Y, and therefore without disturbing their marginal products. (Since the price of the product of industry Y is unchanged, unchanged marginal products mean unchanged prices of factors.)

Once, however, the technical coefficients are not proportional, an increased output of X must lead to a rise in its supply price. This can be seen as follows. If the demand for X rises relatively to the demand for Y, this will now involve a change in the ratio of factor prices. The price of that factor which is more used in X will rise. But since the price of Y is to remain unchanged, this means that the price of that factor more used in Y must fall. But it has to fall only so far as to keep the Y combination of factors unchanged in total price (per unit of product) and there is (*ex hypothesi*) less of the factor, whose price has fallen, in the X combination than in the Y combination. The X combination, containing more of the factor whose price has risen, and less of the factor whose price has fallen, must therefore rise in price.

This argument is unaffected by the fact that the change in demand will have an influence upon the actual ratios in which the factors are combined in the two industries. For the change in the technical coefficients in each industry may be regarded as small compared with the initial difference in their ratios.

The mathematical expression of this case is facilitated by using the elasticity of substitution. If σ_x, σ_y are the elasticities of substitution between the factors in the two industries; if k_x, k_y are the same as before; if h_{ax}, h_{bx} are the proportions in which the cost of production in industry X is divided between the two factors, and h_{ay}, h_{by} similar expressions for industry Y; then the corrected elasticity of supply

$$e_x = \frac{h_{ax} h_{bx} \sigma_x + (k_y/k_x) h_{ay} h_{by} \sigma_y}{(h_{ax} - h_{ay})^2} \tag{2}$$

This expression obviously tends to infinity when k_x is negligible, and also when $h_{ax} = h_{ay}$. Since $h_{ax} + h_{bx} = h_{ay} + h_{by} = 1$ this latter condition could also be written $h_{ax}|h_{bx} = h_{ay}|h_{by}$; that is to say, it implies equality between the ratios of technical coefficients.

In all other cases, e_x will be positive and finite, so that the supply curve will slope upwards. (This follows from the fact that σ_x and σ_y must be positive, from the law of diminishing returns to a factor.)

3. The corrected supply curves which result from the analysis of the preceding section have their use, in that they are strictly comparable with Marshallian demand curves, and can thus be treated as proper correlatives with those demand curves, where it is desired to regard the Marshallian construction as a part of a system of general equilibrium. Apart from this, however, they are not of much importance. For the actual type of change which they describe is not one which is likely to be very frequent. They assume an increase in total expenditure, which is associated with such a shift in demand in favour of X as to leave the demand for other goods diminished to an extent just equal to the diminution in their supply.

A more interesting type of change, from this point of view, is that in which total expenditure is kept constant. In the case of two industries only, this condition is sufficient to define exactly what must happen to the demand for Y, and consequently to its price. A supply curve for X could therefore be drawn up on this assumption, and it may be profitable to examine the properties of such a curve. It must be emphasised, however, that this case, too, has extremely limited application; for the condition of constant total expenditure is insufficient to define the supply curve exactly where more than two industries are present.

If e'_x is the elasticity of supply of X under this assumption, then in Case I, where one factor only is transferable:

$$\frac{1}{e'_x} = \frac{k_y}{\epsilon_x} + \frac{k_x}{\epsilon_y} \tag{3}$$

e'_x therefore necessarily lies between ϵ_x and ϵ_y. In Case II, where both factors are transferable,

$$e'_x = \frac{(1/k_x)\, h_{ax} h_{bx} \sigma_x + (1/k_y)\, h_{ay} h_{by} \sigma_y}{(h_{ax} - h_{ay})^2} \tag{4}$$

It will be observed that both of these expressions (3) and (4) are symmetrical between x and y. It therefore follows that e'_x must equal e'_y (the elasticity of supply of Y, under the same assumption of constant total expenditure).

II

1. I now proceed to the proofs of propositions (1) to (4). It will be convenient, for reasons which will subsequently appear, to begin with (2). The two products are here produced, under constant

returns to scale, by the same two factors, and both factors are transferable.

a, b, are amounts of factors used in the first industry, to produce x units of product; a', b' amounts used in the second industry to produce y units of product. p_a, p_b are prices of factors; p_x, p_y are prices of products.

Total supplies of factors are fixed, so $da + da' = 0$, $db + db' = 0$. Marginal productivity conditions give

$$(p_a) = p_x x_1 = p_y y_1 \qquad (p_b) = p_x x_2 = p_y y_2$$

writing x_1 for $(\partial x / \partial a)$, y_1 for $(\partial y / \partial a')$ and so on.

Differentiating the first of these (holding p_y constant)

$$x_1 \, dp_x + p_x (x_{11} \, da + x_{12} \, db) = p_y (y_{11} \, da' + y_{12} \, db')$$

or

$$x_1 \, dp_x + (p_x x_{11} + p_y y_{11}) \, da + (p_x x_{12} + p_y y_{12}) \, db = 0$$

and similarly from the second

$$x_2 \, dp_x + (p_x x_{12} + p_y y_{12}) \, da + (p_x x_{22} + p_y y_{22}) \, db = 0$$

From these, and from the identity

$$dx = x_1 \, da + x_2 \, db$$

we can eliminate da, db, giving

$$\begin{vmatrix} -(dx/dp_x) & x_1 & x_2 \\ x_1 & p_x x_{11} + p_y y_{11} & p_x x_{12} + p_y y_{12} \\ x_2 & p_x x_{12} + p_y y_{12} & p_x x_{22} + p_y y_{22} \end{vmatrix} = 0$$

Multiply the first row and first column of this determinant each by p_x, so that we have $-p_x^2 (dx/dp_x)$, or $-(p_x x) \, e_x$, in the top left corner, p_a, p_b in the remaining places of that first row and column. Then divide the second and third rows and columns by p_a, p_b respectively. The determinant can then be written

$$\begin{vmatrix} -(p_x x) \, e_x & 1 & 1 \\ 1 & -L & M \\ 1 & M & -N \end{vmatrix} = 0 \qquad\qquad (5)$$

so that $(p_x x) \, e_x = (L + 2M + N)/(LN - M^2)$.

What remains is to evaluate L, M, N in terms of the TW elasticities of substitution between the factors. On that definition σ_x (the e.s. between the factors in the x industry) $= x_1 x_2 / x x_{12}$ and similarly for σ_y.

Each of L, M, N, consists of two terms, one for each industry. The first term in M is

$$(p_x x_{12})/(p_a p_b) = (p_x x_1 x_2)/(p_a p_b x \sigma_x)$$
$$= 1/(p_x x \sigma_x)$$

and similarly for the other. For L we make use of the Euler conditions $ax_{11} + bx_{12} = 0$, $a'y_{11} + b'y_{12} = 0$; we can then reduce L in a similar manner. The results of these operations are more neatly expressed if we agree to use capitals for the *values* of the factors and products; thus $A = p_a a$, $A' = p_a a'$, $X = p_x x$, and so on. We then have

$$\left.\begin{aligned} L &= (B/A)(1/X\sigma_x) + (B'/A')(1/Y\sigma_y) \\ M &= \qquad (1/X\sigma_x) + \qquad\qquad (1/Y\sigma_y) \\ N &= (A/B)(1/X\sigma_x) + (A'/B')(1/Y\sigma_y) \end{aligned}\right\} \qquad (6)$$

When these values are substituted in (5) above, we have, for the denominator

$$LN - M^2 = [(AB'/A'B) + (A'B/AB') - 2]/(X\sigma_x Y\sigma_y)$$
$$= (AB' - A'B)^2/ABA'B'XY\sigma_x \sigma_y$$

and for the numerator

$$L + 2M + N = (X/AB\sigma_x) + (Y/A'B'\sigma_y)$$

since $A + B = X$, $A' + B' = Y$.

Dividing, we have, for the coefficient of σ_x:

$$XY^2 AB/(AB' - A'B)^2 = X h_{ax} h_{bx}/\Delta^2$$

h_{ax}, h_{bx} being factor-shares, as defined in part I, and Δ being

$$h_{ax} h_{by} - h_{bx} h_{ay} = h_{ax} - h_{ay} \qquad \text{(since } h_{ay} + h_{by} = 1)$$

Finally, therefore,

$$X e_x = (X h_{ax} h_{bx} \sigma_x + Y h_{ay} h_{by} \sigma_y)/\Delta^2 \qquad (7)$$

which is the formula given as (2) in part I.

2. If it is only the first factor that is transferable, the determinant (5) reduces to

$$\begin{vmatrix} -X e_x & 1 \\ 1 & -L \end{vmatrix} = 0 \qquad (8)$$

whence $(1/X e_x) = L$. The expression for L that was given in (6) is still valid; but the reduction to intra-industry σs is not necessary.

We may well prefer to work in terms of marginal costs (at given factor prices) thus avoiding dependence on constant returns to scale. The elasticities of supply at given factor prices, are the ϵ_x and ϵ_y of (1). Noting that here $a_x (= da/dx) = (1/x_1)$, so that $x_1 = (1/a_x)$, we have

$$x_{11} = - (a_{xx}/a_x^2)\, x_1 = - (a_{xx}/a_x)\, x_1^2$$

so that

$$L = - (p_x x_{11} + p_y y_{11})/p_a^2$$
$$= p_x (a_{xx}/a_x)/p_x^2 + p_y (a_{yy}/a_y)\, p_y^2$$
$$= (1/X\epsilon_x) + (1/Y\epsilon_y)$$

which gives (1).

3. For the derivation of (3) and (4) no more is needed than to observe that if $p_x x + p_y y$ is constant, we must have

$$x\, dp_x + y\, dp_y = 0$$

since (in equilibrium) $p_x\, dx + p_y\, dy = 0$. It follows from these two equations that $e_x' = e_y'$ (as previously defined).

Now if S_{xy} is the elasticity of substitution along the (x, y) frontier, defined (as is here inevitable) in the Joan Robinson manner, e_x (with p_y constant) will be $k_y S_{xy}$, by the usual rule. When both p_x and p_y are variable, but $x\, dp_x + y\, dp_y = 0$, it can readily be calculated, from that definition, that

$$e_x' = S_{xy}$$

This relation will hold, whatever the position about transferability of factors. That is all that needs to be said.

III

That the basic formulae, (1) and (2) are best considered as expressing S_{xy} (the e.s. between the products) in terms of σ_x and σ_y (the intra-industry e.s. between the factors) had already been observed in what corresponded, in the original version, to the previous section. But I suppose I did not see this until nearly the end of my work, so I did not give it the attention it deserved. Once one perceives that $e_x = k_y S_{xy}$, it becomes apparent that the formulae are *symmetrical* expressions for S_{xy}, as they should be.

Let us write them in this form, using the reduction to intra-industry σs in each case, for greater comparability. We then have, for (1)

$$(1/k_x k_y S_{xy}) = (h_{bx}/h_{ax})(1/k_x \sigma_x) + (h_{by}/h_{ay})(1/k_y \sigma_y) \qquad (9)$$

and for (2)

$$k_x k_y S_{xy} = (k_x h_{ax} h_{bx} \sigma_x + k_y h_{ay} h_{by} \sigma_y)/\Delta^2 \qquad (10)$$

Thus in (10) S_{xy} is linearly related to σ_x and σ_y, while in (9) there is a linear relation between their reciprocals.

The economic meaning of this is quite interesting. Consider the conditions for S_{xy} to be infinite (the two products to be perfect substitutes) in the one case and in the other.

If S_{xy} is infinite, its reciprocal is zero; (9) tells us that, under its assumption of the single transferable factor, this cannot happen (apart from trivial cases when some h or some k is zero) unless *both* σ_x and σ_y are infinite – or, what comes to the same thing, unless *both* products are producible at constant cost in terms of the trans-ferable factor. Any shift in demand must lead to a change in relative price, if marginal cost is non-constant in *either* industry.

It follows, however, from (10) that S_{xy} may be infinite, so that the products are perfect substitutes on the supply side, *either* if there is perfect substitutability in *either* of the industries, *or* if Δ is zero, so that factor proportions in the industries are the same. How much easier it is to get high substitutability among products when there is much transferability is striking.

Notice that it is only in (10) that Δ appears. It could not appear in (9) since there is there no reason to suppose that the non-transferable factors in the two industries are identical; one might be one sort of land, the other another sort of land. It is only when factors are transferable that they must be expressible in comparable quantities.

Does it not look as if (9) belongs to what one might call a Marshallian world, which is also the world of Keynes and of their successors at Cambridge, while the world of (10) is that of Walras, of Hechscher–Ohlin, and of their many successors? My own preference, in latter days, is to go with the Marshallians. But I am rather proud to be able to show that, so long ago, I had found a vantage-point from which one could look in both directions.

19

Linear Theory

This essay was written as one of the *Surveys of Economic Theory* which had been commissioned by the American Economic Association and the Royal Economic Society. It first appeared in the *Economic Journal* in December 1960 and was then included in the third volume of these *Surveys* (1966). Thus it is fairly easily available, and I began by doubting whether it should be included here. But it is not just a summary of the work of others; much of it is a version I had had to make for myself. For my purpose was different from that of the text books which already abounded. I was not trying to teach a technique; I was trying to write up its story, as an episode in the history of economics. As such it belongs in this volume.

It was quite a labour to write it. But it was useful preparation, first for the paper on the 'Turnpike' which follows, and then for the 'von Neumann' chapters in *CG* (XVIII–XIX). It will be noticed that the scepticism which is expressed in the last section of this paper (p. 289 below) is matched by that expressed at the end of those von Neumann chapters (*CG*, pp. 235–7) and, most explicitly, at the end of one of the new papers in this collection: 'It is the assumption of a *given technology* which is the joker' (volume 1, p. 282).

Two difficult passages, which I expect that many readers would prefer to omit, have been marked out, in this version, from the rest of the text.

The subject which I shall be discussing in this survey concerns the group of techniques – Linear Programming, Activity Analysis, Input–Output and Theory of Games[1] – which have come to us, chiefly from America, since 1945. It is apparent, from the most casual inspection of these topics, that they are very closely related. Further examination shows that they can be set around a recognis-

[1] I shall have much less to say about game theory than about the others.

able core, which may be regarded as a restatement of a central part of conventional economic theory. It will be my object, in what follows, to isolate this core; and to consider what there is that the economist, who has no intention of becoming a practitioner of the techniques, may yet have to learn from it.[2]

This being the intention, it will obviously be proper to put what I have to say into a form in which the mathematics are kept down as much as possible; but it is useless to conceal from the reader that we are dealing with a mathematical subject. The phenomenon which we are to examine is the application to economics of a new kind of mathematics. The most obvious difference between this new mathematical economics and the older variety (which goes back to Cournot) lies in the kind of mathematics that is being used.

All through the first period of mathematical economics — the age of Marshall, of Pareto, of Wicksell, even that of Pigou and Keynes — the economist's main mathematical tool was the differential calculus, expressed (when necessary) in the form of symbols, reduced (when possible) to the form of curves. This, of course, was perfectly natural; most economic problems were problems of maxima and minima, and (since the days of Newton and Leibniz) the differential calculus has been the standard method by which such problems had been approached. It has, however, long been known that there are some quite elementary maximum problems (such, for instance, as those concerned with perimeters of triangles) for which the calculus method is not at all well suited; they may, however, give no trouble if they are tackled on an *ad hoc* basis, usually in Euclidean terms. The development of systematic methods for the study of such cases as these has been an object to which, in our time, quite formidable mathematical ability has been devoted. And the new methods, once

---

[2] My purpose is therefore quite different from that of the numerous text books which seek to teach the techniques to the practitioners. It is, however, not far from that which might have been expected from the authors of *Linear Programming and Economic Analysis* (Dorfman, Samuelson and Solow); it is certainly true that without their work the present paper could not have been written. My main criticism of their performance is that they did not sufficiently differentiate their task from that of the text books. I accordingly propose to begin in quite a different way from that in which they begin, though in the latter stages of my work I shall draw on them very heavily. (It would then be a great nuisance not to have a single name for this composite author; I shall make bold to christen him, when I need to do so, DOSSO.)

Reference must also be made to the excellent survey by W. J. Baumol ('Activity Analysis in one Lesson', *American Economic Review*, December 1958). His purpose has been nearer to mine, but I think he would be the first to admit that there is room for both of us.

The text books from which I have derived most benefit are those of S. Vajda (*Theory of Games and Linear Programming*) and S. I. Gass (*Linear Programming*). Both of these are highly mathematical; but they have helped me to grasp the structure of the theory (with which I shall be largely concerned) more clearly than I could get it elsewhere.

248   *Linear Theory*

found, have often proved to be more satisfactory than the old, even in fields where it is possible for both to be applied.[3] The linear theory, which we are to examine, derives much of its character from the fact that it is an application of some of these newer mathematical methods to economics.[4]

So much must be said, even at the start; though it is inevitable that by saying it one raises the suspicion that economics is being used as a mere opportunity for mathematical exercise, valuable enough to the mathematicians who disport themselves upon this parade-ground, but with a marginal product (in terms of the things in which economists are interested) that is, after all, infinitesimal. I would not myself deny that there is something in this. It is easy to find pieces of 'activity analysis' that do no more than re-state a fairly obvious point in esoteric terms. Nevertheless, after all discounting, there are substantial things that remain. Most obviously, there are the contributions which have been made by the associated techniques to the solution of certain kinds of business (or other practical economic) problems; but these, though their importance is unquestionable, will not be our main concern in what follows. The contributions which have been made by the new methods to economic theory look, at first sight, much slighter. One cannot claim much more for most of them than that they are improvements in the statements we can now make of familiar points: things of which we were (more or less) aware, but which one can now realise that we were putting rather badly. I shall consider such matters in some detail. I would, however, maintain that they are chiefly worth considering because they do carry with them a deepening in our understanding of something that is rather central — nothing less than the ends–means relationship which is what so much of economics is about. Something of that will, I hope, emerge before I have finished.

[3] Thus Hardy, Littlewood and Polya (*Inequalities*, p. 108), writing (in 1934) of a distinct but related field: 'The (calculus) method is attractive theoretically, and always opens a first line of attack on the problem; but is apt to lead to serious complications in detail (usually connected with the boundary values of the variables) and it will be found that, however suggestive, it rarely leads to the simplest solution.' As we shall see, it is much the same story here.

[4] Since my own formal mathematical education (such as it was) ended in 1923, I do not pretend that I myself feel at all at home with these newer methods. I can, however, feel fairly confident about the use which I have had to make of them, because of the advice which I have received from a number of experts. My greatest debt is to Dr H. W. Kuhn (of Princeton), who was spending the year of 1958–9 in London, and who was kind enough to criticise a first draft in considerable detail. Afterwards, in California and in Japan, I had the benefit of consultations with Michio Morishima, with Kenneth Arrow and with George Dantzig himself. To each of these (and also to R. C. O. Matthews, who called my attention to a qualification not easy to disentangle from the literature) I offer my thanks.

I. Origins

It is convenient to let the story begin from a simple pedagogic point.

Anyone who has attempted to put the Walrasian theory of general equilibrium (with fixed coefficients of production) on to a classroom diagram will have had something like the following experience. One cuts it down to the simplest possible case – two goods and two factors. Measuring quantities of the two goods along two axes, one gets a diagram such as that shown in figure 19.1. The quantities of the two goods that can be produced with a given supply of factor A are shown by the straight line AA'; the quantities that can be produced with a given supply of factor B are shown by the line BB'; thus it is *only* the set of quantities represented by P, the point of intersection, that *can* be produced, so long as one assumes (as Walras assumed) that both factors are to be kept fully employed. The quantities of products, and the quantities of factors employed in the production of each, seem therefore to be determined, before anything has been said about prices, or about demands. The general equilibrium system, which is supposed to show the way in which output adjusts itself to demand through the price-mechanism, has the serious defect, when it is regarded as a means of teaching economics: that in the simplest example, the example which it is most natural to take as an illustration, it does not work.

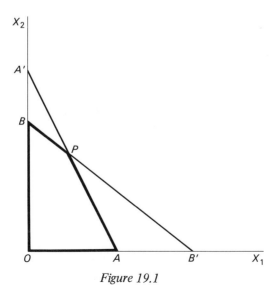

Figure 19.1

Now, it is, of course, true that as soon as we introduce another product (or, more generally, so long as we keep the number of products greater than the number of factors) the difficulty disappears, or at any rate becomes less acute. The quantities of products cease to be technologically determined, so that the price-mechanism can begin to function. For many Walrasians[5] that has been enough. The case of fixed coefficients, with fixed supplies of factors, has been for them no more than a stepping-stone on the way to something more general; the rigidities which appear in the elementary case have not therefore seemed to be so very interesting. Yet it must be admitted to be a defect in a theory that it does not clear up its own elementary cases. Mere consideration of the elementary case is enough to show that the Walras theory cannot be quite right.

It does not appear that much attention was paid to this weakness in the days of Walras and Pareto.[6] What brought it to the surface was Cassel's simplification of the Lausanne system;[7] in Cassel's version it rather stood out. As is well known, there was a phase (in the 1920s) when Cassel's treatise was displacing those of the 'historical' and 'Austrian' schools in the curricula of Central European universities; during such a struggle its weaknesses would be carefully watched. It is not surprising that this particular difficulty was noticed;[8] and it is also intelligible that by some of those who came to Cassel with an *Austrian* background the way in which the difficulty has to be met was noticed too.[9]

For there is a memorable section in Menger's *Grundsätze*[10] in which he distinguishes between 'economic' and 'non-economic' goods – the latter, in his terminology, being goods which have no value, because the amount of them which is desired, when no value is set upon them, is less than the quantity of them that is available. There is a general tendency (so Menger maintained) for the range of goods that are 'economic' to widen in the course of development; minerals, for instance, that have no value at an early stage of development become valuable when more capital is accumulated.

[5] Including the present author, when he wrote *Value and Capital* (1939).
[6] It should be noticed that Walras's basic fixed-coefficient model did not assume fixed factor-supplies.
[7] *Theory of Social Economy*, part II.
[8] See the discussion of W. L. Valk's *Principles of Wages* (1928) in D. H. Robertson, 'Wage Grumbles' (*Economic Fragments*, p. 52).
[9] Articles by Neisser (*Weltwirtschaftsliches Archiv*, 1932), Stackelberg (*Zeitschrift für Nationalökonomie*, 1933) and Zeuthen (also in *Zeitschrift für Nationalökonomie*, 1933) are widely quoted.
[10] Chapter 2.

Accordingly, to a follower of Menger, the determination of economic equilibrium would not merely involve the determination of the prices of those goods that have prices (as in Walras); it should also involve the determination of which goods are to have prices, and which are to be free. The weakness of the Walras–Cassel construction lies in the implied assumption that the whole amount of each available factor is utilised; once that assumption is dropped, the awkwardness of the construction (even in the two-good, two-factor case) can be shown to disappear.

It is at once apparent, if we drop the assumption that both factors must be fully utilised, that the possible combinations of products that can be produced from available resources are not confined (in figure 19.1) to the point P; they comprise all those combinations that àre represented by the whole area $OAPB$. Nor is P the only *efficient* combination; for if product X_2 were not *wanted*, OA would be the maximum amount of X_1 that could be produced; there would be a sense in which production would be maximised all along the broken line APB. The only peculiarity of the point P is that it is the only point at which both factors are scarce. It we do not assume that, the whole of APB becomes a *frontier*. As demand varies, the equilibrium point can move from one end of this frontier to the other. Throughout the whole of this process the price-mechanism is working.

It is easy for the 'intuition' of the 'literary' economist to get that far; but there would have been little progress beyond that point if it had not been for the mathematicians. It was the fact that mathematical methods were being prepared, which were capable of dealing with the equilibrium of a system which is restricted by inequalities, that made it possible to go on. The next events to be recorded are therefore the appearance of two mathematical papers, which I shall make no attempt to discuss in detail, but which must be mentioned, since from them everything subsequent has sprung. An attempt will be made later to describe the substance of their contributions in different terms.

The first of these papers, in order of publication, was the 'proof', by Abraham Wald, of the existence of an equilibrium of the Walras–Cassel system, extended (as just explained) so as to allow for the possibility of free, as well as scarce, factors. This was not in fact a satisfactory proof, since it assumed that the demands for products would not fall to zero, however high prices rose – an assumption that can hardly be admitted. It did nevertheless establish that the 'extended' system is capable of mathematical manipulation; it may therefore be said to mark the first stage in the process by which the 'Austrians' had their mathematical revenge on the followers of Walras.[11]

Much more important, for what followed, was the other; the famous paper by John von Neumann 'A Model of General Economic Equilibrium' (to give it the title by which it is known to English readers).[12] It has been the extraordinary achievement of this work that it has had a profound influence on the development of economic thinking in several different directions. As a dynamic model of an expanding economy, it has been the father of many growth models; but it also has some more static aspects (which alone concern us in this place[13]); as things have turned out so far, the influence of these has been at least as important. The dynamic model is built up as a sequence of 'single-period' links; each of these links, since there is no opportunity for adjustments over time *within* it, can be regarded as a static (or timeless) system. The form in which von Neumann studies this static system is substantially that which we have been calling the 'extended Walras–Cassel'; but in his hands this is already passing over into *activity analysis*. He does not content himself with allowing for the possibilities that available inputs may not be used, feasible outputs may not be produced; he allows for the possibility of joint products, and that available processes may not be employed. Besides, there is included in von Neumann's construction a first statement of what was to become known as the Duality

---

[11] Wald's paper was presented (with an introduction by Karl Schlesinger) to a seminar in Vienna presided over by Karl Menger (mathematician son of the economist Menger) in March 1934. It was printed in *Ergebnisse eines mathematischen Kolloquiums*, Heft 6, 1935. There is a further paper in the following issue of the same publication, and an article (which, among other things, summarises the results of these mathematical papers) in *Zeitschrift für Nationalökonomie*, 1936. The *Zeitschrift* article was translated into English (*Econometrica*, 1951).

The reasons which led Wald to make his curious assumption about demand functions have been explored by Dr Kuhn ('On a Theorem of Wald', in *Linear Inequalities and Related Systems*, Annals of Mathematics Studies 38, Princeton, 1956). I shall be returning to this matter later. (See below, p. 280n.)

[12] There is an awkward question of priority. The von Neumann paper was also published in the Menger *Ergebnisse* (Heft 8, for 1935–6, published 1937). (The English translation is in *Review of Economic Studies*, No. 33, 1945–6.) It is, however, understood that it was originally presented to a seminar at Princeton in 1932, which puts it before Wald, and even before such things as the Neisser article above mentioned. (I know, from personal recollection, that he had these things in mind in September 1933, when I met him with Kaldor in Budapest. Of course, I did not understand what he was saying!)

[13] Although all the theories we shall be discussing have (or can have) dynamic aspects, the static side will give us quite enough to deal with. [But see essay 20 below.]

principle (of which I shall have much more to say later). It is singularly appropriate that it was von Neumann who introduced that principle into the theory of economic optimisation, for it is the link which establishes a connection (we shall be examining later what sort of connection) between that theory and the Theory of Games.

From this point, the later developments begin to branch out; but before discussing these later developments, it will be well to attempt a statement of the stage so far reached. There is indeed no single work which can be said to correspond at all exactly to the stage I have in mind. New ideas tumble out one after another with such rapidity in von Neumann's few pages, that he is already in the middle of the next chapter before he has finished with the first. It will be useful here to take things more slowly. The 'prototype' theory which I shall describe in the next section will still run in terms of 'extended Walras–Cassel'; that is to say, it is solely concerned with the allocation of given factor supplies in the production of a number of products, each of which is to be made by combining factors in proportions that are technically given. Only afterwards shall I go on to the reinterpretations, by von Neumann and others, which have not merely allowed for variable proportions of factors, for joint supply and for intermediate products (all of which things are left out in the prototype), but have enabled the analysis to be applied to problems of business management which are at first sight of quite different kinds. One of the main difficulties with later writings is that they are (rightly) so impressed by these reinterpretations that they insist on beginning their exposition on a high plane of generality. I find it easier to take one thing at a time; though the theory which will now be described is mainly interesting because it can be generalised, it is easiest to put it, at the first round, in a rather conventional setting.

II. The Prototype

1. Given amounts of M factors of production are available; we will call these amounts $b_1, b_2, \ldots, b_M$. There are N products which can be produced by the utilisation of these factors; the (as yet undetermined) amounts of these products we call $x_1, x_2, \ldots, x_N$. There are fixed technical coefficients; that is to say, the amount of each factor required to make a unit of each product is given. The amount of the ith factor needed to make a unit of the jth product we call a_{ij}.

It is clearly implied, when the problem is stated in these terms, that the constants (a's and b's) must obey certain restrictions if they are to make economic sense. Though these restrictions look terribly obvious, we shall get into serious trouble if we do not put them down. (1) Every b_i must be positive; negative factor supplies are meaningless, and a product that required a factor that was in zero supply could not possibly be produced. (2) The technical coefficients a_{ij} cannot be negative; we may, however, allow some of them to be zero – not every factor need be required for every product. (3) But some amount of at least one factor must be required for every product; there can be no j for which $a_{ij} = 0$, for all i. Mathematically, these restrictions define what we are calling the prototype problem. Since they were (I believe) first set out formally by Wald, I shall call them (together with a fourth rule to be mentioned later) the *Wald rules*.

If a set of outputs $(x_1, x_2, \ldots, x_N)$ – or, more briefly (x_j) – is to be *feasible* it must satisfy two sets of conditions, or *constraints*. First, no x_j may be negative (though some or all may be zero); this again looks obvious, but again it is vital that such obvious matters are not overlooked. Secondly, the amount of any factor that is required to produce the set (x_j) must in no case exceed the amount of that factor that is available. The first set of constraints – that $x_j \geqslant 0$ for all j – might be called product constraints, but (with an eye on subsequent generalisation) I prefer a more general description. I shall therefore call them *sign constraints*. The second set, which imply that

$$a_{11}x_1 + a_{12}x_2 + \ldots + a_{1N}x_N \leqslant b_1$$
$$a_{21}x_1 + a_{22}x_2 + \ldots + a_{2N}x_N \leqslant b_2$$
$$\cdot \qquad \cdot \qquad \cdot \qquad \cdot \qquad \cdot$$
$$a_{M1}x_1 + a_{M2}x_2 + \ldots + a_{MN}x_M \leqslant b_M$$

I shall for the same reason call *specific constraints*. There are N sign constraints and M specific constraints, $M + N$ in all. There are N xs to be determined. Thus the number of constraints is always *greater* than the number of unknowns, when all constraints are taken into consideration.

As always in such cases, it is a great help to make as much use as we can of a diagrammatic representation. The problem which has just been set out, for M factors and N products, is precisely that which was expressed, for two factors and two products, in figure

19.1. The feasible *region*,[14] as drawn, was bounded by straight lines that corresponded to the four constraints: two sign constraints (*OA* and *OB*), two specific constraints (*AA'* and *BB'*). The Wald rules have made it necessary that we should get a feasible region that is something like *OAPB*. It is clearly not excluded that one of the specific constraints might have been ineffective (if *AA'*, *BB'* had failed to meet within the positive quadrant) so that the feasible region might have been reduced to a triangle. And it is clearly not excluded that one (or both) of the specific 'arms' might have been parallel to an axis; what is excluded is that they should both be parallel to the same axis, for that would mean that there was a product which did not require any factor, and that is ruled out. It would therefore seem that the polygonal form (such as *OAPB*), or something like it, is going to be typical.

2.   It would now be possible to pose the problem before us in the form of asking for a determination of all feasible solutions: the answer to that question, in the case illustrated, would be the definition of the whole area *OAPB*. But out of all these points, it is only those that lie upon the frontier *APB* which are really interesting; it is only these which, in some sense or other, 'maximise output'. How do we distinguish between these frontier points and the rest of those that are feasible? There are, in principle, two ways of making the distinction.

One is to say that a feasible point is a frontier point if it is a terminus of a vector from the origin; that is to say, if it is laid down that the various outputs are to be produced in fixed proportions, the quantity of any product (and hence of the composite product) that is produced must be maximised. The other is to say that if the products are valued at fixed prices ($p_1, p_2, \ldots, p_N$) the value of output ($\Sigma p_j x_j$) must be maximised. (It must be clearly understood, if we adopt this second distinction, that the ps must be non-negative; we may allow some of them to be zero, but it will be nonsense for all to be zero. This is the fourth of the Wald rules.)

There are economic purposes for which the difference between these two approaches is very important; the whole theory of increasing

---

[14] I am aware that for mathematicians the term *region* has connotations of continuity which are not necessarily implied in the uses I shall be making of it. A more correct terminology would, however, involve explanations which for present purposes are largely irrelevant. In this, and some other cases, I must ask forgiveness for a use of terms in something looser than the strict mathematical sense.

returns may be said to depend upon it. It can, however, be shown[15] that under present assumptions they come to the same thing, so it does not matter which we use. It has proved to be more convenient to work with the test by value of output, according to which a position on the frontier is found by maximising Σpx for given (p). A set of outputs which does this, subject to the constraints is called an *optimum*.

It is at once apparent that for the case which is shown in our diagram there are two sorts of optima. (1) The optimum may be *at a vertex*, such as A, P or B. (2) The optimum may be, as we shall say, *on a flat* – on AP or PB. There will be several values of the price-ratio (p_1/p_2) which will correspond to each vertex optimum; but it is only particular values of the price-ratio which will give a flat optimum – but for those values any point on the flat can be optimum. It will now be shown that the distinction between vertex optima and flat optima is quite generally valid; but for that purpose we need some more general definitions.

3. Let us begin by looking at the vertices on our diagram more closely. At P the two products are both being produced, and the two factors are both scarce; thus we have two positive products (as we may call them) and two scarce factors. At A (and at B) there is only one positive product, and one scarce factor. At O (which must be reckoned as a vertex, though – so long as the Wald rules hold – it cannot be an optimum) we have no positive product and no scarce factor. Thus at all the vertices the number of positive products is equal to the number of scarce factors.

When a factor is scarce the corresponding specific constraint becomes an equation; we may then say that the constraint is *operative*. Thus the vertex P is determined by two specific constraints which are operative. At A there is only one specific constraint which is operative; but the place of the other is taken by a sign constraint, which now becomes operative $(x_2 = 0)$. At O it is only the sign constraints which are operative. Thus each of the vertices is determined by two operative constraints – two equations to determine the two unknowns. A general rule for the determination of a vertex is accordingly suggested: a vertex is a set of N outputs (x_j) which is determined by N operative restraints, to be selected from the total number of constraints $(M + N)$. But this is not quite the whole story.

---

[15] See below, p. 267n.

For (as is again apparent from the diagram) the list of points which would be calculated by this rule is longer than the list of vertices. When the above procedure is applied to that elementary case it would not only throw up the true vertices (A, P, B and O); it will also throw up the pseudo-vertices (A' and B'). These must clearly be excluded; what excludes them? They are excluded by their failure to satisfy some of the constraints which in their determination have been taken as non-operative. A true vertex is a set of outputs which is determined by selecting N of the $M + N$ constraints to be operative, and which also satisfies (as inequalities) the remaining non-operative constraints. Thus, when the optimum is at a vertex, the number of positive outputs should be equal to the number of scarce factors; and the non-scarce factors should be in excess supply.

4. So much for the vertices; now for the optima which lie *on the flat* between the vertices. It is clear that the number of scarce factors cannot ordinarily[16] be greater than the number of positive products; for if it was, we should have more equations than unknowns, and the system would be over-determined. But it is perfectly possible that the number of scarce factors may be *less* than the number of positive products. (Thus for an optimum between A and P, on figure 19.1, we have two positive products, and only one scarce factor.) It will later be shown that this is a general characteristic of flat optima; but it will be more convenient, for the moment, to define them, and to get out their properties, in another way.

It is a well-known rule that if α, β are two points on a line, with co-ordinates (x_α, y_α) (x_β, y_β), the co-ordinates of any other point on the line can be expressed as $(k_\alpha x_\alpha + k_\beta x_\beta, k_\alpha y_\alpha + k_\beta y_\beta)$ where $k_\alpha + k_\beta = 1$. In terms of these *weights*, the point α is $(1, 0)$; the point β is $(0, 1)$; any point on the line *between* α and β will have both weights positive; any point outside $\alpha\beta$ will have one weight negative. There is therefore a sense in which we can regard any point on the line between α and β (including α and β) as being a *weighted average* of α and β; it being understood that the weights are non-negative, and add up to 1.

The points on the flat between A and P (on figure 19.1) can thus be regarded as weighted averages of A and P – two vertices which, in the case where the optimum is on the flat, must be such that at them the value of output $V(= \Sigma px)$ is the same. It is accordingly

---

[16] It will later appear that there is a qualification to this statement which is of some importance.

suggested that we might define the flat optimum as a condition in which two (or more) vertices give the same value of output; any weighted average of these vertices may then be an optimum. It is evident that if V takes the same value at each of the points $(\alpha, \beta, \ldots, \lambda)$, it will also take the same value at any weighted average of $(\alpha, \beta, \ldots, \lambda)$. But before we can accept this definition there is a further matter to be cleared up.

If a point is to be an optimum it must be feasible; how do we know that these points, defined as weighted averages of vertices, are feasible? It can in fact be shown that they must be; this is a special case of a general, and very important property – *any weighted average of a set of feasible points must be feasible*. The mathematical name for this property is *convexity*;[17] what we have to show is that the feasible region is convex. The proof is as follows.

Let $(\alpha, \beta, \ldots, \lambda)$ be feasible points. Take the point which is expressible as the weighted average $(k_\alpha, k_\beta, \ldots, k_\lambda)$. Substitute its co-ordinates (written in full) into any one of the specific constraints, say the ith. Then

$$a_{i1}x_1 + a_{i2}x_2 + \ldots a_{iN}x_N = k_\alpha(a_{i1}x_{1\alpha} + a_{i2}x_{2\alpha} + \ldots + a_{iN}x_{N\alpha})$$
$$+ \ldots + k_\lambda(a_{i1}x_{1\lambda} + a_{i1}x_{2\lambda} + \ldots a_{iN}x_{N\lambda})$$
$$\leqslant k_\alpha b_i + k_\beta b_i + \ldots + k_\lambda b_i$$

since $(\alpha, \beta, \ldots)$ satisfy the constraints, and the ks are non-negative. Then, since the ks add up to 1, the last sum is b_i. Thus any weighted average satisfies the specific constraints, and can be shown to satisfy the sign constraints in the same way. Thus it is feasible.

It is accordingly safe to lay down that when there is a 'tie' between vertex optima any weighted average of these vertex optima is itself an optimum. That is what the *flat optimum* means.

5. So far we have (basically) been arguing from analogy; the method described in the last paragraph can, however, be used to give something which is a bit nearer to a proof of the properties in question.

It is not only the points *on the flat* which can be regarded as weighted averages of vertices; if we bring all the vertices into account, any point within the feasible region (inside the region, or on its boundary) can similarly be expressed as a weighted average of

---

[17] For a further discussion of this concept, see below, p. 266.

vertices. (This can often be done in several ways, but that does not matter.) Further, in view of the convexity of the region, it is *only* points that are within the region that can be thus expressed. Suppose that we now take $(\alpha, \beta, \ldots, \lambda)$ to be the vertices, and consider a point which can be expressed by $(k_\alpha, k_\beta, \ldots, k_\lambda)$. Substituting its co-ordinates into the value of output, as we have previously substituted into the constraints, we get

$$V = \Sigma px = k_\alpha V_\alpha + k_\beta V_\beta + \ldots + k_\lambda V_\lambda$$

where $V_\alpha, V_\beta, \ldots, V_\lambda$ are the values of output at the vertices. Then, since the weights are non-negative and add up to 1, it is obvious that in the case where there is one of the Vs which is larger than any of the others, the optimum is reached if the whole weight is placed at the vertex; while in the case where there is a 'tie', an optimum will be reached by dividing the weight between the tying vertices *in any manner.* That is all that there is to be said.

6. So far as the determination of the optimum is concerned, that completes the prototype theory; the most remarkable development of the theory is nevertheless still to come. This is concerned with the determination of factor prices.

Let us go back, for a moment, to the 'Walras' model, of the two factors and two products, with which we began. It is not merely the case that if we analyse it in Walras's manner, outputs appear to be established independently of demands; it is also the case that (if product prices are assumed to be given),[18] factor prices appear to be determined independently of the supplies of the factors. Corresponding to the *equations*

$$a_{11}x_1 + a_{12}x_2 = b_1, \qquad a_{21}x_1 + a_{22}x_2 = b_2$$

(which make outputs seem to depend upon technical coefficients and factor supplies only), there are the equations of prices and costs (that there is no profit that cannot be imputed to some factor); these will read

$$w_1 a_{11} + w_2 a_{21} = p_1, \qquad w_1 a_{12} + w_2 a_{22} = p_2$$

Taken by themselves, they seem to make the factor prices w_1, w_2 depend upon product prices and technical coefficients only.

---

[18] Walras, of course, did not assume that they were given. That this is an important assumption has nevertheless been brought to the attention of economists by Samuelson (see his Factor Price Equalisation Theorem).

As we have seen, the first set of equations is not universally valid. It needs to be completed so as to allow for the possibility of a factor being in excess supply; when that is done, demands come back into the picture. An exactly analogous argument, applied to the second set, uncovers the assumption that the outputs of both products are positive. If that is not so, if (say) $x_2 = 0$, there is no reason why the cost of the second product should equal its price. A possible combination of factor prices would be such that price equalled cost for the first product, but fell short of cost for the second. The second would not then be produced; it would not pay to produce it.

This simple example is sufficient to show that the theory of imputation (derivation of factor prices from product prices) needs to be completed by an inclusion of 'inequality' cases, just as has been done for the theory of quantity optimisation. It also suggests (what proves to be true) that there is a sense in which the one theory is a mirror image of the other. Let us look at this more generally.

7.   Suppose that at a particular optimum, n of the N possible products are positive products, the remaining $N-n$ having zero outputs. And suppose that m of the M factors are scarce factors, the remaining $M-m$ having zero factor prices.[19] Then it would appear from our preceding discussion (though there is qualification to this to be made in a moment) that at a vertex optimum $m = n$, while at a flat optimum $m < n$. We must again look at these two cases separately.

At the vertex optimum we have $m = n$ equations of the form $\Sigma a_{ij}x_j = b_i$ to determine the n positive outputs; and (since price equals cost for each of these n products) we have an equal number of equations, of the form $\Sigma w_i a_{ij} = p_j$, to determine the $m = n$ prices of the scarce factors. Corresponding to the other factors, where $w_i = 0$, we have the inequalities $\Sigma a_{ij}x_j < b_i$. Corresponding to the other products, where $x_j = 0$, we have the inequalities $\Sigma w_i a_{ij} > p_j$. Apart from the difference in sign of the two sets of inequalities, there is complete symmetry.

The flat optimum is at first sight more perplexing. Here we have $m < n$; there are only m equations to determine the n positive outputs; these outputs are therefore under-determined, but that (it will be remembered) is what they should be. On the other hand, we have n equations $\Sigma w_i a_{ij} = p_j$ to determined the m prices of the scarce factors; these seem therefore to be over-determined. The explanation

---

[19] I take it for granted that the factor prices of the non-scarce factors are zero.

is that it is not possible for a flat optimum to occur at any arbitrary set of prices (p); it can only occur at particular sets of (p), which are related in such a manner that the n equations of prices and costs can be simultaneously satisfied. (The *labour theory of value*, regarded as a statement that the prices of positive products must be proportional to their labour costs, when labour is the only scarce factor, may be regarded as a particular case of this proposition.) If we have begun with an appropriate (p), we can get a flat optimum, with a corresponding (w). The constraints on the (x) will be operative, for all factors where w_i is not zero; and the constraints on the (w), as we may begin to call them, will be operative, for all products where x_j is not zero. Where w_i is zero, and where x_j is zero, we have the same inequalities as before.

But now, having found a way of overcoming the obstacle of over-determinateness in the case where $m < n$, we should look back to see whether we have not been too precipitate in the other case. Would it not have been possible to have found a way round, in a similar manner, which would have salvaged the possibility that $m > n$? The factor prices would then have been under-determined, so that there would have been 'flatness' on that side – there is no difficulty about that; but the only way in which m operative equations on n positive products can all be satisfied, when $m > n$, is for there to be some special relations between the factor supplies (b), just as there had to be suitable relations between the (p) in the opposite case. There is no doubt that this way out is mathematically valid, and it is useful as showing how we may complete the symmetry; but I have refrained from bringing it in until now, since I think that the economist is justified in feeling a little shy of it, at least in the present application. He is undoubtedly interested in the optima that will be reached at various (p), some of which will certainly be inter-related, so that the case where $m < n$ is important to him; but he had begun by thinking of the factor supplies as *given*, so that inter-relations between them, which would enable more than n factors to be scarce simultaneously, would be rather a fluke. Still, it is a possibility, and it is a possibility which, at this stage, has important consequences.

For what we now come to is the Principle of Duality. The conditions which govern the outputs (x) and the factor prices (w), in an optimum position, correspond exactly. We had, however, determined the (x) in a way which could be completely described without introducing the (w); since the constraints on the (w) are so remarkably similar, it is strongly suggested that the (w) might themselves have been *independently* determined in a similar way. That is in fact so; it is not easy to prove it, but a sketch of a proof is given below.[20]

8. The Duality Principle is chiefly important, to an economist, for the following reason. It is rather a defect of the foregoing treatment that it has had to introduce the factor prices, in Walras's manner, as elements in a model of competitive capitalism, in which the factor prices govern *distribution*; in the other part of the theory, in which the optimum *quantities* had been determined, no such assumption as this had been required. It would in fact have been possible to have introduced the factor prices, without reference to distributive shares, as instruments of quantity optimisation; though it would not have been so easy to carry through the argument in detail, we might have proceeded on something like the following lines.

Suppose that arbitrary (non-negative) prices are set upon the factors, and that an entrepreneur (or planner) is provided with a

[20] We started with the condition that the (x) should be *feasible*: in the sense that they are non-negative, and that their factor requirements do not exceed the available factor supplies – that is to say, that $\Sigma a_{ij}x_j \leqslant b_i$ for all i from 1 to M (the specific constraints). We found ourselves imposing a parallel set of constraints on the (w): that they should be non-negative, and that the costs of the products, at these factor prices, should equal or exceed the given product prices – that is to say, the $\Sigma w_i a_{ij} \geqslant p_j$, for all j from 1 to N (which we may now regard as specific constraints on the (w)). Evidently we may say that the (w) are *feasible* if they satisfy the constraints just laid down.

Now take the specific constraints on the (x), multiply each of them by the corresponding w, and add. Since if the (w) are feasible, they must be non-negative, the resulting inequality will hold, whenever both (x) and (w) are feasible. What it states is that the cost of the set of outputs (x_j), valued at the factor prices (w_i), cannot exceed the aggregate value of the factors, at those same factor prices. If this cost is C, and this factor value B, we have $C \leqslant B$, whenever (x) and (w) are both feasible.

Then take the specific constraints on the (w), multiply each by the corresponding (x), and add. If both (x) and (w) are feasible, the inequality which results from this operation must also hold. What it states is that the aggregate value of the products, at prices (p), cannot exceed the aggregate cost of those products, at factor prices (w). $V \leqslant C$, when (x) and (w) are both feasible.

So far we have made no use of the optimum conditions. But it is easy to show that when (x) is optimum, $C = B$; for when w_i is positive the corresponding restraint is then an equation, and when it is not an equation, the corresponding $w_i = 0$. Similarly, when (w) is optimum – or such as to correspond to an optimum (x) – we have $V = C$. Thus, when (x) and (w) are both optimum, we have $V = C = B$. (The social accounts come out right!)

For any feasible (x) and (w), $V \leqslant B$; no feasible V can exceed any feasible B. The feasible Bs lie above the feasible Vs, except for the possibility that some feasible Vs and some feasible Bs may be equal. At the optimum, $V = B$, so that at the optimum this equality is realised. It follows that no feasible V can exceed the optimum V, so that at the optimum V is maximised; that, of course, does no more than confirm the definition with which we started. But it also follows that no feasible B can be less than the optimum B, so that at the optimum B is minimised. We could have determined the 'equilibrium' factor prices as an *independent* optimum problem: by seeking those factor prices which minimise factor value, subject to the condition that the unit cost of no product shall fall below its given (product) price.

fund which is just sufficient to enable him to employ the whole of the available supplies of the factors at those given factor prices. Suppose that he seeks to maximise the value of output, under the single (specific) constraint that the cost of output is not to exceed the value of his fund.[21] The outputs which he will select will, very likely, not be feasible; they will infringe some or other of the *separate* specific constraints, which (we are of course supposing) do still in fact hold. It does, however, follow from our previous analysis (it would be nice if there were some simple *direct* proof, but I do not see one) that there will be some set of factor prices, our optimum (w), at which the optimum that he selects will in fact be feasible, and that will indeed by an optimum of the whole system. The optimum factor prices are the *right* factor prices in this sense.

On this approach, distribution only comes in, if at all, in a secondary manner. If all the factor prices are changed in the same proportion the above constraint[22] is unaffected *in real terms*; just the same combinations of outputs are open, or appear to be open, as before. Thus, by the preceding test, the optimum (w) remains indeterminate, to the extent of a multiplier; in order to determine its level, we have to impose some additional condition, and the condition that the value of output, at the optimum, should be equal to its cost is one that will obviously be convenient to impose. Then it all falls out as explained.

This is more the way in which economists have thought of the determination of factor prices belonging in with that of product quantities; the discovery that factor-price determination is an optimum problem in its own right, so that we can begin at either end, is distinctly harder to place. One can see that it makes sense in economic terms (when the possibility of zero outputs is allowed for); but it is hardly a formulation which would have occurred to the economist if it had not been suggested to him by the mathematician. The nearest thing which might have occurred to him would have been to say that the maximisation of output is a minimisation of the scarcity of the resources applied. That is a way in which an economist might want to talk, but he would hardly have believed that he was quite correct in doing so. What he is now to learn is that there is a way in which he is justified in doing so, after all.

---

[21] That is to say, in terms of the previous note, $C \leqslant B$.
[22] $C \leqslant B$.

III. Beyond the Prototype

The summary which has just been given has been confined to a state-ment of the Linear Theory in Walras–Cassel terms; it should, however, be emphasised that none of the standard works does put it in those terms, and the reason why is fairly evident. The reactions which we have appeared to be analysing so minutely – the changes in the sorts of factors that are scarce, and of producible products that are actually produced – are hardly so important in the real world, as to be deserving of such elaborate attention. Certainly it seems odd to deal with them in such detail before we deal with more important matters. The Walrasian habit of taking these things as settled, *before* the equilibrium system is set up, is not (in direct application) so very unreasonable. The chief reason why the prototype theory is very well worth having is that, once we have it, it can so easily be interpreted in other ways.

On the way to these economic reinterpretations there are, how-ever, some mathematical reinterpretations and extensions which need to be noticed. To the mathematician these are rather obvious; they are the reason why no mathematician would ever stop at the proto-type theory. But since they have been excluded from the prototype theory, they must be set down before going further.

1.   It will be remembered that in our formulation of the prototype we began by imposing certain 'economic' restrictions on the constants – the Wald rules. The *a*s were to be non-negative (with the qualifica-tion that some factor must be required for every product); the *b*s were to be positive; and then there was the supplementary rule that the *p*s were to be non-negative (but not all zero). Useful as these restrictions were to begin with, it may have been noticed that by the end of our discussion they were wearing rather thin. The minimisa-tion problem, which emerged as the dual, could itself have been stated as a maximisation problem, in the same form as the original (or 'primal', as it is coming to be called); but in that case the signs of *all* the constants would have had to be reversed. We took it for granted that a problem of that kind could be dealt with in much the same way. But this raises the broader question: do we need to put any restrictions on the constants?

Mathematically, the answer is no. Almost the whole of the fore-going can be re-worked without the Wald rules; so that any *a*, *b* or *p* can be allowed to be positive, zero or negative. The chief trouble which arises if this is done (it is the reason why it seemed best to begin with the Wald rules) is that we have to allow for some side possibilities, which are obviously excluded in many economic interpretations, so that it was rather a convenience to be able to ignore them at a first round. I shall not attempt, even here, to work them in properly; some brief description must, however, be given.

It is possible, in the first place, if no restrictions are set upon the constants, that there may be no feasible solution, no 'feasible region'. The specific constraints may be mutually contradictory, or they may contradict the sign constraints. (For example, $x_1 \leqslant -6$ is a possible specific constraint if we allow any constants; but it contradicts the sign constraint $x_1 \geqslant 0$.)

Secondly, even if there is a feasible region, it is not necessary that it should be optimisable for a given (p). Clearly, if there were no specific constraints (only sign constraints), while the ps were positive, there would be no optimum, since V could be indefinitely increased. The same thing may happen if there are specific constraints, when they fail to confine the feasible region in some direction.

Neither of these things can happen under the Wald rules; they cannot happen with the primal,[23] nor (it is important to notice) can they happen with the prototype dual.[24] This is a particular case of a general theorem, the general *Duality Theorem*, which states that if an optimum exists for the primal, it exists also for the dual. I shall make no attempt to prove this theorem, which is true for any values of the constants. There is also an extension of the theorem, which connects the two exceptions: it states that if the primal, though feasible, is unoptimisable, the dual will not be feasible.[25] Since (of course) either problem may be regarded as primal, the correspondence holds (in a sense) both ways. It is, however, worth noticing that the possibility remains open that both primal and dual may not be feasible.[26] This is a rare case, but it can arise.

[23] Under the Wald rules the origin (all outputs zero) is always feasible. That is enough to show that a feasible region must exist. Increasing (x) along any vector will always encounter a restraint; V must therefore have a maximum value.

[24] Under the Wald rules a zero value for all w is *never* feasible; but a feasible solution can always be found by giving the ws sufficiently large *positive* values. Between the corresponding value of B and the zero value (which is not feasible) a minimum value must exist.

[25] This can easily be illustrated by a slight variation of our Prototype case.

If we maintain the other rules, but allow the existence of one product which does not require any factor to make it, the primal will be unoptimisable, if that product has a positive price. But the cost of that product must be zero, at any factor prices; so it must fall short of the positive product price; the dual cannot be feasible.

[26] An example is given in Vajda, *Theory of Games and Linear Programming*, p. 78.

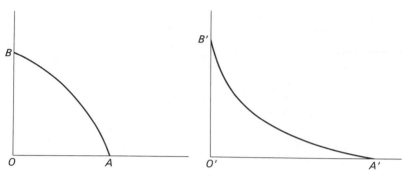

Figure 19.2

2.   *Convexivity.* If a feasible region exists it must be convex; for the proof of convexity (which was given above[27]) is independent of the Wald rules; it will hold for any values of the constants.[28] We are still dealing with convexity properties, and shall continue to do so in all the forms of the linear theory. Since this has the effect of setting a sharp limitation on the range of economic problems to which the theory is applicable, it will be well to consider the concept a little more deeply before going further.

What is the relation (we may begin by asking) between this convexity concept and that which has hitherto been more familiar to economists, in the works, for instance, of Pareto or Joan Robinson? We are accustomed to say that a curve such as AB (figure 19.2) is 'convex outwards' if its steepness continually increases as one moves downwards along it. This definition is clearly different from that to which we have here come, since the one is a property of a region, the other of a curve; but since the region OAB is convex on the new definition,[29] while $O'A'B'$ is not, it does look as if there would be some sense in saying that a convex region is one that is bounded by something like a 'convex outward' curve.

It is indeed true that a convex region can be defined in something like this manner. The convexity of the curve AB (figure 19.2) could have been indicated by the fact that the tangent, at any point of the curve, lies outside the region OAB except at the point of con-

---

[27] See above, p. 258.

[28] Other parts of the 'prototype' argument would require more modification; but I shall not go into that here.

[29] It is sufficient to observe that if α and β are two points within the region (or on its boundary) any point between them on the line joining them will be within the region in the same sense.

tact. We can get rid of the exception about the point of contact (rather awkward in the case of linear boundaries) if we put the same property a little differently. We can define a convex region as one which is such that through any point *outside* the region a line[30] can be drawn so that the whole of the region lies on one side of the line (with no point of the region lying on the line). It is obvious that if a region is 'dented' (like $O'A'B'$), this condition will not be satisfied at a point which lies within the 'dent'. It can be proved that this 'no dent' definition amounts to the same thing as the 'weighted average' definition which we used previously.

I shall not attempt to prove this equivalence; it is one of the things which economists may reasonably take over from the mathematicians.[31] It is nevertheless of much use to the economist to know that the equivalence exists. For once we have it, we can at once see that the convexity, which is so important in the linear theory, is fundamentally the same thing as that which we are accustomed, in our diagrams, to think of as a phenomenon of *diminishing returns*. Convexity, in the new sense, covers constant returns as well as diminishing returns (if AB were a straight line, the region OAB would still be convex). What it does not cover is increasing returns (as illustrated by $O'A'B'$). We can check this by observing that, under increasing returns, an output of zero at a cost of zero may be feasible, an output of x at a cost of c may be feasible, but an output of $\frac{1}{2}x$ at a cost of $\frac{1}{2}c$ will *not* then be feasible.

Under increasing returns, also, there will be a lack of correspondence between the two senses of optimum. A position which maximises output in the quantity sense (that it is the maximum that can be produced when the output of commodities are to be combined in fixed proportions) will not necessarily be one which maximises the value of output at *any* set of product prices. It is a convexity property (a consequence of the equivalence of the two definitions of convexity) that the two senses of optimum come together.

We are accordingly in sight of a rather powerful re-statement of a distinction which has long been known to be crucial for economics. The reason why constant-returns assumptions, and diminishing-returns assumptions, are so much more manageable than increasing-

---

[30] In two dimensions; plane, or whatever corresponds, in more than two.

[31] To prove that 'convexity no-dent' implies 'convexity weighted-average' is not difficult; to prove it the other way (the 'theorem of the supporting hyper-plane') is distinctly more awkward. There is a proof in von Neumann and Morgenstern, *Theory of Games*, pp. 134 ff; see also Vajda, *Theory of Games and Linear Programming*, p. 22. The neatest proof which I know is that given by Debreu in an appendix to Koopmans and Bausch, *Selected Topics in Economics involving mathematical reasoning*, Cowles Foundation Paper No. 136, p. 96.

returns assumptions, is that in the former cases we can use convexity properties, while in the latter we cannot. There is in fact not much difficulty in dealing with phenomena of diminishing returns by linear methods (a curve can always be approximated by a polygon);[32] but the linear theory, since it is based upon convexity, cannot be extended, without losing most of its virtues, into the realm of increasing returns.

3. *The equational form.* This is a convenient point at which to mention another complication – that the form in which we have been posing the optimisation problem is by no means the only form in which what is in substance just the same problem can be put.

The excess supplies of the factors (which are zero in the case of scarce factors, and have to be positive when the factor is not scarce) are themselves a part of the (primal) problem; they are determined, along with the outputs (x_j), when we maximise V subject to the constraints. If they had been introduced explicitly, the primal problem could have been expressed as a maximisation of V, subject to the *equations*

$$a_{i1}x_1 + a_{i2}x_2 + \ldots + a_{iN}x_N + e_i = b_i$$

(for all factors), together with the sign constraints on the outputs and on the excess supplies $(x_j \geqslant 0, \ e_i \geqslant 0)$. Now, as soon as we have left the Wald rules behind us (so that we do not have to worry about the signs of the constants), this is exactly the same thing as maximising

$$\Sigma q_j x_j + \Sigma q_i' e_i$$

where q and q' are new sets of price-weights; for the *e*s could always be eliminated from the latter sum with the aid of the given equations. (It would then reduce to the familiar form $\Sigma p_j x_j$, with *p*s depending on the given q and q' and on the given *a*s.) The optimisation problem is therefore the same as the maximisation of a

---

[32] I do not mean that we have to introduce a linear re-statement in order to make use of the 'weighted-average' concept of convexity. It is indeed obvious from the diagrams of figure 19.2 that we do not. It is possible (and useful) to re-state Paretian economics (with curved frontiers and indifference curves) in terms of convexity properties. This has been done, in a manner which should become classic, in the first of Tjalling Koopmans's *Essays on the State of Economic Science* (1957). I should like to take this opportunity of expressing the debt which I owe to that admirable work, which has had more effect upon the present paper than may appear on the surface. (The companion piece, that is mentioned in the previous footnote, did not appear until after this survey had been substantially written.)

'weighted sum' of s variables, *all* of which are to be non-negative, and which are connected by t equations $(t < s)$.[33]

The 'equational' formulation, which reduces all the constraints to sign constraints, at the expense of increasing the number of variables, is indeed that which is most commonly used in works on Linear Programming.[34] I have preferred to put the matter the other way, which (since it operates with fewer variables) offers more scope for geometrical illustration. Besides, the equational method is less obviously in touch with traditional economics. It is, however, well suited for some economic applications (as we shall see in a moment). There is much to be said for being ready to work either way.[35]

IV. Linear Programming

Our sketch of the underlying theory is now complete; we can return to the story.

In order that Linear Programming should be born, two more things were necessary.

1. It had first to be realised that there are problems, other than the straightforward 'economic' maximisation of the value of output from given resources, which are formally equivalent to economic optimisation. Opportunities, that is, for the application of the generalised theory (which has been described in the preceding section of this survey) had to be discovered. It is usual to associate this stage with two examples that have become classic – the 'transportation problem' posed in 1941 by F. L. Hitchcock,[36] and the 'diet problem', which was posed in a paper by Jerome Cornfield that

[33] If $t > s$, and the equations are independent, the problem would be over-determined, and could not have a solution. If $t = s$, and the equations are independent, they will themselves determine a single solution, which will be the actual solution if it satisfies the sign constraints.

[34] The reason for this is mainly computational. If a problem is presented in inequality form it is easily converted into equational form by the introduction of 'slack' variables (such as our es). The reverse process involves solving the equations, which may well be extremely laborious.

[35] If the primal variables (x) are completed by the introduction of the excess supplies of the factors, the dual variables (w) must be similarly completed by introducing the differences in the dual inequalities. These, in our prototype formulation, are the differences between cost and price – the *unprofitabilities* of the products, we may call them. When these are included the dual problem is in turn reduced to the minimisation of a weighted sum of N variables, subject to sign constraints, and connected (now) by $N - M$ equations.

[36] In the *Journal of Mathematics and Physics* (Massachusetts Institute of Technology), vol. 20, pp. 224-30.

was circulated in the same year.[37] But it is probably more correct to regard these as no more than forerunners. The true begetters of Linear Programming were those who perceived the opportunities in question in connection with war production: Tjalling Koopmans, who rediscovered the transportation problem in connection with shipping, and G. B. Dantzig, who encountered similar questions in his work for the US Air Force.[38] It was when Koopmans and Dantzig got together, after the Second World War, that things really happened.[39] Here, however, we may content ourselves with a word about the conventional examples.

The *diet* problem – to determine the cheapest diet by which a minimum intake of given nutrients can be achieved – is very near to our prototype; indeed, when set out, it fits exactly into the prototype dual. (The amounts of nutrients in each food are the *a*s; the quantities of foods are the *w*s; the minimum intakes are the *p*s; and the costs of the foods are the *b*s. Every nutrient must be contained in some food, or – as is at once apparent – the problem cannot be feasible.) The *transportation* problem – to determine the cheapest pattern by which given demands of m markets can be supplied from n sources, with given unit costs of transport from any source to any market – is in a sense more interesting, since it is a beautiful example of a problem that sets itself up in terms of *equations* between non-negative variables. (The amount to be delivered from *each* source to *each* market has to be determined; these are connected by equations, since the total supply from each source, and demand from each market, is given.) Though some of the variables can be eliminated by means of the equations, so that it may be thrown back to the determination of $(m-1)(n-1)$ variables, connected by $m+n-1$ specific constraints, the choice of variables to be eliminated is very arbitrary; and though the initial unit costs are all positive, there is no guarantee that the same will hold for the coefficients which take their places, after elimination. Thus the

[37] These have been described in innumerable places. There is a simple account in G. Morton, 'Notes on Linear Programming', *Economica*, 1951; and a fuller in DOSSO, chs. 2 and 5.

[38] The influence of Leontief's work in demonstrating the practical applicability of one form of allocative theory, and in turning the attention of economists to a model in which produced commodities figure as inputs (this, as we shall see, itself means going beyond the Wald rules) also requires recognition.

[39] See their (indigestible) volume, *Activity Analysis of Production and Allocation*, ed. Koopmans (1951).

transportation problem already requires the more general theory, while for the diet problem the prototype is sufficient.

2. The mere posing of these problems would not have been an advance if there had existed no method by which the problems could have been solved. The main development in that direction was to follow a little later. It should, however, be made clear that, even before the invention of the Simplex method, the problems were *in principle* solvable; as soon as it is known that the optimum (if there is an optimum) must be at a vertex, or between *tying* vertices, identification of the vertices (and there was a rule for that) and calculation of the cost (as it was in these examples) at the vertices, would always lead to a solution *in the end*. With simple classroom examples, that is often by no means an impossible undertaking. But in any practical instance the amount of work to be done piles up very rapidly.[40] Even with the aid of computers (the simultaneous development of which has been a most important element in the practical success of Linear Programming), the solution of most real problems would still have been out of reach without the invention of better methods.

Any detailed discussion of such methods must clearly lie outside the scope of this survey. Reference must, however, be made to the Simplex method (discovered in 1947 by Dantzig[41]), which was historically the means by which this difficulty was sufficiently overcome to make Linear Programming a usable technique. Effectively, what the Simplex method provides is a means by which we can recognise an optimum when we have reached it; and by which, once any vertex (true vertex) has been identified, we can move from it in the *direction* of the optimum. It is itself a consequence of convexity. If one was trying to climb a mountain, and one knew that it was a convex mountain (without valleys or saddles), the shortest way of getting to the top would be to be straight up, from wherever one

---

[40] It may be useful to take an example from the transportation problem. If there are no more than 5 sources and 4 markets there are 20 variables to be determined; even after elimination, these cannot be reduced to less than $4 \times 3 = 12$ variables, subject to 12 sign constraints and $5 + 4 - 1$ specific constraints, 20 in all. The number of *possible* vertices is the number of ways in which 12 can be selected from 20; this is no less than 127 920. Thus if the thing were gone at bull-headed, more than an eighth of a million calculations, each of considerable size, would be necessary.

[41] Set out by that author in ch. 21 of *Activity Analysis*. Versions are, of course, to be found in all the text books.

happened to be. That is (more or less)[42] what the Simplex method does – in n dimensions!

The weakness of the Simplex method (as so far described) is that it requires the identification of some (true) vertex as a starting-point. Sometimes this can be found by inspection (for a problem which satisfied the Wald rules it would present little difficulty); but very often it cannot, save by luck. If it cannot, there is a preliminary investigation which must be carried through before the above process can start. Various methods have been suggested whereby this preliminary stage can be systematised; that which seems to be most generally useful is an adaptation of the Simplex method itself. By introducing extra variables into the original problem, a subsidiary problem can be written down which is such that: (1) a true vertex of the subsidiary can be found by inspection, and (2) an optimum of the subsidiary is a true vertex of the original problem. Thus the subsidiary can be solved by the Simplex method; once the subsidiary is solved, the Simplex method can be applied to the original problem without difficulty.[43]

Other methods are, however, in use. It is sometimes useful to begin by tackling the dual to the original problem; the dual can, of course, be written down immediately, and once the dual is solved, the primal can be solved at once. (An obvious case of this is when the primal has many variables but only two specific constraints; for the dual can then be reduced to two variables, and can be solved graphically.) There is also a Dual Simplex method, in which the dual is kept in sight all the time. A direct attack on the difficulty of finding a vertex from which to start is made by the 'Multiplex method'

---

[42] More accurately, it may be described as follows. As we have seen, any vertex A is a solution of n of the constraints (sign and specific) considered as equations. A vertex *neighbouring* to A can be defined as one which is a solution of $(n-1)$ of A's equations, together with *one* of those which were not taken when A was determined. (A must, of course, be a true vertex, and the neighbouring vertices must be true vertices.) If A is an optimum the value of $V(=\Sigma px)$ at A must, of course, be no less than the value at any of the neighbouring vertices. It is less obvious, but it is true (as a result of convexity) that if A is not an optimum there must be at least one of the neighbouring vertices where the value of V is greater than it is at A. (This is the same principle as that which is familiar to economists, that – under universal diminishing returns – a maximum is sufficiently determined by looking at marginal conditions.) Thus in order to discover whether A is an optimum it is only necessary to look at its relation with its neighbouring vertices. And in order to proceed as rapidly as possible to the optimum, from a given vertex, it is only necessary to select that one of the neighbouring vertices along the 'edge' to which V increases most rapidly; then to repeat the operation with the vertex so reached; continuing until a vertex has been found from which there is no increase to any neighbouring vertex. That is the Simplex method.

[43] For a description of this device, see Gass, *Linear Programming*, pp. 61–6.

(published in 1957 by Ragnar Frisch).[44] This requires only a feasible point (not a vertex) as a starting-point; from that it identifies a 'centre' of the feasible region; if one moves from the centre, in the direction of increasing V, one should arrive somewhere near the optimum.

These are the basic tools which are at the disposal of the Linear Programmer; by these means a problem is soluble, if it can be cast into appropriate form, and of problems that can be so cast there appears to be an ample supply.[45] Most of them (like the diet problem and the transportation problem) are problems of the least cost method of carrying through a given programme; problems (both military and civil) of the public sector do often fall fairly naturally into that form. But since the coefficients in the weighted sum that is to be maximised (or minimised) may (when we have left the prototype) be either positive or negative, there is no reason why the determination of a maximum profit combination of inputs and outputs (prices of the inputs and outputs being given) should not be tackled in a similar way. Thus the uses of Linear Programming are not confined to the public sector, but can be extended, at least to some extent, to the field of private enterprise.

There is, however, a doubt which creeps in at this point; and it seems proper that in a survey like the present, such doubts should be mentioned. What is the relation between this new technique and the process of market adjustment by the price-mechanism, on which economists have been accustomed to rely for the solution of what are, after all, for the most part much the same problems? One can understand that there are problems of 'economic maximisation' which are unsuitable, for social or institutional reasons, for solution by a competitive process; the 'public sector' problems just mentioned are obvious examples of this, but no doubt there are others. Here, where the reason for the non-availability of the market mechanism is non-economic, it is an obvious gain to have found an alternative. What seems distinctly less clear is the usefulness of the technique in those cases which have so much troubled economists, where there are economic reasons why the market mechanism will not work. It looks only too likely that in these cases the Linear Programming technique will also be unsatisfactory.

[44] It is briefly described by van Eijk and Sandee in *Econometrica*, January 1959, pp. 9–13.

[45] A fat bibliography has been published by Vera Riley and S. I. Gass (Johns Hopkins Press, 1958). It is summarised in nine pages at the end of Gass, *Linear Programming*.

Competitive theory (it has often been remarked by Linear Programmers) takes it for granted that the individual firm is maximising its profits; that, so they say, means that the Linear Programming problem, inherent in the firm's own production, has already been solved. That, they naturally maintain, is a big assumption. It has been shown by experiment that any complex problem of this sort requires a technique for its solution; without that technique it is too much to expect that the individual firm will be able to maximise its profits; now that the technique has been provided, the gap in the traditional theory can be filled. One would not deny the merits of this argument as a piece of salesmanship; but its deeper significance seems to come out more clearly if it is stood the other way up.

The traditional case for competition can be put into the form of saying that it is a way of avoiding the Linear Programming problem (the macro-problem, we might call it) which is involved in the co-ordination of production over the whole economy. The macro-problem is broken up, by the market, into little bits, each of which should be too simple to warrant the application of elaborate technique; the co-ordination between the bits (which would have otherwise to be provided by a supertechnician) is provided by the market mechanism. If this process were to be carried through fully there should be no scope for Linear Programming within the firm; for the firm's problem should be reduced to that of optimising against a set of constraints, so few and simple that the solution would be obvious. In practice, of course, the fragmentation is rarely carried so far as this; at the most, the market takes over a part of the task of co-ordination; a significant part is left to be done within the firm. The application of Linear Programming to business problems does therefore remain open as a useful possibility. We should, however, ask: why is it that the fragmentation does not proceed so far as to prevent this happening? What is it that stops the market from taking over the whole job?

Doubtless there are many reasons. But surely one should not overlook the reason which has, after all, most commended itself to economists: the diseconomies of small scale. Now if it is true that small-scale diseconomies are the main economic reason why fragmentation does not proceed to the limit it will follow that the same force which restricts the application of the market mechanisms will also restrict the application of the linear technique. For the presence of scale economies implies the absence of convexity: some qualification (which may be more or less serious) to the convexity which Linear Programming requires.

One is driven to the conclusion that Linear Programming and the price mechanism are rather close substitutes – both in the things they can do and in those they cannot. But the fact that two things are close substitutes does not exclude the possibility that there may be a part for each to perform.

V. Activity Analysis

There is a wide sense of the term 'Activity Analysis' in which it would include the whole of the theory (as opposed to the practical technique) of Linear Programming. I am using it here in a narrower sense, to which its title is (I think) more appropriate.

Let us go back to the prototype theory (which is subject to the Wald rules), and concentrate attention (this time) on its economic interpretation. As given so far, that economic interpretation was rather narrow. The prototype theory was presented as nothing more than a re-working of the Walras–Cassel system; the 'fixed coefficients' and other basic restrictions, which notoriously limit the applicability of that system, were retained. It was, however, already shown by von Neumann[46] that there is an easy way in which they can be relaxed. All that is needed is a slight change in point of view.

It is convenient to begin with a rather special problem – that of products in joint supply. It is implicit in the Walrasian assumptions that the processes of production of the various products are *independent*: in the sense that the output of any product can be increased, by the absorption of additional units of the factors, without affecting the supplies of other products, except in so far as factors are withdrawn from the production of these other products. Though this independence assumption is not a bad approximation to reality, it is certainly not true universally; it is better, therefore, to do without it. There are indeed various ways by which that could be done.

It would, for instance, be possible to observe that joint supply relations can be reduced to (linear) equations connecting the various outputs (x); we have a regular technique for dealing with such equations. By their aid, for instance, some of the xs could be eliminated; we could then proceed, with the remaining xs, as before. That is the procedure which would be suggested by what has been said previously; but if we do proceed in that way, we are raising the question – what is the status of those xs, which remain as variables

[46] In the article cited, in note 12.

of the system, after the others have been eliminated? They are outputs, but they are not all the outputs – they *represent* both themselves and the others. The notion accordingly presents itself that it will be easier to work, from the start, with indices of outputs, which are to be distinguished from the actual outputs of the commodities, and which will spare us the (arbitrary) choice of which variables to eliminate. It is from that idea that Activity Analysis arises.

An *activity* is a process whereby certain quantities of inputs are transformed into certain quantities of outputs. There are *constant returns to scale* (this is an essential assumption of Activity Analysis) so that an activity can be carried out at any *intensity*; by increasing the intensity, one simply increases all inputs and all outputs in the same proportion. Thus the kth activity, carried on at unit intensity, transforms $a_{1k}, a_{2k}, \ldots, a_{Mk}$ of the factors into $\alpha_{1k}, \alpha_{2k}, \ldots, \alpha_{Nk}$ of the products; if carried on at intensity X_k it transforms $a_{1k}X_k, \ldots, a_{Mk}X_k$ of the factors into $\alpha_{1k}X_k, \ldots, \alpha_{Nk}X_k$ of the products. (The as and αs are non-negative constants, which define the activity. Of course, where there is no joint supply, all but one of the αs will be zero.)

If there are R activities, carried on at intensities (X_k) the total input of the ith factor is $\Sigma a_{ik}X_k$ (summed over all k); the total output of the jth product is $\Sigma \alpha_{jk}X_k$ (summed over all k). Thus V, the total value of output (at prices p_j), is $\Sigma\Sigma p_j \alpha_{jk} X_k$ (summed over all j and all k – all products and all activities); this may be written $\Sigma P_k X_k$, where P_k (being $\Sigma p_j \alpha_{jk}$ summed over all products) is nothing else but the value of the output of the kth activity, when that is carried on at unit intensity. Everything can now be expressed in terms of the Xs. The sum to be maximised is $\Sigma P_k X_k$ (where the Ps, since they depend upon given ps and given αs, are given constants). The specific constraints take the usual form

$$a_{11}X_1 + a_{12}X_2 + \ldots + a_{1R}X_R \leqslant b_1$$
$$\cdots\cdots\cdots\cdots\cdots\cdots\cdots\cdots\cdots\cdots\cdots\cdots\cdots$$
$$a_{M1}X_1 + a_{M2}X_2 + \ldots + a_{MR}X_R \leqslant b_M$$

where there are the usual sign constraints. Thus the whole of the prototype theory can be reinterpreted, so as to allow for the possibility of joint products, without requiring any formal (or mathematical) change.

That, I think, is the best way to introduce the 'activity'; but the idea would be much less important than it is if it could only deal with joint products. As a result of this restatement, there is a further extension, much more far-reaching, which is automatically at our disposal. In the prototype theory, we maintained the Walras–Cassel assumption of the 'fixed technical coefficients' – that there is just one way of producing each product, so that the a_{ij}s are all constants. It may well have appeared that we were putting too much weight upon this assumption (it was, after all, abandoned long ago by those who worked in the Walras tradition[47]); it was nevertheless convenient to maintain it, for purposes of exposition, and it was safe to do so, because it would be so easy to abandon it when the time came.

The Activity Analysis model, just described, is in fact no longer tied down by the assumption of fixed technical coefficients. Just as the possibility was left open, in the prototype, that some possible products would not be produced; so it is left possible here, for exactly the same reason, that some possible processes (for a product that is produced by another process) will not be employed, so that the intensities of these processes (X) are zero. The condition for this to happen can be worked out at once from the condition for zero output in the prototype. The intensity of the kth activity will be zero if $P_k < \Sigma w_i a_{ik}$; that is to say, if the activity is unprofitable at the imputed factor prices. Thus, while some of the unused activities will represent products that it does not pay to produce, others (and probably in practice these will be the more interesting) will represent methods of production that it does not pay to employ. Accordingly, by a sufficient widening of the range of possible activities, everything which economists are in the habit of saying about factor substitution can be brought in.

It must be emphasised that the resulting model is mathematically identical with our prototype model; the Wald rules are still in force; all that has happened is that it has been given a different economic dress. Nevertheless, by that simple change it has been converted into a general theory, with a range which is comparable to that of the Paretian theory of general equilibrium. The Activity Analysis approach is indeed in the end not so dissimilar from the Paretian approach; their strengths, and their weaknesses, are much the same. We get no help from Activity Analysis in dealing with increasing returns, the nut which is hardest to crack by Paretian methods; indeed, it may be said that the Activity Analyst is more completely dependent upon the hypothesis of constant returns to scale than the Paretian. There is nothing to prevent the Paretian from exploring the realms of increasing returns, to the very limited extent to which

---

[47] By Walras himself in his last edition; by Pareto already in the *Cours* (1898).

they can be explored by his methods; to the Activity Analyst they are forbidden territory. Each is beset by the temptation to make excessive use of the price parameters, which are associated on the one side with the assumption of perfect competition, on the other with convexity assumptions, which amount (in practice) to much the same thing. The possibility of methods that it does not pay to employ can be dealt with on either method; where Activity Analysis gains is in its more explicit attention to the possibility of products that it does not pay to produce, and of factors that it does not pay to use. For any problem where these latter possibilities are not important (and that is surely the case with the majority of economic problems) it will not matter which method one uses. If either is applicable, both will be applicable; each will give the same results.

This being so, it is not surprising to find that particular problems, for the solution of which the new method has a decided advantage, are far from common. It can indeed happen — it is already happening — that people who have learned to think in the new way will begin by getting their problems out in that way; but it usually appears in the end that they could have been got out in the old way just as well.[48] This is not to deny that there are things which it is easier to notice if one is thinking in the new manner; one wonders whether Samuelson would have put forward his famous Factor-price Equalisation Theorem just when he did, if he had not been working, at the same time, at the development of Activity Analysis.[49] It would, however, appear that (apart from Input–Output applications, which I shall be considering in the next section) the principal achievement of the new method had been the establishment of very general theorems, which are mainly valuable because, when we have them, we can go on in our old ways with a better conscience. The chief of these is the proof of the existence of a competitive equilibrium (the solution of Wald's problem) which is contained in a most remarkable passage of the DOSSO book.[50] The general character of this proof (too important a matter to be omitted from this survey) will be sketched out, very roughly, as in the rest of this section.

[48] A nice example is to be found in the papers by Farrell and Champernowne (*Econometrica*, July 1954).

[49] There is a family resemblance between the Factor Price Theorem and the Input–Output Substitution Theorem (see below, pp. 284–5) due to the same author.

[50] Pp. 366–73. It appears that in its final form this proof is due to Solow; but it was built up by stages, that are to be associated with the names, first of Wald himself, then of Lionel Mackenzie, of Samuelson and of Harold Kuhn. (There is another discussion in Baumol, *American Economic Review*, 1958, pp. 859–65.)

From the Wald rules about the constants – as, bs and ps (or Ps) – which are carried over into Activity Analysis, it follows (as we have seen) that production is optimisable; there is a set of quantities of products (x) which maximises the value of output for given product prices (p), and there is a set of imputed factor prices (w) which belongs to that optimum. If production is organised (as it should then be possible for it to be organised) into firms which operate under perfect competition, the earnings of the factors will be such as correspond to these imputed factor prices. Thus on the 'supply' side the equilibrium exists; but nothing has yet been said about the demands for the products. These must now be brought in. All we assume, at this stage, is that the demands depend, in some way, upon the product prices and factor earnings; then, since the factor earnings depend on product prices, both the demands (x') and the supplies (x) of the products have been shown to depend upon the product prices (p).[51] The difficulty is to show that there must be some set of product prices which makes demands equal to supplies. This is tackled in the following way.

Starting from any arbitrary set of product prices (and derived factor prices), we have an (x') determined by the demand functions; but this (x') may not be feasible, or, if feasible, it may not be efficient – there may be no (p) for which it would be optimum. What DOSSO then does is to diminish (or increase) all the x' in the same proportion, until the resulting set of quantities, $k(x')$, does lie on the frontier of the feasible region. To this $k(x')$ there will correspond a set of prices (p'), being a set of prices for which $k(x')$ is an optimum. (Usually, indeed, as when $k(x')$ is at a vertex, there will be many such sets of prices; but that does not – too much – matter.) These (p') prices are rather analogous to 'supply prices', to be put against the 'demand prices' (p) with which we began.

A rule has therefore been evolved by which a set (or sets) of supply prices can be associated with the given demand prices. At this point it is possible to invoke the aid of a powerful mathematical tool, *the fixed-point theorem*,[52] according to which (provided that a number of conditions, which can be shown to hold in this case, are satisfied) there must be some (p) which is itself included among the sets of (p') which, in this manner, it generates. Once that is established, the rest is simple. For since the total earnings of the factors (which, by 'Walras's law', are all spent) are equal to the total value of output,[53] it follows that at this (p), $\Sigma px' = \Sigma p(kx')$. Since the ks are the same for all products, $k = 1$. The quantities demanded are optimum quantities; supplies and demands are equal. Thus the competitive equilibrium exists.

[51] The (p) are, of course, to be understood as *relative* prices; if all ps, and consequently ws, are multiplied by the same multiplier, they will generate the same (x) – and the same (x').

[52] The general idea of a fixed-point theorem is well explained in Courant and Robbins, *What is Mathematics?*, pp. 251–5. It should, however, be noticed that what is there described is the original Brouwer theorem, not the slightly more complicated Kakutani theorem, which is what is needed for the above purpose. See the passage in DOSSO, just cited; also Baumol, *American Economic Review*, 1958, p. 859.

[52] See above, p. 262n.

The most interesting thing about this proof, to the economist, is the little that has to be assumed about the demand functions.[54] It is necessary that there should be some set of demands, some (x'), that is generated by every (p) and the (w) that belongs to it; but little more is necessary.[55] There is nothing that corresponds to the 'downward slope of the demand curve'. The explanation of this rather surprising omission is that nothing has been said about the uniqueness of the equilibrium. Multiple equilibria are perfectly possible. Sufficiently strong 'downward slope' assumptions (what Samuelson calls 'the weak axiom of revealed preference' — what I should prefer to describe in terms of the absence of net-income effects) do, however, prove uniqueness. That is where they come in. It is, of course, familiar, from simple examples, that the presence of net-income effects may lead to such things as 'upward sloping demand curves' and multiple equilibria.

VI. Input–Output

Throughout our discussion of Activity Analysis we have maintained the Wald rules; with the implication, which they carry, that factors and products (inputs and outputs) are fundamentally different sorts of things. Analysis of that kind can deal with most aspects of a static system (under constant returns to scale); but it cannot deal with intermediate products, which are outputs from one angle and inputs from another. What it must be assuming about such products is that they have been 'netted out' by vertical integration. It is, however, uncertain whether actual production is capable of such integration, without being involved in lateral integration also; in any case, the intermediate products which certainly exist are worthy of study on their own account. It will not be expected that any very serious discussion of the Input–Output theory, invented by Leontief as a means of studying such linkages,[56] can find a place at the end of this

---

[54] It is quite unnecessary to make the peculiar assumption, which Wald made in 1934, that demands do not fall to zero, however high prices rise. As Kuhn has shown in the paper that was previously mentioned (p. 252n) the reason why Wald made this assumption was that he did not have the duality theory. He took it for granted that all of the *given* list of outputs must have prices equal to costs; and that meant that he had to exclude the possibility of zero outputs. Though he allowed for the possibility of factors with zero prices, he did not allow for the other zero, which is dual to it.

[55] It has to be assumed that the demand functions are continuous — that there are no jumps in demand as prices change. This is necessary, if we are going to insist on making it a condition of equilibrium that demands should *equal* supplies. If we were prepared to be content with some sort of approximate equality this continuity condition could presumably be loosened a bit.

[56] *Structure of the American Economy* (1st ed., 1941; 2nd ed., 1951); *Studies in the Structure of the American Economy* (1953). I have made extensive use of the chapters on Input–Output in DOSSO (IX and X); it does, however, take some effort to disentangle from these chapters the essential points.

already lengthy survey; it has, however, proved so attractive a field[57] for the application of the developments which we have been considering that it cannot be left altogether on one side.

It is characteristic of Leontief's model that it reduces the primary factors to one only – homogeneous labour; apart from labour, the inputs of each industry are the outputs of other industries. We define x_i as the *gross* output of the ith commodity, including that which is absorbed as inputs of other industries, or indeed (for the seed-corn must come out of the harvest) as input in the production of x_i itself. The amount of the ith commodity which is needed as input of the jth (per unit of the latter) is taken as given, like the corresponding coefficients in the prototype; it will cause no confusion if we write it a_{ij}, as before. The demand for the product x_i, as input in the production of other commodities, will then come to $\Sigma a_{ij}x_j$ (summed over all j); the net, or final, output is the difference between this and gross output, that is to say, it is $x_i - \Sigma a_{ij}x_j$. The amount of labour that is required (per unit of product) for the jth product we will simply write a_j. Then the demand for labour is $\Sigma a_j x_j$ (over all products).

What are the constraints under which this system operates? There are, of course, first of all the usual sign constraints (all x_i non-negative). If we suppose that the supply of labour (b) is given, we have a specific constraint, of the usual kind, due to the limitation of the supply of that factor; here it will appear as $\Sigma a_j x_j \leqslant b$. It is, however, further necessary that the *net* outputs of the products should be non-negative. It is possible, that is, for the whole output of a particular product to be absorbed as inputs in the production of other products; but it is inconsistent with static equilibrium for more than the whole output to be so absorbed. Thus we have another set of specific constraints, of the form $\Sigma a_{ij}x_j \leqslant x_i$ (for all i), or, written in full,

$$a_{i1}x_1 + a_{i2}x_2 + \ldots + (a_{ii} - 1)\, x_i + \ldots + a_{in}x_n \leqslant 0$$

It is the appearance of these 'Leontief constraints', as we may call them, in addition to the labour constraint, which marks the Leontief system off from those we have considered hitherto.

It may be assumed, for the same reasons as before, that the *a*s (of every kind) are non-negative; but that cannot mean that all of the coefficients in any Leontief constraint can be non-negative. If they

[57] As will be apparent to anyone who turns the pages of *Econometrica* or the *Review of Economic Studies*, it is one of the fields of application on which interest has been centred in the most recent years.

were, it would follow at once (because of the zero on the right-hand side) that outputs of all commodities with non-zero coefficients must be zero. For the Leontief system to the feasible at all, it is first of all necessary that the 'feedback coefficient' a_{ii} (of any output into its own production) should be less than unity. But that means that we are bound to have one negative coefficient in each of the Leontief constraints; accordingly, the Wald rules, and their consequence — assured feasibility — will not apply.

The situation which emerges can easily be illustrated diagrammatically (figure 19.3). If gross outputs x_1 and x_2 are measured on the two axes, the labour constraint will appear as a downward sloping line of the usual kind (LL); while the Leontief constraints will appear as upward-sloping lines (because of the negative coefficient) through the origin (because of the zero on the right-hand side). The feasible region is accordingly cut down to the triangle OAB. Evidently it will continue to take the same sort of form — a pyramid or 'cone' with apex at the origin — in more than two dimensions.

There are two things, which are already visible in this construction, which require to be noticed. In the first place, the mere condition that $a_{ii} \leqslant 1$ (which keeps the Leontief lines upward sloping) is not sufficient to ensure that there exists a feasible region. The line OA could easily be swung up (or OB swung down) so that the feasible region disappeared. What this would mean (in the two-goods case) is that the amount of x_2 absorbed in making x_1 was greater than could be replaced by absorbing all of the x_1 in the x_2 industry (so that if

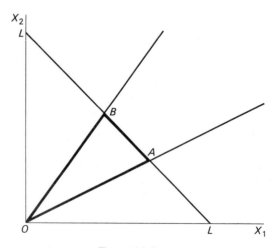

Figure 19.3

net x_1 were zero, net x_2 would still be negative); with a coefficients chosen at random that would certainly be possible, and it would certainly mean that the system would not work. The same thing can naturally happen in more complicated ways when there are more than two commodities. The conditions (upon the a coefficients) for it *not* to happen are called the Hawkins–Simon conditions;[58] it is unnecessary to write them out here. It is sufficient to observe that some such conditions must be satisfied if the Leontief system is to be feasible.

Secondly, if the system is feasible, efficiency requires that the 'point' selected should lie on that part of the boundary which is formed by the labour constraint. From any other point of the feasible region, gross outputs can be increased proportionately, and therefore all net outputs in the same proportion. It is accordingly to be expected that any optimum (in the sense so far used) will lie on that part of the boundary. But this needs checking up.

It is natural to take, as the thing to be maximised, the value of *net* output (at given prices p). But it is easy to show that the value of net output at 'gross' prices is the same as the value of gross output at 'net' prices – the 'net price' of a product being interpreted as the *value added* per unit of output in its production. For

$$V = \Sigma p_i(x_i - \Sigma a_{ij}x_i) = \Sigma(p_j - \Sigma p_i a_{ij})\, x_i = \Sigma \pi_j x_j$$

where π_j (the 'net price') is $p_j - \Sigma p_i a_{ij}$. With ps and as given, the πs are given. It is accordingly correct to maximise $\Sigma \pi_j x_j$ against the constraints.

An optimum, as we know, must either lie at a vertex or 'between' vertices. Now the vertices of the Leontief region are: (1) the origin, which – since we do not now have the Wald rules to support us – cannot be excluded as a possible optimum; (2) the points such as A, B on the diagram, which are intersections of Leonteif constraints with the labour constraint. At the origin, however, V is necessarily zero, while at the latter vertices V will necessarily be positive[59] (if there is a feasible region), so that it is only the latter vertices which we need consider. Each of these vertices will represent a position in which there is a zero net output of all but one of the commodities, and a maximum net output of the one that remains. Possible optima (all of which, it is now confirmed, must lie on the

---

[58] They were worked out, with a little trouble, by the eponymous authors, in *Econometrica* during the year 1949.

[59] We keep the 'extra' Wald rule, that the ps are non-negative, and not all zero.

Linear Theory

labour constraint part of the boundary) are weighted averages of these vertices.

If there are positive net outputs of all the n commodities, V must have an equal value at all of these vertices, so that $\Sigma \pi_j x_j$ must be the same all over the 'plane' $\Sigma a_j x_j = b$. This can only happen if π_j bears the same proportion to a_j for all commodities. This we may write $\pi_j = w a_j$, where w is easily recognisable as the (imputed) price of labour. Thus we have n equations

$$p_j - \Sigma p_i a_{ij} = w a_j \qquad \text{(for all } j)$$

to determine the gross prices (p) relatively to the wage of labour. It will only be at these prices that the net outputs of all N commodities can be positive.

How do we know, it may, however, be asked, the prices (p) that are determined by these equations will be non-negative? It turns out that the conditions for this to be so are the same Hawkins–Simon conditions as we had formerly to invoke to establish feasibility. Thus, granted these conditions, the internal coherence of the Leontief model is established.

Substitutability in Leontief Models. There are a few more points to be noted. The prices which have just been determined are independent of the demands for the commodities; however demands change, the optimum point must keep on the 'labour constraint' plane, so that the prices just determined must continue to hold. Thus, in spite of the 'fixed coefficients' at which products are transformed into one another, the fact that there is (ultimately) only one scarce factor keeps the 'labour theory of value' in operation, with the system operating under constant cost. It follows from this that even if the net outputs of some commodities are zero (so that they are pure intermediate products, only produced in order to be re-absorbed into the productive process) their 'net prices' must still be equal to the value of their labour coefficients: the condition $\pi_j = w a_j$ must still hold for such products. Equality does not require, as seemed at first sight, that net output should be positive; it is sufficient that gross output is positive.

There is a more remarkable consequence of the same property, that has been pointed out by Samuelson – his 'substitution theorem'.[60] It is not necessary, in the Leontief model, to start, as hitherto supposed, with given technical coefficients – given methods of producing the commodities. There may be a choice of methods,

[60] Originally stated in ch. VII of *Activity Analysis* (ed. Koopmans).

and it will yet follow that there is one method which has to be adopted for each product; the method chosen is independent of the demands for the products. Thus the Leontief system produces under constant cost, even if methods are (in principle) variable.

This, it will be recognised, is again a generalisation of the labour theory of value. If all labour was applied directly to the making of finished products (and labour was the only factor), there might be a choice of methods, but efficiency would dictate that the most efficient method should be used for each product – as Marx (for instance) knew very well. The choice of method would be independent of the demand. What Samuelson has shown is that the same continues to hold, so long as labour is the only primary factor of production, even if labour is applied indirectly as well as directly. Put in this way, his result is by no means surprising.

There is, however, an exception to the classical doctrine, that has been familiar since the days of J. S. Mill. If some of the products are joint products, the relative prices of the joint products will depend upon demand; it is then possible that a shift in demand will lead to the substitution of one method of production for another, even though labour is the only primary factor. The Leontief system excludes such joint production, so that in the Leontief system this complication cannot arise. It is, however, to be expected that it will arise if we attempt to extend the Samuelson principle to cases in which joint production is allowed.[61]

It may be useful to show in detail how this is. In terms of Activity Analysis, the general problem may be posed as follows. There are R activities, capable of producing the N commodities (by input of some and output of others, and, of course, by input of labour). Since the activities include many alternative possible methods of producing the commodities, R may be supposed to be larger – if we like much larger – than N. We may generalise our notation, and write α_{ik} as the *output* of the ith commodity by the kth activity, when it is operating at unit intensity; inputs can be covered by the same symbol, α_{ik} being negative when the ith commodity is an input. Here we will write β_k for the input of labour. Then, if X_k is the intensity of the kth activity, the net output of the ith commodity, over the whole system, is $\Sigma\alpha_{ik}X_k$. We have to maximise $\Sigma\Sigma p_i\alpha_{ik}X_k$, subject to the constraints: $X_k \geqslant 0$ for all k; $\Sigma\alpha_{ik}X_k \geqslant 0$ for all i; $\Sigma\beta_k X_k \leqslant b$. Formally, the problem is almost the same as before. Since some αs are positive, and some negative,

---

[61] The point of the elaborate investigations by Koopmans and Arrow (chs. VIII and IX of the *Activity Analysis* volume) was to clear up this exception.

there is still the same question of determining whether or not there exists a feasible region; in order that it should exist the αs will have to be suitable. We will suppose that they are suitable.

Following the same argument as before, it would be necessary, if all activities were utilised, that $\Sigma p_i \alpha_{ik} = w\beta_k$ for every activity. But this gives us R equations to determine N prices; if $R > N$, as we have supposed, the system is over-determined.[62] Thus, in general, it will not be possible for more than N activities to be utilised; the rest will have $\Sigma p_i \alpha_{ik} < w\beta_k$, and intensity zero. Optimisation involves the selection of a particular set of not more than N activities, which are to be employed; an optimum set of activities must satisfy the conditions just stated. If the optimum set consists of the whole number of N activities the prices at which these activities can be employed will be determinate; any demands for final outputs which the system is capable of satisfying can be satisfied at these prices and with these activities. Now if there is no joint supply, at least N activities will be required to produce the N commodities; this therefore is Samuelson's case. But if there is joint supply it will be possible for the N commodities to be produced in positive quantities with less than N activities; the prices are then not determinate, and it is possible that as demands vary, the activities that are utilised may change.

The matter may be illustrated, and the argument made more precise with the aid of a diagram (figure 19.4). Suppose that there are two commodities being produced and three possible activities: $N = 2$ and $R = 3$. Measuring the intensities of the activities along three axes, the labour constraint becomes a plane; as we have seen, the optimum must lie upon that plane: let us therefore take it to be the plane of the paper. The intersections of this plane with the co-ordinate planes will accordingly appear on the paper as a triangle XYZ. The sign constraints and the labour constraint limit possible optima to points within or on the sides of this triangle. The *two* Leontief constraints (which will also be shown as straight lines — the intersections of the Leontief planes with the labour plane) will limit the possible optima further. If they are to be operative at all they must intersect the triangle: there are then two main cases, in one of which they intersect the same two sides (figure 19.4(a)); in the other there is only one side which they both intersect (figure 19.4(b)).

Now in either case, for the reason above stated, it is not possible that all three activities should be used in an optimum position; the

---

[62] This assumes (and it is assumed throughout the argument) that the activities are 'linearly independent' — that we are not including any activity which is a mere combination of other activities. In economic applications that (I think) may be taken for granted.

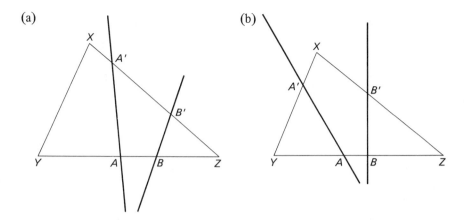

Figure 19.4

optimum cannot therefore lie *within* the triangle XYZ; it must lie *on* one of the sides. Accordingly, in figure 19.4(a), possible optima lie along AB or along $A'B'$; one of these stretches will be more efficient than the other. If it is AB the system will be at A when the demand for one commodity is zero, at B when the demand for the other is zero; they can be combined (efficiently) in any proportions by moving along AB.

In this case, therefore, the Samuelson theorem is verified; but now consider figure 19.4(b). Possible optima now lie along AB, or along the broken line $A'XB'$. If AB is optimum, all is as before; but if the other is the optimum stretch there is a change in the combination of activities as demand varies from one extremity to the other. But this exception can only arise if the point X is on the optimum path – if positive net outputs of the *two* commodities can be secured by using only *one* activity. Joint production is accordingly a necessary condition for the exception to arise.

VII. Conclusion – The Theory of Games

There remains one further topic which needs consideration before we have exhausted the list of specialisms which, in their relations to one another, we set out to examine. It will, however, be convenient, before I take up that topic, to interpose some general remarks upon the field we have already covered.

The methods of analysis (if indeed they are more than one method) that have been described are rather tied down by the assumption of constant returns to scale, or (perhaps even more fundamentally) by the convexity which is associated with an absence of scale economies; nevertheless, subject to that restriction, the field with which they deal is dealt with very thoroughly, more thoroughly than it was dealt with by the methods previously in use. As I have explained, I do not think that the new methods need displace the old methods; it may indeed be said that one of the services of the new methods is to provide a justification for the use of the older methods, which was previously lacking. Granted convexity (the necessary condition for the new methods to operate) it has now been fully *proved* that a general optimum must also be a local optimum – that marginal conditions are therefore sufficient to establish its general optimality. Consequently if one is prepared to grant (as in many cases one is) that the changes one wants to consider will not involve any change in the number or specifications of the kinds of goods that are to be produced, or of the resources that are used, the old-fashioned marginal rules are all that have to be considered. The occasions on which the economist will want to go further, so as to have to use the new methods in relation to particular problems (while being able to retain the convexity conditions which enable him to use them) are really rather infrequent.

It must nevertheless be recognised (and this is the point on which I now want to lay stress) that the new methods are a great advance upon the old in the understanding which they convey of the *raison d'être* of the price mechanism. The rather inappropriate mathematical methods, which have been employed (at all levels of mathematisation) by the school of Cournot and Walras – and of Marshall – did in this respect rather let us down. For they caused it to appear that the price system is just one way of organising an economy efficiency; that it is, in a sense, exterior to the economic problem, something that is brought in from outside. What the linear theory has shown – and this, speaking as a theoretical rather than as a practical economist, seems to me to have been its greatest service – is that, so long as the convexity assumptions hold (and though I have constantly emphasised that they do not hold universally, I would certainly admit that they hold, to a fair approximation, over a large part of the economic field), the price mechanism is something that is inherent. It did not have to be invented, or brought in from outside. It belongs.

This indeed is what was first perceived, after a fashion, by Menger and his followers; but they did not have the power of explaining, in a manner which would compel communication, the truth that they had seen. Now it has all been set down in black and white. It has been made apparent, not only that a price system is inherent in the problem of maximising production from given resources but also that something like a price system is inherent in any problem of maximisation against constraints. The imputation of prices (or 'scarcities') to the factors of production is nothing else but a measurement of the *intensities* of the constraints; such intensities are always implicit – the special property of a competitive system is that it brings them out and makes them visible. It is through its power of developing the intensities (in the photographic sense of developing), so that they are available for use as instruments in the process of maximisation, that the competitive system does its job.

To have taken so much economics, and to have reduced it to a problem in pure mathematics, is no doubt in many ways a most notable achievement; to many economists it will be a rather shattering achievement, but it is (after all) the kind of thing that has happened in one after another of the natural sciences. It is not surprising that it should happen to us also. Nevertheless, the question persists: how much of economics is it that is being thus absorbed? If we take the famous definition, given so many years ago by Lord Robbins – 'the relationship between ends and scarce means that have alternative uses'[63] – economics, in that sense, is very well covered by the linear theory. It has, however, been shown that in that sense it has very little to do with 'human behaviour' – a phrase that Robbins did allow to creep in. The 'logic of choice', now that it has been fully mathematised, appears as nothing else but pure technics – the distilled essence of a general technology.

Economics, surely, is a social study. It is concerned with the operations of human beings, who are not omniscient, and not wholly rational; who (perhaps because they are not wholly rational) have diverse, and not wholly consistent, ends. As such, it cannot be reduced to a pure technics, and may benefit by being distinguished from a pure technics; for we can then say that its concern is with the use that can be made of pure technics by man in society. And that looks like being a distinctly different matter.

[63] *Nature and Significance of Economic Science*, p. 15. The 'Austrian' credentials which are presented in the footnote to that page should be noticed.

But is it? Here I come to my last topic, on which I propose to be brief. In the Theory of Games we have a subject (evidently related to those which we have been discussing, at least in the sense that it uses some of the same mathematics) which is specially concerned with the analysis of behaviour when ends are different, either completely or partially opposed. Are we to say that the rest of economic theory, which is not pure technics, is nevertheless capable of being treated in much the same way by the sister subject – the Theory of Games?

I do not pretend to know the answer to that question. I am not equipped to answer it; the Theory of Games now covers a vast territory, and there is far too much of it that I make no pretence of understanding. I shall confine myself to one point which I think I do see clearly – namely that the relation of economics to the Theory of Games is an entirely different matter from those which we have been discussing. There is no doubt that the theory of optimisation (whether or not it *is* economics) is highly relevant to economics; it may well be that the Theory of Games is highly relevant; but one does not follow from the other.

This is worth stating, because it is easy to get the impression that the connection is closer. One of the neatest ways of proving the general Duality theorem[64] (which, it will be remembered, has not been proved in this paper) is to develop it as a consequence of the fundamental theorem of Game theory – the Minimax theorem, as it is called.[65] If this is done, it looks as if the theory of optimisation is being swallowed up by Game theory – as if the Theory of Games was not merely swallowing that part of economics on which it has obvious designs, but was ready to absorb the lot! But that, I am convinced, would be a mistake.

Though the Minimax theorem is usually stated as a theorem in Game theory (and no doubt it is that application which to mathematicians is the most fruitful), it is not necessary to state it that way. It can easily be stated in a more abstract manner – as a pure property of numbers that are arranged in a rectangular matrix. Any such matrix has a minimax (the minimum of row maxima) and a maximum (the minimum of column minima). It is easy to prove that the minimax must always be greater than, or equal to, the maximin. What von Neumann's Minimax theorem states is that there is a process of 'enlarging' the matrix by which the gap between minimax and maximin (if it initially exists) can be so reduced that it

---

[64] See above, p. 265.
[65] See, for instance DOSSO, ch. 16.

ultimately disappears. This process of enlargement is simply the addition of new rows and columns which are weighted averages (in the sense in which we have been using that term) of the former rows and columns. By sufficient enlargement, minimax and maximin can be brought together.

What I want to emphasise is that this enlargement is a purely abstract operation, which can be given all sorts of meanings, that have nothing but a formal connection with one another. When the Minimax theorem is used as a means of proving Duality the matrix is a matrix of technical coefficients; the enlargement (in one direction) is carried out by varying outputs, in the other by varying factor prices. When it is used in Game theory the matrix is a matrix of pay-offs; the enlargement is performed by mixing strategies. The mixing of strategies has nothing necessarily to do with the Minimax theorem; it is one of the ways in which the theorem can be applied, and no more. That the Minimax theorem can be used in the theory of optimisation does not show that 'Outputs *v.* Factor Prices' is in any sense a Game.

20

Prices and the Turnpike:
The Story of a Mare's Nest

This essay was published in *Review of Economic Studies*, 28 (1961). How it came to be written is explained in the text. There was attached to it, when it appeared in *RES*, a companion piece by M. Morishima, which gave more general proofs, this, being entirely his work, is not included here. References to it, which would make no sense without it, have therefore been suppressed. But that makes it all the more necessary that I should acknowledge, and indeed emphasise, the help that I had from him in writing my own paper, help which continued in the work that grew out of it — chapters 18 and 19 of *CG*, and the appendices there attached.

The investigation that is described in this paper began from an attempt to explain the Turnpike Theorem, of Samuelson and Solow,[1] in a way that would be moderately comprehensible to not-so-very mathematical economists. For this purpose I made a simplification, which looked as if it was a permissible simplification; I then found, to my surprise, that the Turnpike Theorem did not seem to come out right. I supposed, at one point, that I had thereby refuted the Turnpike Theorem, at least in one of its manifestations; and indeed it took some time, and the combined efforts of quite a number of interested economists,[2] to find where it was that I had gone wrong. The trap is in fact not one that it was at all easy to suspect; it would therefore seem that it needs to have a sign-post put upon it, lest

[1] I began from the version in Dorfman, Samuelson and Solow, *Linear Programming and Economic Analysis*, p. 330 and thereabouts. As elsewhere, I shall in future refer to this composite author as DOSSO.

[2] Acknowledgements are due to (1) Edmond Malinvaud, at the time of his visit to Oxford in November 1959, (2) correspondence with DOSSO and with Tjalling Koopmans, (3) discussions in California with Roy Radner, Dale Jorgensen and Kenneth Arrow (March 1960). But it was not until I was working with Morishima and Nikaidô at Osaka in April–June 1960 that light finally dawned.

others fall into it also. For this reason, and because there are some interesting and rather unfamiliar properties of the model in question which emerge in the course of the argument, the story is one which it seems useful to set down.

I

Most of the assumptions on which we shall be proceeding in what follows are the same as von Neumann's. We are to examine the behaviour of an economy in a sequence of unit periods, in each of which certain quantities of goods are absorbed as inputs, while other quantities of the *same* goods emerge as outputs at the end of the period. Thus, for the period that runs from t to $t+1$, X_{0t}, X_{1t}, ..., X_{Nt} – which we shall write (X_t) – are inputs, and correspondingly (X_{t+1}) are outputs. When we pass to the next period, no new factors are brought in, but no consumption is taken out. The same (X_{t+1}) which emerge as outputs of the period t to $t+1$ are therefore available as inputs for the period $t+1$ to $t+2$. There are the usual Activity Analysis assumptions of convexity and constant returns to scale. We begin with a given (X_0); we have to determine the optimum path of the system, on some criterion or other.

This general set-up is common to all writers on the subject; beyond this there are certain divergences. For one thing, the optimum itself may be defined in two ways. On the one hand, we may seek for the path which maximises final output: in the sense that, when the proportions in which the outputs are to emerge at the end of n periods (n being large) are given, the output of the composite commodity (combined in these proportions) that is then produced is to be as large as possible. This, we may say, is the orthodox interpretation; it was in terms of this interpretation that the Turnpike Theorem was first formulated. But there is another interpretation which crops up now and again in the literature,[3] and which certainly seems very natural to anyone who approaches the problems as one of Linear Programming. According to this alternative, what would be maximised would be the *value* of final output at given price-weights – $\Sigma P_n X_n$ where (P_n) is given. It normally follows from convexity that 'quantity-optimisation' (on the first test) and 'value-optimisation' (on the second) are equivalent; but whether the equivalence continues to hold in a sequential model of

[3] As in DOSSO, p. 330.

the von Neumann sort is a thing that may possibly need some verification.

The other difference, that requires notice, concerns the treatment of fixed capital. In his original paper[4] von Neumann insisted that the capital goods employed are to be included both in (X_t) and in (X_{t+1}): 'wear and tear of capital goods are to be described by introducing different stages of wear and tear as different goods'. If one adopts this device, capital goods do not need any explicit attention in the subsequent analysis; formally, of course, this is a great simplification. DOSSO, however, prefers to introduce capital goods explicitly; so that there are required, for the production of current output, not only the current output of the preceding period (as before) but also the use of capital goods, the supply of which can be increased as an alternative use of current resources. Inevitably this complicates the model; and for the purpose that I have in mind the gain in (apparent) realism is hardly worth the complication. I shall therefore revert to the von Neumann convention, with capital goods figuring as inputs and as outputs (after whatever wear and tear occurs to them in the process of production).

There is, however, another complication which forces itself upon one's attention as soon as one has made this decision. On the von Neumann convention, every act of production (every 'activity') must use some current products of the preceding period, together with capital equipment left over from the preceding period, both included as inputs; and there must be included among its outputs, both its current product (or products) and the capital goods (at appropriate stages of wear and tear) which are carried forward for use in the next period. It is therefore inevitable, if we are to make sense of an actual process of production in these terms, that the 'activity' should be multi-product — that particular pairs (at least) of the outputs (X_{t+1}) should be jointly produced. von Neumann did, of course, assume that this was so; but if we try to simplify his system, this is a complication which it is very tempting to leave out. The particular model which I am going to discuss in this paper is one that does leave it out.

Economically, as I would freely admit, this is illegitimate. Nothing can therefore be argued, from the *special* properties of such a model, about anything that could happen in the real world. It does nevertheless seem clear that if the Turnpike Theorem is true in the general case, it must be true in this special case also. I have therefore felt justified in giving some attention to this special model, which has the

[4] *A Model of General Economic Equilibrium, RES,* 1945–6, p. 2.

merit of being easy to think about without using too much mathematics; thus it can hardly fail to have some classroom use, when the
Turnpike Theorem comes to be fitted in to general courses of
economic teaching.[5] If, as we shall find, it is rather a tricky case, it
is important that that should be known.

The problem before us may therefore be re-stated as follows.
Assuming no fixed capital (or no explicit attention to fixed capital)
and no joint production, is there any tendency for the optimum
path, that begins from an arbitrary (X_0) and extends over a
sufficiently long period, to approximate for most of its course (as
the Turnpike theorem maintains) to the von Neumann path of
balanced growth? In particular, does this tendency exist if our test
for the optimum is that of value-optimisation?

II

Now that prices have been mentioned, it is possible to set out the
basic conditions, by which the optimum path is determined, in a very
simple form.

It is, in the first place, a necessary condition for efficient growth
that in every period the (X_{t+1}) should be the maximum outputs
obtainable for given (X_t); maximum may here be understood in
either sense, but it will be more convenient to take it in the value
sense – that for some given set of price-weights (P_{t+1}), the value of
output, $\Sigma P_{t+1} X_{t+1}$, is to be maximised. That is the first condition;
but in a sequential model of this sort, an intra-period condition like
this is not sufficient for optimality. It is further necessary, when two
successive periods are looked at together, that the marginal rates of
substitution between the (X_{t+1}), considered as outputs of the period
t to $t+1$, should correspond with their marginal rates of substitution,
when they are considered as inputs of the period $t+1$ to $t+2$. That
is to say, when we consider the combined period t to $t+2$, the prices
(P_{t+1}) that are used in maximising $\Sigma P_{t+1} X_{t+1}$ are not to be arbitrarily
selected; they must be the same prices (or, more strictly, they must
be proportional to the prices) which emerge as input prices (or

[5] It was only after this paper was completed that I read the book by Piero Sraffa,
Production of Commodities by means of Commodities (Cambridge, 1960). It was exciting
to find that he had broken up his analysis of a parallel problem in just the same way as I
had found myself wanting to break up this: beginning with no fixed capital *and* no joint
production, and then introducing fixed capital and joint production together. The advantages of that approach are well illustrated by Sraffa's book; one can now expect with some
confidence that it will be widely used. But it will be safer to use it if the dangers that are
attendant upon it are also realised.

'resource values' as the Activity Analysts call them) for the period $t+1$ to $t+2$. Such consistency of the system of relative prices will be sufficient (it has been often shown) to preserve intertemporal optimality. It is indeed no more than a dynamic translation of the principle, so familiar in statics, that maximisation at consistent prices by independent units yields a Pareto optimum.

It will be convenient, in what follows, to get rid of the proportionality factor, by which these prices are indeterminate, in the usual economic way, by taking one of the commodities (that with index 0) as a standard of value. The price of this commodity will therefore be taken at unity throughout, and can be suppressed. And, while we are at it, there is no reason why we should not adopt the same device on the quantity side also. By constant returns to scale, an increase in all inputs in the same proportion makes it possible to increase all outputs in the same proportion; accordingly, while we are working out the effects of the above stated optimum conditions, we may simply look at the ratios of quantities. The simplest way of doing this is to measure the quantities of all other commodities by their proportion of the contemporaneous quantity of the standard commodity. The 'quantity' of the standard commodity will accordingly be kept at unity in our subsequent work, and can also be suppressed.

The general problem of optimisation, in a von Neumann system, may therefore be expressed as follows. We are to start from given supplies at time 0; but from those given supplies we cannot determine any more than a set of alternative collections of output at time 1. To select a particular collection, expressed by (X_1), we to know (P_1); and (P_1) is not yet determined. We are to take it that (X_n), the final set of quantity-ratios, or (P_n), the final set of price-ratios, is given. The problem is to determine the intermediate (X)'s and (P)'s, given the initial (X_0) and the final (X_n) – or (P_n) only.

A general solution of this problem, which takes into account the possibility of zero outputs and zero prices, but maintains the 'no joint supply' assumption, was beyond my capacity;[6] I was therefore obliged, when I got to this point in my own thinking, to make do with something simpler. I accordingly *assumed* (as I thought that DOSSO assumed) that there were no zero outputs or zero prices; that one starts with the same list of commodities, all fully employed, that are produced and used in the von Neumann equilibrium, and

---

[6] It was given in the Morishima paper, which was attached to this.

continues with positive outputs of the same commodities. Granted that assumption (we shall examine later how far it is a permissible assumption) the procedure to be followed is fairly obvious.

What we must do is to assume, for the moment, that (P_0) is given as well as (X_0). It will then follow, under the assumptions just made, that (P_1) can be deduced. For the techniques of production (the technical coefficients) which minimise unit cost in each industry are determined by the input prices (P_0); from (P_0) and these technical coefficients the relative unit costs are determined; and (P_1) must correspond to these unit costs if there are to be no zero outputs. Next, having determined (P_1), we can deduce (either by the production possibility 'curve', or by the conventional Linear Programming technique) the outputs – that is, the *relative* outputs – (X_1). Thus, given (P_0) and (X_0), we have (P_1) and (X_1) determined.

We can then run down the sequence, until we have 'determined' (P_n) and (X_n). But (X_n) – if we are quantity-optimising – is given; what this must mean is that when, by the above process, we have determined (X_n) as a 'function' of the arbitrary (P_0), we must invert the process so as to determine a (P_0) which will generate an (X_n) equal to the given (X_n). If we are value-optimising, so that (P_n) is given, we must do likewise for (P_n). If there are $N+1$ commodities, there are N prices in (P_0) and N quantities in (X_n). Thus there are N equations for N unknowns (and similarly if terminal prices are given). That these equations must have a solution is by no means directly obvious; it is nevertheless clear that a solution must exist, if there is to be an optimum path in the conditions supposed.

The basic equations by which the path is determined may be written $(P_{t+1}) = H[(P_t)]$ and $(X_{t+1}) = F[(X_t), (P_t)]$; each of these being symbolic expressions for N equations, incorporating suitable functions $H_1, \ldots, H_N, F_1, \ldots, F_N$. These equations are valid for the optimum path that corresponds to any initial (X_0) and terminal (X_n) or (P_n). We are, however, particularly interested in von Neumann's equilibrium path (nicknamed the 'Turnpike') which is an optimum path such that along it relative quantities and prices can remained unchanged. In the notation just described, it will be determined by the equations $(\bar{P}) = H[(\bar{P})]$ and $(\bar{X}) = F[(\bar{X}), (\bar{P})]$. Thus it is the equilibrium path of the system in the usual 'difference equation' sense. The relation between this equilibrium path, and the path which is determined by an arbitrarily given starting point and arbitrarily given terminus, is the matter with which the Turnpike Theorem is concerned.

III

The method of analysis which I shall employ at the next round is substantially that used by DOSSO. If the differences between the 'actual' and the equilibrium paths are small, we may take first-order approximations to the functions in the above equations, thus reducing the recurrence relations to a linear form, which can readily be solved by well-known methods. It would be perfectly possible to set out the resulting analysis for the general case of any number of commodities, by using known properties of matrices; it will, however, be sufficient for the purpose in hand, if it is written out for the case of two commodities, which can be treated in a relatively elementary manner.

With two commodities (numbered 0 and 1, 0 taken as standard), we have only one price in each period $- P_t -$ and one quantity-ratio $- X_t$. I shall write $p_t = P_t - \bar{P}$; $x_t = X_t - \bar{X}$.

If these differences are small, we can take

$$p_{t+1} = P_{t+1} - \bar{P} = H(P_t) - (H\bar{P}) = hp_t$$

and

$$x_{t+1} = X_{t+1} - \bar{X} = F(X_t, P_t) - F(\bar{X}, \bar{P}) = fx_t + gp_t$$

where f, g, h are the values of the partial derivatives of F and H along the equilibrium path. These values can be calculated in terms of the technical coefficients along the equilibrium path, as follows.

Written in full, the H and F functions are given by

$$P_{t+1} = \frac{a_{10} + a_{11}P_t}{a_{00} + a_{01}P_t}, \qquad X_t = \frac{a_{01} + a_{11}X_{t+1}}{a_{00} + a_{10}X_{t+1}}$$

where the as (the technical coefficients) are to be regarded as functions of P_t. Nevertheless, since f is a partial derivative of F with P_t constant, it can be calculated by holding the as constant, at their equilibrium values. Further, since costs are to be minimised at P_t, the terms involving change in the as will cancel out in the calculation of h also; so that also can be calculated with as constant at their equilibrium values. Remembering that $\bar{P}$ and $\bar{X}$ must satisfy the above equations, with $\bar{P}$ written for P_t and P_{t+1} (and similarly for $\bar{X}$), we have, after a little manipulation,

$$f = \frac{S + \sqrt{(S^2 - T)}}{S - \sqrt{(S^2 - T)}}, \qquad h = \frac{S - \sqrt{(S^2 - T)}}{S + \sqrt{(S^2 - T)}}$$

where $S=\frac{1}{2}(a_{00}+a_{11})$, $T=a_{00}a_{11}-a_{01}a_{10}$. f and h are accordingly reciprocals, being both positive when T is positive, both negative when T is negative.[7] But in either case the absolute value of f is greater than 1, of h less than 1.

g will clearly be zero in the case of fixed technical coefficients (when there is no choice of methods). It becomes negative when the coefficients are variable, being larger in absolute size the larger are the elasticities of substitution between the inputs in the two industries.

With this information at hand, we can return to our linearised equations

$$x_{t+1} = fx_t + gp_t, \qquad p_{t+1} = hp_t$$

If g is not zero, we can eliminate the ps, and get

$$x_{t+2} - fx_{t+1} = h(x_{t+1} - fx_t)$$

or

$$x_{t+2} - (f+h)x_{t+1} + fhx_t = 0$$

This can be solved by the usual procedure for difference equations; its characteristic roots are obviously f and h; so that the general solution is $x_t = Af^t + Bh^t$, where A and B are constants.

To determine A and B, we have x_0 given; if we are quantity-optimising, we also have x_n given. The solution can then be written

$$x_t = \frac{(x_n - x_0 h^n)f^t + (x_0 f^n - x_n)h^t}{f^n - h^n}$$

If n is large, h^n can be neglected (since $|h|<1$). This formula therefore reduces to

$$x_t = x_0 h^t + x_n h^{n-t}$$

(remembering that $fh=1$). Thus, if t is small, x_t behaves like $x_0 h^t$; this continually diminishes (in absolute size) as t increases; the 'actual' path moves closer to the equilibrium path. When t approaches n, the second term takes over; the actual path therefore moves away from the equilibrium path towards its objective. The Turnpike property is thus confirmed.

[7] We must, of course, take the positive roots of the quadratics for $\bar{X}$ and $\bar{P}$; and therefore the positive root of S^2-T. (It will be noticed that S^2-T is necessarily positive.)

IV

I do not think that the preceding can possibly be regarded as a proof of the Turnpike Theorem (for quantity-optimising), even for the special case marked out by our simplifying assumptions; for the use of 'smalls', first for linearising, and then in quite a different way in the latter part of the argument, does not carry conviction without careful defence. How easy it is to argue on these lines and to go off the rails will appear from some examples which we shall proceed to consider.

Take, to begin with, the case of fixed technical coefficients, where $g = 0$. The price equation and the quantity equation then become independent of one another; the quantity equation becomes $x_{t+1} = fx_t$, and the solution of that is $x_t = x_0 f^t$; any initial displacement from the equilibrium must therefore (or so it seems) increase indefinitely. But the path which is generated in this way pays no attention to the terminal x_n which has been prescribed for it; it cannot therefore be the solution to the problem proposed. Something, it seems clear, has gone wrong.

It is in fact not difficult to deal with this case from first principles (without any linearising). Suppose that we put the optimisation problem the other way up (as is permissible by constant returns to scale). So far we have maximised terminal outputs, to be produced in prescribed proportions, after n periods, from initially given resources fixed in amount. Let us now take the terminal quantities to be given, and enquire into the minimum quantities that are to be available at time 0 *in fixed proportions*, and to be such that after n periods the given terminal quantities can be produced from them. In the latter form the solution of the fixed coefficient case is rather obvious.

For with fixed coefficients the quantities of inputs needed in the *last* period to produce the given outputs of that period are at once deducible from the given techniques. We cannot get to our objective unless the penultimate period has produced at least this amount of each commodity; while if it has produced more of any commodity, it must have used more inputs than were necessary, so that it could not have been producing with full efficiency. Jobbing backward in this manner, one can see that the efficient inputs and outputs of each period are determined from the terminal outputs; and so on right back to the beginning. But the inputs of the initial period, so determined, will not (in general) be in the prescribed proportions; all that can be efficiently used are nevertheless those that are in such proportions. If we have them in other proportions, we cannot use them in those other proportions; the superfluous amounts must be thrown away. Thus the optimal path (whether we are minimising initial input in fixed proportions, or maximising final output in fixed proportions) is found by throwing away superfluous quantities in the first period; then proceeding, by repeated use of the given technique, to the final objective.

That this solution is correct may be confirmed by considering prices. A commodity cannot be in excess supply unless its input price is zero; but it is necessary that the input prices of each period should correspond to the output prices of the preceding period; thus if a commodity were in excess supply in period $t + 1$ to $t + 2$, it could not be produced in period t to $t + 1$. There can therefore be no excess supplies, except in the period 0 to 1; for the input prices of that period are not output prices of any period, so that some of them may be zero. The throwing-away must therefore be confined to the first period.[8]

All this is generally valid, when we have fixed coefficients. For the last step let us go back to the two-commodity model.[9] If we start from the given X_n, and calculate X_{n-1} from it by means of the quantity-equation (in its unlinearised form); then repeat the operation many times, so as to get back to X_0, interpreted as the proportions in which the commodities are to be *used* (not thrown away) in the initial period; we shall find[10] that this X_0 approximates closely to $\bar{X}$. (This is in fact what our equation $x_t = x_0 f^t$ – whence if follows that $x_0 = x_n h^n$ – was trying to tell us.) Thus, after the initial throwing-away, the path starts very near the Turnpike, gradually shearing off from it towards its objective; the path is therefore of the same character as that previously considered, only the initial

---

[8] To this there is the formal exception that a commodity could have a zero output price, if all the inputs that were required for it had zero prices. But of course in such a case it would not matter whether the excess supplies of the commodity were made or not.

[9] The same result could be demonstrated for many commodities by matrix methods. (There are, however, certain exceptions in the general case, the counterparts of which in the two-commodity case are obviously trivial; for these see Morishima's paper.)

[10] It can readily be shown algebraically, without any linearising, that if X' is the other (negative) root of the quadratic determining $\bar{X}$, the quantity-relation (for as which are constant at their equilibrium values) is equivalent to

$$(X_t - \bar{X})/(X_t - X') = h(X_{t+1} - \bar{X})/(X_{t+1} - X')$$

Thus for the initial inputs (after throwing away)

$$(X_0 - \bar{X})/(X_0 - X') = h^n(X_n - \bar{X})/(X_n - X')$$

which is approximately zero when n is large. Thus X_0 (for the actual initial inputs) is approximately equal to $\bar{X}$.

approach to the Turnpike is done all at once, not by degrees. So far, then, the Turnpike Theorem is confirmed.

V

So far we have been concerned with quantity-optimisation; let us now turn to value-optimisation, with P_n (in the ratio sense) given instead of X_n. (Here I shall *not* be assuming fixed coefficients.) If we apply the linearisation method to this problem, it appears to give the same kind of trouble.

For now we cannot eliminate the prices from our linearised equations. We must solve the price-equation directly; obviously $p_{t+1} = hp_t$ gives $p_t = p_0 h^t = p_n h^{t-n}$ (p_n being given). Substituting from this in the quantity equation, and summing from 1 to t, we get

$$x_t - x_0 f^t = gp_n h^{-n} (h^{t-1} + h^{t-2} f + \ldots + h f^{t-2} + f^{t-1})$$

$$= gp_n h^{-n} \frac{f^t - h^t}{f - h}$$

The x_t that is given by this formula does not appear to have any tendency to be small at intermediate t, when n is large.

Let us therefore proceed as we did formerly, and see if we can get any further by a verbal argument. We shall only be able to do that in a special case; the case which suggests itself for investigation is that in which the terminal P_n is the same as the equilibrium $\bar{P}$, so that $p_n = 0$. So all p_ts are zero. The linearisation solution would then give $x_t = x_0 f^t$, which is the same diverging path as we seem to get in the case of fixed coefficients, previously discussed. We were then able to dismiss this solution; but we cannot dismiss it so easily in the case to which we have now come, for the reason which will now be explained.

Consider the price-sequence in its original form $(P_{t+1}) = H[(P_t)]$. This equation holds so long as there are no zero outputs; then, if (P_n) is the same as $(\bar{P})$, $H[(P_{n-1})] = H[(\bar{P})]$; and though it is possible that this latter equation (or rather set of equations) may have multiple solutions, we may reasonably neglect that possibility, and conclude that if (P_n) is the same as $(\bar{P})$, (P_{n-1}) must be the same as $(\bar{P})$ also.[11] And so on, back to (P_0). That is to say, under the assump-

---

[11] The logic of this is the same as that of the Factor-price equalisation theorem in international trade. So long as there are no zero outputs, the prices of factors are determined from prices of products, independently of the supplies of the factors (of course assuming constant returns to scale).

tions that we have made – and though they are no more than a special case, they seem to comprise a perfectly fair set of questions to put to the model – the same relative price $(\bar{P})$ must obtain over the whole of the sequence.

But if the same relative prices obtain, then – regarding them as input-prices – the same techniques (the same technical coefficients) must obtain. We can therefore determine the path that is to be followed by supposing that the system begins from an arbitrary (X_0), while the technical coefficients, by which (X_{t+1}) is derived from (X_t) are given. That is to say, we are back at the former case of fixed technical coefficients. But the way in which we got out of the difficulty presented by that case, when we met it formerly, is here *not* open.

For in the former case the fixed technical coefficients were *given*; there was only one technique of production (in each 'industry') that was available to use. It was therefore entirely possible that, for the proportions in which outputs had to be produced in the initial period, some of the initially available resources could not be used. Here, however, techniques are potentially variable; there is no reason why they should not be so variable that the marginal products of the initially available commodities cannot sink to zero. If that is so, excess supplies in the initial period will be inconsistent with efficient organisation in that period; there cannot be excess supplies in the initial period along the optimum path.

I must confess that when I reached this point in my thinking I was very puzzled. I thought at one time that I had disproved the Turnpike Theorem, for the case of value-optimisation. But indeed the inconsistency, which appears to have been discovered, does not merely upset the Turnpike Theorem, if it is taken at its face value. What it seems to show is that value-optimisation, in this model, is quite different from quantity-optimisation; the static equivalence between the two ceases to hold. That (though it was a possibility that had to be held open) was not easy to believe; is there any other way out?

There is another way out, and (knowing the answer) it has been hard to write out the foregoing without revealing it. The equations $(P_{t+1}) = H[(P_t)]$, on which this puzzling argument was based, only hold if there are no zero outputs. Now it is clear that there can be no zero outputs in the initial period, if we assume (as I think we may justifiably assume) that some quantities of all commodities are necessary for the continuance of the process – every output is a necessary input in the production of *some* commodity.[12] For the same reason, there can be no zero outputs in each subsequent period; until we come to the last period, the outputs of which are not inputs for any period. Some of these may be zero. What we have in fact learned is that some of them *must* be zero, if we impose a (P_n) equal to $(\bar{P})$.

There is in the end no other bolt-hole that is open. This is the solution; but what a solution of this kind must mean is by no means obvious. I did not bring myself to accept it, and I cannot expect the reader to accept it, without some way of elucidating it further. What is needed for that is to find a case, which raises all the difficulties that have been perplexing us, but which is simple enough for us to be able to work out its optimum path (or paths) in as much detail as we require. Such a case can in fact be found.

VI

What we need is a case in which the range of techniques available is so wide that any quantities of inputs can be absorbed without input prices falling to zero; and in which all inputs are necessary inputs, in the sense that some quantity of every input is necessary for every output.[13] There is a very well-known case which satisfies these conditions: that in which the 'production function' of every 'industry' is of Cobb–Douglas type. Let us assume that this is so, and see what happens.

As before, I shall confine attention to a two-commodity model, though (as before) it could be generalised without great difficulty.

What has first to be determined is the form of the H and F functions in this Cobb–Douglas case. It can be shown, in a manner which is sketched out in the attached footnote,[14] that the price-relation (the H function) takes the form

$$\log P_{t+1} = h \log P_t + \beta$$

where β is a constant, and h (which corresponds to our old h, but is not identical with it) is also a constant, depending on the indices in

---

[12] This assumption was *not* made in the original Samuelson–Solow article, 'Balanced Growth under Constant Returns to Scale' (*Econometrica*, 1954). It was made in the Morishima paper (his Assumption 4).

[13] This is more drastic than is necessary, but that does not matter.

[14] The genesis of these relations may be demonstrated as follows.

Let a_{ij} (consistently with our previous notation) be the amount of the ith input used per unit of output in the jth industry. The Cobb–Douglas function for that industry may be the Cobb–Douglas functions, in such a way that its absolute value is less than 1. The equilibrium price-ratio $(\bar{P})$ must also satisfy this equation, so β may be eliminated by subtraction. Here it will evidently be more convenient to write $p_t = P_t/\bar{P}$. So we get

$$\log p_{t+1} = h \log p_t$$

the solution of which is

$$\log p_t = h^t \log p_0$$

p_t therefore converges very rapidly to unity, as t increases.

---

written (after dividing by output, and taking logs) as

$$\sum_i \alpha_{ij} \log a_{ij} = \text{constant}$$

(The αs are the Cobb–Douglas indices; thus we may take $\sum_i \alpha_{ij} = 1$).

In each industry, unit cost is to be minimised; this gives the 'constant factor-shares' conditions for that industry; if for the moment we put W_i for input prices and P_j for output prices, these may be written

$$W_i a_{ij} = \alpha_{ij} P_j$$

Taking logs, multiplying by α_{ij} and summing for all inputs, we get (for each industry)

$$\sum_i \alpha_{ij} \log W_i + \sum_i \alpha_{ij} \log a_{ij} = \sum_i \alpha_{ij} \log \alpha_{ij} + \sum_i \alpha_{ij} \log P_j$$

Of these four terms, the second is constant (by the production function); the third is constant; the fourth is $\log P_j$ (since the indices, in each industry, add to unity). We therefore get

$$\log P_j = \sum_i \alpha_{ij} \log W_i + \text{constant}$$

(for each industry).

This may now be re-written to give a recurrence relation for the von Neumann process. In the two-commodity case, for P_j we have $P_{0,\,t+1}$ and $P_{1,\,t+1}$; for W_i we have $P_{0,\,t}$. Thus

$$\log P_{1,\,t+1} = \alpha_{01} \log P_{0,\,t} + \alpha_{11} \log P_{1,\,t} + \text{constant}$$

$$\log P_{0,\,t+1} = \alpha_{00} \log P_{0,\,t} + \alpha_{10} \log P_{1,\,t} + \text{constant}$$

Subtracting, and measuring relatively to commodity 0 as standard,

$$\log P_{t+1} = h \log P_t + \text{constant}$$

since $\alpha_{11} - \alpha_{10} = \alpha_{00} - \alpha_{01} = h$ (say). h is clearly less than unity in absolute value.

Returning to the constant factor-shares conditions for the individual industries, we have only to multiply by outputs and add, to get constant factor-share conditions for the economy as a whole. If we write $P_t X_t$ as V_t, these would be expressed in terms of the von Neumann process as

$$V_{1,\,t} = \alpha_{10} V_{0,\,t+1} + \alpha_{11} V_{1,\,t+1}$$

(and similarly for $V_{0,\,t}$). From these the F-function used in the text can be at once derived.

The quantity-relation (or F function) may be similarly shown to take the form

$$P_t X_t = \frac{\alpha_{10} + \alpha_{11} P_{t+1} X_{t+1}}{\alpha_{00} + \alpha_{01} P_{t+1} X_{t+1}}$$

where the αs are the Cobb–Douglas indices. This is mathematically the same relation as we got in the fixed coefficient case, save that PX is written for X; it must have the same properties. Thus if we suppose $P_n X_n$ to be taken arbitrarily, and work backward to time 0 (n being large), we are bound to find that $P_0 X_0$ is very near to its equilibrium value $\bar{P}\bar{X}$.

This is independent of what we are fixing, terminal quantities or terminal prices. It always holds that P_n must be near to $\bar{P}$, $P_0 X_0$ near to $\bar{P}\bar{X}$.

X_0 being given, P_0 must equal $\bar{P}\bar{X}/X_0$ (nearly); there is a rapid convergence, as time goes on, from this initial value of P_t to the final value which is nearly $\bar{P}$.

If we are quantity-optimising, so that X_n is given, $P_n X_n$ must be close to $\bar{P}X_n$; while $P_0 X_0$ is close to $\bar{P}\bar{X}$. Until t approaches n, $P_t X_t$ will remain close to $\bar{P}\bar{X}$; while, after the first few periods, P_t will be close to $\bar{P}$. Therefore, in the middle stretch, X_t will be close to $\bar{X}$; the optimum path approaches the equilibrium path, as the Turnpike Theorem maintains.

If we are value-optimising, we are setting P_n; but we now see that we cannot set P_n, and have no zero outputs, unless we set P_n very close to $\bar{P}$. If we set the right $\bar{P}$, we shall get just the same result by value-optimisation as we did by quantity-optimisation. (There is no discrepancy, after all!) But the P_n which we can set and get this result is very closely confined.

What was shown by the argument that caused all the trouble (it turns out to be a perfectly valid argument, with a validity which is by no means confined to the case of Cobb–Douglas functions) is that $P_n = \bar{P}$ (terminal prices the *same* as the equilibrium prices) is not one of the P_n's that can be set to yield all positive outputs. This is confirmed by the present analysis. For if $p_n = 1$, $\log p_n = 0$, and (by the price-relation) all $\log p_t$ must be zero (so long as n is not infinite). All P_t must therefore be equal to $\bar{P}$. In particular P_0 must be equal to $\bar{P}$; so that $P_0 X_0$ cannot be close to $\bar{P}\bar{X}$, unless X_0 is close to $\bar{X}$. Thus if X_0 is not close to $\bar{X}$ – if we do not start from a position which is near to the equilibrium path – we cannot have all terminal outputs positive.

VII

The result to which we have come can easily be expressed in a simpler manner. The 'production possibility curve' which results from the end of a von Neumann process (with arbitrary initial position) is very nearly linear. The various goods are available, at the end of the process, at nearly constant costs in terms of one another. Thus if we set prices which correspond to these constant costs, we can get all sorts of product-mix for hardly any change in prices; but if we set prices that do not correspond, the outputs of some commodities (those with the lower prices, relatively to these costs) must fall to zero. These relative prices are nearly the same as those which hold along the equilibrium path, but (in finite time) they are never quite the same. They continue to be influenced by the initial position, to ever so slight an extent (less and less as n gets larger).

This *tendency towards constant cost* is a consequence of the 'no joint supply' assumption; in general it will go if that assumption is removed. In the form in which we have used it, the assumption is clearly unrealistic; thus it cannot be inferred that there would be any such approximation in a model which got a little closer to the real world. On the other hand, there is certainly something suggestive about it; to find out how much would be left of it if the 'no joint supply' assumption were *partially* relaxed, seems a promising line for further enquiry.

21

Direct and Indirect Additivity

This is (in substance) a note that was published in *Econometrica* in April 1969. It was a comment on a paper by Paul Samuelson, which had appeared in a previous issue of that same journal (October 1965). He claimed to have shown that there was just one case in which a utility function could be both directly and indirectly additive, namely that in which the share of the budget, devoted to the purchase of each particular commodity, remained constant however prices changed. By direct additivity (DA) was meant that the utility function was the sum of *independent* utility functions of the amounts of the various commodities; by indirect additivity (IA) was meant that if the utility function was converted into a function of prices (at given spending power) it was similarly separable into functions of the prices of the individual commodities.

My first reaction, on reading Samuelson's paper, was that his proof of his proposition was unnecessarily lengthy; so I tried to find something simpler. I think I did find a simpler approach; but it seemed to throw up an exception, which he had not noticed. I tested this for a simple case, which appeared to confirm it. My note thus began with a statement of the simple case, where the exception is evident. It then proceeded to give the general proof (which of course was the route by which I had found the exception).

I make no claim that this note is of importance. I nevertheless take the opportunity of including it here, in a slightly improved form. For the point is correct, and should go on the record, and it can be made a little clearer than it was as originally published.

I

Consider an *additive* utility function of two goods

$$U = u(x_1) + \alpha \log x_2$$

where u is *any* well-behaved utility function of the single quantity x_1, and α is a constant.

I take the budget constraint in the form $p_1 x_1 + p_2 x_2 = 1$, standardising prices as Samuelson did. We have the usual conditions for maximisation

$$u'(x_1) = \lambda p_1 \tag{1}$$

and

$$\alpha/x_2 = \lambda p_2 \tag{2}$$

From the budget constraint

$$\lambda = \lambda(p_1 x_1 + p_2 x_2) = x_1 u'(x_1) + \alpha \tag{3}$$

so that λ is a function of x_1 only. Then, from (1), we have

$$\frac{1}{p_1} = x_1 + \frac{\alpha}{u'(x_1)} \tag{4}$$

This, under the above assumption about $u(x_1)$, should be solvable for x_1, giving x_1 as a function of p_1 only. It then follows from (3) that λ also is independent of p_2.

Further, from (2)

$$\log x_2 = \log \alpha - \log \lambda - \log p_2$$

so that

$$U = u(x_1) + \alpha \log x_2$$
$$= \alpha \log \alpha + [u(x_1) - \alpha \log \lambda] - \alpha \log p_2$$

The bracketed expression has just been shown to be independent of p_2, so the utility function U has been shown to be also *indirectly additive*.

While $p_2 x_2$ is constant for a change in p_2, it is clear from the demand function (4) that there is no reason why $p_1 x_1$ should be constant for a change in p_1.

II

The reason for the exception (and the reason why it is in effect the only exception) emerges at once when the matter is looked at more generally.

U is now to be taken to be a *general* utility function of the amounts of n commodities: $U(x_1, \ldots, x_n)$. By application of the equilibrium equations and of the budget relation the xs can be eliminated, giving $U = U^*(p_1, \ldots, p_n)$ – the *indirect* formulation. It is well-known that while

$$(\partial U/\partial x_i) = \lambda p_i \qquad (5)$$

we have

$$(\partial U^*/\partial p_i) = -\lambda x_i \qquad (6)$$

From these is immediately follows that

$$x_i(\partial U/\partial x_i) + p_i(\partial U^*/\partial p_i) = 0 \qquad (7)$$

So much is valid, quite generally. But if we have DA, the first term in (7) is a function of x_i only; while if we have IA, the second is a function of p_i only. Thus if there is both DA and IA, and we differentiate (7) with respect to $p_j(j \neq i)$, the second term vanishes, while from the first, which is a function of x_i only, we have

$$(\partial x_i/\partial p_j)[(\partial/\partial x_i)(x_i \, \partial U/\partial x_i)] = 0 \qquad (8)$$

Now go back to (6). If there is IA, and we differentiate with respect to $p_j(j \neq i)$, the left-hand side vanishes, so

$$(\partial/\partial p_j)(\lambda x_i) = 0$$

or

$$x_i(\partial \lambda/\partial p_j) + \lambda(\partial x_i/\partial p_j) = 0 \qquad (9)$$

Thus if

$$(\partial x_i/\partial p_j) = 0, \quad (\partial \lambda/\partial p_j) = 0$$

Then from (8) we have the two alternatives for every i: either

(i) $(\partial \lambda/\partial p_j) = 0$ when $j \neq i$; λ, as a function of prices, is a function of p_i alone, or
(ii) $x_i(\partial U/\partial x_i)$ is independent of x_i, while by DA it is independent of the other xs; so it is a constant. Thus $\lambda p_i x_i$ is constant.

Now if it is the first of these alternatives which holds for every i, λ must be constant. And if it is the second which holds for every i, since $\Sigma px = 1$, λ must also be constant. It is at once apparent in the second of these cases that $p_i x_i$ must be constant for every i; and it can readily be shown that the same always happens when λ is constant. Thus in each of these cases the Samuelson rule is verified.

But why should not the first alternative hold for some commodities, and the second for others? If there were *two* commodities for which the first alternative held, λ would have to be constant, and we should be back where we were. But suppose that there is just *one* commodity for which the first alternative held, while it was the second which held for all the rest. Number that one commodity 1. λ would then not be constant; it would be a function of p_1 though independent of all the other ps. For anyone of those other commodities, it would be $\lambda p x$, not $p x$, which would have to be constant.

This is the exception which was illustrated in the first section of this note.

22

Elasticity of Substitution Reconsidered

This is based upon a paper entitled 'Elasticity of Substitution again: Substitutes and Complements', which appeared in *Oxford Economic Papers* in November 1970. It led to some comments in the pages of that journal; Sato and Koizumi extended my three factor analysis to and *n*-factor case, while Syrquin and Hollender discussed a possible generalisation which admitted of increasing returns to scale.[1] In the meantime, I had myself made some use of the opportunities which my 1970 paper had opened up, in a chapter on the Production Function in *Capital and Time*.[2] I do not find that what I said in the paper is much disturbed by these developments, though they have made me see that I might have made the foundations of my analysis a little clearer, and there are ways in which the mathematics, as presented, were clumsy. In consequence, a most instructive formulation of the Fundamental Formula, to which they led up, was missed. For these reasons I have thought it well to make a new version, which shall incorporate improvements in these respects, and shall begin with a survey of the earlier literature, which should help to bring the discussion into focus for the modern reader.

I

The e.s. first made its appearance in my *Theory of Wages* (1932). It came up there in two contexts, one micro, the other macro.

In the micro sense I used it to make an extension of Marshall's formula[3] for the elasticity of derived demand – the elasticity of demand for a factor (or input) used in producing a particular

---

[1] Sato and Koizumi, *OEP*, 1973, pp. 44–59; Syrquin and Hollender, *OEP*, 1982, pp. 515–19.
[2] *CT* (1974), pp. 177–82.
[3] Marshall, *Principles*, Math. App., Note XV.

product, the elasticity of (consumer) demand for that product being given. There was in his version just one co-operating factor, the supply of which might vary with the price (per unit) offered for it. He also supposed that the proportion in which the factors were to be combined was invariable ('blades' and 'handles' was his example). I wanted to allow for possible variability, though I kept the rest of Marshall's assumptions. If one factor became too expensive, the other might to some extent be substituted for it. The e.s. first came up as a measure of that substitutability, and that was how it got its name.

The macro use was more ambitious, and much more contentious. The model here was a model of a whole (closed) economy, which was supposed to be representable as the production of a single product by two factors. A production function, representing 'the' technology, was given. The factors were paid by the value of their marginal products; such payments exhausted the whole value of the product, so that, at least at a point of equilibrium, the economy would be working under constant returns to scale (CRS).[4] It was easy to show that under these assumptions (the MP assumptions I shall call them) an increase in the use of one factor, that of the other being constant, would increase or diminish its share in the product (in value terms) according as the e.s. between the factors, as I there defined it, was greater or less than unity. For an increase in the relative share of factor 1 must (with two factors) diminish the relative share of factor 2. But if a_1, a_2 are quantities of factors, x is quantity of product, x_1, x_2 are marginal products (or first partial derivatives), the relative share of factor 2 is $a_2 x_2/x$. So the condition for this to fall as a_1 increases is that x_2 should increase less rapidly than x when a_1 increases (since a_2 is constant). That is to say, $x_{12}/x_2 < x_1/x$, or $x_1 x_2/x x_{12} > 1$. So it was this latter expression which I took, in 1932, as my definition of the elasticity of substitution.

It was a formula which (as has been shown) arose out of the macro model; it depended, in consequence on the MP assumptions. I could nevertheless show that, again under those same assumptions, it could be used for the micro problem also.

A few months after the publication of *TW* (1932) appeared *Economics of Imperfect Competition* (*EIC*) by Joan Robinson. (There was not time for her to have seen my book before hers was substantially completed.) She also had a concept called e.s., but she

---

[4] For the 'Wicksellian' argument by which I sought to justify CRS, see *TW* (either edition), pp. 238–9.

used it only in a micro sense, and the definition which she gave arose out of that context. She kept the assumption of two factors only, but she did not make (she would certainly have been most unwilling to make) the MP assumptions. She accordingly defined the e.s. as 'the proportionate change in the ratio of the amounts of the factors employed divided by the proportionate change in the ratio of their prices'.[5] This gave results which were consistent with mine, in the micro application. Even in the macro application, if she had been willing to make it, it would have given similar results. For if the e.s. between the factors, in her sense is greater than unity, a relative increase in the price of one factor must diminish its relative share in the product. (Just as a rise in the price of a commodity will diminish the receipts of its producers if the elasticity of demand for that product is greater than unity.) This could be shown, from her definition, without any MP assumptions.

So it long continued to be taken for granted, by those economists who were willing to accept the MP assumptions, that her definition and mine were equivalent; while those economists who were unwilling to accept them, retained her definition as *the* definition of e.s., but had no use for mine.[6] But it turned out, in the end, that there was much more to be said.

II

The first step forward, in my own thinking, was when I noticed, when preparing the second (1963) edition of *TW*, that the 'extended Marshallian' formula for elasticity of derived demand, which I had given in 1932, was itself a hybrid between two expressions with sharper and clearer meanings.[7] I had written

$$\lambda = \frac{\sigma(\eta + e) + ke(\eta - \sigma)}{\eta + e - k(\eta - \sigma)}$$

where η is the elasticity of demand for the product, k the cost-proportion of the factor, e the elasticity of supply of the 'other'

---

[5] *EIC*, p. 256.

[6] It will be noticed that it was from my definition that the 'constant e.s.' production functions, as one time so popular among econometricians, were descended. If my σ is set equal to 1 *everywhere*, it gives the Cobb–Douglas function, already familiar before 1932. If it is made constant everywhere, but not equal to 1, it generates a function, of apparently different form, which appears to offer an extra degree of freedom. For my part, I have never been able to see why any e.s. should be constant everywhere.

[7] *TW* (1963), p. 374.

factor, and σ the e.s. between them. Now if in this cumbrous expression one had set e infinite, so that the price of the other factor was fixed, it would have reduced to

$$\lambda = k\eta + (1 - k)\sigma$$

while if one had set $e = 0$, so that the quantity of the other factor was fixed, it would have reduced to

$$(1/\lambda) = k(1/\eta) + (1 - k)(1/\sigma)$$

Attention was drawn to the duality between these two equations, and also to that between the corresponding equations for cross-elasticities, which I there wrote

$$\mu = k(\eta - \sigma) \quad \text{and} \quad (1/\mu') = -k(1/\eta) + k(1/\sigma)$$

But, in 1963, I stopped there.

If one was to get further, one needed a better notation. Keeping a_1, a_2 for quantities of factors, and k_1, k_2 for factor-shares, let p_1, p_2 be prices of factors. Now use the E notation for elasticities. Thus

$$(Ea_1/Ep_1) = (p_1/a_1)(da_1/dp_1) \quad \text{with } p_2 \text{ constant}$$

and

$$(Ep_1/Ea_1) = (a_1/p_1)(dp_1/da_2) \quad \text{with } a_2 \text{ constant}$$

thus each of the derivatives is an (appropriate) partial derivative. It will be noticed that with this notation, the elasticity of a downward-sloping curve is negative. I shall nevertheless keep η for the Marshallian elasticity of (consumer) demand, so that η is positive.

The four equations (from *TW*, 1963) can then be written in a more revealing form. If p_2 is constant

$$Ea_1/Ep_1 = -k_1\eta - k_2\sigma \tag{1a}$$

$$Ea_2/Ep_1 = -k_1\eta + k_1\sigma \tag{1b}$$

while if a_2 is constant

$$Ep_1/Ea_1 = -k_1(1/\eta) - k_2(1/\sigma) \tag{2a}$$

$$Ep_2/Ea_1 = -k_1(1/\eta) + k_2(1/\sigma) \tag{2b}$$

When the equations are written in this form, several things emerge.

Take first the (1) equations. If $\eta = 0$, so that output is constant, nothing is left in these but the σ terms. So what this σ measures is the e.s. along the isoquant, which is geometrically identical with the e.s. along an indifference curve, which plays the same part in consumer theory. So the form of (1a) is the same as the form of the Slutsky equation.

Further, for these (1) equations, the *EIC* definition exactly fits. For, p_2 being constant, that reduces to

$$(Ea_2/Ep_1) - (Ea_1/Ep_1) = (k_1 + k_2)\,\sigma = \sigma$$

by (1a) and (1b). Whence, if this σ is zero, a_2/a_1 is constant; the factors are combined in fixed proportions, so they can be treated as a single 'composite' factor. The effect of a change in p_1 on the 'price' of this composite factor is given by k_1. η will then register the effect of the change in this 'price' upon output. That squares up; it should, however, be noticed that if, on this interpretation (1a) and (1b) are to hold, the increase in the composite factor and the increase in output must be in a constant proportion – a CRS assumption which has crept in even here.[8]

Now take the (2) equations. The $(1/\sigma)$ in these equations is isolated by setting $(1/\eta) = 0$, so that the price of the product (p_x I shall write it) is fixed. The MP assumption gives $p_2 = p_x x_2$, so if p_x is constant,

$$(Ep_2/Ea_1) = (Ex_2/Ea_1) = (a_1 x_{12}/x_2) = k_1(x x_{12}/x_1 x_2)$$

the latter being the reciprocal of the *TW* definition of σ.

So the σ in (2b) belongs to the *TW* definition. (To get this identification we do not need the full force of the MP assumption; it would be sufficient that p_2 and $p_x x_2$ were in a constant ratio.)

Nevertheless, to proceed to (2a) we do need MP, including CRS. For $(Ex_1/Ea_1) = a_1 x_{11}/x_1$; and this is equal to $-a_2 x_{12}/x_1$, as it needs to be if we are to have (2a), only if we have CRS.

So each of the four equations has some relation to MP (and so to CRS) assumptions; but it is not the same relation in each.

III

There is another difference between the (1) equations and the (2) equations which needs to be emphasised. While the former are concerned with the effects of prices on quantities, the latter are concerned with the effects of quantities on prices. That is why the (1) equations run in terms of η and σ, while the (2) equations run in terms of their reciprocals. Now when we pass to the reciprocals, the meanings of the questions asked do not exactly correspond. This

[8] 'Efficiency units' were introduced in *EIC* to meet just this difficulty.

holds even for η and $(1/\eta)$. The former registers the effect of a change in price on quantity purchased; but the latter registers the effect on price of a change in supply *in a competitive market*. There should surely be a corresponding change in the meaning of σ, as we pass from (1) to (2).

It might have been noticed that in extreme cases, this can be serious. As has been shown, it follows at once from the *EIC* formula that if the e.s. between two factors is zero, the ratio in which the factors are combined is unaffected by a change in their price-ratio. This is confirmed by the *TW* formula, which would represent that case as one where an attempt to change the ratio (increasing the use of one factor when the supply of the other was fixed) would cause the MP of the fixed factor to shoot to infinity – so that in equilibrium the use of the first factor could *not* be increased. There is no trouble about that, but at the other end there is. On the *EIC* definition, if σ becomes infinite, the factors are perfect substitutes; but on the *TW* definition, it implies that x_{12} is zero – the MP of the one factor is *independent* of the quantity of the other. That is a useful meaning, which we should want to keep. But what has it to do with *perfect substitutes*? The solution to the puzzle is CRS. If the factors are independent, *and* there is CRS, there must be constant returns to each factor separately. If that is so, then, in a formal sense, they are perfect substitutes. But that is a very special case of perfect substitution, not in itself of much use.

Though it is evidently impossible for two factors to be more substitutable than perfect substitutes, it is not so obviously impossible for the corresponding limit, on the side of the *TW* definition, to be breached. It is surely not impossible, *in general*, for an increase in one factor to diminish the MP of the other. That is impossible, in the two factor case, with CRS, but from a more general consideration it should surely not be ruled out. One would judge that with two factors and *increasing* returns to scale, it would be unlikely to arise, but between two factors, when there are other factors beside the two, it could quite readily arise.

We have come to contemplate that possibility by consideration of the *TW* definition of σ; but the *TW* formula, as it stands, is ill-adapted to deal with it. It is $(1/\sigma)$ which appeared in equations (2). $(1/\sigma)$ goes to infinity when the factors are *perfectly complementary*; it is zero when the cross-effect is zero; in the case just discussed it could go negative. It would thus appear to be proper, in a more general theory, to work with the reciprocal of the *TW* σ, regarding it as an *elasticity of complementarity*. I shall denote it by c_{12}. In the particular case of two factors with CRS, $c_{12} = (1/\sigma_{12})$; but in general, as we shall see, there is no such relation.

IV

Let there now be three factors, which we seek to distinguish. It is sufficient, I find, to take three factors. For we only need a third factor to serve as background, a background which in the two-factor case is so lamentably missing. We have to generalise equations (1), in which prices are parameters, and (2), in which quantities are parameters. In the first case any number of factors, besides the two which are our special concern, can be treated as a single factor, since their (relative) prices will be held a constant. In the second we can again treat them as a single factor, since their (relative) quantities will be held constant. Thus for a complete theory of substitute-complement relationships, three factors should be enough.

We should then have, in place of (1), three equations. I shall write them in the form they would take along the isoquant (x constant) since it is only the σ terms in which were are interested. They would naturally be written (p_2 and p_3 being taken as constant)

$$(Ea_1/Ep_1) = - k_2 \sigma_{12} - k_3 \sigma_{13}, \quad (Ea_2/Ep_1) = k_1 \sigma_{12},$$

$$(Ea_3/Ep_1) = k_1 \sigma_{13} \tag{1'}$$

The second and third of these equations are matters of definition; the first follows from them, as in consumer theory, since x is constant (and maximised at given prices). We may take it that, as in consumer theory, these σs (now *partial* elasticities of substitution) are reversible; thus $\sigma_{21} = \sigma_{12}$.

It will be noticed that these partial elasticities cannot now be defined in an *EIC* manner, for that definition pays no attention to what is to happen to the price of the third factor. If p_2 and p_3 were constant, it would reduce to

$$(Ea_2/Ep_1) - (Ea_1/Ep_1) = (k_1 + k_2) \sigma_{12} + k_3 \sigma_{13} = \sigma_{12} - k_3 (\sigma_{12} - \sigma_{13})$$

so that it will not work unless $k_3 = 0$, or unless factors 2 and 3 are indistinguishable.

It will also be noticed that, just as in consumer theory, it is possible for all of the triad σ_{12}, σ_{13}, σ_{23} to be positive, but it is also possible that *one* should be negative. It is not possible for two to be negative, since that would mean that a rise in the price of one of the factors would lead to a substitution *in its favour*.

Let us now turn to the (2) equations. In place of them we should now like to write

$$Ep_1/Ea_1 = -k_2 c_{12} - k_3 c_{13}, \quad Ep_2/Ea_1 = k_1 c_{12}, \quad Ep_3/Ea_1 = k_1 c_{13}$$
$$(2')$$

a_2 and a_3 being here taken as constant, and p_x constant (to eliminate the η term). The second and third of these equations are immediately valid, with the definition of the cs that has been given. But for the first to be valid from them, we need CRS, otherwise we should have to write $(Ep_1/Ea_1) = k_1 c_{11}$. Only if we have CRS do we have what is in effect the Euler condition

$$k_1 c_{11} + k_2 c_{12} + k_3 c_{13} = 0 \qquad (3)$$

and so can proceed to the first equation in $(2')$.

If we do have that condition, it will follow, just as on the other side, that not more than one of the c_{12}, c_{13}, c_{23} can be negative. For c_{11}, c_{22}, c_{23} may each be taken to be negative (diminishing returns to each factor separately). (There is no question that if the production function is mathematically well-behaved, $x_{21} = x_{12}$ and so $c_{21} = c_{12}$.) I doubt, however, if this rule about signs is much dependent on CRS, for it is much more intelligible that the Euler expression (3) should be positive, when there are increasing returns to scale, than that it should be negative. It would have to be *strongly* negative for the rule about signs to fail.

V

What now is the relation between the cs and the σs? It will be proved, in the Appendix to this paper, that under MP assumptions, they are connected by a simple formula which I call the Fundamental Formula. It is

$$\sigma_{12} = (A - c_{12})/B \qquad (4)$$

where A and B are symmetrical functions of c_{12}, c_{13}, c_{23}; and these, so long as all cs and σs are finite, can be shown to be necessarily positive.

This is actually a formula which is more symmetrical than it looks. For it follows from it that

$$c_{12} = A - B\sigma_{12} = (A' - \sigma_{12})/B' \qquad (4')$$

if $B' = (1/B)$ and $A' = (A/B)$. Now it can be shown that A' and B'

are the same functions of the σs as A and B are of the cs. So the cs are transformed into σs and the σs into cs by the *same* transformation.

It is at once apparent from (4) and (4′) that while it is possible (as we have seen), for one, but no more than one, of the σs to be negative, and for one, but not more than one, of the cs to be negative, *the exceptional cases do not correspond*. If c_{12} is negative, σ_{12} must be positive and if σ_{12} is negative, c_{12} must be positive.

The pattern which emerges may thus be summarised as follows. We have the two partial elasticities, σ the elasticity of substitution, c the elasticity of complementarity. It is possible for either to be negative, but it is not possible for both to be negative. Let us say that when σ is positive, the factors are p-substitutes (substitutes in the production of a fixed output) but when c is positive, the factors are q-complements (complements in the production of a variable output). The range of possible relationships, between two factors, in the presence of a third factor, can then be divided into a middle range, in which the factors are p-substitutes and also q-complements, with two 'wings', in one of which the factors are p-substitutes *and* q-substitutes, while in the other they are q-complements *and* p-complements. When there are no more than two factors, the middle range alone can be present; so when that case was the only case envisaged, it seemed possible to make do with a single e.s., σ and the reciprocal of c coming together. As soon as a third factor is introduced, even as background, that will not do; we have to accommodate the 'wings'.

This all falls out from formulae (4) and (4′) when σ and c are finite. For the fully extreme cases of *perfect substitution* and *perfect complementarity*, it is best to go back to (1′) and (2′) directly. If the factors are perfect substitutes, in the sense that σ_{12} is infinite, (Ea_2/Ep_1) is infinite when p_2 is fixed, so the price-ratio (p_1/p_2) cannot in equilibrium change. (That of course is what we normally mean by perfect substitutes.) An increase in a_1, with a_2 and a_3 constant, will diminish the MP of factor 1, and will diminish that of its substitute factor 2 also. Thus, in this extreme case, the factors are q-substitutes also. This extreme case appears where it should do, at the extremity of the 'wing'.

In just the same way, when the factors 1 and 2 are perfect complements, so that c_{12} (as we have seen) is infinite, a_1/a_2 is constant, so a substitution in favour of a_1 must carry with it one in favour of a_2. So the factors are p-complements. This also fits in, at the extremity of the other 'wing'.

Though all this can be shown most tidily when we have CRS (as will be done in the Appendix) it is hard to believe that we need CRS in order for this pattern to be established. The extremes, just discussed, would seem to stand firm, even without CRS; while all we need for the rest of the pattern is the impossibility of two factors being p-complements *and* q-subsitutes. The construction of a model with increasing returns to scale which would make that possible looks quite difficult.[9]

VI

There is a further proposition, of some importance, which (as will be shown in the Appendix) is connected with my Fundamental Formula (4). It concerns relative shares. Out of three factors, if 2 and 3 are perfect substitutes, or perfect complements, they are effectively one factor, and the familiar two-factor theory of relative shares applies. Putting those limiting cases aside, the proposition in question can be stated as follows. It will be easier for factor 1 to increase its relative share in the product when its amount (a_1) increases if the other factors (2 and 3) are available at a fixed price-ratio than if the relative quantities of these factors to be used are fixed.

To get a fair comparison, we must impose a constraint on the scale of operations. Since p_2 *and* p_3 constant will satisfy the first condition, while a_2 *and* a_3 constant will satisfy the second, for total expenditure on these factors $(p_2a_2 + p_3a_3)$ to be constant is a suitable constraint to be imposed. Then in the fixed price case, factors 2 and 3 can be freely substituted for one another at the fixed price-ratio, so long as the expenditure constraint is maintained; there is a range of alternatives that is open, of which to employ a_2 and a_3, the given amounts of the other case, is just one. To maximise output with given a_2 and a_3 must be more difficult than to maximise it in the other case, for in this fixed-quantity case, an extra constraint is imposed. So the fall in x_1 (the MP of factor 1) when its quantity increases will regularly be less in the fixed-price case than in the fixed-quantity case. So it must be easier for factor 1 to increase its relative share in the former case than in the latter. More elasticity in the rest of the productive system must make it easier for a change in the supply of one factor to be accommodated.

[9] There is a further point about these extremes which is worth noticing. If 1 and 2 are perfect complements so that a_1/a_2 is fixed, $(Ea_1/Ep_3) = (Ea_2/Ep_3)$, so that $\sigma_{13} = \sigma_{23}$. Similarly, if they are perfect substitutes, $c_{13} = c_{23}$.

This result will be confirmed algebraically in the Appendix (under CRS assumptions). But it would seem from the considerations just advanced that it should be quite generally true.[10]

Appendix

The Fundamental Formula of section V of the preceding, and the proposition of section VI, can be established as follows. Here I keep the full force of the MP assumptions, including CRS; the prices of the factors are *equal* to the values of their marginal products. How far the results can be extended when we abandon these restrictions has been considered in the text.

1.   The problem is to express the σs in terms of the cs. To get the σs, we must take x, p_2, p_3 constant, while keeping (for all Es) p_1 as the independent variable. This common variable can be suppressed when writing, so for (Ea_1/Ep_1) and so on, I shall in this section just write Ea_1.

With MP assumptions, we have $p_2 = p_x x_2$; so, from p_2 constant, we have $Ep_x + Ex_2 = 0$.

For the first of these terms, since

$$x\,dp_x = d(xp_x) \qquad\qquad \text{(since } x \text{ is constant)}$$

$$= a_1\,dp_1 + p_1\,da_1 + p_2\,da_2 + p_3\,da_3 \qquad (p_2, p_3 \text{ constant})$$

$$= a_1\,dp_1 + p_x\,dx \qquad\qquad \text{(from the MP conditions)}$$

$$= a_1\,dp_1 \qquad\qquad (x \text{ constant again})$$

$$Ep_x = k_1$$

For the second

$$Ex_2 = (1/x_2)(x_{12}\,da_1 + x_{22}\,da_2 + x_{23}\,da_3)$$

$$= k_1 c_{12} Ea_1 + k_2 c_{22} Ea_2 + k_3 c_{23} Ea_3$$

These Es may now be expanded (by $1'$ in the text) since x, p_2, p_3 are all constant. Dividing through by k_1, we thus have, from p_2

---

[10] The form of the preceding argument which was set out in *TW* (1963), pp. 379–81, made it appear that the proposition was less general than I now think it is. This was remarked on by Samuelson, in his paper in the Festschrift in my honour (*Value, Capital and Growth*, 1969, p. 478) and in my 1970 paper I accepted his criticism. But on further consideration it seems to be easy to re-state my argument so as to meet it.

constant,

$$1 = c_{12}(k_2\sigma_{12} + k_3\sigma_{13}) - c_{22}(k_2\sigma_{12}) - c_{23}(k_3\sigma_{13})$$

Re-arranging this, and replacing $k_2 c_{22}$ by the Euler equation (5 in the text), we have finally

$$1 = \sigma_{12}[(k_1 + k_2) c_{12} + k_3 c_{13}] + \sigma_{13}[k_3(c_{12} - c_{23})$$

The corresponding equation to this, derived from p_3 constant, is evidently

$$1 = \sigma_{12}[k_2(c_{13} - c_{23})] + \sigma_{13}[(k_1 + k_3) c_{13} + k_2 c_{23}]$$

From these two equations σ_{12} can readily be calculated.

It is the result of this which comes out in such a surprisingly simple form. For the numerator, we get

$$(k_1 + k_3) c_{13} + (k_2 + k_3) c_{23} - k_3 c_{12} = A - c_{12}$$

if we write A for the *symmetrical* expression

$$\sum (k_2 + k_3) c_{23}$$

But it appears from the Euler equation that A could also be written

$$-(k_1 c_{11} + k_2 c_{12} + k_3 c_{13})$$

so, since there must be diminishing returns to each factor separately if the factors are to be combined in cost-minimising proportions (cost-minimising proportions for a given output), and thus each c_{11}, c_{22}, c_{33} is negative, A must be positive.

The denominator, which I call B, is a determinant, which, (when multiplied out) reduces to

$$k_1 c_{12} c_{13} + k_2 c_{12} c_{23} + k_3 c_{13} c_{23}$$

This is another symmetrical expression which (excepting in a limiting case, to which I shall be coming) can also be shown to be positive. For – again by Euler – $B = (k_2 k_3 / k_1)(c_{22} c_{33} - c_{23}^2)$, or either of the other expressions symmetrical with this. But these are proportional to $(x_{22} x_{33} - x_{23}^2)$ and so on; the *second-order conditions* for minimisation of cost are that these terms should be positive, and the conditions must be satisfied if the factors are fully distinct. Generally, therefore, we may take it that B is positive.

The Fundamental Formula

$$\sigma_{12} = (A - c_{12})/B \tag{4}$$

with A and B both positive, is therefore to hand.

2.   From this formula may be drawn a number of consequences.

(i) If the production function is well-behaved, so that $c_{21} = c_{12}$ — as we have been assuming throughout — it follows that $\sigma_{21} = \sigma_{12}$.

(ii) If we use (4) and the corresponding formulae for σ_{13} and σ_{23}, to calculate

$$\sum (k_2 + k_3)\, \sigma_{23}$$

which has the same form as A, with cs replaced by σs (so I shall call it A') we find that

$$BA' = \sum (k_2 + k_3)\, A - A = 2A - A = A$$

and so

$$c_{12} = A - B\sigma_{12} = B(A' - \sigma_{12})$$

Then, substituting these values of the cs into the original formula for B, we find

$$B = B^2 \sum k_1 (A' - \sigma_{12})(A' - \sigma_{13}) = B^2 \sum k_1 \sigma_{12} \sigma_{13}$$

since the other terms cancel. So if we write B' for the sum on the right (the dual to B), we have

$$BB' = 1$$

and

$$c_{12} = (A' - \sigma_{12})/B' \qquad\qquad (4')$$

the Fundamental Formula in its alternative (dual) form.

(iii) In order to get $BB' = 1$ by this method, we have had to assume that B was not zero; but there is a limiting case in which that is not true. Suppose B is zero. It then follows from the formula for B that at least one of the cs must be negative; but not more than one can be negative, so one must be negative and the others positive. Let c_{12} be negative. It must still be true that A is positive, so, from (4), σ_{12} must be (positive) infinite; the factors 1 and 2 are perfect (p) substitutes. σ_{13} and σ_{23} are essentially arbitrary, since there is here no reason why a substitution against 3 should be in favour of one or the other of the perfect substitutes. There is certainly no reason why either should be negative. But if both are positive, it follows from σ_{12} being infinite that B' is infinite. So the rule that $BB' = 1$ is not infringed, even in the case where one pair become perfect substitutes.

The case of perfect complements, with $B' = 0$, could be treated analogously.

3.   There remains the question of relative shares. We know that if there are only two factors, $\sigma > 1$ is the condition for a factor to increase its relative share when its use is (relatively) increased; and since with two factors $\sigma = (1/c)$, that c should be < 1 is then an equivalent statement.

Now when there are three factors, but the second and third are available at a fixed price-ratio, we could analyse what happened to the first by treating the complex as a single factor, so writing the first equation of $(1')$

$$(Ea_1/Ep_1) = -(k_2 + k_3)\,\sigma_1$$

with σ_1 playing the part of a two-factor e.s. Comparing this with the original form of $(1')$,

$$(k_2 + k_3)\,\sigma_1 = k_2\sigma_{12} + k_3\sigma_{13} \tag{5a}$$

Similarly, when the quantity ratio a_2 to a_3 was constant, we would have

$$(k_2 + k_3)\,c_1 = k_2 c_{12} + k_3 c_{13} \tag{5b}$$

σ_1 and c_1 would then play the parts of σ and c in the two-factor case, when it came to establishing conditions for an increase in the relative share of factor 1 – in the fixed price-ratio and fixed quantity-ratio cases, respectively.

What now is the relation between c_1 and σ_1? In the two-factor case $\sigma c = 1$. It will now be shown that in the three-factor case (when perfect complements and perfect substitutes are excluded, for these effectively reduce the three-factor to a two-factor case) $\sigma_1 c_1 > 1$.

Applying (4) to (5a) and using (5b), we have $B\sigma_1 = A - c_1$ as we should indeed expect. Then

$$B(\sigma_1 c_1 - 1) = c_1(A - c_1) - B$$

but B can be written

$$k_1 c_{12} c_{13} + (k_2 + k_3)\,c_{23} c_1$$

so that

$$B(\sigma_1 c_1 - 1) = c_1[A - c_1 - (k_2 + k_3)\,c_{23}] - k_1 c_{12} c_{13}$$

Now the expression in square brackets

$$= (k_1 + k_2)\,c_{12} + (k_1 + k_3)\,c_{13} - c_1$$

which, when multiplied by $(k_2 + k_3)$ becomes

$$k_1(k_3 c_{12} + k_2 c_{13}) \qquad \text{(since } k_1 + k_2 + k_3 = 1)$$

Then, multiplying again by $(k_2 + k_3)$, we have finally

$$(k_2 + k_3)^2 B(\sigma_1 c_1 - 1)$$
$$= k_1[(k_2 c_{12} + k_3 c_{13})(k_3 c_{12} + k_2 c_{13}) - (k_2 + k_3)^2 c_{12} c_{13}]$$
$$= k_1 k_2 k_3 (c_{12} - c_{13})^2$$

Thus $\sigma_1 c_1$ is always > 1, excepting in the cases when $B' = 0$, and when $c_{12} = c_{13}$, which are readily identified as the cases when factors 2 and 3 are perfect complements and perfect substitutes,[11] respectively.

The proposition about relative shares which was advanced in the concluding paragraph of the text is thus (somewhat laboriously) confirmed.

---

[11] See note 9 above. It will be noticed that

$$B'(c_{12} - c_{13})^2 = B(\sigma_{12} - \sigma_{13})^2$$

by the Fundamental Formula.

Part V
Reviews

Most of these are reviews of modern editions, or translations, of writings by classical or post-classical, economists; they are thus presented as supplementary to the essays in part I above. There are appended, however, two or three which are of a different character.

23

Dupuit

In this review, which appeared in *Economica* (1935) I welcomed the appearance of what is now the standard edition of Dupuit's writings, *De l'utilité et de sa mesure par Jules Dupuit: écrits choisis et republiés par Mario de Bernardi* (Turin, La Riformia Sociale, 1934). How great was the service done for economics by the preparation of this Einaudi edition was appreciated by one who had been through the trouble of extracting the originals from the library of the British Museum.

Of all great economists, Dupuit must have been one of the most unfortunate in the manner of publication of his work. It has long been recognised that he deserves a place with Cournot and Gossen among the most important forerunners of the modern theory of exchange value, but so long as his work remained hidden away in ancient and dusty volumes of the *Annales des ponts et chaussées*, his readers must have been few and far between. These articles, together with a few contributions to other publications, have now been reprinted with great care in this elegant volume.

Although Dupuit's work cannot compare with Cournot's for subtlety of analysis or range of problems treated, he did examine those subjective factors lying behind the demand curve which Cournot neglected. Like Cournot, he was attracted by problems of monopoly; but here again his work is complementary. He came to utility from public utilities; the problem which most concerned him was that which arose in his own engineering experience, the social significance of discriminating charging. In order to deal with this question he was led to invent the concept of consumers' surplus. His ideas on consumers' surplus are crude; but, in spite, or perhaps indeed because of, their crudity, they repay study. For one cannot help feeling that a great many of the criticisms that have been made of Marshall's consumers' surplus doctrine are valid enough against

Dupuit, but are not valid against Marshall. (The earliest of such criticisms, Walras's criticism of Dupuit, is quoted in the introduction to this book.) It would be generally agreed that the gain, in money terms, which accrues to the purchaser of tea, from his being able to buy it at so much per pound, can be most satisfactorily measured by the difference between what he actually pays and what he would be prepared to pay for the same quantity of tea, if the only choice confronting him was between having that quantity or no tea at all. If the marginal utility of money is constant, this difference can be measured by the area under the demand curve; but the equation stands or falls with that condition. This is the point that Dupuit, and also some of Marshall's critics, failed to observe.

Reading these essays in so pleasantly readable a form, one is impressed by the excellence of the writing. It was not obscurity which prevented Dupuit from revolutionising economics. If only he had not hidden his light under a bridge, Jevons might have found himself twenty years out of date.

24

Jevons

This was a review, published in the *Economic Journal* (1978), of volumes 3–5 of the *Papers and Correspondence of W. S. Jevons*, edited by R. D. Collison Black (*RES*, 1977). I have omitted a passage dealing with bibliographical matters.

The twenty years over which these three volumes extend span practically the whole life of Jevons economist. Quite early in 1863, when he is still an unemployed and impecunious graduate, he publishes his *Serious Fall in the Value of Gold*; in 1865, when he is no more than a 'tutor' at Owens College, Manchester, he publishes his *Coal Question*; in 1871, when he has become Professor at Manchester, comes the *Theory of Political Economy*. There are many other publications during the twenty years; but one can see, as one reads the letters, what turning-points these particular dates are.

It was the *Serious Fall* which gave Jevons his first recognition; already, arising out of that, we find Cairnes, Fawcett and Thorold Rogers among his correspondents. But it was the *Coal Question* which made him a public figure. When he came to submit his application for the Chair at Manchester (in 1866) he could attach a galaxy of testimonials. They came from those just mentioned, who particularly speak of his *Gold*; from Bagehot, Farr and Newmarch, who also speak of *Gold*; but it was *Coal* which enabled him to attach the glittering names of Mill and Gladstone. No wonder he had a walkover! We have to see him, from that point, as one of the nation's leading applied economists. It was from the eminence which he had reached in that way that he was able to launch his Utility theory.

So it ran no danger of being overlooked, as others had been overlooked; it is indeed to him that Dupuit, and Cournot, and Gossen owe their fame. Walras, and even Marshall, must have found it easier to attract attention from the publicity that Jevons gave them.

However we now judge Jevons's work in comparison with theirs (or some of theirs), it was Jevons who was the standard-bearer.

One learns more in these volumes about the spreading of Jevonian ideas (both in theory and in applied economics) than one does about the man himself. There are not many instances where we see his mind at work. One is accustomed to seeing it in his published writings, but in his correspondence he rarely has much to add. One instructive example may, however, be mentioned. It is the case of the sun-spot theory. We see how it begain – the ten-year sunspot cycle and the trade cycle which in Jevons's day seemed to have a similar ten-year period. Jevons had a good eye for such statistical parallels. We see him working upon the series, pushing his ten-year trade cycle back into the eighteenth century, and simultaneously corresponding with astronomers so as to make the sun-spots give a better fit. Then, since he recognises that he has to posit some causal connection, he starts to work on harvest figures, finds that they don't fit very well, but he is not to be choked off. Perhaps it is the Indian monsoon which is affected by the sun-spots! So he starts collecting data about prices in India, though he is conscious that he will be hard put to it, even if the sun-spot–monsoon connection is established, to make Indian trade so powerful a force as he requires, so as to swing the state of trade in Europe and in America. It is not an impressive example of scientific method, but perhaps it is worth recalling as a cautionary tale for econometrists.

It is pleasant to make the acquaintance of some of Jevons's correspondents. There are actual letters from E. Laspeyres, whose ghost has survived, for most of us, only in the form of an index number. 'I cannot express me very well what it is because I mean it better' (III, p. 81); suddenly he comes alive. The Baron d'Aulnis de Bourouill, the Jevonian missionary in Holland, does not appeal to me as much as he seems to do to Professor Black. But I am decidedly impressed by the obscure American, R. O. Williams, whose excellent letters (IV, pp. 130ff.) extend marginal utility to deal with quality differences, using as examples the market for houses and (curiously) tobacco; they quite remind one of Menger. But isn't it remarkable that the great drag-net, which we see here organised by Jevons and by Walras, and which was extended into the German area (so that von Thünen and Gossen were fished up) never fished up Menger? Jevons, it seems clear, never heard of Menger. This is confirmed by the fact that there is no reference to Menger in *Mathematical Psychics* (1881); Edgeworth, in these last years of Jevons's life, was his most faithful follower.

25

Menger

This is an extract from my review, in the *Economic Journal* (1951), of the English translation of Carl Menger's *Principles of Economics*, translated by Dingwall and Hoselitz (Illinois, 1950). As the translators rightly said in their preface, the book was 'more than normally difficult to translate'. So they tried to dress it in a more modern terminology. This I thought to be wrong.

Menger was a good deal more than a 'primitive'. He was writing on a subject which was just beginning to acquire a considerable literature in English, and which has by now a vast literature. But he had a different approach from the one which has become dominant in English. Nearly all modern English writing on value theory is at least semi-mathematical, while Menger's is as non-mathematical as is consistent with clarity of argument. A semi-mathematical argument is easily translated from one language to another; terms have exact equivalents, ultimate reference to mathematical symbolism serving to keep the equivalence exact. The translator of Menger does not have this advantage. He has to face the ordinary difficulties of literary translation, with the added difficulty that the words which he can hardly help using are words with regular meanings that have been given to them by a school of economists whose habit of thought is different from Menger's. Menger's thinking refuses to fit into these categories. The obvious translation of his terms is therefore very frequently a wrong one. The English expression has acquired implications which the corresponding expression in Menger does not have.

There is, however, no need to be mystical about the difference between Menger's thought-language and ours. His lack of mathematics led him to overlook some important things which leap to the eye as soon as one uses the mathematical method; his innocence of any suspicion of the problem of oligopoly is one of the great contrasts between his theory and those of (say) Cournot or Edgeworth. But, on the other hand, the absence of mathematical simplification gives him a beautifully direct approach to some problems which are again in our own day being forced upon the attention of economists — problems which do not go into mathematics easily, so that we are tempted to deal with them by the use of higher and higher mathematics! Menger never attempts to simplify by assuming continuity and divisibility; this cuts him off from Cournot and the followers of Cournot, but makes him much less remote than most of his contemporaries from some of our own modernists, such as (shall we say?) Samuelson or Arrow. Menger never assumes a perfect market, with consumers confronting a definite list of exactly defined and standardised commodities; he does indeed claim that it is a special virtue of the marginal utility approach that it can allow for variations in quality as well as in quantity. To re-acquire this sensitivity of Menger's we have had to wait for Chamberlin. Perhaps most important of all is his theory of marketability, which again fails to go easily into mathematics, but may still provide the easiest way of integrating into the body of a general economic theory such things as the Liquidity Preference of Keynes.

A book such as Menger's cannot be effectively translated into English by being forced into a terminology which is strange to it, and which — at its best — it transcends. To have invented new terms would have been difficult, and when so many near-equivalents are to hand, seems hardly worth the trouble. But it would have been the safer course.[1]

[1 A leading example of the kind of thing I had in mind — which I did not give in this review — is the key word *Wert*. These translators go straight at it, and make it *Value*; but that by now has other connotations in English, so it goes all wrong. It would have been much better to have made it *Valuation*.]

26

Marshall

This is the substance of a review, published in the *Economic Journal* (1976), of *The Early Economic Writings of Alfred Marshall (1867–1890)*, edited in two volumes by J. K. Whittaker (*RES*, 1975).

Adam Smith, as is well known, gave orders on his death-bed that his papers should be destroyed; Alfred Marshall, in this respect at least, was less prudent. He instructed his successor to edit from his manuscripts 'such material as he may think to be of value' (whence the *Memorials*); but he gave no instructions as to the disposal of the remainder. They have remained in boxes in the Marshall Library at Cambridge, but in a state (in the words of his present editor) of 'confusion ... Many pages are missing, and many sheets are simply the relics of old working notes, whose meaning is now elusive'. Professor Whittaker·has clearly had a stupendous task to bring his selection from them into any sort of order. Dating has been difficult, and the piecing together of bits that belong together has also been difficult. By no means the least valuable part of what emerges are the editor's own extensive comments, from which (as much as from the texts) we get a significant impression of the development of Marshall's thought in the decades before the first edition of the *Principles*. One can at least appreciate the *Principles* a little better now that one can follow, at least in outline, the route which Marshall took on his way to his major work.

All that can be done by the present reviewer is to indicate a few points which he personally found to be of interest.

The famous statement by Keynes (*Memorials*, p. 21) about the relation between Marshall and Jevons now needs some qualification. 'The publication of [Jevons's *Theory of Political Economy* – 1871] must have been an occasion of some disappointment and annoyance to Marshall. It took the cream of novelty off the new ideas which

Marshall was slowly working up.' More, perhaps, has been read into this statement than Keynes intended; it has been supposed that what Marshall was 'working up' was the 'Marginal Utility Revolution', in which he was anticipated by Jevons, and of course by Walras and Menger also. It is now quite clear that that is all wrong. Marshall began, as one would expect, from Mill. He does not stress the filiation to Mill, since he was conscious of moving on from Mill, and wished to call attention to his differences from Mill. Yet Mill is the basis from which he starts. It has always been obvious that there is a close relation between Marshall's *Pure Theory of Foreign Trade* and Mill's chapter on International Values; we can now see that Marshall, in his early work, began from Mill on a much wider front. We can see the outline of an early Marshall who is really pre-Jevons, and much more like Mill than he is like Jevons. Consumer's rent, to take a leading example, begins as the difference between value in use and value in exchange, much as in Mill; it is, initially, a sum of 'money', not of 'utility'. It only takes on the latter form when Marshall goes Jevonian, perhaps not until about 1880. It might have saved later writers a lot of trouble if this transmogrification had not taken place.

Perhaps the most important way in which even the early Marshall differs from Mill is over the Wage Fund. Mill himself, of course, had 'abandoned the Wage Fund' just at the date of the earliest Marshall writings; but it is clear that for Marshall, Mill's recantation did not go far enough. For already at that date Marshall was a marginal productivitist (long before he became a marginal utilitist). It is marginal productivity (that, and nothing else of substance) which is implied in the debt which he so often acknowledges to von Thünen. And marginal productivity, in Marshall, is the fully fledged production function concept, not the 'discounted marginal productivity' of Taussig or Wicksell, which is much less far from the Classics. It is indeed true that in later work the marginal productivitism of Marshall was drastically qualified, but it is central to his thought in this early period, up to (and probably including) the first edition of the *Principles*.

It is hard to believe that his marginal productivitism is not to be associated with his concept of capital — his 'materialist' concept of capital, to be contrasted with the classical 'fund' concept. The fragments on capital that are printed here are in themselves disappointing; they give no clear lead. But it is surely implied in the full marginal productivity doctrine that capital is thought of as being embodied in instruments; the typical 'piece' of capital is a machine. That Marshall should have thought in this way has had consequences for later economics that have not been too fortunate; it would have been wonderful to have found in these pages a reasoned defence of his viewpoint, but that no doubt is too much to expect. What we do get, very strikingly, is a revelation of the state of mind which led Marshall to this point of view. He was intensely concerned to be realistic. As we know, he visited factories and looked at their working; so his economics was to be an economics of the shopfloor, not, like that of the Classics, an economics of the counting-house. This was an approach that had many virtues, but it was essentially myopic. So it is not surprising that Marshallian economics is at its best when it is dealing with the firm or with the 'industry'; it is much less capable of dealing with the whole economy, even the whole of the national economy. This is already a characteristic of the early Marshall, and this time it was to remain with him throughout.

In the Essay on Value, 'believed' by Marshall himself to have been written about 1870, there is a fascinating first sketch (vol. I, pp. 134–9) of what was to become the great Marshallian classification of equilibria. Market equilibrium, short period, long period – all are present; but here they are marked as B, C, and D. They are preceded by A, which has dropped out of sight, or at least out of emphasis, in the *Principles*. It is the case of 'retail trade' where 'the buyer is influenced merely by considering whether he can afford to pay the price at which the commodity is offered, and does not in general look forward to either a rise or fall in the price; the seller fixes his price in general without much thought merely following the prices which rule in some large market and which are themselves determined by considerations such as those discussed under B or C'. One can understand why this A was suppressed, because it is not an equilibrium and hence plays no part in determining prices; but here again how much we should have gained if Marshall had gone on a little further in the direction in which we now know he set out!

27

Pareto

A review of the collection of *Pareto's Letters to Pantaleoni*, published in three volumes by the Banca del Lavoro in 1960. It appeared in *Economica*, under the title 'Pareto Revealed', in 1961.

There are contained in these volumes 785 letters of Pareto, the largest collection of Pareto letters that has come to be published, and on most counts probably the most important. All but 47 of them were directed to Pantaleoni; this is, in fact, the Pantaleoni collection of Pareto letters. If Pareto kept Pantaleoni's replies (as it is not unlikely that he did) they have not survived. All that have survived (and are here printed) are a few, of which Pantaleoni kept copies, or which were returned to him with Pareto's comments. The Pareto letters, not directed to Pantaleoni, which are included in these volumes, are also letters that came into Pantaleoni's hands in one way or another.

It must first of all be said (by a reviewer in *Economica*) that to the economist, whose interest in Pareto is centred on the *Manuel*, and especially on those parts of the *Manuel* which have been fruitful in later economics, these letters will be rather disappointing. The proportion of them that is concerned with economic theory, in such a way as to throw light upon the development of Pareto's ideas in that field, is rather small. One may perhaps allude to the long letter of December, 1899 (no. 438), in which Pareto declares that he is now proceeding *from* the indifference curve ('given by experience'), instead of proceeding *to* it from something beyond experience ('pleasure, marginal utility, rareté, ophelimity'), as Edgeworth had done, and as he himself had done in the *Cours*. This is interesting, in view of its date; but it is perhaps more interesting that the change is presented as a means of getting away from the old preoccupation with exchange, so as to base economics upon something more general.

An animal cannot exchange, but even an animal, or a (weighing) machine can be indifferent. And so he draws a picture of Buridan's ass!

There are a few more things of this kind, but it was clearly not for their sake that these sumptuous volumes were prepared, nor that the editor fulfilled his task with such elaborate scholarship. The chief interest of these letters is distinctly different. It has more to do with the *Sociologia* than with the *Manuel*; more with politics than (directly) with economics. This, it is evident at a glance, has been the editor's interest; it is the references to political history which he has been chiefly concerned to elucidate in footnotes and in appended essays, which are a notable contribution to the history of Italy during the relevant period. All that side of Pareto has been distinctly distasteful to most of those who have come under his influence as an economist. We knew that he began as a (very dogmatic) liberal, and ended (nearly, if not quite) as a Fascist; one did not feel proud of him, at this date, in either of these capacities. It has, of course, been the peculiar merit of his teaching in economics that one can profit by it while rejecting the political views that in Pareto's own mind went with it. The systematic extrusion of subjective elements, which was the centre of his contribution to mathematical economics, has the fortunate effect of allowing his economics to be used by many who would find his politics deplorable. We know the high grounds of scientific method on which he justified the extrusion; on those grounds we may well be prepared to accept it for ourselves. The problem does nevertheless remain: how did it sit, in Pareto's mind, with these other things that seem so much less acceptable? The principal thing which we may get from these letters is the best chance, which is likely to come to us, of finding out.

The correspondence of Pareto and Pantaleoni begins in 1890, when Pantaleoni was already a professor of economics, Pareto a railway engineer who was beginning to dabble in that subject. It continues, sometimes intensely (letters following one another at intervals of days), sometimes more sparsely (but there are few years that are not represented by a dozen letters) until the death of Pareto in August, 1923. At the start, Pantaleoni is the professional, Pareto the amateur; but the rôles are soon reversed. Pareto came to economics later, but he was in fact the older man; and soon it is he who is the teacher. Though Pantaleoni's contributions to economics are of some importance (he saw some things better than Pareto did), it soon becomes evident, in this correspondence, that he is jogging along behind. But whatever the intellectual relation, there is every

indication, at all times, of close personal friendship. Pantaleoni was
in Pareto's confidence, as others (such as Walras or Barone, whom
outsiders might have associated with him more closely) were not. It
was in these letters, if anywhere, that Pareto put down what he really
thought and felt.

The subject of the correspondence is, however, to a large extent,
the doings of Pantaleoni. It is through Pantaleoni's activities that
Pareto is brought into relation with Italian politics. He had himself
been active in political journalism in the days before he left Italy; but
after he settles at Lausanne (in 1893) that begins to fade away. He
prefers his seat on the side-lines, and will not be tempted to go back.
But Pantaleoni, though he also is persuaded to take refuge in Switzer-
land after he has been deprived of his chair at Bari, cannot resist the
temptation of returning, when he sees an opportunity of entering the
Italian parliament. Pareto tries to dissuade him (no. 462):

Don't you believe that you can support yourself in Italy on speculations like
your acetylene business. How much, by the way, did you make on the other one,
your electric furnace? You will end by throwing away the money you have, not
making more. If you didn't have all those sons to support – and that large dog –
you could risk your future on the throw of a card. . . . For a chap like you, to
get elected deputy is a luxury.

But it is no good; the chance of a fight is too appealing.

At the beginning, in the nineties, both Pareto and Pantaleoni are
'liberisti' – liberals in political matters, economically free traders,
even unto laissez-faire. 'Liberismo', we must however understand,
was then a creed of the left; it was for preaching the dangerous
doctrine of free trade that Pantaleoni was turned out from Bari (in
1892). In the war with Abyssinia (1896) they are both of them
strongly anti-imperial, anti-colonial. It is as a deputy of the *extreme
left* that Pantaleoni (in 1900) finally takes his seat in the Chamber.
When, that summer, the King is assassinated, Pantaleoni gets into
trouble (and shocks his more cautious friend) by saying 'serve him
right!'[1]

But then the change begins. If one looked at Pareto alone, one
would say that it came from reading Marx. He is convinced by the
class-war but not (of course) by Marx's economics. So he joins in on
the class-war, on the other side. (It becomes the circulation of élites,
in his Sociology). But when we see what Pantaleoni is doing, things

---

[1] 'Considerant sa morte sanglante comme un dernier et terrible avertissement', was what
he wrote in a Swiss paper (no. 463).

look rather different. After 1900, it is not the oppressiveness of the Italian government, but its weakness, which becomes alarming. Pantaleoni breaks with his socialist allies, because the government is giving way to them too easily. So long as they were hopelessly in opposition, socialists, syndicalists, anarchists – and even 'liberists' – could stick together; but the moment that the walls of Jericho look like falling, the conquering army falls apart. A socialist Italy, Pantaleoni begins to fear, will be even more tyrannical than the ramshackle regime which he has been fighting, so he gravitates towards the nationalists, has to put his 'liberismo' into second place, and (soon) almost to forget about it. This is what was happening to his friend while the corresponding change was taking place in Pareto.

He, as we can now see, was affected by the same political shift, but on a different plane. 'Liberismo' is finished, but it cannot be replaced for him (as it could by Pantaleoni) by a simple shift in political alignment. He sets himself to re-think his liberal principles; and even on grounds of formal economic theory finds them wanting. But instead of attempting to find a new set of principles (as other economists have done when finding themselves in the same theoretical predicament), he forswears the use of political principle altogether. It is not only on the scientific level that everything that comes from 'beyond experience' should be cut away. All such principles, he now holds, are mere 'derivations' (in the terminology of his Sociology); they are nothing but rationalisations of individual or of group self-interest. When he and Pantaleoni were 'liberists', they were merely following the interest of their group, and rationalising it. Now that their interest has shifted, it is natural that they turn their politics another way.[2] So he rationalises his decision to go, at least part of the way, with Pantaleoni (for even now, he cannot quite stomach the alliance with the nationalists). Surely that is what he is doing, though he does it in the sophisticated way of proving to himself that his new course does not need rationalisation!

The path from such 'inverted Marxism' to the Fascism, with which Pantaleoni formally, and Pareto less formally, ended, looks only too easy. Nevertheless, I have the impression, from reading these letters, that Pareto was nearer to what came to be Fascism in (say) 1912 than he came to be in his last years. Self-interest, given its head, was very strong; but there are signs, at the last, that the scientific spirit – the detachment of the scientific spirit – was even stronger. Even Pantaleoni, in spite of his adventure with d'Annunzio at Fiume, and

---

[2] Like so many intellectuals, he prefers to convict himself of unworthy motives than to admit to intellectual error.

his acceptance of a senatorship from Mussolini, shows signs that his old spirit is not extinct. 'I go on saying that I have one lady-love, the Lady Independence; we have been together all these years, and I am not going to leave her now'. That is what he writes in the last of the letters here preserved, *after* the March on Rome. One cannot rationalise the whole of Pantaleoni in terms of self-interest.

One of the things which become easier to understand, once we have this background, is the reason for those tiresome polemics between 'Lausanne' and 'Cambridge'. It was not merely a matter of language, though that had something to do with it. Chiefly it was because the English appeared to Pareto to be so cosily ensconced in their utilitarian principles; they had not eaten of the Tree of Knowledge, as he had. (His attitude to Walras, we now know, was not at bottom dissimilar; but in view of personal debt to Walras, with whom he had to live at Lausanne, he kept his feelings about Walras's *Economie Sociale* more to himself.) He would not bother to get to the bottom of Marshall's theory (quite a job, in view of his imperfect English); for he knew that a man who sermonised like that must be wrong. Edgeworth had once shown signs of sense, but Edgeworth had now ganged up with the others. These people were ethicists, humanitarians, democrats; they were selling the pass to the enemy; they were on the wrong side in the class-war.

All this is indeed a sad story. There is, however, no need to let go of the strong part of Pareto's teaching, the fruit of his 'scientific' approach to social studies, because of the way in which it degenerated in his own case. It *is* true that there is a sense in which the student of society should take himself outside society; he should forget that he himself is a part of what he studies. Human relations between the scientist and his material are a weakness. Sympathy is therefore a weakness; but if sympathy is a weakness, antipathy is also. When Pareto allowed himself to slip into the misanthropy, into which (by his own confession) he often came, he was slipping away from his own doctrine.

> Io son fatta da Dio, sua merce, tale
> Che la vostra miseria non mi tange.[3]

Being human, we cannot at the most do more than attain to that celestial abstraction on one side of our minds. The moral of the story that is told in these letters seems to be that, if we do so, we should look well to see what happens on the other.

---

[3] Beatrice to Virgil (*Inferno*, 2.91).

28

Myrdal

A review, published in the *Economic Journal* (1954), of *The Political Element in the Development of Economic Theory*, by Gunnar Myrdal, translated from the German by Paul Streeten (London, 1953).

This important book appeared in Swedish in 1929. It was soon afterwards translated into German, and in its German version it had a wide influence. The appearance of an English translation (which will henceforward be the only version that is readily available, since both the Swedish and the German editions are out of print) is therefore to be welcomed. It has been a nuisance that a book, which can now be seen to mark a very significant stage in the development of economic thinking, has been so long out of reach.

The English reader, coming to Myrdal's book for the first time, will naturally bracket it with Robbins's *Nature and Significance of Economic Science*, though it should be noticed that it is a little earlier than Robbins's book. Both can now be regarded as classics of the positivist, anti-normative tendency, which (never quite unrepresented among economists) came into particular prominence at that particular time. Many of the arguments advanced in the two books run very closely parallel. But Myrdal is more of an extremist than Robbins; he carries his agnosticism to greater lengths. Robbins wields his axe with gusto, but at the end of his operations it is only the undergrowth that has been cleared away; the tree still stands. When Myrdal has finished, it lies flat. Some will feel that this carriage of arguments to their logical conclusion is a sign of Myrdal's superiority; others, including the present reviewer, that Myrdal's is a *reductio ad absurdum* which proves no more than that Robbins also went too far. It must nevertheless be granted that in our search for an acceptable standpoint in these difficult matters Myrdal has at least performed the function of putting up a flag at one corner of the field.

As Robbins is to Cannan, so Myrdal is to Cassel; the positivist tendency, already apparent in Cassel's work, is given by Myrdal a more explicit statement. There is indeed one respect in which the derivation from Cassel is a weakness; for it leads Myrdal to take over Cassel's view that demand theory (positive demand theory) can be entirely based, in Cournot's manner, upon the simple demand curve or price–quantity relationship, without any assumption about a scale of preferences, even an ordinal scale, lying behind it. The rejection of cardinal utility, which is common to Myrdal and Robbins, is accordingly extended by Myrdal into a more thoroughgoing rejection of subjective valuation theory altogether. This is, no doubt, one of the sources of his extremism; but there would seem to be some indication, from the (very brief) preface that the author has contributed to the present edition, that he may have changed his mind to some extent upon this question. If so, one of the more obvious differences between Myrdal's approach and Robbins's would fall to the ground.

Much more important than this is the fact that the normative economics, which Myrdal attacked, was that which provided, in the hands of the older British economists, and of contemporary economists on the Continent, an intellectual foundation for economic liberalism; while that which Robbins attacked was itself on the way towards an abandonment of liberalism, at least in its pure form. Politically, therefore, the books appear to be in opposite camps. While Robbins is, ultimately, a traditionalist who is not concerned to do more than lop off what he conceives to be excrescences on the main tradition of economic thinking, Myrdal attacks the tradition itself. The similarity of the weapons employed does not conceal this radical difference.

The core of Myrdal's argument may be summarised in the following propositions. Every economic change affects distribution as well as production, and the two aspects can never be disentangled. There are no economic grounds on which we can say that one system of distribution is better than another; and since every change affects distribution, this means that there are no economic grounds on which we can say that one state of affairs is better than another, or that any change can be made with advantage. In order to come to conclusions about advantage, we must introduce value-judgments from outside economics. The economists of the past have always implicitly introduced such value-judgments; but because they have done so implicitly rather than explicitly, they have arrived at conclusions which do not follow from their overt premises, and have therefore exhibited a concealed political bias. That bias Myrdal desires to expose, in the interests of an economics which is to be purely scientific, which is to explain, but is not in any way to prescribe. This is the ouline of his contention; further details are perhaps hardly called for, since (though hardly anyone has carried it as far as Myrdal) the general nature of the argument which he advances has now, a quarter of a century later, become quite familiar.

One or two comments upon his position may, however, be made. It is one of Myrdal's merits that he makes the issue hang so directly upon the dichotomy between production and distribution; for it is here, rather than in any side-issue about the measurability of utility, that the crux is really to be found. It is accordingly no accident that the part of his anaiysis which will be most readily accepted – which is indeed already most widely accepted – is that which deals with public finance. For in tax questions the distribution aspect is primary; effects on production, if they come in at all (and they may be quite unclear), are of secondary importance. The attempt to lay down canons of taxation which are free from 'value judgments', which are independent of political principles, was always a vain one. Neither the utility theory of Edgeworth and Pigou nor the benefit theory of Wicksell and Lindahl have much power to carry their readers with them.

But surely, in relation to economics as a whole, taxation is a somewhat special case. There is no shortage of economic problems which lie at the other extreme, problems in which the production aspect is clear, while the distribution aspect (when long-term as well as short-term effects on distribution are considered) is rather hazy. It would be wrong to claim that even these problems are entirely unaffected by Myrdal's indeterminateness; but there is a respectable case for the classical (and modern) practice of treating them, as a first approximation, as if they were. As soon as there is allowed to be some justification in this procedure, even over a limited field, the whole picture changes.

It should be noticed that the concepts which Myrdal must banish do not only include such obvious targets as utility and welfare; they also include the *real national income*. He cannot even grant that maximisation of real income (in any sense) is a proper economic norm. Now one can readily admit that real income is a tricky concept, and (with Pigou) that its maximisation does not have unconditional priority over other objectives; but the abandonment of these ideas is precisely the point at which the present reviewer (and no doubt many others) would desire to stop short. The efforts which some of us have been making to find a new basis for 'Welfare Economics' (efforts which are usefully summarised by Mr Streeten in an appendix to his translation) have been a search for a way by which one can avoid that abandonment. Though they have suffered by claiming greater success than they have attained (or than is perhaps attainable), one modest claim may still be made for them. They have shown that there exist a fair number of problems for which the concept of real income is a useful guide, and the increase of real income a reasonable objective. Once this is granted, the development of economic principles recovers its unity. We can respect our forebears, not merely because they incidentally discovered some things which we think to be important, but because the things which to them seemed central retain their importance to us also.

When one is dealing with those later writers who take what is substantially Myrdal's view, one is tempted to ask, in view of their insistance that policy must depend upon value-judgments that are extra-economic, where in fact do these value-judgments come from? If they are to be wisely formed, they must be based upon some discipline; if not on science, then on philosophy. Why should we assume that economics has nothing to contribute to that philosophy? But in Myrdal's case the answer to these questions is clearer than it is with some others; it becomes clearer still if we read this book with some thought of his later work. What he is doing here is to turn away from economics towards sociology. It is because he conceives of a sociology that will give him some basis for value-judgments that he is willing to go so far in extruding them from economics. The admiration which one feels for his accomplishment in that wider field sweetens the taste of this book. But we economists, who will never be sociologists, must make our philosophy, not neglecting what he can teach us, from what we can learn by ourselves.

29

Positive Economics?

This comes from a review, published in *Economica* (1965), of that deservedly successful textbook, *An Introduction to Positive Economics*, by R. G. Lipsey (London, 1963). Some of the points I here make against Lipsey are further developed in essay 32.

Such criticisms as I have to offer spring from a basic reservation which I feel, in the end, about the whole approach. 'Positive Economics' means, of course, Not Welfare Economics; the processes and the institutions, that are under consideration, may be analysed, but they may not in any systematic manner be assessed. Some assessment there inevitably is; something has to be said about Monopoly versus Competition, about Fixed versus Fluctuating Exchanges, about Growth versus Current Opulence. The views that are expressed on these matters seem to me to be sound; there is nothing the matter with Lipsey's 'judgement', much as he dislikes the term. Yet they hang in the air; for they are – deliberately – not based upon regular analysis.

One can understand the aversion which is felt by our *Optimus Secundus* from the cruder kinds of Welfare Economics: his conviction (expressed even here in one or two places) that the whole of that branch is better postponed for more advanced treatment. But when one considers how far he has gone in this 'elementary' work, it is a question whether this denial is well-advised. It would not have been necessary to get seriously involved in the more sticky sort of 'welfare' question in order to analyse the gains and losses that may accrue *to the various parties* from the passage (say) to a more monopolistic structure of industry. To set gains against losses is elusive, but something definite can surely be said on what determines how large the gains and losses are. I cannot help feeling that a little less purism on this point would have made the discussion of some controversial matters quite a bit more interesting.

If all this is ruled out, what is left for 'Positive Economics'? As Lipsey handles it, it is neither more nor less than a Propædeutic to Econometrics. The insistence that each of the propositions advanced is a hypothesis to be tested must surely lead that way. Yet if one is going that way, I think one should go a bit further in that direction than Lipsey has gone.

We are told, time and again, that here is a thing that ought to be tested, but has not been tested. Surely, the reader will conclude, economists have been very lazy. It is all very well to talk about a 'young science', but look at the money that gets spent on economic research. Why is there not more to show?

Doubtless there should be more to show, but I am worried that the reader of this book should have so much encouragement to look in that direction, without being given more idea what the difficulties are. If the student is to look at economics in the way that Lipsey proposes, something should be learned, quite early on, about econometric method. There are some apologetic remarks (on p. 20) about an 'error term', but we hardly hear of it again. Some simple examples of its use (perhaps in relation to demand theory, which might then have appeared less arid) would have helped a good deal. If one is leading up to econometrics, it is terribly one-sided to approach econometrics entirely from the traditional economic-theoretical angle.

There is another gap, which from the same point of view is still more important. We are told in the last sentence of the book, that 'when theory and fact come into conflict it is theory, and not fact, that must give way'. This is a dangerous proposition, particularly in economics. For as Hume taught long ago,[1] all that is shown by such a conflict is that *either* the theory *or* the fact is wrong. A theory is not to be rejected because it has been tested against the wrong facts – facts that are defective, or inappropriate. The choice of the right facts is as important a part of the testing process as any other. But here, when, as occasionally happens, numerical 'facts' are presented, no indication is given of the criticism, and elucidation, which needs to be performed on them, before they are used. If one is to set up a fence against Welfare, need one also set up a fence against Applied Economics?

---

[1] In his essay on Miracles: 'When anyone tells me that he has seen a dead man restored to life, I immediately consider with myself, whether it be more probable, that this person should deceive or be deceived, or that the fact, which he relates, should really have happened', Hume, *Enquiry*, in his *Philosophical Works*, ed. Green and Grose, vol. 4, p. 94.

30

Micro and Macro

From a review, published in the *Journal of Economic Literature* (1979), of *Microfoundations: The Compatibility of Microeconomics and Macroeconomics*, by E. Roy Weintraub (Cambridge, 1979).

It is convenient to begin from the pedagogic problem, which is where (I think) Weintraub himself starts. The student goes to 'micro' lectures on Mondays and to 'macro' lectures on Thursdays, and they just do not fit. Not because the Monday lectures were concerned with the firm and the individual, the Thursday lectures with the whole economy, as the micro–macro distinction apparently implies. If that were all, there would be no problem. The trouble is that the approach is different, the Monday lectures being in some sense classical, the Thursday lectures being Keynesian.

So there are two lines of division, not one; is it not part of the trouble that they have got superimposed? Once they are separated, we should have four sets of lectures, not two: macro-classical on Tuesdays, micro-Keynesian on Wednesdays, as well as the two that were already being given. Would these help to build a bridge?

Macro-classical is easy to recognise; it has a great tradition, going back, at least, to Ricardo. It is rather surprising that Weintraub has so little to say about it. For it is by no means a 'degenerating research programme'; it is still quite alive. For suitable purposes, the study of the causes of long-term economic growth, or of differences in the wealth of different countries, we still want to use it. It would have helped if it had been brought in.

Micro-Keynesian is more surprising; is it an empty box? Why should it be? There is, of course, no question that the *General Theory* itself is macro; but when one sets it beside the classical macro, one sees that it cannot be its macro-ness that distinguishes it from the latter. It must be something else. It must be marked off by a line that cuts across the micro–macro distinction. So it should have a place in micro.

It has not been easy to find it. A great part of the work that is described by Weintraub can be looked on as a hunt after it. One can distinguish in that story several stages – as he does, though I myself would arrange them rather differently.

There was a first stage, which I can follow him in associating with my own *Value and Capital*, when one thought that one could draw the line as *statics* against *dynamics*, in the simple sense in which those terms were used in that book. *Statics* out of time; in *dynamics* all quantities dated. When I got into my *dynamics*, I did, at least sometimes, find myself moving in what seemed to be Keynesian country; that was the reason why I ventured to claim that I had built the bridge (in the passage from my introduction, which Weintraub quotes). It was the analogy between my case of unity-elastic expectations and Keynes's wage-theorem that I think I had mainly in mind. But I ought certainly to have recognised that there was a good deal of my *dynamics* that was not at all Keynesian; it was nearer in spirit to the very 'classical' Austrians than it was to Keynes.

The book as a whole, however, was Walrasian. *Static* theory, as presented, was, in the Walras sense, general equilibrium theory; my *dynamics* was an endeavour to push general equilibrium forward into that other field.

The further history of that endeavour, culminating in the 'neo-classical synthesis', which has become so fashionable, is narrated in some detail by Weintraub. It was partly a matter of the refinement of the static foundations; but more important, in the present context, was the colonisation of more and more of the *dynamic* territory by 'classical' (if Walrasian was classical) methods. At the height of its success, the colonisation seemed to be complete; 'Keynes' had been pushed right over the edge. The quarry of the hunt had just disappeared.

Weintraub, I am glad to find, does not think that it had disappeared; there are two places in his book where he begins to catch sight of it.

One is his discussion of what he calls 'Chapter 12 Keynesianism' – the famous chapter on long-term expectation, which he rightly perceives has to be read in the light of Keynes's work on probability. I have myself, fairly recently, gone on record[1] in saying that I think this chapter to be 'rather wicked'; and I do not withdraw that statement, though I have since done some work on probability,[2] which has enabled me to understand Keynes's standpoint better. My present

[1] *EP*, p. 126.
[2] *CE*, ch. 8.

view is that Keynes was entirely right in emphasising that there is an element in economic judgements about the future that is not reducible to mathematics, but I still think he was wrong in making it so irrational. It can be quite rational, so that it can be influenced by policy, without being expressible in terms of a probability calculus. This is important, but it is not so important as Weintraub's other point.

This emerges towards the end of his book, when he comes to 'Edgeworthian disequilibrium'. His 'Edgeworthians' are those who seek to go beyond the admittedly artificial structure of the Walrasian market, with its price-takers and its auctioneer; and so to consider market forms more generally. The beginning is from isolated exchange between two parties, with a *core* of equilibrium bargains, as Edgeworth effectively showed nearly a century ago.[3] The introduction of additional parties, as Edgeworth also showed, narrows the core. The extension to many commodities, made by more modern writers, does not seem to introduce any new principle, so far as the determination of an equilibrium is concerned.

Where things become more interesting is when the question is faced: how is such an equilibrium to be reached, or even approximated? One must not assume 'transparency', everybody knowing everything about everybody; they must just find out, more or less, what they need to find out. It is reassuring to find that when such questions are posed, even in the rarified way that is favoured by the writers in whose work Weintraub is interested, they lead to results, such as the need for intermediaries and the need for a money as unit of account, which to more pedestrian thinkers[4] are not unfamiliar. One can welcome their appearance, at the end of the book, as an indication that at last the quarry is coming into sight.

To my mind, however, there are still some things missing. 'Edgeworthian disequilibrium' is still conceived as a problem of exchange; it has not yet taken on a temporal colour, so it is not yet in the *Value and Capital* sense *dynamic*. What about borrowing and lending, in a non-transparent market? What therefore about credit? I have come to believe that one of the main divides, between *classical* theory and (shall one say?) *meta-classical* − for Keynes's is only one version of the meta-classical theory we ought to be contemplating − is just here. The market economy, in practice, is a credit economy; so it depends upon trust, between man and man. There are numerous ways which have been invented for diminishing that dependence; but

[3] *Mathematical Psychics* (1881).
[4] My own work on the matter is in *CEMT*, ch. 1 and in *TEH*, chs. 3 and 5.

it cannot be eliminated. Among the faceless individuals who populate our pure models there is no place for it; but the market economy can- not exist, as anything more than a random sequence of bargains, without it.

It is not only to the capital market that this applies. For consider, from this angle, the difficult Keynesian doctrine of equilibrium with unemployment. If equilibrium is to be taken to be a continuing condition, the unemployed must be kept alive; there are various ways in which they may be kept alive, and we should distinguish them. There is the modern way, of unemployment 'benefit'; but if this is assumed, it should be made explicit. There is the 'disguised unem- ployment' when labour is sent back to the farms. But there is also the way that was so sadly common in the great cities of the nineteenth (and early twentieth) century, when the 'unemployed' picked up a living by casual labour. It is quite instructive to take this last case as a standard case, from which the others are treated as variants. Employ- ment then means *regular* employment, such that employer and worker expect their relation to have some continuance; there is that degree of confidence between them. If this confidence is to be main- tained, wages, in the regular sector, must be rather rigid; they cannot swing about with 'demand and supply' for labour. So when effective demand improves, more labour is drawn into the regular sector. When it diminishes, there is more 'unemployment'; and it could happen that as a consequence the wage that can be got by casual labour will fall – though it is not very easy to see what the mechanism is that will bring this about. It will certainly take a great fall in wages in the casual sector for that to be able to compete at all effectively with the regular sector; there will surely be quite a long 'short run' over which it is fair to assume that this does not happen much. So here again, once the element of confidence is emphasised, we find ourselves moving in the direction of Keynes.

It will now be apparent what I think should go into those Wednes- day lectures. Monetary institutions, certainly; but also a look at other markets, labour markets, and product markets to see how they really work, and can work. Not in the same way in all times and places; so it will widen the mind to turn to some of the older economists, to see how they thought that markets worked, in their time.[5]

---

[5] I have myself got particular help from Henry Thornton (*Paper Credit*, 1902) – (see my essay on Thornton in *CEMT* – and from Marshall – see ch. 5 in *CG*).

Part VI
Summings-up

31

The Formation of an Economist

This was written as one of a series of recollections by internationally known economists. It appeared in the *Banca Nazionale del Lavoro Quarterly Review*, September, 1979.

If I am asked how it was that I became an economist, I can give nothing better than the regular economic answer: in order to earn my living. At the moment when the decision had to be made, I had just taken my first degree at Oxford. I had had a very good general education, but a very unspecialised education, which did not clearly point in one direction rather than another. It had been paid for by 'scholarships', awarded on competitive examination (at the ages of 13 and 17); at that stage my main subject was mathematics. But I had turned away from mathematics; I took my degree in 'philosophy, politics and economics', a new course just established at Oxford, a course which was perhaps better devised for the training of politicians than of academics. (Hugh Gaitskell, Harold Wilson, Edward Heath and Reginald Maudling all had that background.) But I wanted to be academic; and though I had done very little economics, I was advised that economics was an expanding industry, so I would have a better chance of employment if I went that way. So I did.

Economics, at Oxford, was very 'social'; so they started me working on labour problems. I did my thesis on skill differentials in the building and engineering trades. But I had been well advised that there was a market for economists; so when I came to seek employment for myself, I was able to get what I wanted. From 1926–35 I taught at the London School of Economics; and I learned at the London School of Economics. Within those nine years I passed from the state of appalling ignorance, from which I started, to my first theoretical achievements: the invention of the elasticity of substitution (*Theory of Wages*, 1932), the distinction of income and substitution effects ('Reconsideration of the Theory of Value', in collaboration with Roy Allen, *Economica*, 1934)[1] and the liquidity spectrum ('A Suggestion for Simplifying the Theory of Money', *Economica*, 1935).[2] Already, before I left LSE, I had done what I still feel to be some of my best work.

How had this happened? Those nine years at LSE fall very sharply, from my point of view, into two parts. They are separated, in 1929, by the arrival of Lionel Robbins as head of department. In the three years before that time I had been working mainly by myself. I had access to that already splendid library, and I got advice from my colleagues on what I should read, but I was not a member of a group. After 1929 I was a member of a group, the group which Robbins built up around him. We were all of us quite young people and most of us are still surviving. Apart from Robbins himself, there were Hayek and Roy Allen, Richard Sayers, Nicholas Kaldor and Abba Lerner, together with Marian Bowley and Ursula Webb (Ursula Hicks after 1935). So the work which I did in these latter years was in large measure a collective work.

I go back to the years of preparation which preceded. There were two things which happened during those years which need to be recorded.

One of them, in the first of those years, was that Hugh Dalton[3] (then temporary head of the economics department) said to me 'you read Italian, you ought to read Pareto'. So it was reading the *Manuale* which started me off on economic theory.[4] I was deep in Pareto, before I got much out of Marshall.

---

[1] Essay 1, in volume I of this collection.

[2] Essay 5, in volume II of this collection.

[3] Dalton had learned his economics at Cambridge, where he was a pupil of Pigou; but by the time I knew him his interest in economics was waining. He had started upon his political career, and was aiming at being Foreign Secretary in a future Labour government. It is well known that when the time came, he was disappointed in that ambition, and had to go back to economics as Chancellor of the Exchequer. But by 1945 his economics was seriously out of date.

His lectures, which I attended in 1926, were a bit like political speeches. 'I always begin with population – good spicy subject, gets 'em interested' he said to me himself.

He had learned Italian when serving with the British army in Italy in 1918. He had a great affection for Italy, but felt himself unable to visit Italy during fascism. My Italian had begun by stumbling through Dante, while I was still at school; I had gone on to read fairly widely in Italian literature. But it was not until 1933, after I had published *Theory of Wages*, that I made my first contact with Italian economists, visiting, in Turin, Einaudi and Cabiati, del Vecchio at Bologna and Marco Fanno at Padua.

[4] I was naturally led from Pareto to Walras and Edgeworth. My time at Oxford was too late for me to have been able to go to Edgeworth's lectures; and I doubt if by my teachers at Oxford he was even mentioned. So it was not until I got to LSE that I found *Mathematical Psychics*.

The other was a long interlude in the second year, when I went to South Africa. The professor at the University at Johannesburg (their sole teacher of economics!) had died very suddenly. The authorities sent to London for a temporary replacement, while they made up their minds on the appointment of a successor. No one senior to me would take it, but I was tempted – on the whole very fortunately. I had to lecture on a wide variety of subjects, from statistics to economic history; but somehow I managed.

My own interest, at that time, was still in labour problems; and from that angle South Africa was a revelation. I came from a country where Trade Unions could still be thought of, by their well-wishers, of whom I had been one, as agents for the advancement of labour in general. But in South Africa they stood for no more than the interests of a minority, for White labour only. So much has been heard, in later years, of the colour problem in South Africa that it will hardly be credited that Dalton had given me an introduction to his 'fellow-socialist', the leader of the South African Labour Party, then in coalition with the Nationalists, the begetters of *apartheid*, with whom I could soon see that they belonged. Thus I got a new view of Trade Unions, I began to think of them as monopolists, so that it was by the application of monopoly theory that their effects were to be understood. The reservation of skilled jobs to White labour, and the confinement of the best land in the country to White ownership, were the economic obstacles in the way of progress for the Black majority. In a free market system these would wither away, so I became a free market man, even before I left South Africa.

Thus, when the Robbins circle began to form, I fitted in. I readily accepted his rejection of inter-personal comparability of utilities (then considered as a rationale for progressive taxation), for the rejection was in line with the ordinalism I had got from Pareto. And I was readily seduced by the great 'neo-classical synthesis' (as it effectively was, though that name has been mainly applied to later varieties), according to which a competitive system, free of monopoly elements, which would only grow if they were buttressed by state 'interference', would easily find an 'equilibrium'. I was willing to apply this doctrine, even to the labour market; though there I had some reservations, which survive in some chapters of *Wages*. My *Wages* book, however, is in its main lines thoroughly 'neo-classical'.

It was surprising, to outside observers, that these very Right-ish doctrines could have had such a vogue at the London School, which was popularly considered to be a hotbed of socialists. We did indeed have our eminent socialists, such as Laski and Tawney (Dalton, by now, had gone off into politics); but it was significant of the tolerant atmosphere of the School that personal relations with them were friendly. There was indeed a substratum of 'liberal' political principles which our socialists and our free market men had in common.

LSE was not only tolerant, it was also, to a high degree, international. (It has become even more international since that time!) What we economists thought we were doing was not only to bring to life the inheritance of the British Classical Economists, but also to widen the horizons of the British economists of our own time by bringing in a refreshment from what was being done, and had been done, in other countries. I got mine, as has been seen, from Walras and Pareto; Robbins, on the other hand, was looking to the Americans (Chicago was already another home of free market economics) and even more to the Austrians. Books written in other languages had not then been translated into English; but I managed enough German to read the Austrians, and also Wicksell and Myrdal (at that time only available to me in German). I have never learned Swedish, but, as will be seen, I have been deeply influenced by Swedish economics.

It was not only through books that one made these contacts. Eminent economists, from many countries, would pass through London, and when they came to London they would come to the School. Thus it was that I made the acquaintance of Taussig and Viner, of Mises and Schumpeter, of Ohlin and Lindahl; as well as of a younger generation of Austrians, often on their way to exile, for Austria was already falling under Hitler's shadow.[5] Hayek himself came to London before the Hitler revolution; he came to tell us about Austrian economics; and he did.

My reaction to Hayek's teaching, at that time, I have described elsewhere;[6] and I have also set out, in another place,[7] the change in

---

[5] Ursula spent a semester at the University of Vienna in 1931, so she had first-hand experience of the incipient Nazification. But it was not difficult for the rest of us, associating with German and Austrian exiles, to have a feeling of what was coming. When I went to Cambridge in 1935 (of which more below) I found an atmosphere that was very different. I remember how shocked I was to hear Pigou, a very great economist but curiously insular, remarking at that time that he supposed that Hitler was going to 'bomb the frogs' (i.e. the French). None of our business! And it was even later that Claude Guillebaud (Marshall's nephew and later editor) wrote a book on the *Economic Recovery of Germany*, praising the economic policy of Hitler as an application of Keynesian economics. (I would not like to leave that reference without saying that Guillebaud was a good friend of mine in Cambridge; he was the only other British economist I have known who knew the last canto of the *Paradiso* by heart.) The vogue of appeasement at Oxford during those years is notorious; but the sleep at Cambridge was still more profound.

[6] 'The Hayek Story', in *Critical Essays in Monetary Theory* (1967).

[7] 'Recollections and Documents', *Economic Perspectives* (1977). [See also the paper on 'LSE and the Robbins Circle', which I have included in volume II.]

my own ideas which was intertwined with it. Here I will merely say that I began, once again, from Pareto, making an attempt, first of all a very crude attempt, to make the Paretian system less static, so as to be able to incorporate planning over time, planning for a future which was not known in advance. Hayek was making us think of the productive process as a process in time, inputs coming before outputs; but his completest, and most logical, account of intertemporal relations was confined to a model in which everything worked out as intended – a model of 'perfect foresight'.[8] In his *Prices and Production* (1932), the lectures through which we first got to know him, things were allowed to go wrong, but only for monetary reasons; it was only because of monetary disturbances that an exception was allowed to the rule that market forces must tend to establish an equilibrium. If money could only be kept 'neutral', all would be well. (An anticipation of latter-day monetarism!) In the models I tried to construct, in which people did not know what was going to happen, and knew that they did not know what was going to happen, there was no place for 'neutral money'.

I was aware, before I left LSE in 1935, and before the appearance of Keynes's *General Theory* at the beginning of 1936, that the direction in which my mind was moving was not dissimilar to his. (He told me so himself, in some correspondence I had with him.[9]) But I did not begin from Keynes; I began from Pareto, and Hayek.[10] But I had gone on by 1935 to draw consequences from my new approach; and I had realised that I had separated myself from the faith in the free market which had been dominant among my colleagues. After I had read them my *Simplification* paper (at the end of 1934) they must have been aware of what was happening; but, as I have said, the atmosphere at LSE was tolerant, and I have been able to keep them among my friends.[11]

It was not because I was becoming Keynesian (as in a sense I was) that in the summer of 1935 I removed to Cambridge. I went there in consequence of an invitation from Pigou, and it was because of the friendship I had already formed with Robertson[12] that I was attracted.

---

[8] ('Das intertemporale Gleichgewichtsystem', in *Weltwirtschaftliches Archiv*, 1928).

[9] Reprinted in 'Recollections and Documents', cited.

[10] There is evidence for this, in the paper on 'Equilibrium and the Cycle', which is reprinted in volume II.

[11] I think that Hayek, and perhaps Vera Lutz, have been the only ones of us who in later years have been fully constant in the old faith. Even Robbins has departed from it, to a considerable extent.

[12] I have described my early relations with Robertson in 'Recollections and Documents'. See also the memoir of him which I wrote for the British Academy, and which is reprinted as a preface to the selection of his *Essays on Money and Interest* (1966).

Cambridge, however, was already riven by disputes between Keynesians and anti-Keynesians; and since I was associated with Pigou and
Robertson, I found myself regarded, at least by some Keynesians, as
being in the 'anti' camp. The ISLM version of Keynes's theory,[13]
which I myself produced, but which has never been highly regarded
by orthodox Keynesians, did not help me.

My chief occupation during those years at Cambridge (1935–8)
was the writing of *Value and Capital*. This is not at all a Cambridge
book; it is a systematisation of the work I had done at LSE. It is
represented as a work of bridge-building, not so much between micro-
and macro-economics (as others have often regarded it) as between
the static neo-classical system, which has been regarded as the
foundation of free market economics, and the 'dynamic' models
where past and future are properly distinguished, in which I had by
that time become more interested. My own dynamic model is presented in terms that have some relation with Keynes's work; but it is
not very Keynesian. It owes much more to what I had got from the
Swedes, from Myrdal and Lindahl. It was from Myrdal that I got the
idea of 'temporary equilibrium', a momentary market equilibrium in
which price-expectations are taken as data; it was Lindahl, with his
pioneering work on the social accounting framework, who taught me
how (formally at least) to string my temporary equilibria together.[14]

I do not now think that the monetary chapters in *Value and
Capital* are at all good; it is not from them, but from the *Simplification*
paper of 1935, that my later work on money has proceeded. There is
little about liquidity in *Value and Capital*.

By the time *Value and Capital* was published, I had removed to
Manchester, where I remained during the war years. The British
universities were only partly closed down, so there still was work to
be done, though most of the teaching I had to do was rather elementary. I took advantage of this to write my *Social Framework*, which
seems to have had the widest circulation of any of my books. It
should have been called *The Social Accounts*, for its novelty consisted
in the systematic use of social accounting material for elementary
teaching; but the idea of social accounting was then unfamiliar, so I
was persuaded to fall back on that unsatisfactory title.

[13] 'Mr Keynes and the Classics', *Econometrica* (1937); reprinted in volume II.
[14] I read Myrdal's *Monetary Equilibrium*, in German, at the beginning of 1934; it was
through Myrdal's references to him that I first heard of Lindahl. I found these references
very exciting; but I could not follow them up, since I could not read Swedish. So it was a
great moment when I actually met him at LSE. He had come to London to get help in the
translation of his essays into English; I was able to find a helper for him. A year later, on
another visit to see that helper, she had to tell him that we had decided to get married.
'Ah!' he said in his imperfect English 'I had my doubts'.

Value and Capital had been published at the beginning of 1939; so it got distributed throughout the world before the War broke out. But I was thereafter cut off from the reactions that were forming to it; it was only after the War that I found out what had been happening.[15]

In the second half of 1946, I made my first visit to the United States. I there met again some old friends, such as Schumpeter and Viner; but I also made my first contacts with the younger generation, who were soon to become famous. At Cambridge (Mass.) I met Samuelson; in New York I met Arrow; and at Chicago Milton Friedman and Don Patinkin. I did not know them, but they knew me; for I was the author of *Value and Capital*, which (as has since become obvious) was deeply influencing their work. They regarded it as the beginning of *their* 'neo-classical synthesis' – no more than the beginning, for they and their contemporaries, with far more skill in mathematics than mine, were sharpening the analysis I had merely roughed out. But I am afraid I disappointed them; and have continued to disappoint them. Their achievements have been great; but they are not in my line. I have felt little sympathy with the theory for theory's sake, which has been characteristic of one strand in American economics; nor with the idealisation of the free market, which has been characteristic of another; and I have little faith in the econometrics, on which they have so largely relied to make their contact with reality. But I make no pretence that in 1946 I was even beginning to get clear about all this. It took me many years before I could even begin to define my new position.

I can see, looking back, that there is quite a gap between my early contributions, substantially completed by 1950, and the work on which I have been engaged from 1960 onwards. It is not that in the gap I was idle. There was work to be done in Oxford, where from 1946–52 I took part in the formation of Nuffield College; and where from 1952–65 I held the Drummond Professorship, with some general responsibilities for the organisation of post-graduate studies. And I was also much engaged in other activities, which sprang initially from Ursula's work in Public Finance, and from other work in that field in which I joined her. I have always held (as I said in the preface to *Value and Capital*) that theory should be 'the servant of applied economics'; but I have also been aware that theory gives one

[15] Years later, when visiting Japan, I was assured that my book had been a set book at Kyoto University since 1943. I was astonished, and asked them how it could have been possible for them to get copies. They reminded me that until December 1941 they could import through America; and then, they said, we captured some in Singapore!

no right to pronounce on practical problems unless one has been through the labour, so often the formidable labour, of mastering the relevant facts. Those which have to be mastered before one can pronounce on the macro-economic problems of developed countries are so extensive that the task of mastering them has usually to be left to specialists; but there have been simpler cases where it has appeared more manageable. During the years when the British Empire was breaking up, there were many such opportunities for British economists; they were often called on for advice in easing the transition to self-government and then independence. We have done a bit in that field, in Nigeria and in the Carribbean, in India and in Ceylon; during the fifties it was a major interest.

I pass on, as here is appropriate, to the years about 1960, which I reckon as the time of my *Risorgimento*. The first thing I had to do, on resuming my former work, was to bring myself up-to-date with what others had been doing; and I knew that I could not understand what others had been doing unless I could re-state it in my own terms. I did two exercises of that kind,[16] which took a good deal of time. But I do not feel that these things are fully my own work; they are just 'translations'.

Nevertheless, with these behind me, I could go on. I could start to build on the work I had done in the thirties, but I could do so in my own way. I could take those parts of Keynes's system which I wanted, and could reject those which I did not want. I then found myself led, only incidentally to formal models, but chiefly to new analytical concepts, which may have some power to improve understanding of what has happened in the world, and what is happening.

There are three of these which I now feel to be important enough to be distinguished.

The first is the contrast between what I have called flexprice and fixprice markets: the former being those in which prices are made by the market (by demand and supply, as in the textbooks), the latter being those in which prices are made by producers, a change in price being an act of policy. This already appears in *Capital and Growth*,[17] but its fruits have been gathered throughout my later work. I contend that flexprice markets, as they have existed in practice, depend upon the existence of intermediaries, neither producers nor final consumers

---

[16] The first was published as 'A Survey of Linear Theory' (essay 19 in this volume); the second is embedded in the middle chapters of *CG* (1965). The writing of the latter owed much to the tuition which I received from Michio Morishima, while he was a Visiting Fellow of All Souls College in 1963–4.

[17] Especially in ch. 5.

of the products in which they trade. My *Theory of Economic History* is largely an attempt to see the main lines of economic development as a matter of the evolution of the merchant-intermediary, and its consequences. But I have fully recognised that in the most modern times it is the fixprice market which is taking over. Thus, when I am concerned with contemporary problems, I have tried to think in terms of a *mixed* fixprice-flexprice economy.

The second is a deepening of the concept of liquidity, which, though it is Keynes's concept, was (I now feel) imperfectly explored by Keynes. He did not (at least in the *General Theory*) sufficiently stress the relation between liquidity and time. 'Liquidity is not a matter of a single choice; it is a matter of a sequence of choices, a related sequence. It is concerned with the passage from the unknown to the known – with the knowledge that if we wait we can have more knowledge'.[18]

The third is the concept of the Impulse, which grew out of *Capital and Time*, but which did not finally emerge until the essay on 'Industrialism' in *Economic Perspectives*. I think of a major invention, or other major change in circumstances, like the opening up of a new market, as generating a chain of consequences, some of which by theory can be followed out. I did not have this idea when I wrote my *Theory of Economic History*; it is needed to complete the analysis which I gave in that earlier book.

During the years since 1965, while I have been writing my later books, I have been a retired professor; but I have been allowed to continue to work at Oxford, at All Souls College. Though I have useful discussions with colleagues at Oxford, I have not been a member of a group, as I was in early days at LSE. Those who have worked closest with me have been visitors to Oxford, and post-graduate students, who themselves come and go. For though in Oxford our first degree students are mainly British, most of our post-graduate students come from abroad. When they have done their two or three years, they go back to places, often very distant places, from which they have come. Such contact as one can then maintain with them must be largely by correspondence – unless one can go and see them at their homes or places of work. I have indeed done a good deal of that.

It has so happened that a considerable number of economics post-graduates, and of other economists who have visited Oxford, have come from Italy. And it is not so far from England to Italy as it is to

[18] *CKE* (1974), pp. 38–9. See also my *EP* (1977), essay 3, and *CE* (1979), chs. 6 and 7.

places further afield! I have explained the importance of my knowledge of Italian (which is still, I fear, little more than a reading knowledge) in the beginnings of my economics. It has been a great thing for me that I have again been able to use it in the contacts with Italian economists which I have been able to develop during the last twenty years. We now feel that a year which does not contain a visit to Italy is a year in which there is something missing. And now, when we come to Italy, we come to see our friends.

32

A Discipline not a Science

Anyone who has been through these three volumes of essays, here drawing to a conclusion – even if he has done no more than glance at the bits and pieces of prefatory notes and so on, which he may properly take to represent my present opinions – can be forgiven for thinking that the position to which I have come is distinctly sceptical. I would not altogether deny that that is so, though *critical* is the adjective I would myself prefer. I do think it is a besetting vice of economists to over-play their hands, to claim more for their subject than they should. As will have been seen, I have on occasion fallen into that vice myself; but I think, or hope, that as the years have gone by, I have learned more wisdom.

I

There were examples of this in the field of welfare economics, with which the first of the three volumes was largely concerned. That is often said to be 'normative' or 'prescriptive'; I have passed through a stage, as when I wrote my first welfare essays,[1] when I would not have refused those words for it. 'Optimum' and its derivatives, words which one is bound to use, even when one is trying to keep them as un-prescriptive as possible, are bound to lend themselves to that interpretation. My final conclusion, however, was that 'Welfare Economics is itself a critique'.[2]

What that means, in application, is the identification of welfare economics with cost–benefit analysis, in the widest sense. The function of the analyst is comparison between alternative policies. (The policies may be such as to imply executive decisions, by public or by private bodies; or they may be expressed in legal enactments –

[1] Volume I, essays 2 and 4.
[2] Volume I, p. 239.

what is said applies to each.) There is in most cases one policy which can be described as doing nothing; the alternative is to take action according to some plan. Where that first proposal for action comes from we do not have to specify; it is the next stage with which the analyst is concerned.

It is his business to estimate, so far as he can, the gains and losses that are likely to accrue, to various classes, or sections of the population, from the proposed action; maybe also some gains, or losses, of a 'social' character, which cannot readily be imputed to a particular class. It is *not* his business, I would now maintain, to weigh up those gains and losses against each other. He can, nevertheless, most usefully, take advantage of his estimates to suggest improvements in the proposal with which he is confronted. Formally, that is to say, he can suggest a second plan, which he thinks will have a prospect of offering smaller losses, and larger, or not much smaller gains, so that in comparison with the first, it has some claim to be more attractive. He cannot prescribe this second plan; arts of persuasion will still be required; but he has some grounds for his persuading.[3]

When welfare economics is looked at in this light, it becomes apparent that it is essentially forward looking; and that does not square very well with the static manner in which its principles have usually been set out.[4] I still think it is right, as a matter of exposition, to begin with the static principles; but to stop there is terribly wrong. Something has been learned, since I began to write on the subject, about the extension to 'dynamics'; I have done a bit of that myself.[5]

However, there remains a point, which, in my later work in this direction, I fear I have not sufficiently stressed. Even if one is only concerned with the differences, in effects, on various classes, between adoption and non-adoption of the proposal, these differences are in the future, they are likely to be modified by things that will happen in the future and which cannot now be foreseen. So there is not just one outcome that is at issue; there are various outcomes, in different 'states of the world'. How do we weigh up the set of outcomes which may be expected in different eventualities, if the proposal is adopted, against that which may be expected if it is not? This is a weighting problem, quite similar in character to the distributional weighting problem, which was the centre of attention on the static approach.

---

[3] This is essentially what is left of the 'some gaining none losing' criterion, which came so much to the fore on the static approach. As between sophisticated and unsophisticated plans, it may often be more nearly satisfied than in arbitrary applications.

[4] As in volume I, essays 2 and 4.

[5] Chiefly in chs. XVII–XXII of *CG*, from which a passage is quoted in volume I, p. 77.

As between one pattern of risks and another, it is hard to prescribe. It is nevertheless often possible to suggest amendments, which at reasonable cost should diminish the risks. One which does that, and no more than that, may often be readily accepted as an improvement.[6]

II

I have so far been talking as if the welfare economist (or cost–benefit analyst) could proceed *directly*, from the project submitted to him, to an assessment of the gains and losses which are his special concern. But there is, of course, a step which must precede the assessment of such subjective differences; ascertainment of the objective effects (on prices, quantities and so on) which are to be expected on the one course and on the other – or rather, here also, of the differences between them. So far as this is a question of economics,[7] it is a question of Positive Economics. That used to be thought to be a less contentious field, for it is untroubled by those inter-personal comparisons, which are such a bother on the welfare side. Yet it is now to Positive Economics that controversy seems to have shifted. I find myself taking a very definite view about it, which is different from that which many economists appear to hold.

Why should one believe in Positive Economic Theory? Or, more precisely, what is the kind of belief in it which it is proper to have?

Long ago, in *Value and Capital*, at the end of my first chapter on Consumer Theory, I raised what is in effect this question.

Pure economics has a remarkable way of producing rabbits out of hats – apparently *a priori* propositions which apparently refer to reality. It is fascinating to try to discover how they got in; for those of us who do not believe in magic must be convinced that they got in somehow.

I had two tentative answers, or beginnings of answers. One (and I am glad to think that I got that far) was to insist on the importance of the *ceteris paribus* clause. All economic laws depend for their validity – their applicability to particular real situations, which I take to be the same thing – on the correctness of the supposition that the variables of which they have taken account are the only ones which matter. How much is hidden away in that will appear as we proceed.

---

[6] I would like the remarks of this section to be read in conjunction with my prefatory note to my review of Scitovsky, p. 153 above.
[7] Engineers, and others, will of course have someting to say about it.
[8] *VC*, p. 23.

The other (to be no more than noticed here – I shall return to it later) was stated, in the old passage just cited, in a form which later work has shown to be too restrictive. It can now be taken more generally. The actions, consequences of which are to be analysed, are the results of decisions, decisions made for some purpose. The purposes may vary, but they have a common form. So (it is claimed) they can always be represented as the maximisation of some index (utility, profit or earnings). They are consequences of action being taken on a maximisation criterion. These two lines of thought will have to be separately examined.

III

Any economic 'law' – take the demand curve as the simplest example – though it may be stated as a functional dependence between price and quantity, which may be read either way – must always, in application, be a one-way affair. The assertion that q depends on p, and the assertion that p depends on q, are obviously, when one thinks of it, quite different assertions. The latter depends on the behaviour of producers, the nature of the market, in a way that on the former does not arise or hardly arises. If then we decide to distinguish them, and look at the former alone (since it is the simpler) what the demand curve asserts is that a change in price is a reason for a change in quantity demanded. But it does certainly not assert that it is the only possible cause – that if q has changed from one year to the next, then p must have changed. There are other reasons, many other possible reasons, for a change in q.

Some of these can be readily specified; changes in the incomes of the consumers, in the prices of related goods, to take accepted examples. These can be introduced as additional parameters into the 'demand function', but we can never be sure that all those needed have been included. However complex we make the function, we can never be sure that something else will not come up which invalidates it.

One can accept that there is less danger of this in simple cases, such as the demands for 'breakfast-table commodities' with which econometrics began. It is with the more ambitious undertakings that it becomes really formidable. (The 'demand for money' is a notorious case.) But there is always some danger of it, so that it is never wise to claim that our economic laws can offer complete explanations. But if we cannot offer more than partial explanations, how can we predict?

There are indeed two kinds of prediction: prediction of what will happen, and predictions of what will probably happen. It is useful to distinguish them, though they slide into each other. Let us call the first sort strong predictions and the other weak predictions; thus accepting (if need be) that even the strongest prediction is not perfectly strong.

It is indeed true that in the natural sciences there are some predictions which we take to be perfectly strong; predictions of the dates of eclipses are perhaps the oldest example. We do in such cases have a practically complete explanation; the phenomenon has been so circumscribed it has been possible to collect just about the whole of the information that can be relevant to it. But even in the natural sciences, most predictions are not of this type. Experiments are being made; but what will happen at the next experiment is uncertain. It is nevertheless claimed that over a long sequence of experiments, the average outcome will be much more predictable. In many cases, many important cases, that is enough.

But is it enough in economics? We do have our own forecasters, whose business it is to foretell the future; but the best they can do is to tell us what value of a variable, at some date in the future, it is wisest to expect. That such expectations have to be formed, as a basis for current action, is undeniable;[9] also that it is most important that they should be as good as possible. But however much they are improved, they are always weak predictions; so it is also important that a judgement about their reliability should be made. The issue is whether that reliability is suitably assessed by the method that is appropriate in experimental sciences, by a statistical standard error.

That has been calculated on the basis of past experience, taking just those things into account which on past experience have seemed to be relevant; but there are always, or nearly always, other things which may come up which affect a wise judgement, and the confidence which it is wise to have in it. The great historical, or structural, changes which have occurred with such dismaying frequency in the present century cannot plausibly be treated as random disturbances. It is no wonder that the general floating of exchange rates, since 1971, has upset so many projections. The applicability of the probability calculus to economic forecasting cannot be taken for granted; it always requires defence.[10]

---

[9] p. 116 above.
[10] For a fuller discussion, see the chapter on 'Probability and Judgement' in *CE* (ch. 8). Much of what I am saying here is based on what is said in that chapter.

IV

I now turn back to the maximisation postulate.[11] This was defended in *Value and Capital* (in the passage a part of which I was quoting) as the simplest alternative available to us. I do not now feel that that is at all compelling. Maximisation, when properly understood, is not simple. So I do not now feel that that will do.

There is a passage in one of my later writings where the issue is brought up more sharply.[12] I was there confining myself to the econometric application of consumer theory, but that serves to bring out the point. We seek to explain a time-series of consumptions, by a particular population of consumers, over a particular time. That some of the causes would be non-economic was granted; among the economic explanations would be some that run in terms of current prices (including incomes). The function of demand theory, in this context, would be to help in separating out the current-price explanations from the others. It is proper to do this by postulating an ideal consumer, who *by definition* is only affected by current prices, and asking how we should expect such a consumer to behave.

We can have no direct experience of such a consumer, for we have not met him; but there is a well-established view[13] that we can deduce his behaviour from introspection, asking how we ourselves would behave if we found ourselves in such a position. That is a possible procedure, but I do not feel happy about it. When I have thought of it in historical applications, I have wanted to qualify it. 'What should I do if I were in that position, *and* if I were the kind of person who is being considered? If I were a medieval merchant, or a Greek slave-owner?[14] There are internal constraints, as well as external, that have to be considered.

Even in more modern applications, the subjective approach does not necessarily lead in the direction of simple maximising. The chooser may fail to maximise (profit, for instance) just because it is too troublesome. I had already observed in my old paper on Monopoly[15] that a monopolist 'may well exploit his advantage by not

---

[11] The 'Economic Principle' as I ventured to call it in *CE* (pp. 43ff.). But it is chiefly in relation to the classical concept of equilibrium (see above p. 39) that it is there discussed.

[12] *RDT*, pp. 16–17; quoted, rather extensively, in volume I, p. xiii.

[13] The outstanding modern representative of it is Hayek; see his famous paper on 'Economics and Knowledge', reprinted in his *Individualism and Economic Order* (1949). Though I disagree with Hayek on this point, there are many others in this field where I am with him.

[14] *TEH*, p. 6.

[15] Above, p. 139.

bothering to get very near to the position of maximum profit than by straining himself to get very close to it'. I would not be afraid to maintain that the alternatives to maximisation, in price and production policy, which have been investigated by Professor H. A. Simon and his associates,[16] can, if we desire, be interpreted in this manner.

Even in the field of consumer behaviour, there are similar short-cuts which deserve attention. Instead of going to the trouble of thinking through his whole budget, whenever there is a change in prices, he may use the marginal utility of money (to him) in Marshall's manner as a measuring-rod. In common language, he makes his decisions, to buy or not to buy, according to what he thinks he can afford.[17]

There are these qualifications to the maximising principle, but I doubt if they should be regarded as exceptions. They can readily be treated as forms of maximisation, when that is sufficiently widely defined. It may indeed be claimed that all decisions, or choices, imply the rejection of one alternative in favour of another; it is necessary, if the rejection is to be explained, that the alternative selected should be expected to bring some (relative) advantage. The conclusions which follow from this are admittedly *a priori*; but no more is needed to bring them down to earth than the fact, the surely undeniable fact, that choices are made. Any choice can be exhibited as a maximisation against constraints; what I have just been saying is that the constraints may be internal to the chooser, as well as external to him.[18]

V

What has so far been said does not exhaust the uses of economic theory. There is much more to come, which sets it in a different perspective.[19]

Once it is accepted that economic theories (those which are not mere tautologies) can offer no more than weak explanations – that they are always subject to a *ceteris paribus* clause – it becomes clear that they cannot be verified (or 'falsified') by confrontation with fact. We have been told that 'when theory and fact come into conflict,

[16] Cyert and March, *The Behavioural Theory of the Firm* (1963) is the standard presentation.

[17] See volume II, pp. 285–6 for a fuller discussion.

[18] See again *CE*, pp. 43ff. Also p. 139 above.

[19] I have been much helped in what follows by Amartya Sen's paper 'Description as Choice' (*OEP*, Nov. 1980).

it is theory, not fact, that must give way'.[20] It is very doubtful how far that *dictum* applies to economics. Our theories, as has been shown, are not that sort of a theory; but it is also true that our facts are not that sort of fact.

It is usually possible, in the natural sciences, for the reliability of a fact to be tested by repeated experiment (or repeated observation, for observation, under precaution, is one kind of experiment). It is perfectly true that when a theory, which claims to offer a strong explanation, comes into conflict with a fact that has been in that way securely established, the theory requires amendment. But the facts of economics are not in that way fortified. An economic time-series is a sequence of observations of a historical process, each item having its own distinct individuality. Each of them is a historical fact; like other historical facts, it depends on someone's testimony. It is reported by someone that this is what happened. One of the possibilities that is then open is that he may have been wrong. He did not perceive what he said he had perceived. This is a possibility that is very familiar to the professional historian; it is why he has to *criticise his sources*. (The monkish chronicler, or the present-day reporter, may be careless, or may be credulous.) One does find cases of that in economics, but it is usually more important, in economics, that the reporting of a fact is a description of the fact; and the description may well be defective.

A lack of consilience between theory and fact, in economics (when that cannot be ascribed, or readily ascribed, to the weakness of the theory, in the light of the preceding discussion) is most commonly due to a lack of correspondence between the terms in which the theory runs, and the terms in which the fact is described. (Theories, and descriptions of facts, in which the terms *cost, profit* or *quantity of money* appear, are obvious examples.) When that clash occurs, it may be that the theory should be improved, so as to run more closely in the terms in which the relevant facts are commonly described but it may also be that the description of the facts should be improved, so that we may think about them more clearly. I believe it is this last, much more than anything which is suggested by analogy with the physical sciences, which is the special function of economic theory. Though the concepts of economics (most of the basic concepts) are taken from business practice, it is only when they have been clarified,

---

[20] Quoted from Lipsey, in my review of his book, p. 348 above. He was, of course, deriving it from Popper.

and criticised, by theory, that they can be made into reliable means of communication.[21]

Now once one recognises that this is what economic theory very largely is doing, one sees that the use of models, which are themselves quite unrealistic, may be entirely defensible. In order for a concept to be clarified, it has to be set to work; it has to be shown how it operates in some context. Its working is most easily clarified if it is taken in some simple context, which we are at liberty to construct as we please. When that has been done, if it has been done successfully, the clarification, which so far has only been achieved within the model, will help us much more generally.

VI

There are many examples of this in economic theory. I will just take three, from bits of my own work, which have appeared in these volumes.

(1) In the essay on business income (essay 14 of this volume) it is shown that the meaning of *capital gains*, which in practice is used so very confusingly, can be greatly clarified by the use of a model. The model, in this case, is not entirely unrealistic; it depicts a situation which could occur, though obviously rarely. It serves to show that in common usage two quite different meanings are superimposed.

(2) In my 'second theorem' on portfolio selection (volume II, essay 19, part II), the commonsense view, that an operator may be expected to shift his portfolio in a more risky direction when his circumstances become easier, is sharpened and made more clearly defensible, by the use of a model that is itself artificial.

(3) In my new paper on 'Elasticity of Substitution' (essay 22 of this volume) the clarification of substitute–complement relationships is at last, I believe, brought to a conclusion. It had long ago been shown, in the old Hicks–Allen paper on Value (volume I, essay 1) that complementarity, on an indifference level, can only arise if the two goods, so related, are being looked at

---

[21] It is indeed by no means uncommon for economic concepts to be taken up by business, and given a rough ride in the world of affairs; especially since business men, and administrators, have taken to reading articles in newspapers, written by journalists with economics degrees. How this has happened with the concept of liquidity, which I claim to have been invented by Keynes, is discussed in volume II, pp. 238–47.

against a background of other goods. The other goods, in this consumer case, are taken to be available at constant prices. What is shown in the new paper is that when quantities, not prices, of the other goods (or factors) are taken to be fixed, it is complementarity which becomes the normal relation; so that two, by themselves, in the sense which is then appropriate, must be complements. It is the substitute relation which requires more than two for it to appear. The pattern thus identified seems to be quite generally valid; but it would hardly have been possible to establish it clearly save by a detour into the theory of a constant returns to scale production function – a hypothesis which has been much over-used, but which, for such clarification as this, could hardly have been avoided.

I might indeed go on to maintain that the *Value and Capital* model, of General Equilibrium under Perfect Competition, can be defended in much the same way.[22] Save with reference to a few quite limited sectors of actual economies, it can make no claim to be realistic; but it is a model of a whole economy which in all its details can be understood. Thus it is a laboratory, in which ideas can be tested. There are several such which could be mentioned; two will suffice. One is the distinction between income and substitution effects, which first came up in the study of individual behaviour, but which could be shown, by the use of the model, to have a much wider reach. The other is the elucidation of Keynes's wage-theorem, which appears in Keynes to be based upon a very arbitrary assumption (that the marginal efficiency of capital curve is fixed in wage units); when this is related to unitary elasticity of expectations it can be understood much better.[23]

It may also be observed that on this interpretation, the *VC* model is not much affected by the criticism, made against it by some mathematical economists, that the existence of an equilibrium, at positive prices, is not demonstrated. I admire the elegance of the Samuelson–Solow proof of existence;[24] but I still do not think that for my purpose I needed it.[25] Existence, from my point of view, was a part of the hypothesis; I was asking, if such a system existed, how

---

[22] This is not how I would have defended it when I wrote the book; see p. 1132 above.
[23] See what is said about the wage-theorem in *CKE*, pp. 72–4.
[24] Described on pp. 278–80 above.
[25] It may be said that I took it for granted that no free good would become priced, and no priced good would become free, in any of the changes under discussion. This does not seem unreasonable. See also above, p. 288 note.

would it work? I can understand that for those who are concerned with the defence of 'capitalism', to show the possibility of an arm's length equilibrium (an 'Invisible Hand') is a matter of importance. But that was not, and still is not, my concern.

VII

It would be wrong to conclude with these details. The main thing I have been trying to say is the thing Keynes himself said, in the preface that he wrote for the series of Cambridge Economic Handbooks:[26]

> The Theory of Economics does not furnish a body of settled conclusions immediately applicable to policy. It is a method rather than a doctrine, a technique of thinking, which helps its possessor to draw correct conclusions.

It is a Discipline, as I have ventured to call it. Keynes wrote that preface in the early twenties, long before the *General Theory*. But I do not believe that he would have abandoned the principle he there laid down. For it is significant that the date of that preface is very near to the date when his *Treatise on Probability* was published (1921). Much of what I have been saying in this essay has arisen out of work which I myself have been doing on Probability[27] – work which has led me to a view on that subject which I think is quite near to the view of Keynes. So I think I can see the connection. I see no reason to suppose that he fundamentally changed his mind on these matters, though like other economists, he often overplayed his hand. We know that he would have hated to be taken up by econometrists.[28]

---

[26] This preface was omitted from some of the later Handbooks, so it is doubtless less familiar now than it was to economists of my generation.

[27] *CE*, chapter 8.

[28] See his famous review of Tinbergen in *EJ*, 1939 (*Collected Writings*, vol. XIV, p. 306).

The Published Works of John Hicks

The following abbreviations are used:

Books by the author

CE	*Causality in Economics* (1979)
CEET I	*Collected Essays on Economic Theory*, vol. I: *Wealth and Welfare* (1981)
CEET II	*Collected Essays on Economic Theory*, vol. II: *Money, Interest and Wages* (1982)
CEET III	*Collected Essays on Economic Theory*, vol. III: *Classics and Moderns* (1983)
CEMT	*Critical Essays in Monetary Theory* (1967)
CG	*Capital and Growth* (1965)
CKE	*The Crisis in Keynesian Economics* (1974)
CT	*Capital and Time* (1973)
EP	*Economic Perspectives* (1977)
EWE	*Essays in World Economics* (1959)
TEH	*A Theory of Economic History* (1969)
TW	*The Theory of Wages* (1932; second edition, 1963)
VC	*Value and Capital* (1939)

Journals and publishers

AER	*American Economic Review*
BNDLQR	*Banca Nazionale del Lavoro Quarterly Review*
BOUIS	*Bulletin of the Oxford University Institute of Statistics*
CJE	*Canadian Journal of Economics*
CUP	Cambridge University Press
Ec	*Economica*
Eca	*Econometrica*
EHR	*Economic History Review*
EI	*Economic Inquiry*
EJ	*Economic Journal*
ER	*Economic Record*
GER	*Greek Economic Review*
IA	*International Affairs*

IBR	Irish Bank Review
IEA	Institute of Economic Affairs
JEL	Journal of Economic Literature
JMCB	Journal of Money, Credit and Banking
JPKE	Journal of Post-Keynesian Economics
LBR	Lloyds Bank Review
MS	Manchester School
MSS	Manchester Statistical Society
NIESR	National Institute for Economic and Social Research
OUP	Oxford University Press
OEP	Oxford Economic Papers
QJE	Quarterly Journal of Economics
REP	Revue d'économie politique
RES	Review of Economic Studies
TBR	Three Banks Review
SAJE	South African Journal of Economics
SJE	Swedish Journal of Economics
ZFN	Zeitschrift für Nationalökonomie

Square brackets denote reprints, translations and foreign editions.

1928 'Wage-fixing in the building industry', *Ec*

1930 'Early history of industrial conciliation in England', *Ec*
'Edgeworth, Marshall and the "indeterminateness" of wages', *EJ* [*CEET* III]

1931 'Theory of uncertainty and profit', *Ec* [*CEET* II]
'A reply' (to Dobb, 'A note on "The indetermination of wages" '), *EJ*
'Quotas and import boards', in Beveridge *et al.*, *Tariffs: The Case Examined*, Longmans, Green
'The possibility of imperial preference' (with W. Beveridge), in Beveridge *et al.*, *Tariffs*
Review: Amulree, *Industrial Arbitration*, in *Ec*

1932 *The Theory of Wages*, Macmillan [Italian, 1934] (see 1963 below)
'Marginal productivity and the principle of variation', *Ec*
'Reply to Schultz: Marginal productivity and the Lausanne School', *Ec*

Reviews: Goodfellow, *Economic History of South Africa*, in *EJ*
Simiand, *Le Salaire*, in *EJ*
Mises and Spiethof (eds), *Probleme der Wertlehre*, in *EJ*
Bresciani and Turroni, *Le vicende del Marco Tedesco*, in *Ec*

1933 'A note on Mr Kahn's paper' ('Elasticity of substitution'), *RES*
'Gleichgewicht und Konjunktur', *ZFN* [*EI*, 1980; *CEET* II]
Reviews: Taussig, *Wages and Capital* (reprint), in *Ec*
Monroe, *Value and Income*, in *ZFN*
Reichenau, *Die Kapitalfunktion der Kredits*, in *ZFN*

1934 'A reconsideration of the theory of value' (with R. G. D. Allen), *Ec* [*CEET* I]
'A note on the elasticity of supply', *RES* [*CEET* III]
'Léon Walras', *Eca* [*CEET* III]
Reviews: Isles, *Wages Policy and the Price Level*, in *EJ*
Myrdal, 'Monetary equilibrium', in Heyek (ed.), *Beiträge zur Geldtheorie*, in *Ec* [*CEET* II]
Wickstead, *Common Sense of Political Economy* (reprint), in *Ec*

1935 'The theory of monopoly', *Eca* [*CEET* III]
'A suggestion for simplifying the theory of money', *Ec* [*CEMT*; *CEET* II]
'Wages and interest: the dynamic problem', *EJ* [*TW* (2nd edn); *CEET* II]
Reviews: Dupuit, *De l'utilité et de sa mesure* (Turin reprint), in *Ec* (*CEET* III]
von Stackelberg, *Marktform und Gleichgewicht*, in *EJ*
Roos, *Dynamic Economics*, in *EJ*

1936 'Mr Keynes's theory of employment', *EJ* [*CEET* II]
'Distribution and economic progress: a revised version', *RES* [*TW* (2nd edn)]
'Economic theory and the social sciences', contribution to a symposium on the Social Sciences, Institute of Sociology
Review: Pigou, *Economics of Stationary States*, in *EJ*

1937 'Mr Keynes and the "Classics" ', *Eca* [*CEMT*; *CEET* II]
La Théorie mathématique de la valeur, tr. by Lutfalla, Hermann, Paris

1939 *Value and Capital*, Clarendon Press [Spanish (Mexico), 1945; Japanese, 1950; French, 1956; Polish, 1975; Hindi, 1971; Urdu, 1975; Hungarian, 1978]
'Public finance in the national income' (with Ursula Hicks), *RES*
'Mr Hawtrey on bank rate and the long term rate of interest', *MS* [*CEET* II]
'Reply to Hawtrey', *MS*
'Foundations of welfare economics', *EJ* [*CEET* I]
Reviews: Allen, *Mathematical Analysis for Economists*, in *Ec*
Pool, *Wage Policy and Industrial Fluctuation*, in *Ec*

1940 'Valuation of social income', *Ec* [*CEET* I]
'A comment' (on Lange, 'Complementarity and interrelations of shifts in demand'), *RES*

1941 *Taxation of War Wealth* (with Ursula Hicks and L. Rostas), Clarendon Press
'Rehabilitation of consumer's surplus', *RES* [*CEET* I]
'Saving and the rate of interest in war-time', *MS*
Education in Economics, MSS

1942 *The Social Framework: An Introduction to Economics*, Clarendon Press [Swedish, 1945; Spanish (Mexico), 1950; Greek (pirated), 1955; Portuguese, 1956; German, 1962; Sinhalese/Tamil, 1964. Also special editions: American, 1945 and Japanese, 1974 listed separately below]
Taxation of War Wealth (with Ursula Hicks and L. Rostas), 2nd edn, Clarendon Press
'The monetary theory of D. H. Robertson', *Ec* [*CEET* II]
'Maintaining capital intact', *Ec*
'The budget white paper of 1942', *Journal of the Institute of Bankers*
'Consumer's surplus and index-numbers', *RES* [*CEET* I]
Review: Davis, *Theory of Econometrics*, in *EJ*

1943 *Standards of Local Expenditure* (with Ursula Hicks), CUP for NIESR

The Beveridge plan and local government finance (with Ursula Hicks), MSS
Review article: Rist, *History of Monetary and Credit Theory*, in *EHR* [*CEET* II]

1944 *Valuation for Rating* (with Ursula Hicks and C. E. V. Leser), CUP for NIESR
'Four consumer's surpluses', *RES* [*CEET* I]
'Inter-relations of shifts in demand: comment' (on Robertson), *RES*

1945 *The Incidence of Local Rates in Great Britain* (with Ursula Hicks), CUP for NIESR
The Social Framework of the American Economy, adapted by Hart, OUP, New York
'Recent contributions to general equilibrium economics', *Ec*
'Théorie de Keynes après neuf ans', *REP*
Review: Pigou, *Lapses from Full Employment*, in *EJ* [*CEET* II]

1946 *Value and Capital*, 2nd edn, Clarendon Press
'Generalised theory of consumer's surplus', *RES* [*CEET* I]

1947 'World recovery after war', *EJ* [*EWE; CEET* II]
'"Full employment" in a period of reconstruction', *National-økonomisk Tidsskrift* [*CEET* II]
'The empty economy', *LBR*

1948 'Valuation of social income: comment on Kuznets' *Reflections*', *Ec* [*CEET* I]
Articles on consumer surplus, *Economie appliquée*
Review: Sewell Bray, *Precision and Design in Accounting*, in *EJ*

1949 *The Problem of Budgetary Reform*, Clarendon Press [Spanish, 1957]
'Devaluation and world trade', *TBR* [*EWE*]
'Les courbes d'indifférence collective', *REP*
'Mr Harrod's dynamic economics', *Ec* [*CEET* II]

1950 *A Contribution to the Theory of the Trade Cycle*, Clarendon Press [Italian, 1950–1; Spanish, 1954; Japanese, 1954]
   Articles on 'Value', 'Demand', 'Interest', 'Wages' and 'Rent' in *Chambers' Encyclopaedia*

1951 *Report of Revenue Allocation Commission, Nigeria*, part 2 [*EWE*]
   Free Trade and Modern Economics, MSS [*EWE*]
   'Comment on Mr Ichimura's definition' (of related goods), *RES*
   Review: Menger, *Principles of Economics* (Dingwall and ' Hoselitz translation), in *EJ* [*CEET* III]

1952 *The Social Framework*, 2nd edn, Clarendon Press
   'Contribution to a symposium on Monetary Policy and the Crisis', *BOUIS*
   Review article: Scitovsky, *Welfare and Competition*, in *AER* [*CEET* II]

1953 'Long-term dollar problem', *OEP* [*EWE*, *CEET* III]

1954 'The process of imperfect competition', *OEP* [*CEET* III]
   'Robbins on Robertson on utility', *Ec*
   'A reply' (to Morishima, 'A note on a point in *Value and Capital*'), *RES*
   Review: Myrdal: *The Political Element in the Development of Economic Theory* (Streeten translation), in *EJ* [*CEET* III]

1955 *Finance and Taxation in Jamaica* (with Ursula Hicks), Jamaican Government
   The Social Framework of the American Economy, 2nd edn, adapted by Hart and Ford, OUP, New York

1956 *A Revision of Demand Theory*, Clarendon Press [Spanish (Mexico), 1958; Japanese, 1958]
   'Instability of wages', *TBR* [*EWE*]
   'Methods of dynamic analysis', in *25 Economic Essays* (Festschrift for Erik Lindahl), Ekonomisk Tidschrift, Stockholm [*CEET* II]

1957 *National Economic Development in the International Setting,*
     Central Bank, Ceylon [*EWE*]
     Review article: 'Patinkin: a rehabilitation of "Classical"
     economics?' in *EJ* [*CEMT* as 'The classics again']

1958 'Measurement of real income', *OEP* [*CEET* I]
     Development under Population Pressure (Ceylon), Central
     Bank, Ceylon [*EWE*]
     'A "value and capital" growth model', *RES*
     Future of the Rate of Interest, MSS [*CEMT*]
     'World inflation', *IBR* [*EWE*]

1959 *Essays in World Economics,* Clarendon Press (including
     previously unpublished articles: 'National economic de-
     velopment in the international setting'; 'Manifesto on
     welfarism' [*CEET* I]; 'Unimproved value rating (East
     Africa)'; 'A further note on import bias' [*CEET* III]; 'The
     factor-price equalisation theorem' [*CEET* III]) [Japanese,
     1965; Spanish, 1967]
     Review: Leibenstein, *Economic Backwardness and Eco-
     nomic Growth*, in *EJ*

1960 *The Social Framework*, 3rd edition, Clarendon Press
     'Linear theory', *EJ* [*Surveys of Economic Theory*; *CEET* III]
     'Thoughts on the theory of capital: the Corfu conference',
     OEP

1961 'Prices and the turnpike: the story of a mare's nest', *RES*
     [*CEET* III]
     'The measurement of capital in relation to the measurement of
     other economic aggregates', in Lutz and Hague (eds), *The
     Theory of Capital*, IEA [*CEET* I]
     'Pareto revealed', *Ec* [*CEET* III]
     'Marshall's third rule: a further comment', *OEP* [*TW* (2nd
     edn)]

1962 'Liquidity', *EJ* [*CEMT*; *CEET* II]
     'Evaluation of consumers' wants', *Journal of Business*
     Reviews: Meade, *A Neo-Classical Growth Model*, in *EJ*
              Sen, *Choice of Techniques*, in *EJ*

1963 *The Theory of Wages*, 2nd edn, Macmillan [Spanish, 1973]
     International Trade: The Long View, Central Bank of Egypt

'The reform of budget accounts' (with Ursula Hicks), *BOUIS*
Review: Friedman, *Capitalism and Freedom*, in *Ec*

1965 *Capital and Growth*, Clarendon Press [Spanish, 1967; Italian, 1971; Polish, 1982]
      Robertson, A Memoir, British Academy [reprinted as introduction to Robertson, *Essays in Money and Interest*, 1966]
      Review: Lipsey, *An Introduction to Positive Economics*, in *Ec* [*CEET* III]
                Scitovsky, *Papers on Welfare and Growth*, in *AER*

1966 After the Boom, IEA
      'Growth and anti-growth', *OEP*
      'Essay on balanced economic growth', *The Oriental Economist* (Tokyo)

1967 *Critical Essays in Monetary Theory*, Clarendon Press (including previously unpublished articles: 'The two triads'; 'Monetary theory and history'; 'Thornton's "Paper Credit"'; 'A note on the *Treatise*'; 'The Hayek story') [Spanish, 1971; Italian, 1971; Japanese, 1972)]

1968 'Saving, investment and taxation', *TBR*

1969 *A Theory of Economic History*, Clarendon Press [Swedish, 1970; Japanese, 1971; Portuguese (Rio), 1971; French, 1973; Norwegian, 1974; Spanish, 1974]
      'The measurement of capital – in practice', *Bulletin of the International Statistical Institute* [*CEET* I]
      'Autonomists, Hawtreyans, and Keynesians', *JMCB* [*EP* as 'Hawtrey']
      'Direct and indirect additivity', *Eca* [*CEET* III]
      'Value and volume of capital', *Indian Economic Journal*
      Review: Pesek and Saving, *Money, Wealth and Economic Theory*, in *EJ*

1970 'A neo-Austrian growth theory', *EJ*
      'Elasticity of substitution again: substitutes and complements', *OEP* [revised version in *CEET* III as 'Elasticity of substitution reconsidered']
      'Capitalism and industrialism', *Quarterly Journal of Economic Research* (Tehran)

'Expected inflation', *TBR* [*EP*]
Review: Friedman, *The Optimal Quantity of Money*, in *EJ*
[*CEET* II as 'The costs of inflation']

1971 *The Social Framework*, 4th edn (much enlarged), Clarendon
Press [Japanese, 1972; Portuguese (Rio), 1972]
'A reply to Prof. Beach' ('Hicks on Ricardo on machinery'),
EJ

1972 'The Austrian theory of capital and its rebirth in modern
economics', *ZFN* [in Hicks and Weber (eds), *Carl Menger
and the Austrian School of Economics*, Clarendon Press,
1973; *CEET* III]
'Ricardo's theory of distribution', in Preston and Corry
(eds), *Essays in Honour of Lord Robbins*, Weidenfeld and
Nicolson [*CEET* III]

1973 *Carl Menger and the Austrian School of Economics* (edited
with W. Weber), Clarendon Press
Capital and Time, Clarendon Press [Italian, 1973; Spanish
(Mexico), 1976; Japanese, 1973; French, 1975]
'Recollections and documents', *Ec* [*EP*]
'The mainspring of economic growth', *SJE* [*EP*; *AER*, 1981]
'British fiscal policy' (with Ursula Hicks), in Giersch (ed.),
Fiscal Policy and Demand Management, Mohr, Tübingen
'On the measurement of capital', *The Economic Science*
(Nagoya University, Japan)

1974 *The Crisis in Keynesian Economics*, Basil Blackwell [Italian,
1974; Spanish, 1976; Japanese, 1977; Hungarian, 1978]
The Social Framework of the Japanese Economy (with
Nobuko Nosse), OUP
'Preference and welfare', in *Economic Theory and Planning:
Essays in Honour of A. K. Das Gupta*, OUP, Calcutta
'Real and monetary factors in economic fluctuations',
Scottish Journal of Political Economy [EP; in Manti
(ed.), *The 'New Inflation' and Monetary Policy*, Macmillan,
1976].
'Industrialism', *IA* [*EP*]
'Capital controversies: ancient and modern', *AER* [*EP*]

1975 'The scope and status of welfare economics', *OEP* [*CEET* I]
'What is wrong with monetarism', *LBR*

'Revival of political economy: the old and the new' (reply to Harcourt), *ER*

'The quest for monetary stability', *SAJE*

'The permissive economy', in Hicks *et al.*, *Crisis '75?*, IEA

1976 'Some questions of time in economics, in Tang *et al.* (eds), *Evolution, Welfare and Time in Economics* (festschrift for Georgescu-Roegen), Lexington Books [*CEET* II]

'Must stimulating demand stimulate inflation?' *ER* [*CEET* II]

'"Revolutions" in economics', in Latsis (ed.), *Method and Appraisal in Economics*, CUP [*CEET* III]

'The little that is right with monetarism', *LBR*

Review: Whittaker (ed.), *The Early Economic Writings of Alfred Marshall*, in *EJ* [*CEET* III]

1977 *Economic Perspectives*, Clarendon Press (including previously unpublished articles: 'Monetary experience and the theory of money'; 'Hawtrey'; 'The disaster point in risk theory'; 'Explanations and revisions') [Portuguese (Rio), 1978; Italian, 1980]

'Mr Ricardo and the moderns' (with S. Hollander), *QJE* [*CEET* III]

1978 *Le Funzioni della moneta internazionale*, Bancaria

Reviews: Lachmann, *Capital Expectations and the Market Process*, in *SAJE*

Collison Black (ed.), *Papers and Correspondence of William Stanley Jevons*, vols 3–5, in *EJ* [*CEET* III]

1979 *Causality in Economics*, Basil Blackwell [Italian, 1981; Spanish (Buenos Aires), 1982]

'The concept of income in relation to taxation and to business management', *GER* [*CEET* III]

'The formation of an economist', *BNDLQR* [*CEET* III]

'Is interest the price of a factor of production?' in Rizzo (ed.), *Time, Uncertainty and Disequilibrium*, Lexington Books [*CEET* III]

'On Coddington's interpretation: a reply', *JEL*

'The Ricardian system: a comment', *OEP*

Review: Weintraub, *Microfoundations: The Compatibility of Microeconomics and Macroeconomics*, in *JEL* [*CEET* III]

1980 'IS–LM: an explanation', *JPKE* [*CEET* III]
      'Equilibrium and the trade cycle' (re-translation by Schechter of German 1933 article), *EI* [*CEET* II]
      Review: Presley, *Robertsonian Economics*, in *CJE* [*CEET* II]

1981 *Wealth and Welfare*, vol. I of *Collected Essays on Economic Theory*, Basil Blackwell (including previously unpublished articles: 'The rationale of majority rule; 'Valuation of social income – the cost approach'; 'Optimisation and specialisation')

1982 *Money, Interest and Wages*, vol. II of *Collected Essays on Economic Theory*, Basil Blackwell (including previously unpublished articles: 'LSE and the Robbins circle'; 'Foundations of monetary theory'; 'Are there economic cycles?'; 'Limited liability: the pros and cons', in Orhnial (ed.), *Limited Liability and the Corporation*, Croom Helm [*CEET* III]
      Foreword to Andrew Shonfield, *The Use of Public Power*, OUP
      'Planning in the world depression', *Man and Development* (India)

1983 *Classics and Moderns*, vol. III of *Collected Essays on Economic Theory*, Basil Blackwell (including previously unpublished articles: 'The social accounting of classical models'; 'From classical to post-classical: the work of J. S. Mill'; 'Elasticity of substitution reconsidered'; 'A Discipline not a Science')
      Culture as Capital, Supply and Demand, Lincei, Rome
      'Edgeworth', in Murphy, *Studies of Irish Economists*
      The Social Framework of the Indian Economy, with Ghosh and Mukherjee, OUP, India

In course of publication

Index

Square brackets denote references to previous volumes in this collection.